A Complete Guide to C#

David Wayne Bishop

Grinnell College

JONES AND BARTLETT PUBLISHERS

Sudbury, Massachusetts

BOSTON TORONTO LONDON SINGAPORE

World Headquarters
Jones and Bartlett Publishers
40 Tall Pine Drive
Sudbury, MA 01776
978-443-5000
info@jbpub.com
www.jbpub.com

Jones and Bartlett Publishers
Canada
2406 Nikanna Road
Mississauga, ON L5C 2W6
CANADA

Jones and Bartlett Publishers
International
Barb House, Barb Mews
London W6 7PA
UK

Library of Congress Cataloging-in-Publication Data not available at time of printing.

ISBN 0-7637-2249-9

Acquisitions Editor: Stephen Solomon
Production Manager: Amy Rose
Associate Production Editor: Jenny L. McIsaac
Editorial Assistant: Caroline Senay
Marketing Manager: Matthew Bennett
Manufacturing Buyer: Therese Bräuer
Cover Design: Kristin E. Ohlin
Interior Design: Mary McKeon
Composition: Northeast Compositors
Printing and Binding: Courier Westford
Cover Printing: John Pow Company

Printed in the United States of America
08 07 06 05 04 10 9 8 7 6 5 4 3 2 1

To Wilber and Anna Marie Bishop

The time of our life is short and tedious,
And in the end of man there is no remedy.
None are known to have returned from the void.

For we are born of nothing,
And after this it shall be as if we had not been.
The breath in our nostrils is smoke,
And speech a spark to move our hearts which, when put out,
Our bodies shall be as ashes.
Life will pass away like the trace of a cloud,
Dispersed as mist,
Driven away by the beams of the sun,
And overpowered by the heat thereof.
For time is the passing of a shadow,
And there is no going back from our end for it is fast sealed.
None return.

So let us enjoy all the good things,
And let us speedily use the creatures as in youth.
Let us fill ourselves with costly wine and ointments,
And let not the flower of time pass us by.
Let us crown ourselves with roses before they whither,
AND LET NO MEADOW ESCAPE OUR RIOT.
For in time our name shall be forgotten,
And none shall remember our work.
This is our portion, and this is our lot.
- The Bible

Love everlasting
- DB

I would like to also thank Stephen Solomon, Caroline Senay, Jenny McIsaac, and all the employees of Jones and Bartlett for the priceless assistance they provided to me in preparing and refining the manuscript. Also to Teresa Smolinski, the textbook's wonderful artist. **Thank you.**

preface

C# (C sharp) is an exciting new language developed for Microsoft's .NET platform. Development in the .NET platform can be done using multiple languages, including C#, C++, and Visual Basic. Programs written in all of these languages can be compiled to a Common Language Runtime in .NET.

C# was created to provide portability for distributed applications that function over networks and internets. The language is based on C++, but differs from it in significant ways—not so much in appearance, but in the manner in which it is compiled and executed. C# programs do not compile to machine code, but to an intermediate code called Microsoft Intermediate Language (MSIL), which is interpreted. C# provides much of the same functionality as Java, but is optimized for the Windows .NET platform.

This text covers the basic features of C#, and covers what most individuals would learn in a course in C#. To be a useful guide, a text must be more than a dictionary of syntax for a language; it must capture the character and philosophy of the language as well. For example:

- It is useless to talk about threading without discussing race conditions, concurrency, synchronization, deadlock, and all the methods of dealing with these problems;
- Presenting C#'s abilities to access databases isn't worth much if databases are not well understood by the reader. One of the strengths of databases is to reduce redundancy through proper use of primary and foreign keys. A poorly designed database misses the mark entirely, and often makes data access even more inconvenient and error-prone;

- Coverage of network programming must include a discussion of communication protocols. Many students don't understand the difficulties involved in making machines communicate with each other, especially when the machines are run on different platforms.

Specifically, the text will cover these main areas:

- Simple data types
- Predefined classes and structures
- Control statements
- Object-oriented programming (OOP)
- Graphical user interfaces (GUIs)
- Basic algorithm analysis
- Data structures
- Threads and concurrency
- Files, streams, and database access
- Network programming

There are some topics that are related to C# that are not in the text. Specifically:

- C# uses XML for various purposes, including generating documentation. C#/ XML integration is a topic large enought for an entire book; thus, I have left it out, rather than shortchange the reader with basic coverage.
- C# uses Active Server Pages (ASP) for its Web-based browser-oriented applications. ASP is also a very healthy subject to tackle on its own, and hence it is also absent.

This text isn't geared only to the student. Anyone desiring knowledge of C# can understand this book. You will need only a familiarity with the Windows operating system, because all development in this text is done in Windows. Visual Studio .NET tends to be expensive, and you do not need it to develop or follow the programs in this text. The free Framework SDK is sufficient. However, a copy of the standard edition of Visual C# .NET is available from the publisher at a significantly reduced price for students.

Ancillary Materials

This text is intended to work with a Website. Exercises, source code, and instructor's materials are posted online at

http://www.jbpub.com/catalog/0763722499/

Part of the site allows entry only to instructors of the course.

Obtaining the C# Software

There are system requirements for developing and running C# programs. For Windows development, you are required to use any of these platforms:

- Windows NT 4.0
- Windows 2000 (Service Pack 2 recommended)
- Windows XP

The following versions of Windows can run .NET programs, but cannot be used for development:

- Windows 98
- Windows ME

In order to compile and run C# programs, you must have a C# compiler. Microsoft includes a C# compiler in the Microsoft Framework SDK, which you can download from their site:

http://msdn.microsoft.com/downloads/

Click on "Software Development Kits," and then select "Microsoft .NET Framework SDK." A page will open allowing you to download the SDK as one large file, or in separate files. If you select to download as one large file, and choose to save it to your disk, a file called setup.exe will be downloaded to your machine. Run it as you would run any setup program in Windows. Downloading separate files will allow you to distribute the setup program across multiple disks; instructions for constructing the setup program from the separate files is on the Website. The SDK includes tools for the other .NET languages as well.

There are other components you should also install, which can be found at the same site. These are:

- Framework Service Pack 1
- Microsoft Data Access Components 2.7
- ODBC .NET Data Provider

Microsoft also supplies a package called Visual Studio .NET, which is a rapid application development (RAD) tool for quickly developing graphical applications in C# and the other .NET languages. A copy of the standard edition of Visual C# .NET is available from the publisher at a significantly reduced price for students.

Using the Documentation

The Framework SDK installs its own documentation. To see it, locate the Framework SDK documentation link in your Start menu, and click it. This will bring up a document, as shown in Figure 1.

The menu of the documentation application works much like a browser. In the left frame you will see a navigation tool, with tabs for

- Contents
- Index

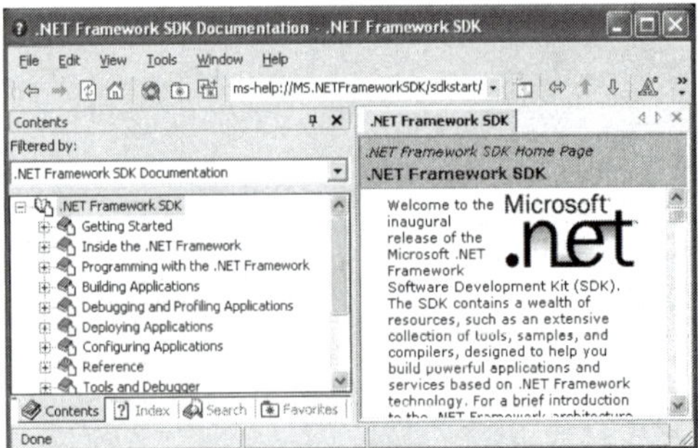

Figure 1

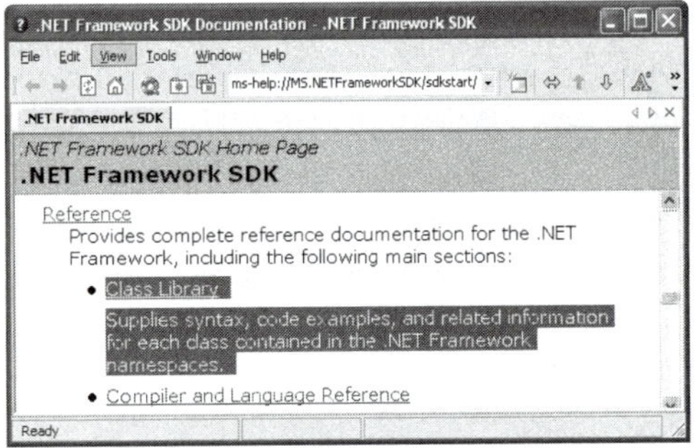

Figure 2

- Search
- Favorites

The Search tab is particularly useful. If you search for a term, another frame will open on the lower right-hand side of the screen displaying documents containing the searched-for term.

You will probably spend most of your time in the Class Library. The link to the class library is on the starting page of the documentation, as shown in Figure 2.

If you click on the Class Library link, the documentation provides a listing of all the namespaces, which contain the classes we use. You may click on any namespace to see the classes it contains. To start with, the System namespace contains most of the classes you'll need in order to learn C#. It contains many of the fundamental classes a beginning programmer would work with (see Figure 3).

Once you have opened this link, you will see a listing of all the classes in the System namespace. Certainly the most fundamental of all these classes is Object, so click on the Object class to see a description of it, as is done in Figure 4.

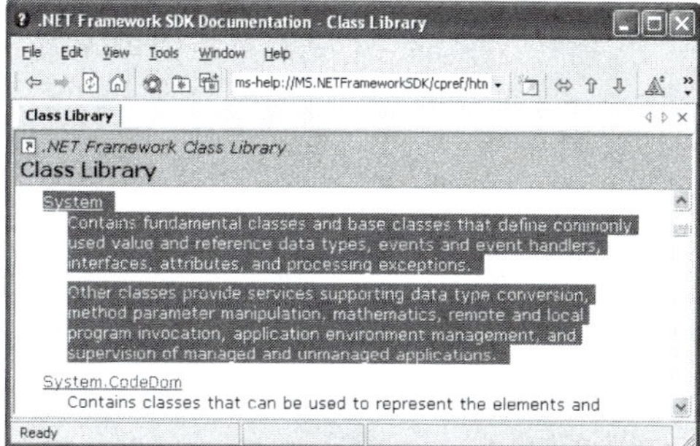

Figure 3

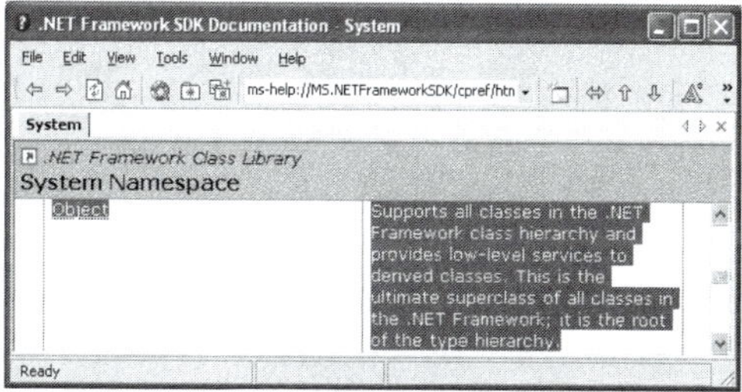

Figure 4

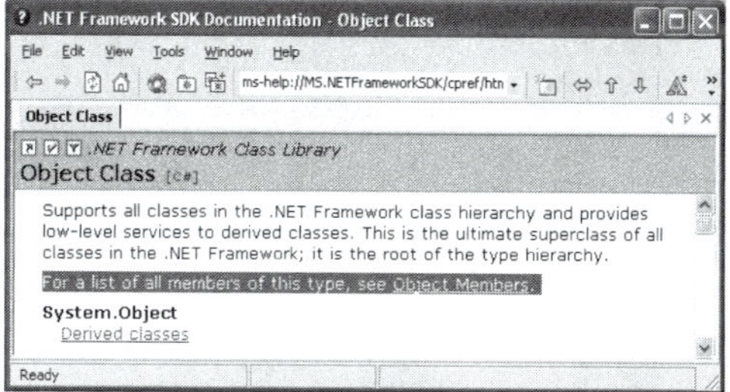

Figure 5

Here you see an overview of the Object class—how it works, how it is used, and so on. A class also has members; these can be viewed if you click the "members" link near the top of the page. In this case, click on Object Members, as is done in Figure 5.

Here you really get to the heart of the class. The members of a class represent the myriad ways to manipulate objects of that type. Figure 6 shows the members in the Object class.

And it doesn't end here. You can get a detailed description of any of these members by clicking on one. For example, by clicking on Object Constructor, we see a description of it, as in Figure 7.

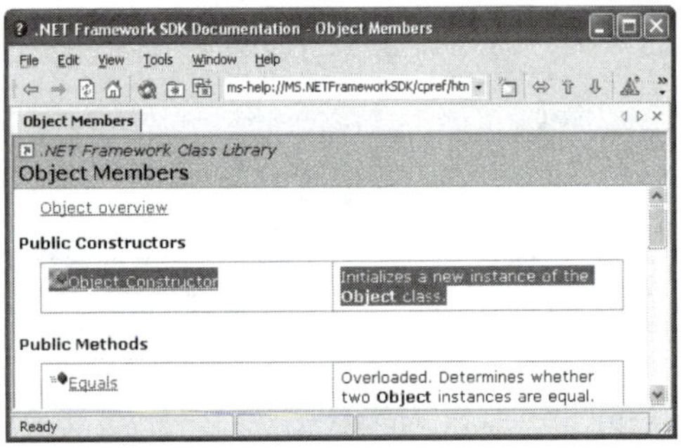

Figure 6

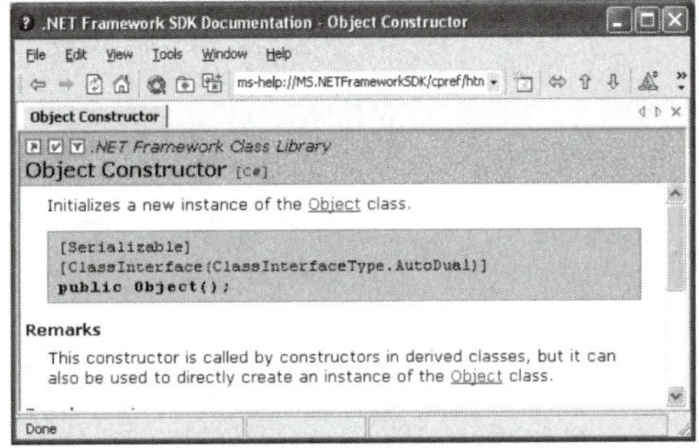

Figure 7

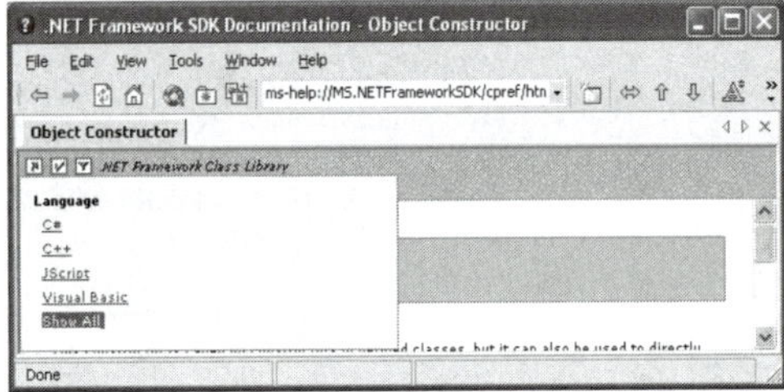

Figure 8

.NET supports multiple languages, so you may see an example of how it is coded not only in C#, but also in Visual Basic, C++, and JScript. To do this, you set the language filter to Show All, as in Figure 8.

When this is done, any page you are viewing shows documentation and examples in all the .NET languages. You can easily switch back to a single language if desired, as shown in Figure 9.

This is the basic manner of chasing down information in the Framework SDK. The C# classes are numerous indeed, and browsing the documentation is a time-consuming

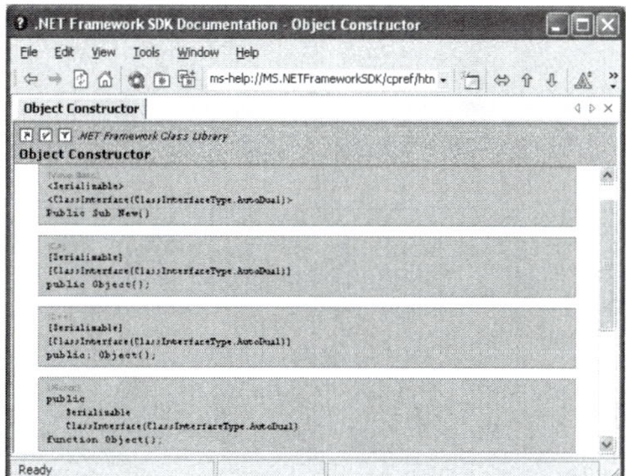

Figure 9

venture. It is worthwhile, however, before you write anything in C#, to look in the documentation for something that does basically (or exactly) what you are looking for. After all, why keep reinventing the wheel?

The publisher offers a free tutorial for learning to use Visual C# .NET standard edition. See the book's Website, or ask your instructor for more details on obtaining this tutorial.

contents

chapter 1

Introduction

C# is an object-oriented language; that is, its programs are based on creating and using objects. Objects are members of classes, which can be thought of as new data types.

Before object-oriented programming, languages dealt with a limited set of data types. There was typically a data type to represent each of the following:

- Integers
- Floating point numbers
- Characters
- Strings of characters
- Boolean values (true or false)
- Arrays of the preceding data types

The processing of these values was done by using functions, or procedures. These functions would accept incoming data as parameters, and manipulate it in some way, possibly returning a value to the calling procedure. These types of languages were called "procedural languages."

Older procedural languages did not allow you to create your own data types. As these languages evolved, constructs were put in place that allowed the programmer to define records, or structures, which were aggregates of the basic data types. These new structures could be passed into functions written to accept parameters of the newly defined type, and could also be returned by such a function.

What these languages did not do, however, was provide some mechanism for naturally grouping these functions with the structures they were intended to handle. Thus, the concept of a class came about. A class groups the data and the functions that manipulate that data together in a natural way. The data members in a class came to be known as fields, and the functions were called "methods." This difference in terminology exists not just to separate object-oriented languages from procedural languages; it has very much to do with the difference in how programs are conceived and written in these two very different paradigms.

■ A SIMPLE C# PROGRAM

The class is fundamental to C# programming. Every program is encapsulated in either a class or a structure, even if it consists of only a single block of code. For C# applications, execution always starts with the main program, or in C# terminology, the `Main()` method.

First, consider what you would like to name your class. At this point, it doesn't matter much, but we will call this class `HelloWorld`, and define it as shown in Listing 1.1.

Listing 1.1

```
//HelloWorld.cs
class HelloWorld {
   /*This is the Main() method
   It only displays "Hello World!" on the screen*/
   static void Main() {
      System.Console.WriteLine("Hello, World!");
   }
}
```

The `Main()` method is encapsulated inside the `HelloWorld` class, and it contains only one statement; that is, to display "Hello World!" on the screen. This source program is saved as the file HelloWorld.cs. It is a good habit to name your .cs (C sharp) files after the class, and to use the same case as the class name. Windows is generally not case sensitive, but C#, like its predecessors C and C++, definitely is.

It is C# convention to capitalize the names of most classes. If a class name consists of multiple words, the first letter of each word is typically capitalized.

To run this program, we must first compile it. To do this, open a command prompt, and go to the directory in which HelloWorld.cs was saved. The C# compiler is invoked with the command `csc`, followed by the file name of the source file.

```
C:\C#>csc HelloWorld.cs
Microsoft (R) Visual C# .NET Compiler version 7.00.9466
for Microsoft (R) .NET Framework version 1.0.3705
Copyright (C) Microsoft Corporation 2001. All rights reserved.
```

By default, this will produce an executable .exe file, with the same name as the .cs file.

```
C:\C#>dir
 Volume in drive C has no label.
 Volume Serial Number is 156F-1503

 Directory of C:\C#

05/12/2002  07:10 PM    <DIR>          .
05/12/2002  07:10 PM    <DIR>          ..
05/12/2002  07:11 PM               136 HelloWorld.cs
05/12/2002  07:16 PM             3,072 HelloWorld.exe
               2 File(s)          3,208 bytes
               2 Dir(s)   3,769,999,360 bytes free
```

To run the HelloWorld.exe program, we invoke it by name.

```
C:\C#>HelloWorld
Hello, World!
```

■ COMMENTING PROGRAMS

The HelloWorld program also contains some comments. Documenting your programs is very important, because it allows others to more easily understand your code, and can even help you understand your own code if you haven't looked at it in a while!

C# provides three basic mechanisms for commenting your programs. The first is the single line comment, which begins with //.

```
//This is a single line comment
```

The compiler ignores everything on a line after it sees the //. You can type anything at all here.

You can insert a comment that spans multiple lines by using the markers /* and */.

```
/*This is a comment that spans multiple lines
The compiler won't even look at me!*/
```

The compiler ignores everything between the /* and */ markers.

A third type of comment can be used to generate documentation for your C# programs; that is, by placing these documentation comments at strategic places and including the appropriate information, you can generate a document that describes the functionality of the program. Others can view this document as a reference. We will not discuss the documentation comment in this text.

■ EXPLANATION OF HELLOWORLD PROGRAM

The HelloWorld program includes a very useful class, called `Console`. In the program, its use is seen in the line

```
System.Console.WriteLine("Hello, World!");
```

The `Console` class has a method called `WriteLine()`, which may take a string (`"Hello, World!"` here) as a parameter, and display it on the console. Because this `WriteLine()` method is in the `Console` class, we invoke it by using

```
Console.WriteLine()
```

The `WriteLine()` method is what is called a "static method," and is called by the class name. Later on we shall see a different type of method called an "instance method." These methods are called by objects, and not by the class name.

Many classes have similar functionality, and so are logically grouped together into what is called a "namespace." The `Console` class is grouped together with other classes used for basic system calls in the `System` namespace. C# requires us to specify the namespace to which the `Console` class belongs, hence we use

```
System.Console.WriteLine()
```

If you look in the SDK documentation, you will find a listing of all the namespaces for the .NET platform. These namespaces serve not only the C# language, but also the other .NET languages. Table 1.1 shows some of the classes in the `System` namespace. You will note that `Console` is among them.

If we know the namespace to which a class belongs, we can avoid having to specify it with each method call by employing what is called the using directive. Listing 1.2 demonstrates the using directive in a modified version of HelloWorld.

TABLE 1.1

`Activator`	Contains methods to create types of objects locally or remotely, or obtain references to existing remote objects.
`AppDomain`	Represents an application domain, which is an isolated environment where applications execute. This class cannot be inherited.
	⋮
`Console`	Represents the standard input, output, and error streams for console applications. This class cannot be inherited.
	⋮
`Version`	Represents the version number for a common language runtime assembly. This class cannot be inherited.
`WeakReference`	Represents a weak reference, which references an object while still allowing it to be garbage collected.

Listing 1.2

```
using System;
class HelloWorld2 {
   static void Main() {
      Console.WriteLine("Hello, World!");
   }
}
```

The output of HelloWorld2 is the same as HelloWorld.

```
Hello, World!
```

There are other terms in the program that will require explanation—for example, the use of the keyword `static`—but we will defer discussion of this until later. For now, assume simply that it must be present when defining the `Main()` method.

Another common question is that of indentation. It doesn't matter to the compiler how you indent your lines in a C# program. Lines are indented for the benefit of humans, so that they may be more readily understandable when reviewed. The convention is to terminate a class or method in the same column as its heading was positioned, and anything it contains is indented further.

▪ CONSOLE INPUT/OUTPUT (I/O)

The `Console` class has other methods we can use. The most useful to us now is the `ReadLine()` method, which can read a series of characters into a program. Listing 1.3 demonstrates its use:

Listing 1.3

```
using System;
class EchoDemo {
      static void Main() {
            //Prompt the user to enter something
            Console.Write("Enter a message: ");
            //Use ReadLine to capture characters and assign
            //to a string
            string s=Console.ReadLine();
            //Send the string back to the console
            Console.WriteLine(s);
      }
}
```

The program prompts the user to enter some characters, reads them into a string, and then echoes the string back to the console.

```
Enter a message: Why?
Why?
```

We will discuss the `string` type at length later. Note that this program also uses `Console's` `Write()` method, which is similar to `WriteLine()`, but does not send the console's cursor to the next line after sending its output.

By perusing the Framework SDK documentation, we can see the methods available in the `Console` class. Table 1.2 is an outline of the `Console` class that shows its properties and its methods. Don't worry if you don't understand some of the terminology.

Any of these methods can be seen in more detail by clicking on its description, which is a hyperlink; for example, clicking on the `WriteLine()` method gives a more detailed description of it, as shown in Table 1.3.

You can see that there are many different flavors of the `WriteLine()` method. Each one has a different parameter list. To carry this one step further, you can click on any of

TABLE 1.2 Console Members

Public Properties

`Error`	Gets the standard error output stream.
`In`	Gets the standard input stream.
`Out`	Gets the standard output stream.

Public Methods

`OpenStandardError`	Overloaded. Acquires the standard error stream.
`OpenStandardInput`	Overloaded. Acquires the standard input stream.
`OpenStandardOutput`	Overloaded. Acquires the standard output stream.
`Read`	Reads the next character from the standard input stream.
`ReadLine`	Reads the next line of characters from the standard input stream.
`SetError`	Sets the `Error` property to the specified `TextWriter`.
`SetIn`	Sets the `In` property to the specified `TextReader`.
`SetOut`	Sets the `Out` property to the specified `TextWriter`.
`Write`	Overloaded. Writes the specified information to the standard output stream.
`WriteLine`	Overloaded. Writes the specified data, followed by the current line terminator, to the standard output stream.

TABLE 1.3 `Console.WriteLine` Method—Writes the specified data, followed by the current line terminator, to the standard output stream.

Writes the current line terminator to the standard output stream.	`public static void WriteLine();`
Writes the text representation of the specified Boolean value, followed by the current line terminator, to the standard output stream.	`public static void WriteLine(bool);`
Writes the specified Unicode character, followed by the current line terminator, to the standard output stream.	`public static void WriteLine(char);`
Writes the specified array of Unicode characters, followed by the current line terminator, to the standard output stream.	`public static void WriteLine(char[]);`
Writes the text representation of the specified decimal value, followed by the current line terminator, to the standard output stream.	`public static void WriteLine(decimal);`

(continued)

TABLE 1.3 (continued)

Writes the text representation of the specified double-precision floating-point value, followed by the current line terminator, to the standard output stream.	`public static void WriteLine(double);`
Writes the text representation of the specified 32-bit signed integer value, followed by the current line terminator, to the standard output stream.	`public static void WriteLine(int);`
Writes the text representation of the specified 64-bit signed integer value, followed by the current line terminator, to the standard output stream.	`public static void WriteLine(long);`
Writes the text representation of the specified object, followed by the current line terminator, to the standard output stream.	`public static void WriteLine(object);`
Writes the text representation of the specified single-precision floating-point value, followed by the current line terminator, to the standard output stream.	`public static void WriteLine(float);`
Writes the specified string value, followed by the current line terminator, to the standard output stream.	`public static void WriteLine(string);`
Writes the text representation of the specified 32-bit unsigned integer value, followed by the current line terminator, to the standard output stream. This method is not CLS-compliant.	`public static void WriteLine(uint);`
Writes the text representation of the specified 64-bit unsigned integer value, followed by the current line terminator, to the standard output stream. This method is not CLS-compliant.	`public static void WriteLine(ulong);`
Writes the specified object, followed by the current line terminator, to the standard output stream using the specified format information.	`public static void WriteLine(string, object);`
Writes the specified array of objects, followed by the current line terminator, to the standard output stream using the specified format information.	`public static void WriteLine(string, params object[]);`
Writes the specified subarray of Unicode characters, followed by the current line terminator, to the standard output stream.	`public static void WriteLine(char[], int, int);`
Writes the specified objects, followed by the current line terminator, to the standard output stream using the specified format information.	`public static void WriteLine(string, object, object);`
Writes the specified objects, followed by the current line terminator, to the standard output stream using the specified format information.	`public static void WriteLine(string, object, object, object);`

these methods in the documentation to get a more detailed description. For example, select the method

```
public static void WriteLine(string);
```

to see the following more detailed description:

Writes the specified string value, followed by the current line terminator, to the standard output stream.

```
public static void WriteLine(
   string value
);
```

☐ Exceptions

Exception Type Condition
IOException An I/O error occurred.

☐ Remarks

If value is a null reference, nothing is written to the standard output stream.

chapter 2

Data Types

There are three different kinds of data types in C#, representing the way data is stored. In C#, data can be stored in the following ways:

- *Value*—In C#, all of the simple types (i.e., integers, floating point numbers, Boolean values, and characters) are stored by value. Assignment to a value type means copying the value. Structures are also stored by value, and, as it turns out, the simple types are actually structures in C#. There are also enumerations, which are likewise stored by value.
- *Reference*—Storage by reference means that the item does not store the value, but a reference to the value's actual location in memory. Assignment to a reference type means copying this reference, and not the value. This can have the effect of producing multiple references to the same item. When an object is created of a class type, the object is said to "instantiate" the class, or the object is called an "instance" of the class. In C#, objects that are instances of a class are stored by reference.
- *Pointer*—C# is derived from the languages C and C++, both of which made extensive use of pointers. To be compatible with these languages in .NET, C# also allows pointer usage, but only in what are called "unsafe blocks." Pointers are actually addresses, and are similar to object references, but there is much more freedom in manipulating pointers. The price for this freedom is usually the introduction of horrendous bugs and general havoc.

First we will discuss data stored by value. C# has a rich set of data types, including the simple types (also known as atomic, fundamental, or primitive types), structures, enumerations, and classes. In this text, we will collectively refer to all of these as types, or data types. First, we discuss the simple types, which can be separated into categories.

▪ THE INTEGER TYPES

The integer types are summarized in Table 2.1.

Note that all of the integer types have a signed version and an unsigned version. For each of these, the signed version has one bit reserved for the sign (negative or nonnegative) and the unsigned does not. Thus, we see that the ranges of the signed types include negative values, but the unsigned types have a larger range of positive values.

□ Binary Numbers

Perhaps a discussion of data representation is in order. A binary computer has no choice but to represent data as a series of bits, where each bit can be either off or on. We will equate off with the value 0 and on with the value 1. Everything, including all data and commands in a program, are ultimately represented in this way.

As far as integers go, this representation is fairly direct. Whereas we humans count in base 10 (because we have 10 fingers), a computer must count in base 2; that is, a computer counts 0, 1, 10, 11, 100, 101, 110, 111, 1000, 1001, and so on. Table 2.2 shows the integers 0 through 15, in both decimal and binary systems.

Note that binary numbers greater than 1 have a "B" suffix. This is simply for readers to differentiate them from base 10 numbers; for example, the number 100B is not the decimal number 100, but the decimal number 4.

TABLE 2.1

Type	Description	Bytes	Range
`byte`	Unsigned byte	1	0 to $2^8 - 1$
`sbyte`	Signed byte	1	-2^7 to $2^7 - 1$
`short`	Signed short	2	-2^{15} to $2^{15} - 1$
`ushort`	Unsigned short	2	0 to $2^{16} - 1$
`int`	Signed int	4	-2^{31} to $2^{31} - 1$
`uint`	Unsigned int	4	0 to $2^{32} - 1$
`long`	Signed long	8	-2^{63} to $2^{63} - 1$
`ulong`	Unsigned long	8	0 to $2^{64} - 1$

TABLE 2.2

Decimal	0	1	2	3	4	5	6	7
Binary	0	1	10B	11B	100B	101B	110B	111B
Decimal	8	9	10	11	12	13	14	15
Binary	1000B	1001B	1010B	1011B	1100B	1101B	1110B	1111B

The smallest amount of information most processors work with is a byte, which is a series of 8 bits. The largest binary integer that can fit in a byte is 11111111B, or 255. Thus, the range of values in an unsigned byte is

00000000 through 11111111B = 0 through 255 = 0 through $2^8 - 1$

If you know the size of the other unsigned types, it is easy to compute their ranges.

Signed integer types reserve one bit for the sign. A 0 means the number is nonnegative, whereas a 1 means it is negative. Thus, the nonnegative range for a signed byte, for example, only goes up to 01111111B = 127 = $2^7 - 1$, but negative numbers can be represented using a signed type.

☐ Converting between Binary and Decimal Integers

It won't take much to convince you that converting between binary numbers and decimal numbers isn't very direct, or even easy. Note that any decimal integer can be easily written as a sum of powers of 10; for example:

$3921 = 3 \times 10^3 + 9 \times 10^2 + 2 \times 10^1 + 1 \times 10^0$

A binary integer can be easily written as a sum of powers of two; for example,

10111B = $1 \times 2^4 + 0 \times 2^3 + 1 \times 2^2 + 1 \times 2^1 + 1 \times 2^0$

To convert a binary integer to a decimal integer, we can simply take the sum of these powers of two:

10111B = $1 \times 2^4 + 0 \times 2^3 + 1 \times 2^2 + 1 \times 2^1 + 1 \times 2^0 = 16 + 0 + 4 + 2 + 1 = 23$

To convert a decimal number to binary, we must express it as a sum of powers of two. There is a relatively easy way to do this: Divide the integer by 2, noting the quotient and the remainder. Continue to divide the quotient by 2 until nothing remains. The remainders generated by this process, when taken in reverse order, yield the corresponding binary integer. For example, convert the integer 25 to binary. First, note that

25/2 = 12 R 1

12/2 = 6 R 0

6/2 = 3 R 0

3/2 = 1 R 1

1/2 = 0 R 1

By listing the remainders in the reverse order in which they were produced, we get the binary integer

11001B = 25

These calculations aren't horrific, but we can eliminate such calculations if we simply learn to count in a different base.

□ Hexadecimal Numbers

Because conversion between base 10 and base 2 involves calculation, computer professionals often count in hexadecimal, or base 16. Such a number system requires 16 symbols, so we traditionally use the symbols (in order)

0, 1, 2, 3, 4, 5, 6, 7, 8, 9, a, b, c, d, e, f

These symbols correspond to the decimal integers 0 through 15. The integer 16 would be represented in hexadecimal (or hex, for short) by 10H. Here, we use the "H" suffix to distinguish hexadecimal numbers from decimal numbers. Table 2.3 shows some decimal integers and their corresponding hex equivalents.

The relationship between hex numbers and decimal numbers doesn't seem very direct, but if you place hexadecimal numbers and binary numbers side by side, you may notice something (see Table 2.4).

Notice that there is a direct relationship between hexadecimal numbers and binary numbers; that is, each hexadecimal digit can be equated with four binary digits. The reason this is true is simply because $16 = 2^4$. Once you realize this, converting between binary and hexadecimal numbers becomes a snap.

Let's do some examples. Begin by converting the hexadecimal number a9bfH to binary. By consulting Table 2.4, we see that

a	=	1010B
9	=	1001B
b	=	1011B
f	=	1111B

TABLE 2.3

Decimal	0	1	2	3	4	5	6	7	8	9
Hexadecimal	0	1	2	3	4	5	6	7	8	9
Decimal	10	11	12	13	14	15	16	17	18	19
Hexadecimal	a	b	c	d	e	f	10H	11H	12H	13H
Decimal	20	21	22	23	24	25	26	27	28	29
Hexadecimal	14H	15H	16H	17H	18H	19H	1aH	1bH	1cH	1dH
Decimal	30	31	32	33	34	35	36	37	38	39
Hexadecimal	1eH	1fH	20H	21H	22H	23H	24H	25H	26H	27H

TABLE 2.4

Hexadecimal	0	1	2	3	4	5	6	7
Binary	0	1	10B	11B	100B	101B	110B	111B
Hexadecimal	8	9	a	b	c	d	e	f
Binary	1000B	1001B	1010B	1011B	1100B	1101B	1110B	**1111B**
Hexadecimal	10H	11H	12H	13H	14H	15H	16H	17H
Binary	10000B	10001B	10010B	10011B	10100B	10101B	10110B	10111B
Hexadecimal	18H	19H	1aH	1bH	1cH	1dH	1eH	**1fH**
Binary	11000B	11001B	11010B	11011B	11100B	11101B	11110B	**11111B**
Hexadecimal	20H	21H	22H	23H	24H	25H	26H	27H
Binary	100000B	100001B	100010B	100011B	100100B	100101B	100110B	100111B

So, a9bfH = 1010100110111111B.

Convert 110100110111111B to hexadecimal. Divide the number into blocks of four binary digits each, padding with leading zeros if necessary:

0110B	=	6
1001B	=	9
1011B	=	b
1111B	=	f

So, 110100110111111B = 69bfH.

■ DECLARING VARIABLES

The variable is the cornerstone of procedural languages and object-oriented languages. By creating a variable, we can assign values and modify them to produce desired results. You create a variable in C# using

```
<type name> <variable name>;
```

or

```
<type> <variable name> = <value>;
```

For example, you would create a signed `int` variable like this,

```
int demoInteger;
```

or like this,

```
int secondDemoInteger = 125;
```

C# uses the assignment operator "=" to assign values on the right-hand side to variables on the left-hand side. In this example, `demoInteger` is automatically assigned the value of 0, whereas `secondDemoInteger` is assigned the value

125 = 00000000000000000000000001111101B

As you can see from the previous example, integer type literals in a program are represented in an obvious way; that is, as decimal constants. Care must be taken, of course, not to assign an integer type a value that is outside of its range; for example, attempting the following assignment will create an error:

```
int tooBig = 3000000000;
```

The largest value that can be placed in a signed `int` is $2^{31} - 1$, or approximately 2 billion. This value could be assigned to a `long`, however. Notice that integer literals contain no commas. You can argue that this makes them harder to read, but it doesn't matter; you cannot use commas.

A `long` literal is the same as an integer literal, but has a trailing "L" after the digits. This signifies to the compiler that the number gets 8 bytes rather than 4. Here is an example:

```
long iAmALong = 5000000123L;
```

In this case, the literal must have the trailing "L", because the integer is too large to be considered an `int`. You may have noticed in previous examples that `int` literals are assigned to `long` variables. If you read the section on data conversion among the simple types, you will see that this is OK.

■ DECLARING CONSTANTS

You may need to declare constants in your program. We do this in C# by using the `const` modifier when declaring a variable:

```
const int mySalary = 300;
```

Once a variable is declared using `const`, its value cannot be changed. Only simple types, strings, and enums can be declared constant.

■ SIMPLE TYPES STORED BY VALUE

All of the simple types are stored by value; that is, the variable stores the value (however it is represented in binary), and assignments copy the value from one variable to another. Consider the following:

```
int first = 65;
int second = first;
```

Figure 2.1 shows that the value that will be stored in the variable first is 65 = 1000001B.

Figure 2.1

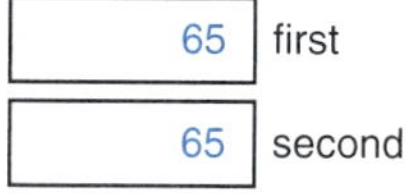

Figure 2.3

Remember that an `int` gets 4 bytes of space. When the second statement is executed, these bytes are copied into the variable second (see Figure 2.2).

For simplicity, in the future we will depict storage of these values in base 10, and disregard the number of bytes the value occupies, unless circumstances require otherwise. (See Figure 2.3.)

Figure 2.2

■ C# IS CASE SENSITIVE

Like everything else in C#, variable names are case sensitive. This means that the variables

```
int hohoho;
int HoHoHo;
int HOHOHO;
```

are all considered different. It is the convention in C# to have variables start with a lowercase letter, but if the variable consists of multiple words, to capitalize the first letter of each subsequent word. Here is an example:

```
long reallyBigHonkinNumber = 3;
```

A variable name can also contain underscores ("_"), but no white space.

It is possible to make multiple declarations of the same type at once, using the comma, as in the following declaration:

```
int zero, one=1, two=2;
```

The variable zero gets the default value of 0.

■ THE `char` TYPE

As with integers and every other data type, characters must be coded in binary. Many different coding schemes exist. In some schemes, like ASCII, characters are one byte long; this allows us to represent a maximum of $2^8 = 256$ characters. In earlier times, this was acceptable, but as computers became more widely used, it was clear that one byte was not nearly large enough to represent all the characters in the myriad alphabets of the world.

C# uses a character representation called "Unicode." This is a coding scheme that assigns each character 2 bytes of space. This allows for the representation of $2^{16} = 65{,}536$ characters. For convenience, the first 256 characters of the Unicode sequence correspond to the ASCII sequence. Table 2.5 shows characters 33 through 127 of the ASCII (and Unicode) sequence.

So, as an example, the character 'A' in the Unicode sequence would be represented in the machine as 65, or rather, its 2-byte binary equivalent:

00000000 01000001

Character literals have multiple formats in C#. We can specify a character in single quotes, as its Unicode, or as an unsigned hexadecimal short. For example, we can assign the character 'A' to `char` variables in all of the following ways, demonstrated by the program CapitalA, in Listing 2.1.

TABLE 2.5

<table>
<tr><td>33: !</td><td>34: “</td><td>35: #</td><td>36: $</td><td>37: %</td><td>38: &</td><td>39: ‘</td><td>40: (</td><td>41:)</td><td>42: *</td></tr>
<tr><td>43: +</td><td>44: ,</td><td>45: –</td><td>46: .</td><td>47: /</td><td>48: 0</td><td>49: 1</td><td>50: 2</td><td>51: 3</td><td>52: 4</td></tr>
<tr><td>53: 5</td><td>54: 6</td><td>55: 7</td><td>56: 8</td><td>57: 9</td><td>58: :</td><td>59: ;</td><td>60: <</td><td>61: =</td><td>62: ></td></tr>
<tr><td>63: ?</td><td>64: [at]</td><td>65: A</td><td>66: B</td><td>67: C</td><td>68: D</td><td>69: E</td><td>70: F</td><td>71: G</td><td>72: H</td></tr>
<tr><td>73: I</td><td>74: J</td><td>75: K</td><td>76: L</td><td>77: M</td><td>78: N</td><td>79: O</td><td>80: P</td><td>81: Q</td><td>82: R</td></tr>
<tr><td>83: S</td><td>84: T</td><td>85: U</td><td>86: V</td><td>87: W</td><td>88: X</td><td>89: Y</td><td>90: Z</td><td>91: [</td><td>92: \</td></tr>
<tr><td>93:]</td><td>94: ^</td><td>95: _</td><td>96: ’</td><td>97: a</td><td>98: b</td><td>99: c</td><td>100: d</td><td>101: e</td><td>102: f</td></tr>
<tr><td>103: g</td><td>104: h</td><td>105: i</td><td>106: j</td><td>107: k</td><td>108: l</td><td>109: m</td><td>110: n</td><td>111: o</td><td>112: p</td></tr>
<tr><td>113: q</td><td>114: r</td><td>115: s</td><td>116: t</td><td>117: u</td><td>118: v</td><td>119: w</td><td>120: x</td><td>121: y</td><td>122: z</td></tr>
<tr><td>123: {</td><td>124: |</td><td>125: }</td><td>126: ~</td><td>127: ⌂</td><td></td><td></td><td></td><td></td><td></td></tr>
</table>

Listing 2.1

```
using System;
class CapitalA {
      static void Main() {
//Three ways of representing 'A'
            char c1='A';
            char c2='\u0041';
            char c3='\x0041';
            Console.WriteLine(c1+" "+c2+" "+c3);
      }
}

A A A
```

C# uses `'\uHHHH'` to represent a Unicode in hexadecimal, and `'\xHHHH'` to represent an unsigned short, also in hexadecimal. The use of the backslash signifies an "escape character," which we will discuss after the next program.

The Display Characters program in Listing 2.2 displays characters numbered 33 through 127. It uses a `for` loop, and the `cast ( )` operator to do this, both of which we will cover later.

Looping is in Chapter 4, and the cast operator is in this chapter.

Listing 2.2

```
using System;
class DisplayCharacters {
   static void Main() {
      for (int i=33; i<128; i=i+1) Console.Write(i+": "+
          (char)i+" ");
   }
}
```

This program was actually used to help construct Table 2.5. Here is the output:

```
33: ! 34: " 35: # 36: $ 37: % 38: & 39: ' 40: ( 41: ) 42: * 43: + 44: , 45: -
46: . 47: / 48: 0 49: 1 50: 2 51: 3 52: 4 53: 5 54: 6 55: 7 56: 8 57: 9 58: :
59:; 60: < 61: = 62: > 63: ? 64: @ 65: A 66: B 67: C 68: D 69: E 70: F 71: G
72: H 73: I 74: J 75: K 76: L 77: M 78: N 79: O 80: P 81: Q 82: R 83: S 84: T
85: U 86: V 87: W 88: X 89: Y 90: Z 91: [ 92: \ 93: ] 94: ^ 95: _ 96: ` 97: a
98: b 99:c 100: d 101: e 102: f 103: g 104: h 105: i 106: j 107: k 108: l 109:
m 110: n 111: o 112: p 113: q 114: r 115: s 116: t 117: u 118: v 119: w 120: x
121: y 122: z 123: { 124: | 125: } 126: ~ 127: ⌂
```

▪ ESCAPE CHARACTERS

There are many characters that we would like to manipulate in our programs, but would have a difficult time typing into the program; for example, how would you tell your program to issue a tab at some point? C# allows us to represent these characters as escape characters; all begin with a backslash '\' (see Table 2.6).

You shouldn't have a problem typing single quotes, double quotes, and backslashes, but single quotes are used to delimit character literals, double quotes are used to enclose string literals, and the backslash is used for escape characters. Thus, to place them in a string, you must precede them with a backslash. Here are examples of assigning special characters:

```
char special1 = '\";  //assigned the single quote ' character
char special2 = '\n'; //assigned the new line character
char special3 = '\\'; //assigned the backslash
```

▪ THE FLOATING POINT TYPES

C# provides some types to do calculations with real type numbers (see Table 2.7).

The `decimal` type is used when exact representation of a decimal is required; for example, in financial calculations. Because everything is represented in binary format in a computer, certain decimals do not have exact representations in binary. Of course, this

TABLE 2.6

Character	Purpose
`\n`	New line
`\r`	Carriage return
`\t`	Horizontal tab
`\v`	Vertical tab
`\f`	Form feed (new page)
`\b`	Backspace
`\a`	Alert (beep)
`\0`	The null character 00000000 00000000
`\'`	Single quote
`\"`	Double quote
`\\`	backslash

TABLE 2.7

Type	Description	Bytes	Range
`float`	Floating point	4	$\pm 1.5 \times 10^{-45}$ to $\pm 3.4 \times 10^{38}$
`double`	Double floating point	8	$\pm 5.0 \times 10^{-324}$ to $\pm 1.7 \times 10^{308}$
`decimal`	Decimal	12	$\pm 1.0 \times 10^{-28}$ to $\pm 7.9 \times 10^{28}$

is true of number systems in general; for example, in base 10, the fraction 1/3 has an infinite decimal representation; that is,

$$1/3 = 0.333\ldots = 3 \times 10^{-1} + 3 \times 10^{-2} + 3 \times 10^{-3} + \ldots$$

Certain fractions that have finite representations in decimal have an infinite representation in binary; for example, 1/5 is exactly represented as $0.2 = 2 \times 10^{-1}$ in base 10, but in binary it has an infinite expansion:

$$1/5 = 0.2 = 0.001100110011\ldots B = 2^{-3} + 2^{-4} + 2^{-7} + 2^{-8} + 2^{-11} + 2^{-12} + \ldots$$

This is not to say that `decimal` types are not stored in binary, because everything must be stored in binary. There is simply some ingenious trickery involved in letting certain bits represent decimal digits in the number.

Creating floating-point variables is done in the same way as earlier described for integer types.

```
double d = -3.4;
float f = 7.11f
decimal dec = 9.99m;
```

Note the "f" suffix following a floating-point literal; this is required. Also, a decimal literal must be followed by "m". Without these suffixes, the compiler will see the literal as a `double`, which cannot be assigned directly to a `float` or `decimal` variable.

Sometimes we would like to enter a number in scientific notation. Humans, of course, use base 10 for this. Consider the number

$$-0.00000000000000000000000000231$$

which is represented in scientific notation as

$$-2.31 \times 10^{-27}$$

In C#, we can represent this number using the letter "E" to separate the mantissa −2.31 from the exponent −27:

```
double littleNum = -2.31E-27;
```

TABLE 2.8

Type	Default Value
All numeric types	0
`bool`	false (=0)
`char`	'\0' (=)
`enum`	0
All referenced types	null (=0)

▪ AUTOMATIC ASSIGNMENT

As we have seen in previous examples, C# automatically assigns values to variables. (Specifically, it assigns a default value to static fields, class instance fields, and array elements not otherwise assigned a value.) In cases where automatic assignment occurs, the default value is zero. Table 2.8 lists the defaults.

▪ DEFINITE ASSIGNMENT

C# demands (rightly so) that variables be assigned a value before they can be used. For example, the following code will not compile:

```
using System;
class CodeTester {
    static void Main() {
    int i;
    i=i+1;
    Console.WriteLine(i);
    }
}

C:\ C#>csc CodeTester.cs
Microsoft (R) Visual C# .NET Compiler version 7.00.9466
for Microsoft (R) .NET Framework version 1.0.3705
Copyright (C) Microsoft Corporation 2001. All rights reserved.
```

```
CodeTester.cs(5,4): error CS0165: Use of unassigned local
variable 'i'
```

If we explicitly initialize the variable `i` to 0 in this example, the program will compile.

■ ARITHMETIC OPERATORS

Numeric variables wouldn't be of much use if we couldn't do arithmetic with them. C# has an assortment of arithmetic operators, shown here in Table 2.9.

In an expression involving multiple arithmetic operators, the order in which operations are done is the way we normally do it—from left to right, with multiplication and division operations done before addition and subtraction. C# allows parentheses to override this order; for example, consider this:

```
int whatAmI = 5 + 9*(17 - 4)/2 % 3;
```

The result would be computed in this way:

$$
\begin{aligned}
& 5 + 9*(17 - 4)/2 \% 3 \\
&= 5 + 9 * 13/2 \% 3 \\
&= 5 + 117/2 \% 3 \\
&= 5 + 58 \% 3 \\
&= 5 + 1 \\
&= 6
\end{aligned}
$$

6	whatAmI

Figure 2.4

After this statement, the variable `whatAmI` contains the value 6 (see Figure 2.4). Because the division operators are working on integers, their results are integers; "/" returns the quotient, whereas "%" returns the remainder.

TABLE 2.9

Operator	Function	Operand Types
+	Addition	All integer and floating-point types.
–	Subtraction	All integer and floating-point types.
*	Multiplication	All integer and floating-point types.
/	Division	All integer and floating-point types. If operands are integers only, result is the integer quotient of division.
%	Remainder of integer division	All integer types.

■ OPERATOR PRECEDENCE

C# has an established precedence among all of its operators. An appendix in the back of the text contains a table of operators and their relative precedences. For convenience, the table is also listed here.

Table 2.10 lists categories of operators, provides the name and example usage of each, and also denotes which operators may be overloaded. (Some of the operators may be unfamiliar to you.) The operators in each category have higher precedence than operators in subsequent categories. Within a category, execution of operators is done left to right.

TABLE 2.10

Name	Usage	May Be Overloaded
Primary		
Parentheses	`(expression)`	
Member Access, aka the dot operator	`object.member`	
Struct pointer member access	`structObject->member`	
Method call	`method(parameters)`	
Indexing	`object[index]`	
Postincrement	`variable++`	Yes
Postdecrement	`variable--`	Yes
Memory allocation	**`new`**	
Array stack allocation	**`stackalloc`**	
Obtaining type	**`typeof`** `object`	
Obtaining struct size	**`sizeof`** `structObject`	
Switch arithmetic checker on	**`checked`**	
Switch arithmetic checker off	**`unchecked`**	
Unary		
Positive value	`+value`	Yes
Negate value	`-value`	Yes
Logical NOT	`!`	Yes
Bitwise complement	`~`	Yes
Preincrement	`++variable`	Yes
Predecrement	`--variable`	Yes
Type casting	`(Type) object`	
Value at address	`*location`	
Address of value	`&variable`	

(continued)

TABLE 2.10 (continued)

Name	Usage	May Be Overloaded
Multiplicative		
Multiply	`a*b`	Yes
Divide	`a/b`	Yes
Remainder of integer division	`a%b`	Yes
Additive		
Add	`a+b`	Yes
Subtract	`a-b`	Yes
Shift		
Left bit shift	`value<<positions`	Yes
Right bit shift	`value>>positions`	Yes
Relational		
Less than	`a<b`	Yes
Greater than	`a>b`	Yes
Less than or equal to	`a<=b`	Yes
Greater than or equal to	`a>=b`	Yes
Type testing	`object is Type`	
Equality		
Equal to	`a==b`	Yes
Not equal to	`a!=b`	Yes
Logical Bitwise		
AND	`a&b`	Yes
OR	`a|b`	Yes
Exclusive OR	`a^b`	Yes
Logical Boolean		
AND	`a&&b`	
OR	`a||b`	
Conditional	`condition?value1:value2`	
Assignment		
Assign	`a=b`	
Multiply/assign	`a*=b`	
Divide/assign	`a/=b`	
Remainder/assign	`a%=b`	

(continued)

TABLE 2.10 (continued)

Name	Usage	May Be Overloaded
Assignment		
Add/assign	`a+=b`	
Subtract/assign	`a-=b`	
Left bit shift/assign	`a<<=positions`	
Right bit shift/assign	`a>>=positions`	
Bitwise AND/assign	`a&=b`	
Bitwise exclusive OR/assign	`a^=b`	
Bitwise OR/assign	`a|=b`	

■ MIXING TYPES IN EXPRESSIONS

It is permissible to mix floating-point types and integer types in an arithmetic expression. The result is generally the type of the higher precision operand; for example, the result of the following expression is a `double`, though it contains `int`s, `float`s, and `double`s.

```
int zippity = 6;
float doo = 1.2f;
double dah = 4.62;
double whatTypeAmI = zippity/doo + 3*dah;
```

The calculation will go as follows:

	zippity/doo + 3 * dah	
=	6/1.2f + 3 * 4.5	
=	5.0f + 3 * 4.5	(`int` divided by `float` = `float`)
=	5.0f + 13.5	(`int` times `double` = `double`)
=	18.5	(`float` plus `double` = `double`)

■ PROGRAM: CHANGEMAKER

The remainder operator (also called the "modulus operator") is very useful for integer arithmetic. Consider the problem of calculating the fewest bills and coins that make up a certain amount of money. Suppose you have 5737 cents, and you want to convert this to dollars and coins. This is equal to

1 fifty-dollar bill + 1 five-dollar bill + 2 dollar bills + 1 quarter + 1 dime + 2 pennies

Of course, we compute this by taking out the larger denominations first, then repeating the process with the remaining cents. The program in Listing 2.3 does just that.

Listing 2.3

```
using System;
class ChangeMaker {
      static void Main() {
            //Initialize the cents here
            int cents=5737;

            //Display cents before it is modified
            Console.WriteLine(cents+" cents in currency
                              is:");

            //Take out the hundred dollar bills
            //Divide cents by 10000
            int hundredBills=cents/10000;
            //Reduce cents to what's left
            //Take the remainder mod 10000
            cents=cents%10000;

            //Repeat this for lower denominations

            int fiftyBills=cents/5000;
            cents=cents%5000;

            int twentyBills=cents/2000;
            cents=cents%20000;

            int tenBills=cents/1000;
            cents=cents%1000;

            int fiveBills=cents/500;
            cents=cents%500;

            int dollarBills=cents/100;
            cents=cents%100;

            int quarters=cents/25;
            cents=cents%25;
```

(continued)

```
            int dimes=cents/10;
            cents=cents%10;

            int nickels=cents/5;
            cents=cents%5;

            //Display the results
            Console.WriteLine(hundredBills+" hundreds,");
            Console.WriteLine(fiftyBills+" fifties,");
            Console.WriteLine(twentyBills+" twenties,");
            Console.WriteLine(tenBills+" tens,");
            Console.WriteLine(fiveBills+" fives,");
            Console.WriteLine(dollarBills+" ones,");
            Console.WriteLine(quarters+" quarters,");
            Console.WriteLine(dimes+" dimes,");
            Console.WriteLine(nickels+" nickels,");
            Console.WriteLine("and "+cents+" cents.");
        }
    }
```

Here is the output of the program:

```
5737 cents in currency is:
0 hundreds,
1 fifties,
0 twenties,
0 tens,
1 fives,
2 ones,
1 quarters,
1 dimes,
0 nickels,
and 2 cents.
```

Of course, the program could use some work. We don't really want to print out denominations that have a value of 0, for example. It also is awkward to display "1 dimes." We will deal with this later when we talk about branching statements in Chapter 5. A more pressing problem is how to enter numbers from the console, so we don't have to modify the program every time we want to try a different value.

■ PARSING NUMBERS

We have already seen the `Console.ReadLine()` method used to capture a string from the console. For now, we can think of a string as a sequence of characters, which are likewise stored in binary format. Consider the string `"-15377"`; this is really the characters

'-', '1', '5', '3', '7', '7'

stored in their Unicode representation. Certainly, this is not the binary integer that corresponds to $-15377 = -11110000010001B$. We would like a method that could read a string consisting of only digits (with possibly a leading minus sign), and convert it to an `int`. The `Parse()` method in the `Int32` structure of the `System` namespace does exactly this. Here is an example of how it is used:

```
int sockItToMe = Int32.Parse("-15377");
```

This turns the string "`-15377`" into the `int` -15377. It would be easy now to modify the ChangeMaker program to read in the number of cents from the user, as shown in Listing 2.4.

Listing 2.4

```
using System;
class ChangeMaker {
      static void Main() {
            //Prompt the user
            Console.Write("Enter the number of cents: ");
            //Read the cents here
            int cents=Int32.Parse(Console.ReadLine());

            //Display cents before it is modified
            Console.WriteLine(cents+" cents in currency
                              is:");

            //Take out the hundred dollar bills
            //Divide cents by 10000
            int hundredBills=cents/10000;
            //Reduce cents to what's left
            //Take the remainder mod 10000
            cents=cents%10000;

            //Repeat this for lower denominations

            int fiftyBills=cents/5000;
            cents=cents%5000;

            int twentyBills=cents/2000;
            cents=cents%20000;

            int tenBills=cents/1000;
            cents=cents%1000;
```

(continued)

```
            int fiveBills=cents/500;
            cents=cents%500;

            int dollarBills=cents/100;
            cents=cents%100;

            int quarters=cents/25;
            cents=cents%25;

            int dimes=cents/10;
            cents=cents%10;

            int nickels=cents/5;
            cents=cents%5;

            //Display the results
            Console.WriteLine(hundredBills+" hundreds,");
            Console.WriteLine(fiftyBills+" fifties,");
            Console.WriteLine(twentyBills+" twenties,");
            Console.WriteLine(tenBills+" tens,");
            Console.WriteLine(fiveBills+" fives,");
            Console.WriteLine(dollarBills+" ones,");
            Console.WriteLine(quarters+" quarters,");
            Console.WriteLine(dimes+" dimes,");
            Console.WriteLine(nickels+" nickels,");
            Console.WriteLine("and "+cents+" cents.");
        }
}
```

Here is an example of the program running:

```
Enter the number of cents: 192222
192222 cents in currency is:
19 hundreds,
0 fifties,
1 twenties,
2 tens,
0 fives,
2 ones,
0 quarters,
2 dimes,
0 nickels,
and 2 cents.
```

TABLE 2.11

Structure	Method	Returns
SByte	Parse(string)	sbyte
Int16	Parse(string)	short
Int32	Parse(string)	int
Int64	Parse(string)	long
Single	Parse(string)	float
Double	Parse(string)	double

There are corresponding structures for all of the integer and floating point types, and each has a `Parse()` method to convert strings and to return the intended type. These can be seen in Table 2.11.

Clearly, these methods will work only if the string can be parsed as an integer or a floating point. For example, this certainly isn't going to work:

```
float screwedUpHere = Single.Parse("THREE");
```

■ DATA CONVERSIONS

You can see from many of the previous examples that C# freely converts some data types into others to do simple work. For example, expressions involving mixed types are permitted, and will produce a result of the type representing the "highest precision." This means that C# will do all of the following conversions automatically:

```
int → long → float → double
char → int
long → decimal
```

It is arguable as to whether a `float` is of higher precision than a `long`, but the conversion from the latter to the former is automatic, for convenience.

Conversions from higher precision to lower precision require use of the `cast( )` operator. Casting, therefore, may cause loss of precision or data, but it is very convenient and safe if precautions are taken. Some of the following statements use casts, and are required where used; that is, those lines which use a cast would not compile without the cast.

```
double d = 65.23;      //d is assigned the double value 65.23
float f = (float) d;   //f assigned 65.23f
int i = (int) d;       //i assigned 65
char c = (char) i;     //c assigned 65 (='A')
decimal dec = (decimal) d;   //dec assigned 65.23m
```

■ PROGRAM: DISPLAYCHARCODE

The DisplayCharacters program developed earlier cast `ints` into characters for display. Sometimes casts are necessary even when there is no loss of precision; for example, you may wish to convert a `char` to an `int` to display its numerical code instead of the character it represents. The program in Listing 2.5 does this.

Listing 2.5

```
using System;
class DisplayCharCode {
      static void Main() {
            //Prompt the user
            Console.Write("Enter a character: ");

            //Read a single character using Read() method
            //Read returns an int (a 4-byte character code)
            char entry = (char) Console.Read();

            //Cast char to int to display its numerical
            //equivalent
            Console.WriteLine("\'"+entry+"\' = "+
                                  (int) entry);
      }
}
```

Here is a sample run of the program:

```
Enter a character: Q
'Q' = 81
```

■ THE `bool` DATA TYPE

C# provides a data type, `bool`, to store Boolean values; that is, true or false. Although this could be represented using a single bit, Booleans are assigned a byte of space, because this is the smallest unit most processors can deal with.

Boolean literals are represented (logically so) by the values `true` and `false`. The default value on initialization is `false`.

```
bool b, b2 = true, b3 = false; //b2 is true, b and b3 are false
```

Boolean values and variables are quite useful for decision making in programs, as you will soon see. It should be noted that no data conversions are allowed between `bools` and the other simple types.

TABLE 2.12

Operator	Meaning
==	Test of equality
!=	Not equal to
<	Less than
>	Greater than
<=	Less than or equal to
>=	Greater than or equal to

▪ THE RELATIONAL OPERATORS

The relational operators are used to compare values. These operators take two operands, and produce a Boolean result. See Table 2.12 for a description of each.

The equality test == should not be confused with the assignment operator =. Types can be mixed when using the relational operators, as you can see here:

```
int i = 10, j = 35;
double d = 5.1, e = 7.0;
char c1 = 'A', c2 = 'Q'; //c1 = 65, c2 = 81 numerically
bool b1 = i != 2*d;       //true; i is not equal to 2 * 5.1 = 10.2
bool b2 = c2 < c1;        //false; 'Q' is not less than 'A'
bool b3 = 10*e <= c1;     //true; 70.0 ≤ 81
bool b4 = 10*e == 2*j;    //true(?); 10 * 7.0 = 70.0 is equal to 2 * 35 = 70
```

Care should be taken in comparing integer types to floating types. The inherent imprecision in floating types could cause a false result; that is, the program may report them as being equal when mathematically they are not, or vice versa.

Note that the arithmetic operators have higher precedence than the relational operators, and the relational operators have higher precedence than the assignment operator. If this were not the case, parentheses would be required in the previous examples.

▪ THE LOGICAL OPERATORS

We often combine Boolean expressions with the logical operators AND and OR, and use NOT to reverse a Boolean value. We can make truth tables to represent how these work. Suppose A and B are Boolean values; A AND B is then defined as in Table 2.13.

Thus, A AND B is true if and only if both A and B are true. A OR B happens to be false if and only if both A and B are false (see Table 2.14).

TABLE 2.13

A	B	A AND B
FALSE	FALSE	FALSE
FALSE	TRUE	FALSE
TRUE	FALSE	FALSE
TRUE	TRUE	TRUE

TABLE 2.14

A	B	A OR B
FALSE	FALSE	FALSE
FALSE	TRUE	TRUE
TRUE	FALSE	TRUE
TRUE	TRUE	TRUE

TABLE 2.15

A	NOT A
FALSE	TRUE
TRUE	FALSE

The NOT operator in Table 2.15 works on only one argument. NOT A is true if and only if A is false.

In C#, the Boolean operators are denoted by "&&" for AND, "| |" for OR, and "!" for NOT. Do not confuse the ! operator with the != relational operator. Here are some examples of using logical operators:

```
int i = 10, j = 35;
double d = 5.1;
char c1 = 'A', c2 = 'Q';         //c1 = 65, c2 = 81 numerically
bool b1 = i != 2*d && c2 > 80;   //true; 10! = 10.2 and 81 > 80
bool b2 = c2 < c1 || !b1;        //false; 'Q' is not < 'A' and !true is false
bool b3 = 10*e <= c1 && d<5;     //false; 70.0 ≤ 81, but 5.1 is not < 5
```

Note that the logical operators have higher precedence than assignment, but lower precedence than the relational operators. If you are unsure of the precedence, parentheses can't hurt.

■ THE CONDITIONAL OPERATOR

A special operator in C# allows us to assign values based on a condition. The format of the operator is

```
<Boolean_value> ? <value1> : <value2>
```

The result of this entire expression is `value1` if `Boolean_value` is true; otherwise, the expression returns `value2`. Here are some examples:

```
char c = 'A';
//c='A'=65

int i = (c<'Q') ? 25 : 50;
//i assigned value 25, since 'A' < 'Q'

double d = (3*i==c) ? 60 : 70;
//d assigned the value 70.0, since 75! = 65
//OK to assign integer 70 to d; it is cast 'upwards'
automatically

float f = (d>c&&d<'Q') ? (float) d : i;
//f assigned 70.0f cast down from a double
//since 70.0 > 65 and 70.0 < 81 (='Q')
```

The operators we have seen until now operate on the simple types. Are there operators that allow us to manipulate the individual bits? As you shall see, C# provides us with such operators.

■ BITWISE LOGICAL OPERATORS

The logical operators, "&&" and "||", operate on the `bool` data type. The bitwise logical operators "&" and "|" can be used on integer types. These operators take two operands, and do an AND or OR for each bit in the operands. For example, suppose we are working with two bytes, a = 00101000 and b = 00110010. If we take a & b we get

a & b = 00101000 & 00110010 = 00100000

The only bit that is set in both a and b is the third (from the left). Thus, it is the only set bit in the result. On the other hand,

a | b = 00101000 | 00110010 = 00111010

The set bits of the result of a bitwise or are exactly those bits that are set in either operand (possibly both).

There is also an exclusive-or bitwise operator, "^". The result of an exclusive-or a^b is, of course, that the result bit is set if and only if exactly one of the corresponding bits in a or b is set. So if byte a = 00110011 and byte b = 00110001, we have

a^b = 00000010.

The only bit set in the result is the single bit in which a and b differ.

☐ Program: TestBitwiseLogicalForm

Here is a program that demonstrates the behavior of the bitwise logical operators. It is a GUI, but you can compile and run it without knowing how a GUI is coded. You enter two `ints` in the top entry boxes, then press one of the AND, OR, or XOR buttons. The result is displayed in the bottom text box.

Note that input and output are done in decimal. This seems to produce strange results, but if you convert the numbers into their internal binary representation, you will see that the results are correct.

Figure 2.5 shows the & operator,

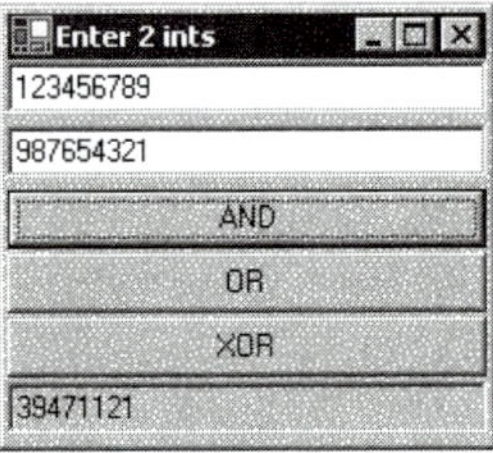

Figure 2.5

while Figure 2.6 shows is the | operator. Finally, Figure 2.7 shows the ^ operator.

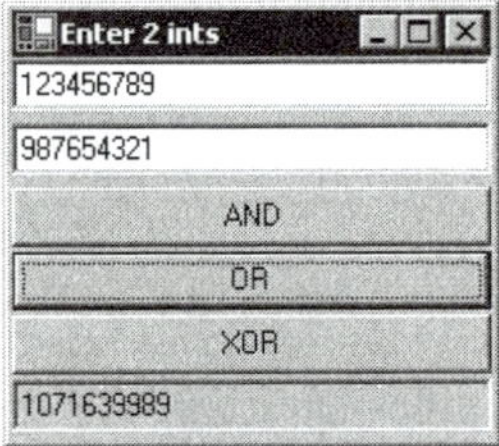

Figure 2.6

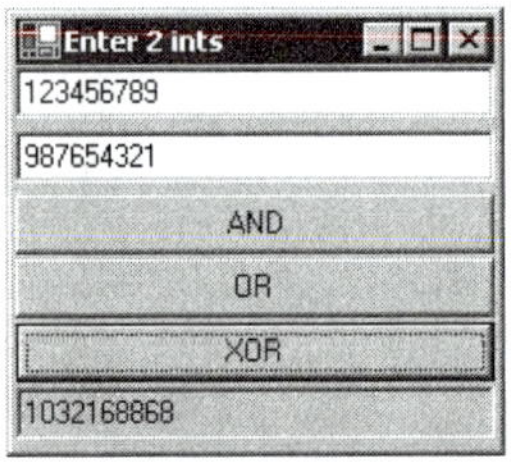

Figure 2.7

▪ SHIFT OPERATORS

The shift operators ">>", ">>>", and "<<" allow us to shift the bits in an integer type to the right or left by a specified number of positions. The following is an example of a left shift:

```
int num = 65;
num = num << 3;
```

After the shift, `num` contains the value 520, because the binary representation of 520 is 65 in binary shifted to the left 3 bit positions.

520 = 00000000000000000000001000001000B

65 = 00000000000000000000000001000001B

When a number is shifted to the left, the left-hand bits are shifted "out of existence," while the right-hand side fills up with zeros. If we are dealing with a signed type, like a `long` or an `int`, this shift may cause the value to turn suddenly from positive to negative, and vice versa, as bits shift left into the sign bit position. For example, consider shifting the value 1090519040 to the left. Here is the number in binary:

1090519040 = 01000001000000000000000000000000B

If we shift this one position to the left, the sign bit is now set, and the result is negative:

10000010000000000000000000000000B = −2113929216

If we shift left again, a zero bit shifts into the sign bit position, and the number becomes positive again!

00000100000000000000000000000000B = 67108864

We can also do right shifts. The behavior of such a shift differs depending on whether we use a signed shift ">>" or an unsigned shift ">>>". With a signed shift, the sign bit does not move as the other bits do, but for an unsigned shift, all bits (including the sign bit) shift to the right. For example, take the signed int −2147483648 and shift it to the right 1 bit:

−2147483648 = 10000000000000000000000000000000B

−2147483648>>1 = 10000000000000000000000000000000B

☐ Program: TestShiftOperatorForm

I have written a GUI that demonstrates these shifts. It will do no good for you to look at the code yet, but you can compile and run it the same way you have done for the previous programs.

Figure 2.8 and Figure 2.9 show 65 shifted left once.

Figure 2.8

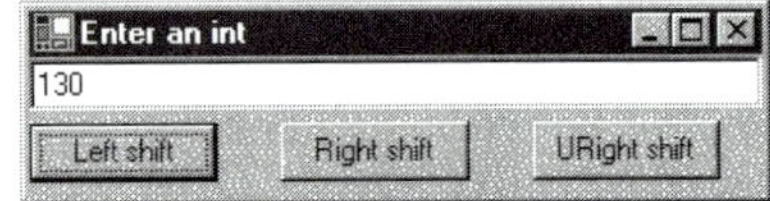

Figure 2.9

Figure 2.10 and Figure 2.11 show 1975308624 shifted to the left one position. Notice that a sign change occurs.

Figure 2.10

Figure 2.11

Figure 2.12 and Figure 2.13 show −344350048 first shifted to the right one position using a signed shift, then again using an unsigned shift.

Figure 2.12

Figure 2.13

■ ASSIGNMENT OPERATORS

We have already seen the basic assignment operator, but C# provides others as a means of shorthand. For example, to perform the assignment

```
a = a + 5;
```

TABLE 2.16

Operator	Usage	Equivalent To
+=	a += b	a = a + b
–=	a –= b	a = a – b
*=	a *= b	a = a * b
/=	a /= b	a = a / b
%=	a %= b	a = a % b

for the variable a, we can simply write

```
a += 5;
```

This type of shorthand exists for the other arithmetic operators as well, as seen in Table 2.16.

▪ INCREMENT AND DECREMENT OPERATORS

The assignments a = a + 1, and a = a − 1 are so common that C# provides special shorthand operators, ++ and ––, for them. For instance

++a is equivalent to a = a + 1

––a is equivalent to a = a − 1

These operators can appear before the variable, known as the prefix form, or after the variable, which is the suffix form. These two forms differ in how they are evaluated. When using the prefix form in an expression, the increment/decrement is performed before the expression is evaluated. The suffix form evaluates the expression first, then performs the increment or decrement. For example, consider the following:

38	i
30	result

Figure 2.14

```
int i = 37;
int result = ++i - 8;
```

The variable result is assigned the value 30, because i is incremented to 38 before subtracting 8 (see Figure 2.14).

But in the next example

38	i
29	result

Figure 2.15

```
int i = 37;
int result = i++ - 8;
```

the variable result is assigned the value 29, because the 8 is subtracted from i = 37 before i is incremented to 38 (see Figure 2.15).

For this reason, care should be taken when using the increment/decrement operators.

chapter 3

Using Classes, Structures, and Enumerations

C# has a bevy of rich data types that are embodied in classes and structures. No matter what you want to do in C#, it is usually just a matter of finding the class that does the job.

■ THE `String` CLASS

Strings are a perfect introduction to objects, which are basically variables of a class type or a structure. Our intuitive definition of a string is that it should be a sequence of characters that can be manipulated in different ways. We should be able to extract characters or substrings from a string, compute its length, search it for patterns, and so on. The `String` class in C# gives us these capabilities.

We have already seen how string literals are represented in C#. A string literal is a sequence of characters (including escape characters) within double quotes, like:

```
"I am a string literal"
"I am a string literal\tcontaining a horizontal tab!"
```

Creating a string in C# is a matter of assigning a string to a `String` object:

```
String s = "Howdy!";
String t = "Hello!";
String u = t;
```

Figure 3.1

A `String` is defined in a class, so it is stored by reference; that is, the object does not contain the value itself, but a "reference" to it. This reference is really a value specifying the location of the string in memory. This has an effect on assignment; for instance, in the previous example, `u` and `t` both reference the same string (see Figure 3.1).

A class usually has a set of fields, properties, and methods we can access. The `String` class is no exception to this. Look up the `String` class in the `System` namespace in the documentation, and you will get a listing of them, shown here in Table 3.1.

If you click on any of these properties or methods, you will get a detailed description.

TABLE 3.1

Public Properties	
`Chars`	Gets the character at a specified character position in this instance. In C#, this property is the indexer for the `String` class.
`Length`	Gets the number of characters in this instance.
Public Methods	
`Clone`	Returns a reference to this instance of `String`.
`Compare`	Overloaded. Compares two specified `String` objects.
`CompareOrdinal`	Overloaded. Compares two `String` objects, without considering the local national language or culture.
`CompareTo`	Overloaded. Compares this instance with a specified object.
`Concat`	Overloaded. Concatenates one or more instances of `String`, or the `String` representations of the values of one or more instances of `Object`.
`Copy`	Creates a new instance of `String` with the same value as a specified `String`.
`CopyTo`	Copies a specified number of characters from a specified position in this instance to a specified position in an array of Unicode characters.
`EndsWith`	Determines whether the end of this instance matches the specified `String`.
`Equals`	Overloaded. Overridden. Determines whether two `String` objects have the same value.

(continued)

TABLE 3.1 (continued)

Public Methods	
`Format`	Overloaded. Replaces each format specification in a specified `String` with the textual equivalent of a corresponding object's value.
`GetEnumerator`	Retrieves an object that can iterate through the individual characters in this instance.
`GetHashCode`	Overridden. Returns the hash code for this instance.
`GetTypeCode`	Returns the `TypeCode` for class `String`.
`IndexOf`	Overloaded. Reports the index of the first occurrence of a `String`, or one or more characters, within this instance.
`IndexOfAny`	Overloaded. Reports the index of the first occurrence in this instance of any character in a specified array of Unicode characters.
`Insert`	Inserts a specified instance of `String` at a specified index position in this instance.
`Intern`	Retrieves the system's reference to the specified `String`.
`IsInterned`	Retrieves a reference to a specified `String`.
`Join`	Overloaded. Concatenates a specified separator `String` between each element of a specified `String` array, yielding a single concatenated string.
`LastIndexOf`	Overloaded. Reports the index position of the last occurrence of a specified Unicode character or `String` within this instance.
`LastIndexOfAny`	Overloaded. Reports the index position of the last occurrence in this instance of one or more characters specified in a Unicode array.
`PadLeft`	Overloaded. Right-aligns the characters in this instance, padding on the left with spaces or a specified Unicode character for a specified total length.
`PadRight`	Overloaded. Left-aligns the characters in this string, padding on the right with spaces or a specified Unicode character, for a specified total length.
`Remove`	Deletes a specified number of characters from this instance beginning at a specified position.
`Replace`	Overloaded. Replaces all occurrences of a specified Unicode character or `String` in this instance with another specified Unicode character or `String`.
`Split`	Overloaded. Identifies the substrings in this instance that are delimited by one or more characters specified in an array, then places the substrings into a `String` array.
`StartsWith`	Determines whether the beginning of this instance matches the specified `String`.
`Substring`	Overloaded. Retrieves a substring from this instance.
`ToCharArray`	Overloaded. Copies the characters in this instance to a Unicode character array.

(continued)

TABLE 3.1 (continued)

Public Methods	
`ToLower`	Overloaded. Returns a copy of this `String` in lowercase.
`ToString`	Overloaded. Overridden. Converts the value of this instance to a `String`.
`ToUpper`	Overloaded. Returns a copy of this `String` in uppercase.
`Trim`	Overloaded. Removes all occurrences of a set of specified characters from the beginning and end of this instance.
`TrimEnd`	Removes all occurrences of a set of characters specified in a Unicode character array from the end of this instance.
`TrimStart`	Removes all occurrences of a set of characters specified in a Unicode character array from the beginning of this instance.

■ CALLING METHODS

C# uses a special operator called the "membership operator," or, more commonly, the "dot (".") operator." We have already used it in some of our previous method calls. The format is either

```
ClassName.MethodName
```

in the case of static members, or

```
objectName.MethodName
```

in the case of nonstatic, or instance, members. Knowing which members are static entails looking at the member's declaration; that is, whether it is preceded by the keyword `static`. Listing 3.1 is a program (StringDemo) illustrating some of the methods from the `String` class.

Listing 3.1

```
using System;
class StringDemo {
      static void Main() {

            String r = " Hello";//Contains leading space
            String s = r.Trim();//Trim leading and trailing whitespace
            String t = "HELLO";
            String u = s.ToUpper();//"HELLO"
            String sub = s.Substring(2,3);//"llo"
```

(continued)

```
            //Length property of strings
            Console.WriteLine(r+" is "+r.Length+" characters long.");
            Console.WriteLine(s+" is "+s.Length+" characters long.");

            //Demonstrate equals method for strings
            bool areEqual=(r.Equals(s))?true:false;
            Console.WriteLine(r+" equals "+s+": "+areEqual);
            areEqual=(s.Equals(t))?true:false;
            Console.WriteLine(s+" equals "+t+": "+areEqual);
            areEqual=(u.Equals(t))?true:false;
            Console.WriteLine(u+" equals "+t+": "+areEqual);

            //StartsWith, EndsWith, and IndexOf
            Console.WriteLine(
                  s+" starts with "+sub+": "+
                  (s.StartsWith(sub)?true:false));
            Console.WriteLine(
                  s+" ends with "+sub+": "+
                  (s.EndsWith(sub)?true:false));
            Console.WriteLine(sub+" appears in "+s+
                  " at position "+s.IndexOf(sub));

            //String concatenation
            Console.WriteLine(s+" + "+t+": "+s+t);

      }
}
```

Here is the output:

```
Hello is 6 characters long.
Hello is 5 characters long.
Hello equals Hello: False
Hello equals HELLO: False
HELLO equals HELLO: True
Hello starts with llo: False
Hello ends with llo: True
llo appears in Hello at position 2
Hello + HELLO: HelloHELLO
```

The program illustrates some important rules to note here:

- String comparisons are case sensitive using the `Equals()` method.
- White space is significant when comparing strings with `Equals()`.
- Note that the characters in a string are numbered 0, 1, 2, and so on. This should be clear because the program reports that "llo" starts at position 2 in "Hello". The

only way this could be true is if "H" is character 0 (not 1). This is true of indexing in general with C#; we shall see this again later when we cover arrays in Chapter 6.

- The "+" operator can be used to concatenate strings. (Of course, we have been doing this all along in nearly every output statement.)

THE `string` ALIAS

C# allows `String` objects to also be referred to by an alias, namely `string`. For example, the following assignment is OK:

```
string s = "Hello";    //string instead of String
```

Other than using the alias where it appears in documentation, the `string` alias is not used in this text. It is more consistent to always use capitalized class names.

CLASS MEMBERS

Everything that a class contains is called its "members." These members fall into many categories. They are

- *Constructors*—These create and initialize objects of the class type.
- *Fields*—These data fields contain information about the object.
- *Properties*—These return specialized information for objects using a "get," and can sometimes be manipulated using a "set."
- *Indexers*—These provide a way to index elements in certain data structures.
- *Methods*—These are procedures/functions that manipulate/return objects.
- *Operators*—These are symbolic operators customized to work with objects.

Collectively, we can refer to all these as the members of a class. The `String` class contains examples of each of these members. If you open the SDK documentation and go to the `String` class, you can see these for yourself.

Constructors

A constructor is a special method specifically used to create and initialize objects. The name of a constructor is always the same name as the class. What distinguishes one constructor from another is the number and type of parameters it accepts. Here is one `String` constructor:

```
public String(
   char c,
   int count
);
```

This constructor creates a string consisting of a char specified by the first parameter, repeated the number of times specified by the second parameter. The keyword `public` means the constructor can be called by any method, inside or outside the class.

Usage:

```
String s = new String('Z',5);
```

This assignment produces the string `"ZZZZZ"`.

Strings are so fundamental to C# that `String` is the only class that does not necessarily require a constructor to create and initialize its objects. A `String` literal can be directly assigned to a `String` object.

```
String ss = "Howdy";
```

This shorthand is possible only for strings . With other classes, we must use constructors to create and initialize the objects. The type of constructors available for the objects depends on the class to which they belong.

☐ Fields

```
public static readonly string Empty;
```

This field represents the empty string. It is `public`, meaning it is accessible from anywhere, and it is `static`; for now, this simply means it is called by class name, in this case, `String`. Members that are not `static` are called "instance members"; they are accessed by objects of the class type, and not by the class name. Instance members have no keyword to identify them; they are instance members merely if they are not preceded by the keyword `static`.

Usage:

```
String t = String.Empty;
```

The previous assignment would be equivalent to

```
String t = "";//This string contains nothing
```

Null References

It is important that you realize the difference between the empty string and the null string, which is created by setting a string to null:

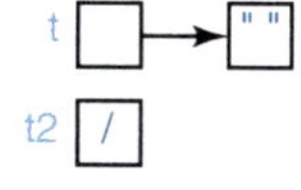

Figure 3.2

```
String t2 = null;//This string points to nothing
```

In the former case, the string points to an empty string, whereas the latter points to nothing (see Figure 3.2). Any object can be set to null, but the programmer must be careful never to call a method that expects a nonnull object with one that is null. C# can often prevent this at compile time, because it will not allow you to use an object that it can prove was never initialized.

☐ Properties

A commonly used property of the `String` class is `Length`.

```
public int Length {get;}
```

Usage:

```
String u = "Howdy";
int theLengthOfU = u.Length;
```

This property obviously returns the length of the string. In the previous example, the variable `theLengthOfU` is assigned the value 5. Note that the `Length` property is not static, so it is called by an object of type `String`, not by the class name.

Indexers

An indexer is a C# feature that allows one to access a datum in a data structure by specifying an index. We will discuss indexers in the chapter on nonlinear data structures.

Methods

There are many methods used to deal with `String` objects. Here is one:

```
public string Insert(
   int startIndex,
   string value
);
```

Usage:

```
String v = "DingDong";
v = v.Insert(4,"Dang");
```

The last statement creates the string `"DingDangDong"`, and assigns it to `v`. Note that this is an instance method, and is called by a `String` object.

Operators

C# allows us to override the default behavior of operators. Note that operators are declared `static`. This is logical, because the redefinition of operators should belong to the class, and not to any particular object.

As an example of overriding ==, consider comparing two strings. When comparing objects using ==, the default behavior is to compare their reference values. If this behavior were used for strings, two lexicographically identical strings stored in different areas of memory would be considered unequal! The `String` class overrides the == operator to actually compare the strings.

```
public static bool operator ==(
   string a,
   string b
);
```

Usage:

```
using System;
class CodeTester {
    static void Main() {
      String w = "Hi";
      String x = "HI";
      w = w.ToUpper();
      bool b = w == x;
      Console.WriteLine(b);
    }
}
```

This code will report the two strings as equal, as it should. This is because the == operator is redefined for strings to compare them as we normally do; that is, character by character.

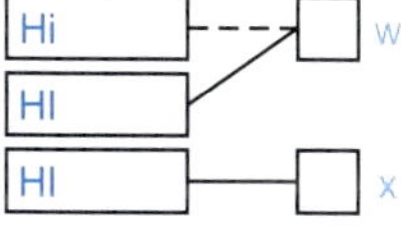

Figure 3.3

```
True
```

This is not, however, the way the == operator normally works; its default behavior is to compare only the reference values of the objects. Figure 3.3 shows that w and x refer to two different strings:

The string w begins by pointing at a string "Hi". By applying the ToUpper() method, it points at a new string "HI". The string x begins by pointing at a different string "HI". When they are compared using ==, it compares each character in one string with each character in the other. If any are unequal, the operator returns false.

If the == operator was not redefined for strings in this manner, it would compare only the references. Because the string references w and x point to different strings, it would say they are unequal. To prove this, modify the code so that the strings w and x are cast into objects (we will discuss casting of objects in Chapter 9).

```
using System;
class CodeTester {
    static void Main() {
      String w = "Hi";
      String x = "HI";
      w = w.ToUpper();
      bool b = (Object)w == (Object)x;
      Console.WriteLine(b);
    }
}
```

When this is done, the test for equality compares w and x as objects, not strings. The result is that the program reports they are not equal.

```
False
```

■ GARBAGE COLLECTION

Consider again the previous scenario:

```
using System;
class CodeTester {
    static void Main() {
      String w = "Hi";
      String x = "HI";
      w = w.ToUpper();
      bool b = w == x;
      Console.WriteLine(b);
    }
}
```

The line `w=w.ToUpper()` causes the reference `w` to move away from the string it was pointing to, and point to a new string in uppercase (see Figure 3.4).

What happens to the old string `"Hi"`, which `w` was pointing to? Because nothing is pointing to it any longer, this object becomes a candidate for garbage collection. When you run any C# program, another program called the garbage collector runs in the background. Whenever an object is left "dangling" like this—that is, when it becomes inaccessible—the garbage collector can run and return the memory back to the operating system.

The garbage collector really decides on its own when to run, though you can force a garbage collection by making the following call:

```
System.GC.Collect();
```

The `GC` class of the `System` namespace represents the garbage collector. Microsoft strongly recommends against explicitly calling the garbage collector. You should really know what you are doing before you force a garbage collection, or you will probably just end up slowing down your program.

There may be times when you want to create some cleanup code before the garbage collector takes your object away. You can do this by defining a destructor for the class; we will cover destructors later.

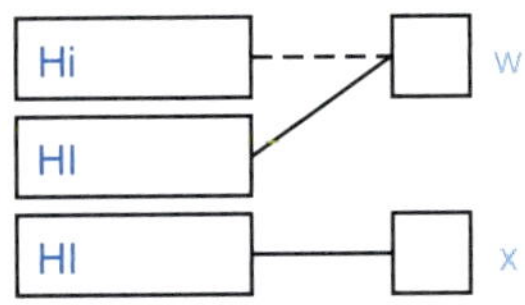

Figure 3.4

▪ PROGRAM: SEARCHSTRINGIGNORECASE

The program in Listing 3.2 prompts the user to enter two strings, then searches for the first occurrence of the second string within the first string. If it appears in the string, the position will be displayed; otherwise, a message stating that the first string does not contain the second is displayed.

Listing 3.2

```
using System;
class SearchStringIgnoreCase {
    static void Main() {
      //Prompt user to enter a string
      Console.WriteLine("Enter a string:");
      String s=Console.ReadLine();

      //Prompt user to enter another string
      Console.WriteLine("Enter another string:");
      String sub=Console.ReadLine();

      //Find first occurrence of 2nd string in 1st string
      //Returns -1 if 2nd string is nowhere in 1st
      int location=s.ToUpper().IndexOf(sub.ToUpper());

      //outString is different depending on result
      //Use ?: conditional operator
      String outString=(location==-1)?"\""+sub+
            "\"\nis not in the string\n\""+s+"\""
            :"\""+sub+"\"\nis in the string\n\""+s+
            "\"\nstarting at character #"+(location+1);

      //Display the output string
      Console.WriteLine(outString);
    }
}
```

Here are sample runs of the program:

```
Enter a string:
Right here is Nirvana
Enter another string:
HER
"HER"
is in the string
"Right here is Nirvana"
starting at character #7
```

```
Enter a string:
Right here is Nirvana
Enter another string:
THE
"THE"
is not in the string
"Right here is Nirvana"
```

▪ STRUCTURES

Structures are similar to classes, but with some important differences. First of all, structure objects are stored by value, rather than by reference. This is useful when assignment needs to copy the values rather than the references. There are other differences between classes and structures, which we will discuss in Chapter 8; however, structures can be treated in much the same way as classes.

☐ The Simple Type Structures

The simple types in C# are actually structures. This makes them objects, the same as objects of any class type. This unified type system of C# allows simple types to be treated as objects. Table 3.2 contains the simple types and their corresponding structure definitions in the `System` namespace.

TABLE 3.2

Type	Structure
`sbyte`	`Sbyte`
`byte`	`Byte`
`short`	`Int16`
`ushort`	`UInt16`
`int`	`Int32`
`uint`	`UInt32`
`long`	`Int64`
`ulong`	`UInt64`
`bool`	`Boolean`
`char`	`Char`
`float`	`Single`
`double`	`Double`
`decimal`	`Decimal`

In each case, the common name is an alias for the class name. Note that the following assignment is OK:

```
Int32 iq = 60;
```

In the case of simple types it is common to use these aliases, whereas for most other structures and classes (like `String`) many programmers prefer not to use them.

■ THE `ToString()` METHOD

Many times we have mixed strings with other types in output statements. For example, consider the following program. Assume we are using the `System` namespace.

```
String greeting = "Hello!";
int age = 3;
int brotherAge = 5;
Console.WriteLine(greeting + " I am " + age + " years old.  My brother is " +
                  (brotherAge - age) + " years older than me.");
```

The last statement joins a string using the + operator to the variable `age`, and to the expression `brotherAge - age`, neither of which is a string. The `WriteLine()` method must convert these quantities to strings. C#'s behavior is to search the structure or the class to which the object belongs for a `ToString()` method, which typically returns a string representation of the object. If the method exists, it will be called implicitly. Of course, we could explicitly make the calls if we so desire:

```
String greeting = "Hello!";
int age = 3;
int brotherAge = 5;
Console.WriteLine(greeting + " I am " + age.ToString() +
                  " years old.  My brother is " + (brotherAge -
                  age).ToString() + " years older than me.");
```

If you check the documentation, you will note that the `Int32` structure has such a method. In fact, it has many methods and properties, as any class does. Table 3.3 shows the `Int32` public members.

Note that even the expression `brotherAge - age` in the previous program is an `int`, and so the `ToString()` method from `Int32` is also called for it. In fact, all of these simple type structures have such a `ToString()` method. Most classes and structures that are worth anything will have a `ToString()` method, for the very purpose described here.

This behavior will become abundantly clear if you consider the next example. Recall that a `bool` takes up 1 byte of memory, and stores the value of either 1 or 0 (true or false). But displaying a Boolean value produces the string output `"True"` or `"False"`.

TABLE 3.3

`Int32` Members

Public Fields	
`MaxValue`	Represents the largest possible value of an `Int32`. This field is constant.
`MinValue`	Represents the smallest possible value of `Int32`. This field is constant.
Public Methods	
`CompareTo`	Compares this instance to a specified object and returns an indication of their relative values.
`Equals`	Overridden. Returns a value indicating whether this instance is equal to a specified object.
`GetHashCode`	Overridden. Returns the hash code for this instance.
`GetTypeCode`	Returns the `TypeCode` for value type `Int32`.
`Parse`	Overloaded. Converts the string representation of a number to its 32-bit signed integer equivalent.
`ToString`	Overloaded. Overridden. Converts the numeric value of this instance to its equivalent string representation.

```
using System;
class CodeTester {
    static void Main() {
      bool meHandsome = false;
      Console.WriteLine("I am handsome: " + meHandsome);
    }
}
```

```
I am handsome: False
```

The `ToString()` method of the Boolean structure is implicitly being called here to return the string `"False"`.

■ THE `CompareTo()` METHOD

The `CompareTo()` method appears in many classes and structures. Many objects can be compared according to an ordering scheme. This is certainly true of numbers, which we can order numerically, and strings, which we can order lexicographically (alphabetically). Most objects in which this type of comparison is possible have access to a `CompareTo(object other)` method. This method always returns an `int`, based on the following criteria:

`CompareTo()` returns:

- A negative integer if the calling object is less than the other
- A positive integer if the calling object is greater than the other
- Zero if the calling object is equal to the other

What is meant by "less than" or "greater than" depends entirely on the type of the objects we are comparing. The type of the objects determines which `CompareTo()` method to call; that is, in which class or structure to look for a `CompareTo()` method.

■ PROGRAM: CompareStringsAndNumbers

The program in Listing 3.3 demonstrates the differences among the various `CompareTo()` methods. The program prompts the user to enter two numbers, which are first stored and compared as strings, then converted to doubles and compared numerically. The output shows the behavior of the comparison methods used.

Listing 3.3

```
using System;
class CompareStringsAndNumbers {
    static void Main() {

      //Prompt the user to enter a number
      Console.Write("Enter a number: ");
      //Read it in as a string of characters
      //this is what happens anyway
      String string1 = Console.ReadLine();

      Console.Write("Enter another number: ");
      String string2 = Console.ReadLine();

      //Assign symbol either <, >, or =
      //Use nested conditional operator ?:
      //First do comparison as strings
      //The CompareTo method from String class will be called
      char symbol = (string1.CompareTo(string2)<0)?'<'
            :((string1.CompareTo(string2)>0)?'>':'=');

      //Display result
      Console.WriteLine(string1+symbol+string2+" lexicographically");
```

(continued)

```
        //Convert both strings to doubles using Parse() from Double
        double number1 = Double.Parse(string1);
        double number2 = Double.Parse(string2);

        //Now compare them as numbers
        //The CompareTo method from Double structure will be called
        symbol = (number1.CompareTo(number2)<0)?'<'
              :((number1.CompareTo(number2)>0)?'>':'=');

        //Display result
        //Convert each quantity to a string manually using ToString()
        //If you don't, interpreter thinks you want to add
        //number1+symbol+number2 as numeric quantities! (not strings)
        Console.WriteLine(number1.ToString()+symbol.ToString()+
              number2.ToString()+" numerically");
    }
}
```

Here is a sample run:

```
Enter a number: 100
Enter another number: 2
100<2 lexicographically
100>2 numerically
```

Take another look at the last output statement:

```
Console.WriteLine(number1.ToString()+symbol.ToString()+
     number2.ToString()+" numerically");
```

Why do we convert `number1`, `symbol`, and `number2` to strings before concatenating them to each other? If we had not, the compiler would interpret

```
number1 + symbol + number2
```

as numerical addition, because all three arguments are basically numeric types. Recall that a `char` is treated as an unsigned `short` in numerical calculations. Another way around this is to insert empty strings between the quantities:

```
number1 + "" + symbol + "" + number2
```

This will cause the compiler to see + as the concatenation operator, and hence the `ToString()` methods of `number1`, `symbol`, and `number2` will be called implicitly.

```
Console.WriteLine(number1+""+symbol+""+number2+" numerically");
```

▪ ENUMERATIONS

An enumeration is basically a set of symbolic constants. They are handy for restricting the user to a set of values, and also to give those values meaning.

For example, suppose we want a data type that represents the days of the week. We could just use the integers 1 through 7, or the integers 0 through 6, or in fact any set of seven integers, but this requires the reader (and you, the programmer) to somehow know and remember that these integers represent weekdays. Instead, we can declare a new data type enumeration called a `Weekday`, as in Listing 3.4.

Listing 3.4

```
using System;
class TestWeekday {

      public enum Weekday {
            Sunday,
            Monday,
            Tuesday,
            Wednesday,
            Thursday,
            Friday,
            Saturday
      }

      static void Main() {

            //Refer to them by name
            Weekday w1=Weekday.Tuesday;
            Console.WriteLine(w1);

            switch (w1) {
                  case Weekday.Monday:
                  case Weekday.Tuesday:
                  case Weekday.Wednesday:
                  case Weekday.Thursday:
                  case Weekday.Friday:
                        Console.WriteLine("Go to work!");
                        break;
                  case Weekday.Saturday:
                  case Weekday.Sunday:
                        Console.WriteLine("Go back to bed!");
                        break;
                  default:
                        Console.WriteLine("Twilight zone!");
                        break;
            }
```

(continued)

```
            //Refer to them by underlying value
            for (int i=0;i<7;i++) {
                  Weekday w2=(Weekday)i;
                  Console.WriteLine(w2);
            }
      }
}
```

The enum `Weekday` basically represents a new data type. It is rather restricted in that it can represent only days of the week, and no operations are defined for `Weekdays`. However, in a program you can create a `Weekday` variable and assign it `Weekday` values. Note that we get an `enum` value by using

```
<enumName>.<enumValue>
```

That is to say, `enum` values are static.

The underlying association of `enums` is nonnegative ints by default; that is, Sunday is actually 0, Monday is 1, . . . , and Saturday is 6. Thus, we can treat `enums` in much the same way we can treat an `int`. Note also from the program that we can cast back and forth between an `enum` and its underlying data type.

■ PUBLIC AND PRIVATE MEMBERS

Here we use `public` when declaring the `enum`. The keyword `public` before a type or a type member means that the type/type member can be accessed from any other class. In contrast, the keyword `private` used in the same manner renders a member inaccessible outside the type in which it is declared.

Because `Weekday` is basically an `int`, we can use it in `switch` statements, for example; we can also easily traverse through `Weekdays` using a loop.

```
Tuesday
Go to work!
Sunday
Monday
Tuesday
Wednesday
Thursday
Friday
Saturday
```

We do not need to use ints as the underlying data type of an enum; we can use any of the following types: byte, sbyte, short, ushort, int, uint, long, or ulong. Also, we do not need to use nonnegative integer values in sequence; we can assign any underlying values we want. The program in Listing 3.5 shows how both these things are done.

Listing 3.5

```
using System;
class TestMonth {
      //sbyte range: -128 thru 127
      public enum Month:sbyte {
            January=5,
            February,   //6
            March,      //7
            April,      //8
            May,        //9
            June,       //10
            July=-10,
            August,     //-9
            September,  //-8
            October=20,
            November,   //21
            December    //22
      }
      static void Main() {
            Console.WriteLine(Month.January
                  +"  "+(sbyte)Month.January);
            Console.WriteLine(Month.February
                  +"  "+(sbyte)Month.February);
            Console.WriteLine(Month.March
                  +"  "+(sbyte)Month.March);
            Console.WriteLine(Month.April
                  +"  "+(sbyte)Month.April);
            Console.WriteLine(Month.May
                  +"  "+(sbyte)Month.May);
            Console.WriteLine(Month.June
                  +"  "+(sbyte)Month.June);
            Console.WriteLine(Month.July
                  +"  "+(sbyte)Month.July);
            Console.WriteLine(Month.August
                  +"  "+(sbyte)Month.August);
            Console.WriteLine(Month.September
                  +"  "+(sbyte)Month.September);
            Console.WriteLine(Month.October
                  +"  "+(sbyte)Month.October);
```

(continued)

```
                Console.WriteLine(Month.November
                      +" "+(sbyte)Month.November);
                Console.WriteLine(Month.December
                      +" "+(sbyte)Month.December);
        }
}
```

The test program reveals these underlying values by casting `Months` to `sbytes`.

```
January 5
February 6
March 7
April 8
May 9
June 10
July -10
August -9
September -8
October 20
November 21
December 22
```

chapter 4

Loops

C# has statements that allow certain portions of code to be executed repetitively. This is useful in many instances; in fact, it would be difficult to conceive of a useful program that did not have a considerable amount of repetitive work involved.

There are three basic looping statements in C#:

- The `while` loop
- The `do . . . while` loop
- The `for` loop

THE `while` LOOP

The `while` loop has the following format:

```
while (booleanValue) {
      <C# statements>
}
```

or, if the `while` loop contains only one statement, the brackets are not required:

```
while (booleanValue) <C# statement>
```

Again, it doesn't matter how we space, indent, or otherwise format the statements, as long as the keywords are present and in the right order. A `while` loop begins by testing the `booleanValue`. If it is true, the loop is entered, and the statements within executed. After this, control returns to the beginning of the `while` loop, and the test is repeated. The program will continue to enter the body of the loop until `booleanValue` eventually becomes false.

The following loop will execute exactly 10 times:

```
using System;
class CodeTester {
    static void Main() {
      int i = 1;
      while (i<=10) {
            Console.WriteLine(i);
            i++;
      }
    }
}
```

```
1
2
3
4
5
6
7
8
9
10
```

The following more condensed version of the same loop also will execute 10 times, but with different output.

```
using System;
class CodeTester {
    static void Main() {
      int i = 1;
      while (i++<=10) Console.WriteLine(i);
    }
}
```

```
2
3
4
5
6
7
8
9
10
11
```

This version uses the prefix form of the increment operator, and it executes only nine times.

```
using System;
class CodeTester {
    static void Main() {
      int i = 1;
      while (++i<=10) Console.WriteLine(i);
    }
}
```

```
2
3
4
5
6
7
8
9
10
```

Obviously, great care must be taken when writing loops to ensure that the control variables have the values we expect. Particular care must be taken when using increment/decrement operators.

It is the programmer's responsibility to see that the `while` loop test eventually becomes false, or the loop will continue indefinitely. This is called an "infinite loop," and sometimes this may be the intent of the programmer. Here is a very simple infinite loop:

```
while (true) {
      //DO ME FOREVER!!!
}
```

Of course, what we would certainly like to avoid is an infinite loop that is unintentional!

You should be careful when using the statement terminator ";", particularly with loops. For example, here is a loop that does nothing but count from 1 to 11, and then exit after `i` is incremented to 12. It executes the output statement only once!

```
using System;
class CodeTester {
    static void Main() {
      int i = 1;
      while (i++<=10); Console.WriteLine(i);
    }
}
```

```
12
```

Because of the semicolon, the program simply does not see `WriteLine()` as part of the `while` loop, which simply increments `i` from 1 to 2 to 3 . . . to 11, and then exits. The fact that `WriteLine()` is on the same line as the `while` statement is irrelevant.

☐ Program: PrimeFactorFinder

Consider a program that finds the prime factors of a number. Recall that a prime is a positive integer greater than 1 whose only positive factors are itself and 1. By this definition, note that 1 is not a prime. A number that is prime obviously has only itself as a prime factor. We would like the output to include this factor, such as:

```
The prime factors of 13 are 13.
```

Positive integers greater than 1 that are not prime are said to be composite. Composite numbers may have multiple factors, but not all of them are necessarily prime factors. For example, 24 has many factors:

```
The factors of 24 are 1 2 3 4 6 8 12 24.
```

Only two of the factors in this list are prime, however; namely, 2 and 3. We would like the program to display only these:

```
The prime factors of 24 are 2 3.
```

This isn't as hard as you might imagine. We proceed in the following manner to extract the prime factors from an integer `n`:

1. Let `x = 2`.
2. If `n` divided by `x` has no remainder, add `x` to the list of prime factors.
3. While `n` divided by `x` has no remainder, let `n = n / x`.
4. Let `x = x + 1`.
5. If `x ≤ n`, go to step 2.
6. Display the list of prime factors.

Note that this algorithm will never add a nonprime factor to the list. For example, if we divide all the 2s out of a number before continuing to 3, no multiple of 2 will divide what is left. The same is true for all other primes greater than 2.

For example, take the number $n = 1764$. Note that 2 divides 1764, so add 2 to the list of prime factors. If we divide all 2s from 1764, we are left with $n = 441$. Neither the number 2 nor any of its multiples will divide 441. If we continue with 3, we see that 3 divides 441. We add 3 to the list of prime factors, then divide n by 3 until it no longer divides what is left. This leaves us with $n = 49$. Now we continue with 4, which does not divide 49. Note that 4 is a multiple of 2 and couldn't possibly divide n at this point, because all 2s were already removed. If we continue with 5, we see that it does not divide 49, and the same is true of 6. When we reach 7, we see that 7 divides 49, so we add 7 to the list of prime factors. When we have divided out all 7s, we are left with $n = 1$. When we increment the test factor from 7 to 8, we see that 8 exceeds $n = 1$, so we display the list of prime factors, 2, 3, and 7, and then stop.

Note that the C# program exactly mimics the algorithm just described, as seen in Listing 4.1. possessive

Listing 4.1

```
using System;
class PrimeFactorFinder {
    static void Main() {
      //Prompt the user to enter the number
      Console.Write("Enter a positive integer greater than 1: ");
      long entry=Int64.Parse(Console.ReadLine());

      //Let num = entry; num will be reduced by division,
      //while entry retains its original value
      long num=entry;

      //Initialize the factor to test as 1
      long testFactor=1;

      //primeString is the list of prime factors
      //It starts out empty
      String primeString="";

      //Start the test factor out at 2 (prefix form)
      //If the test factor exceeds what is left, exit
      while (++testFactor<=num) {
            //If the test factor divides the number
            //add the test factor to the list of prime factors
            primeString+=(num%testFactor==0)?" "+testFactor:"";
```

(continued)

```
            //Divide out the test factor until you are unable to do so
            while (num%testFactor==0) num/=testFactor;
        }

        //Display the list of prime factors
        Console.WriteLine("The prime factors of "+entry+
            " are"+primeString);
    }
}
```

Here are some test runs of the program:

```
Enter a positive integer greater than 1: 1764
The prime factors of 1764 are 2 3 7

Enter a positive integer greater than 1: 123454321
The prime factors of 123454321 are 41 271

Enter a positive integer greater than 1: 101
The prime factors of 101 are 101

Enter a positive integer greater than 1: 724351211
The prime factors of 724351211 are 43 3343 5039
```

Note that this program does nothing to check the input it receives. The user could ignore the directions and enter a negative integer, for example. We will soon discuss how to handle this, but the user could do something even worse, like enter some characters that cannot be parsed as an integer, for example:

```
Enter a positive integer greater than 1: qxy

Unhandled Exception: System.FormatException: Input string was
not in a correct format.
   at System.Number.ParseInt64(String s, NumberStyles style,
NumberFormatInfo info)
   at PrimeFactorFinder.Main()
```

When this happens, the debugging services window will pop up, asking whether we would like to debug the application (see Figure 4.1).

C# has a mechanism called exceptions that deals with these types of problems. We can write programs that handle exceptions, making the program more robust, or equivalently, more difficult to crash. We will defer discussion of this until Chapter 9.

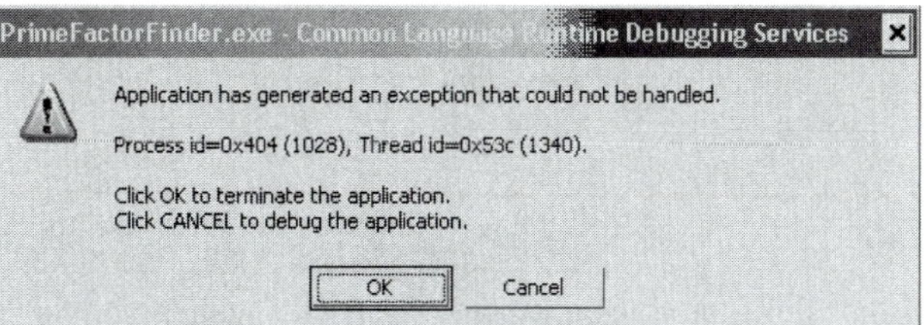

Figure 4.1

□ Nesting Loops

Most C# statements can be nested; that is, there is nothing to prevent us from putting loops within loops, for example. The previous program contains an example of this:

```
//Outer loop
      while (++testFactor<=num) {
            //If the test factor divides the number
            //add the test factor to the list of prime factors
            primeString+=(num%testFactor==0)?" "+testFactor:"";

            //Divide out the test factor until you are unable to do so
//Inner loop - contains only 1 statement
            while (num%testFactor==0) num/=testFactor;
      }
```

■ THE do ... while LOOP

The do ... while loop behaves similarly to the while loop. The format of a do . . . while loop is

```
do {
      <C# statements>
} while (booleanValue);
```

or

```
do <C# statement> while (booleanValue);
```

The statements in a do ... while loop will execute as long as booleanValue evaluates to true. The crucial difference between the while loop and the do ...

`while` loop is that the test for the `do ... while` is performed after the statements execute. Thus, the statements in a `do ... while` loop are guaranteed to execute at least once.

☐ Program: AverageStandardDeviationComputer

This program computes the mean, also known as the average, and the standard deviation of a series of positive scores, say $x_1, x_2, \ldots, x_n$ entered by the user. The mean is simple to compute as

$$m = (x_1 + x_2 + \ldots + x_n)/n$$

We can write a loop that keeps a running total of the scores and keeps count of the number of scores entered, and then divides the total by the number of scores. We do not need to remember the individual scores for this. However, to compute the standard deviation, we need to compute this:

$$s = \sqrt{((m - x_1)^2 + (m - x_2)^2 + \ldots + (m - x_n)^2)}$$

That is, to compute the standard deviation, we must first have the mean. To compute the *i*-th term

$$(m - x_i)^2$$

in the sum, it appears we must remember that the *i*-th score to do this. However, there is another way of computing standard deviation that allows us to compute it at the same time we compute the mean.

Let $u = x_1 + x_2 + \ldots + x_n$
Let $q = x_1^2 + x_2^2 + \ldots + x_n^2$

Notice u and q can be computed simultaneously in the same loop. Then the standard deviation is

$$s = \sqrt{[(q - u^2/n)/(n - 1)]}$$

Note that the mean m is not present in this formula.

The program can be seen in Listing 4.2.

Listing 4.2

```
using System;
class AverageStandardDeviationComputer {
    static void Main() {
      //Set up variables to store the sum of scores
      double sum=0.0;

      //The sum of the square of each score
      double sumsquares=0.0;

      //The number of scores entered
      int size=0;

      //The individual score
      double score=0.0;

      //Prompt the user until they enter a nonnegative number
      do {
            Console.Write("Enter a positive score (0 to quit): ");
            score=Double.Parse(Console.ReadLine());
      } while (score<0);

      //If the score is positive, add it to the totals
      //Loop terminates when score is zero
      while (score>0) {
            //A valid score was entered; increment size
            size++;

            //Increment the running score total by score
            sum+=score;

            //Increment the sum of the squares by score*score
            sumsquares+=score*score;

            //Prompt the user until they enter a nonnegative number
            do {
               Console.Write("Enter a positive score (0 to quit): ");
               score=Double.Parse(Console.ReadLine());
            } while (score<0);
      }

      //Display the mean and standard deviation
      Console.WriteLine("Average: "+sum/size);
      Console.WriteLine("Standard deviation: "+
            Math.Sqrt((sumsquares-sum*sum/size)/(size-1)));
    }
}
```

Here is a test run. Note that it does not include the negative numbers in the calculations, because the inner `do . . . while` loop will continue to prompt the user as long as he or she enters negative values.

```
Enter a positive score (0 to quit): -1
Enter a positive score (0 to quit): 3.1
Enter a positive score (0 to quit): 4
Enter a positive score (0 to quit): -2
Enter a positive score (0 to quit): 4.9
Enter a positive score (0 to quit): 0
Average: 4
Standard deviation: 0.900000000000001
```

Here is the `do . . . while` loop, which repeatedly prompts the user until he or she enters valid data. The `do . . . while` loop is often used in this way.

```
do {
      Console.Write("Enter a positive score (0 to quit): ");
      score=Double.Parse(Console.ReadLine());
} while (score<0);
```

☐ The `Math` Class

The previous program required us to compute a square root. This was done using the static method `Sqrt()` from the `Math` class in the `System` namespace. The `Math` class consists entirely of static members; thus, they are all called by using `System.Math.memberName`. Table 4.1 provides a list of `Math` class members.

■ THE `for` LOOP

The `for` loop is another statement that can perform repetitive tasks. Its format follows:

```
for (<initialization statement(s)>;booleanValue;<modification
statement(s)>) {
      <C# statements>
}
```

or

```
for (<initialization statement(s)>;booleanValue;<modification
statement(s)>)
<Single C# statement>
```

TABLE 4.1

Math Members

Public Fields	
`E`	Represents the natural logarithmic base, specified by the constant, `e`.
`PI`	Represents the ratio of the circumference of a circle to its diameter, specified by the constant, `n`.
Public Methods	
`Abs`	Overloaded. Returns the absolute value of a specified number.
`Acos`	Returns the angle whose cosine is the specified number.
`Asin`	Returns the angle whose sine is the specified number.
`Atan`	Returns the angle whose tangent is the specified number.
`Atan2`	Returns the angle whose tangent is the quotient of two specified numbers.
`Ceiling`	Returns the smallest whole number greater than or equal to the specified number.
`Cos`	Returns the cosine of the specified angle.
`Cosh`	Returns the hyperbolic cosine of the specified angle.
`Exp`	Returns `e` raised to the specified power.
`Floor`	Returns the largest whole number less than or equal to the specified number.
`IEEERemainder`	Returns the remainder resulting from the division of a specified number by another specified number.
`Log`	Overloaded. Returns the logarithm of a specified number.
`Log10`	Returns the base 10 logarithm of a specified number.
`Max`	Overloaded. Returns the larger of two specified numbers.
`Min`	Overloaded. Returns the smaller of two numbers.
`Pow`	Returns a specified number raised to the specified power.
`Round`	Overloaded. Returns the number nearest the specified value.
`Sign`	Overloaded. Returns a value indicating the sign of a number.
`Sin`	Returns the sine of the specified angle.
`Sinh`	Returns the hyperbolic sine of the specified angle.
`Sqrt`	Returns the square root of a specified number.
`Tan`	Returns the tangent of the specified angle.
`Tanh`	Returns the hyperbolic tangent of the specified angle.

The `for` loop can create and initialize variables within the statement. The loop is entered as long as `booleanValue` evaluates to true. Modification of the loop variables occurs after the statements in the body of the loop have executed.

Here is a very simple `for` loop, which displays the squares of 1 through 5:

```
using System;
class CodeTester {
    static void Main() {
      for (int i=1;i<=5;i++) Console.WriteLine(i*i);
    }
}
```

```
1
4
9
16
25
```

Note that `i` is incremented at the end of the loop, not the beginning.

We can put multiple initialization statements and modification statements in a `for` loop, if we separate them with commas:

```
using System;
class CodeTester {
    static void Main() {
      for (int i=1,j=100;i<j;i++,j/=2) {
            Console.WriteLine(i+"*"+j);
            Console.WriteLine("="+i*j);
            Console.WriteLine();
      }
    }
}
```

```
1*100
=100

2*50
=100

3*25
=75

4*12
=48

5*6
=30
```

All of the statements in a `for` loop are optional; you can leave out any of them. For example, here is how you would write an infinite `for` loop:

```
for (;;) {
      //DO ME FOREVER!!!
}
```

☐ Program: PalindromePhrase

A palindrome is a phrase that reads the same forwards and backwards. For example:

A man, a plan, a canal; PANAMA!

We want to write a program that determines whether phrases are palindromes. It should ignore everything but letters, and should compare letters without regard to case. To do this, it is convenient to isolate individual letters in a string, which we can do using the `Chars` property from the `String` class. Suppose we have the following:

```
String s = "Bonjour!";
```

This string has nine characters in it, indexed 0 through $9 - 1 = 8$. To access, say, character #5, which is actually the sixth character, we use this:

```
char sixthChar = s[5];       //assigned the value 'u'
```

We also need to determine whether any particular character is a letter. There is a static method called `IsLetter()` in the `Char` structure that does exactly this. Its definition is as follows:

```
public static bool IsLetter(
   char c
);
```

It is easy to see how it is used:

```
bool isLetter = Char.IsLetter(s[3]);       //True.  s[3] = 'j'
```

Given this, it should be simple to determine whether a phrase is a palindrome. Suppose we are testing the phrase

A Toyota!

which we will store as a string. We will create another working string in uppercase:

A TOYOTA!

Start with two integer variables that will act as indices in this string. One will begin by pointing at the leftmost character, the other indexes the rightmost character. For lack of better names, call them *f* for left, and *r* for right (see Figure 4.2).

Move the indices toward each other until both point at a letter. In this case, *f* stays put, but *r* must be decremented by 1 (see Figure 4.3).

```
A TOYOTA!
|      |
f      r
```

Figure 4.2

```
A TOYOTA!
|      |
f      r
```

Figure 4.3

```
A TOYOTA!
  |   |
  f   r

A TOYOTA!
   | |
   f r

A TOYOTA!
    |
   f=r
```

Figure 4.4

When both indices point at a letter, compare them. If they are not equal, the phrase is not a palindrome and you can exit immediately. If they match, you continue moving the indices toward each other, stopping only on letters, until you find two letters that don't match, or until *f* eventually equals r (see Figure 4.4).

If *f* eventually equals *r*, the phrase must be a palindrome, as is the case here.

The program in Listing 4.3 follows this logic to determine whether a user-entered phrase is a palindrome. It uses an `if` statement; we will cover this type of statement in the next chapter. It should be clear how it works, however.

Listing 4.3

```
using System;
class PalindromePhrase {
   static void Main() {
          bool ispalindrome=true;
          do {
            //Assume the phrase is a palindrome
             ispalindrome=true;

            //Prompt the user to enter phrase
             Console.WriteLine("Input a phrase: ");
             String phrase=Console.ReadLine();

            //Work with an uppercase version
             String phraseUpper=phrase.ToUpper();

            //Set two indices-one each on left and right
            //We will move the indices toward each other
```

(continued)

```
            //until they meet or we find nonmatching letters
            for (int left=0,right=phraseUpper.Length-1;
            left<=right&&ispalindrome;
            left++,right--) {
                  //Move indices in until letters are encountered
                   while (left<=right
                  &&!Char.IsLetter(phraseUpper[left]))
                  left++;
                   while (left<=right
                  &&!Char.IsLetter(phraseUpper[right]))
                  right--;

                  //If left is still left of right
               if (left<=right)
                  //Compare left and right character
                  //If they are unequal, this is not a palindrome
                  ispalindrome=(phraseUpper[left]==phraseUpper[right])
                        ?true:false;
             }

            //outString indicates whether or not phrase is a palindrome
             String outString=(ispalindrome)
            ?"\""+phrase+"\" is a palindrome."
            :"\""+phrase+"\" is not a palindrome.";
             Console.WriteLine(outString);

            //Continue this until a nonpalindrome is entered
         } while (ispalindrome);
    }
}
```

Here is a test run of the program. It repeatedly asks the user to enter phrases, until a nonpalindrome is entered, then it terminates.

```
Input a phrase:
A man, a plan, a canal; PANAMA!
"A man, a plan, a canal; PANAMA!" is a palindrome.
Input a phrase:
Able was I, ere I saw Elba.
"Able was I, ere I saw Elba." is a palindrome.
Input a phrase:
A Toyota!
"A Toyota!" is a palindrome.
Input a phrase:
abababababababa
```

```
"ababababababababa" is a palindrome.
Input a phrase:

"                               " is a palindrome.
Input a phrase:
I don't want to!!!!!
"I don't want to!!!!!" is not a palindrome.
```

■ VISIBILITY

Now that we have covered loops, it is necessary to talk about the visibility of variables and objects. These are basically accessible within the brackets in which they are defined. In the case of loops, a variable declared within the loop is not accessible outside of it. Take the following example:

```
using System;
class CodeTester {
    static void Main() {
      int i = 0;
      while (i++<10) {
            int shift = 5;
            int j = i + shift;
            Console.WriteLine(j);
      }
      Console.WriteLine(shift);
    }
}
```

The last `WriteLine()` statement attempts to display the value of `shift`, but this variable is not visible outside the `while` loop. If we attempt to compile this, we get the following error message:

```
C:\C#>csc CodeTester.cs
Microsoft (R) Visual C# .NET Compiler version 7.00.9466
for Microsoft (R) .NET Framework version 1.0.3705
Copyright (C) Microsoft Corporation 2001. All rights reserved.

CodeTester.cs(10,20): error CS0103: The name 'shift' does not
exist in the class or namespace 'CodeTester'
```

We can fix this easily in this case by declaring `shift` outside the loop:

```
using System;
class CodeTester {
```

```
    static void Main() {
      int i = 0;
      int shift = 5;
      while (i++<10) {
            int j = i + shift;
            Console.WriteLine(j);
      }
      Console.WriteLine(shift);
    }
}
```

This compiles and runs.

```
6
7
8
9
10
11
12
13
14
15
5
```

In the case of a `for` loop, not only are variables declared within the loop accessible only inside the loop, but also any variables declared in the initialization portion are likewise only visible within the loop. For example, the following program will not compile, because it attempts to access the variable `i` outside the `for` loop:

```
using System;
class CodeTester {
    static void Main() {
      for (int i=0;i<10;i++) Console.WriteLine(i);
      Console.WriteLine(i);
    }
}
```

This can be fixed by declaring it outside the loop, and initializing it within the loop:

```
using System;
class CodeTester {
    static void Main() {
      int i;
      for (i=0;i<10;i++) Console.WriteLine(i);
      Console.WriteLine(i);
    }
}
```

The output is

```
0
1
2
3
4
5
6
7
8
9
10
```

This property of visibility is true not only for loops, but also for selection statements, which we will cover in the next chapter. In general, variables and objects are not visible outside the block in which they are declared.

chapter 5

Selection Statements

Selection statements allow programs to execute alternate statements or blocks depending on the value of a variable. There are two selection statements in C#:

- The `if ... else` statement
- The `switch` statement

THE if ... else STATEMENT

The format of an `if ... else` statement is as follows:

```
if (booleanValue) {
      <C# statements>
} else {
      <C# statements>
}
```

As with loops, the brackets are not required if only a single statement is present. The `if` statement works thus: If `booleanValue` evaluates to true, the statements in the `if` portion are executed, and then execution continues past the `else` block; that is, the `else` block is skipped. If `booleanValue` evaluates to false, the `if` portion is skipped, and the statements in the `else` block are executed. Execution then continues past the `else` block.

Here is some code that illustrates how an `if ... else` statement works:

```
using System;
class CodeTester {
    static void Main() {
      int i = 100;
      float f = 3.1f;
      double d = 33.0;
      if (i/f>d) i++;
      else {
      //Brackets optional here too, but they don't hurt
            f*=(float)d;
      }
      Console.WriteLine(i+" "+f);
    }
}
```

The test is whether `i/f>d`; it isn't, because $100/3.1 \approx 32.258 < 33.0$. So, the `else` block is executed, and `f` changes value. Note that `d` must be cast to a `float` in order to assign `f*d` to `f`.

```
100 102.3
```

The `else` portion of an `if ... else` statement is optional:

```
if (booleanValue) {
      <C# statements>
}
```

If the `else` portion is not present, the `if` block is executed if `booleanValue` is true; otherwise, the block is skipped. In the next example, `i/f>d` still evaluates to false, so the statement incrementing `i` simply does not execute.

```
using System;
class CodeTester {
    static void Main() {
      int i = 100;
      float f = 3.1f;
      double d = 33.0;
      if (i/f>d) i++;
      Console.WriteLine(i);
    }
}
```

Note that `i` was not incremented:

```
100
```

☐ Program: GradeComputer

Listing 5.1 shows a program that prompts the user to enter a score. Based on this score, a grade of A through F is computed and displayed.

Listing 5.1

```
using System;
class GradeComputer {
    static void Main() {
      //Prompt user to enter score
      Console.Write("Enter student score:");
      double score=Double.Parse(Console.ReadLine());

      //Initialize grade to the space
      char grade=' ';

      //F range
      if (score<60) grade='F';
      //D range
      if (score>=60&&score<70) grade='D';
      //C range
      if (score>=70&&score<80) grade='C';
      //B range
      if (score>=80&&score<90) grade='B';
      //A range
      if (score>=90) grade='A';

      //Display grade
      Console.WriteLine("Student grade: "+grade);
    }
}

Enter student score:75
Student grade: C

Enter student score:157
Student grade: A

Enter student score:-32
Student grade: F
```

Nested `if ... else` Statements

The `if ... else` statement can be nested within other statements, including `if ... else` statements. We can rewrite the GradeComputer program using a series of nested `if ... else` statements (see Listing 5.2, GradeComputerNested). Its behavior in terms of output is identical to GradeComputer.

Listing 5.2

```
using System;
class GradeComputerNested {
    static void Main() {
      //Prompt user to enter score
      Console.Write("Enter student score:");
      double score=Double.Parse(Console.ReadLine());

      //Initialize grade to the space
      char grade=' ';

      //This is a D or possibly better
      if (score>=60)
            //This is a C or possibly better
            if (score>=70)
                  //This is a B or possibly better
                  if (score>=80)
                        //This is an A
                        if (score>=90) grade='A';
                        //This is not an A; not better than B
                        else grade='B';
                  //Not better than a C
                  else grade='C';
            //Not better than a D
            else grade='D';
      //Not high enough for a D
      else grade='F';

      //Display grade
      Console.WriteLine("Student grade: "+grade);
    }
}

Enter student score:75
Student grade: C

Enter student score:1398457.671
Student grade: A
```

(continued)

```
Enter student score:12
Student grade: F

Enter student score:70
Student grade: C

Enter student score:89.3
Student grade: B
```

Grouping else's with if's

An else is always grouped with the closest if, unless brackets are used to change this. Indentation is not relevant; in fact, it never is in a C# program. Consider the following code:

```
using System;
class CodeTester {
    static void Main() {
      int i = 100;
      float f = 3.1f;
      double d = 33.0;
      if (i/f>d)
            if (i/d>3) i--;
      else i++;
      Console.WriteLine(i);
    }
}
```

By the way the statements are indented, you might think that the else is associated with the outer if, and because i/f is not less than d, the else will execute and i will be incremented. However, the else is associated not with the outer if, but the inner if. The outer if evaluates to false, and the else never executes.

```
100
```

The else here will execute only if the inner if is reached, and evaluates to false. Of course, if this is not what you intended—that is, if you want the else to be associated with the outer if—use brackets:

```
using System;
class CodeTester {
    static void Main() {
      int i = 100;
      float f = 3.1f;
```

```
        double d = 33.0;
        if (i/f>d) {
            if (i/d>3) i--;
        } else i++;
        Console.WriteLine(i);
    }
}
```

```
101
```

Be careful when indenting and/or grouping `else`s. Remember that we indent for readability, and not to satisfy any requirement of the compiler.

■ THE `switch ... break` STATEMENT

The `switch ... break` statement is convenient for selecting among multiple alternatives. This could also be accomplished by using nested `if`'s, but that approach is often hard to read.

The format of the `switch ... break` statement is as follows:

```
switch (value) {
    case value1:
        <C# statements>
        break;
    case value2:
        <C# statements>
        break;
    .
    .
    .
    case valueN:
        <C# statements>
        break;
    default:
        <C# statements>
        break;
}
```

When entering the `switch` statement, `value` is compared against `value1`, `value2`, and so on, until `value` equals one of the `case`s. When a match is found, execution continues with the statements in the matching `case`. If no match is found, the statements in the default case are executed. The break statement is needed to tell C# where to continue execution after the statements in the case are evaluated. Unlike some other languages, like Java and C, execution is not allowed to "fall through" from one case into another.

Here is an example of the switch . . . break statement:

```
using System;
class CodeTester {
    static void Main() {
      String s="Hello";
      switch (s.ToUpper()) {
            case "Hello":
                  s+="1";
                  break;
            case "Hello!":
            case "HELLO!":
                  s+="2";
                  break;
            case "HELLO"://I am a match
                  s+="3";
                  break;//Break to end of switch
            default:
                  s+="default";
                  break;
      }
      Console.WriteLine(s);
    }
}
```

Here is the output:

```
Hello3
```

Notice that multiple cases can be grouped together, as in

```
case "Hello!":
case "HELLO!":
      s+="2";
      break;
```

However, only the trailing case can contain code if you want all cases to be associated with that code.

```
using System;
class CodeTester {
    static void Main() {
      String s="Hello";
      switch (s.ToUpper()) {
            case "Hello":
                  s+="1";
                  break;
            case "HELLO"://I am the match
            case "Hello!":
                  s+="2";
                  break;//Break out
            default:
                  s+="default";
                  break;
      }
      Console.WriteLine(s);
    }
}
```

```
Hello2
```

Here is an example of a situation where none of the `cases` match:

```
using System;
class CodeTester {
    static void Main() {
      String s="Hello";
      switch (s.ToUpper()) {
            case "Hello":
                  s+="1";
                  break;
            case "Hello!":
                  s+="2";
                  break;//Break out
            default:
                  s+="default";
                  break;
      }
      Console.WriteLine(s);
    }
}
```

```
Hellodefault
```

Using `switch` with Other Jump Statements

The `break` statement is a statement in its own right; it isn't necessary to use only the `break` statement to exit a `switch` statement. The jump statements discussed later in this chapter will also work.

Program: DateChecker

The program in Listing 5.3 prompts the user to enter a date in MMDDYYYY format. The program must then determine whether this is a valid date. Some months have 30 days, some have 31, and February has 28 or 29 days.

Determining leap years may be the most complicated part of the program. Leap years are basically years that are divisible by 4. The exception to this are years that mark the end of a century, unless the year is divisible by 400. For example, 1700 was not a leap year, but 1600 was. The logic to accomplish this could be expressed in this way:

```
if ((year%4==0 && year%100!=0) || year%400==0)
numberOfDays=29;
else numberOfDays=28;
```

The next most difficult part of the program may be extracting the month, day, and year from the date entered in MMDDYYYY format. We could do this using substrings, but because everything in the string is a digit, we could use the quotient and remainder of integer division to extract digits. For example, suppose we have the date

12251999

To extract the month, we divide the date by 1,000,000, and keep the quotient:

12251999/1000000 = 12

To extract the year, we can divide the date by 10,000, and keep the remainder:

12251999 % 10000 = 1999

To capture the day, we can first divide the date by 1,000,000 and keep the remainder. This yields the day and the year. We then divide this by 10,000 and keep the quotient to extract the day:

12251999 % 1000000 / 1000 =

251999 / 1000 =

25

Once these problems are solved, programming is rather direct. There is a `switch` statement in the program well suited to discern the number of days in the month.

Listing 5.3

```
using System;
public class DateChecker {
    static void Main() {
              int date, month, day, year, numberOfDays=0;
              bool montherror=false;

            //Prompt the user to enter date
              Console.Write("Enter a date in the MMDDYYYY format: ");
              date=Int32.Parse(Console.ReadLine());

            //Extract first two digits
              month=date/1000000;
            //Extract 3rd and 4th digit
              day=(date%1000000)/10000;
            //Extract last four digits
              year=date%10000;

            //Determine the number of days in the month
            //based on the month
              switch (month) {
                  //31 day months here
                     case 1: case 3: case 5: case 7:
                     case 8: case 10: case 12:
                          numberOfDays=31; break;
                  //30 day months here
                     case 4: case 6: case 9: case 11:
                          numberOfDays=30; break;
                  //February may be 28 or 29 days,
                  //depending on whether or not it is a leap year
                     case 2: if ((year%4==0&&year%100!=0)||year%400==0)
                                  numberOfDays=29;
                             else numberOfDays=28;
                             break;
                     default: montherror=true; break;
              }

            //Display error message if month or day was bad
              if (montherror)
            Console.WriteLine("Error in the month-please check.");
              else if (day>numberOfDays)
            Console.WriteLine("Error in the day-please check.");
            //Display OK message
              else Console.WriteLine("This is a valid date.");
    }
}
```

Here are some sample runs:

```
Enter a date in the MMDDYYYY format: 03312000
This is a valid date.

Enter a date in the MMDDYYYY format: 3412001
Error in the day-please check.

Enter a date in the MMDDYYYY format: 13312000
Error in the month-please check.

Enter a date in the MMDDYYYY format: 12319999
This is a valid date.

Enter a date in the MMDDYYYY format: 02292000
This is a valid date.

Enter a date in the MMDDYYYY format: 2291999
Error in the day-please check.

Enter a date in the MMDDYYYY format: 2291700
Error in the day-please check.

Enter a date in the MMDDYYYY format: 2291601
Error in the day-please check.

Enter a date in the MMDDYYYY format: 2291600
This is a valid date.
```

Notice that the program allows you to omit the leading zero on the month, but not on the day or the year.

■ LABELED STATEMENTS

C# allows you to place a label on a statement in the following way:

```
<label-name>:<statement>
```

Labels are useful when we wish to jump directly from one portion of a program to another. We will see this in the following section when we discuss the jump statements in C#. Here is an example of a labeled statement:

```
comeToMe:Console.WriteLine("WE ARE HERE!");
```

■ JUMP STATEMENTS

There may be situations where you wish to jump directly from one point of execution in a program to another. Older languages allowed great freedom in this regard, by supplying a "go to" statement. C# supplies a `goto` statement, but restricts it in an important way. C# supplies other jumping statements as well.

□ The `goto` Statement

In C#, the `goto` statement allows you to jump from one point in a program to another. The format of a `goto` statement is as follows:

```
goto <statement-label>
```

or

```
goto case <case-value>
```

The first form of the `goto` statement allows the program to jump to a labeled statement. Listing 5.4 is an example of how this would be used.

Listing 5.4

```
using System;
class ZeroIsTheAnswer {
    static void Main() {
      double x;
      Console.Write("Enter the smallest nonnegative number: ");

      while ((x=Double.Parse(Console.ReadLine()))>=0) {
            if (x==0) goto End;
            Console.Write("Nope, try again: ");
      }

      End://Statement label
      if (x==0) Console.WriteLine("KeeRect!");
      else Console.WriteLine("You can't follow directions!");
    }
}
```

Here are some sample runs of the program:

```
Enter the smallest nonnegative number: 3.1
Nope, try again: 0.0001
Nope, try again: -0.0001
You can't follow directions!
```

```
Enter the smallest nonnegative number: .000001
Nope, try again: 0
KeeRect!
```

The program continues to loop until the user enters either a negative number (in which case the test for the `while` loop fails) or zero. In this case, the test

```
if (x==0) goto End;
```

causes execution to continue with the first statement following the label `End:`. In this example, the `if` statement is on a different line than the label. Remember, this is irrelevant to the compiler, and in this case was done to improve readability.

```
End:
if (x==0) Console.WriteLine("KeeRect!");
else Console.WriteLine("You can't follow directions!");
```

The `goto` statement is restricted in C#. It cannot be used to arbitrarily jump from one point to another. Basically, the `goto` can

- Jump to points within the statement block in which it is defined
- Jump to points in outer blocks at a lower level of nesting

For example, the following program demonstrates an illegal use of the `goto` statement. It does not compile.

```
using System;
class CodeTester {
    static void Main() {
      int x=Int32.Parse(Console.ReadLine());
      okeeDokee:
      if (x<3) {
            x++;
            if (x<5) goto okeeDokee;//OK to jump out
            goto cantGoThere;//Can't jump across into another block
      }
      while (x<10) {
            cantGoThere: x++;
      }
    }
}

C:\C#>csc CodeTester.cs
Microsoft (R) Visual C# .NET Compiler version 7.00.9466
for Microsoft (R) .NET Framework version 1.0.3705
Copyright (C) Microsoft Corporation 2001. All rights reserved.

CodeTester.cs(9,3): error CS0159: No such label 'cantGoThere' within the scope
of the goto statement
CodeTester.cs(12,3): warning CS0164: This label has not been referenced
```

Program: LuckyNumbers

Another form of the `goto` statement allows us to jump from one case to another in a `switch` statement. The program in Listing 5.5 uses this form of the `goto` to jump from one case in a `switch` statement to another.

Listing 5.5

```
using System;
class LuckyNumbers {
    static void Main() {
      Console.Write("Enter an integer between 1 and 10: ");
      int x=Int32.Parse(Console.ReadLine());

      switch(x) {
      case 1:
      case 2:
      case 3:
      case 4:
      case 5:goto case 8;
      case 6:Console.WriteLine(x+" is an unlucky number!");
            break;
      case 7:Console.WriteLine(x+" is a lucky number!");
            break;
      case 8:
      case 9:
      case 10:Console.WriteLine(x+" is neither lucky nor
                                   unlucky.");
            break;
      default:Console.WriteLine("Can\'t you listen?");
            break;
      }
    }
}

Enter an integer between 1 and 10: 3
3 is neither lucky nor unlucky.

Enter an integer between 1 and 10: 5
5 is neither lucky nor unlucky.

Enter an integer between 1 and 10: 6
6 is an unlucky number!

Enter an integer between 1 and 10: 9
9 is neither lucky nor unlucky.
```

```
Enter an integer between 1 and 10: 7
7 is a lucky number!

Enter an integer between 1 and 10: 0
Can't you listen?
```

The `break` Statement

The `break` statement is used more often than the `goto` statement. The format is simply

```
break;
```

It is used to jump to the next statement outside the block or statement in which the break appears. We have already seen this use with the `switch ... break` statement, but `break` can be used in other statements as well. It can be used to exit a loop early. The PerfectSquare program in Listing 5.6 shows this behavior.

Listing 5.6

```
using System;
class PerfectSquare {
    static void Main() {
      Console.Write("Enter a perfect square: ");
      double num=Double.Parse(Console.ReadLine());
      double sqrt=0;

      while (num>=0) {
            sqrt=Math.Sqrt(num);
            if (sqrt==(int)sqrt) break;
            Console.Write("Nope, try again: ");
            num=Double.Parse(Console.ReadLine());
      }

      if (num<0) Console.WriteLine("A perfect square is
nonnegative.");
      else Console.WriteLine(sqrt+" squared = "+num);
    }
}

Enter a perfect square: 12
Nope, try again: 3
Nope, try again: -25
A perfect square is nonnegative.
```

(continued)

```
Enter a perfect square: 8
Nope, try again: 81
9 squared = 81
```

The program asks the user to enter a perfect square. A perfect square, by definition, is an integer whose square root is also an integer. By using the `Sqrt()` method from `System.Math`, and the `cast` operator, we can easily tell if the square root of an integer is an integer:

```
sqrt=Math.Sqrt(num);
if (sqrt==(int)sqrt) break;
```

The program loops until the user enters a negative number, in which case the test in the `while` loop fails, or until the user enters a perfect square and we break out of the `while` loop. The `if ... else` statement after the while loop tests which of the conditions caused the loop to end.

The `continue` Statement

The `continue` statement is used to start the next iteration of a loop early; that is, when the `continue` statement is reached, execution jumps immediately to the beginning of the loop. The SumIntegers program in Listing 5.7 demonstrates this; it sums the first 50 integers and the first 100 integers.

Listing 5.7

```
using System;
class SumIntegers {
    static void Main() {
      int sum50=0,sum100=0;

      for (int i=1;i<=100;i++) {
            sum100+=i;
            if (i>=50) continue;//Start next iteration now
            sum50+=i;//This is skipped when i>=50
      }

      Console.WriteLine("Sum of first 50 positive integers: "+sum50);
      Console.WriteLine("Sum of first 100 positive integers: "+sum100);
    }
}

Sum of first 50 positive integers: 1225
Sum of first 100 positive integers: 5050
```

The program calculates two sums, sum50 and sum100. If the integer to be added becomes greater than 50, the continue statement jumps back to the beginning of the for loop, and the statement

```
sum50+=i;//This is skipped when i>=50
```

is skipped.

☐ The try ... catch Statement

You may have noticed that it is quite easy to crash some of the programs developed so far in the text. For example, consider the following program. It asks the user to enter two integers, then divides the first by the second, and displays the results.

```
using System;
class CodeTester {
    static void Main() {
      //Prompt user
      Console.Write("Enter an integer: ");
      int num=Int32.Parse(Console.ReadLine());
      Console.Write("Enter another integer: ");
      int den=Int32.Parse(Console.ReadLine());

      //Do the division
      Console.WriteLine(num+"/"+den+"="+num/den);
    }
}
```

If the user behaves him- or herself (a big if), everything will be OK:

```
Enter an integer: 98
Enter another integer: 3
98/3=32
```

However, suppose the user enters something that cannot be parsed as an integer, or perhaps enters 0 for the denominator.

```
Enter an integer: 3
Enter another integer: 0

Unhandled Exception: System.DivideByZeroException: Attempted to
divide by zero.
   at CodeTester.Main()

Enter an integer: three
```

```
Unhandled Exception: System.FormatException: Input string was
not in a correct format.
   at System.Number.ParseInt32(String s, NumberStyles style,
NumberFormatInfo info)
   at CodeTester.Main()
```

When something like this happens, the program basically chokes, throws up some kind of panic message, and terminates. When a program terminates at any point other than where it should, or if the system has to handle an exceptional condition, the program has crashed.

C# allows us to catch a great number of exceptional conditions that may arise in a program, and to control these conditions in the way we desire, rather than relying on the system's default behavior of simply quitting. (But what else could it do?) C# provides the `try ... catch` statement for this.

Although the `try ... catch` block is not officially a selection statement, it does transfer control from one part of a program to another, so this chapter is a suitable place to discuss it.

The syntax of the `try ... catch` block is

```
try {
      <C# statements>
} catch (<exceptionType> <exceptionName>) {
      <C# statements>
}
```

Each `try` can have multiple `catch` blocks. The `try ... catch` is intended to catch exceptional conditions when they arise; for example, bad input from the console or a file, division by zero, and so on. Special classes called exception classes exit for these conditions. When an exceptional condition arises, an object of the appropriate exception type is generated and immediately transferred to the `catch` blocks, whereupon a sequential search begins for the appropriate block to handle it. When (or if) it is found, the appropriate block executes its statements, and then control is transferred past the end of the last `catch` block.

The `System` namespace, for example, contains many exception types (see Table 5.1).

When you want to catch an exception, it becomes a matter of knowing which kinds of exceptions can be thrown by a particular expression, statement, or type member. This information can be found in the documentation.

Program: TryCatchExample

Listing 5.8 is a simple example of setting up an exceptional condition, and then catching it. We set up the possibility of dividing an `int` by zero, which throws a `DivideByZeroException`. This will occur in a `try ... catch` block. When it occurs, control will transfer to the `catch` block, which sets up a return to the prompt. If the user eventually enters appropriate values, the program will terminate.

TABLE 5.1

`AppDomainUnloadedException`	The exception that is thrown when an attempt is made to access an unloaded application domain.
`ApplicationException`	The exception that is thrown when a nonfatal application error occurs.
`ArgumentException`	The exception that is thrown when one of the arguments provided to a method is not valid.
`ArgumentNullException`	The exception that is thrown when a null reference is passed to a method that does not accept it as a valid argument.
`ArgumentOutOfRangeException`	The exception that is thrown when the value of an argument is outside the allowable range of values as defined by the invoked method.
`ArithmeticException`	The exception that is thrown for errors in an arithmetic, casting, or conversion operation.
`BadImageFormatException`	The exception that is thrown when the file image of a DLL or an executable program is invalid.
`CannotUnloadAppDomainException`	The exception that is thrown when an attempt to unload an application domain fails.
`ContextMarshalException`	The exception that is thrown when an attempt to marshal an object across a context boundary fails.
`DivideByZeroException`	The exception that is thrown when there is an attempt to divide an integral or decimal value by zero.
`DllNotFoundException`	The exception that is thrown when a DLL specified in a DLL import cannot be found.
`DuplicateWaitObjectException`	The exception that is thrown when an object appears more than once in an array of synchronization objects.
`EntryPointNotFoundException`	The exception that is thrown when an attempt to load a class fails due to the absence of an entry method.
`Exception`	Represents errors that occur during application execution.
`ExecutionEngineException`	The exception that is thrown when there is an internal error in the execution engine of the common language runtime. This class cannot be inherited.
`FieldAccessException`	The exception that is thrown when there is an illegal attempt to access a private or protected field inside a class.
`FormatException`	The exception that is thrown when the format of an argument does not meet the parameter specifications of the invoked method.

(continued)

TABLE 5.1 (continued)

`IndexOutOfRangeException`	The exception that is thrown when an attempt is made to access an element of an array with an index that is outside the bounds of the array. This class cannot be inherited.
`InvalidCastException`	The exception that is thrown for invalid casting or explicit conversion.
`InvalidOperationException`	The exception that is thrown when a method call is invalid for the object's current state.
`InvalidProgramException`	The exception that is thrown when a program contains invalid Microsoft Intermediate Language (MSIL) or metadata. Generally this indicates a bug in a compiler.
`MemberAccessException`	The exception that is thrown when an attempt to access a class member fails.
`MethodAccessException`	The exception that is thrown when there is an illegal attempt to access a private or protected method inside a class.
`MissingFieldException`	The exception that is thrown when there is an attempt to dynamically access a field that does not exist.
`MissingMemberException`	The exception that is thrown when there is an attempt to dynamically access a class member that does not exist.
`MissingMethodException`	The exception that is thrown when there is an attempt to dynamically access a method that does not exist.
`MulticastNotSupportedException`	The exception that is thrown when there is an attempt to combine two instances of a noncombinable delegate type unless one of the operands is a null reference. This class cannot be inherited.
`NotFiniteNumberException`	The exception that is thrown when a floating-point value is positive infinity, negative infinity, or not a number (NaN).
`NotImplementedException`	The exception that is thrown when a requested method or operation is not implemented.
`NotSupportedException`	The exception that is thrown when an invoked method is not supported, or when there is an attempt to read, seek, or write to a stream that does not support the invoked functionality.
`NullReferenceException`	The exception that is thrown when there is an attempt to dereference a null object reference.
`ObjectDisposedException`	The exception that is thrown when an operation is performed on a disposed object.
`OutOfMemoryException`	The exception that is thrown when there is not enough memory to continue the execution of a program.

(continued)

TABLE 5.1 (continued)

`OverflowException`	The exception that is thrown when an arithmetic, casting, or conversion operation in a checked context results in an overflow.
`PlatformNotSupportedException`	The exception that is thrown when a feature does not run on a particular platform.
`RankException`	The exception that is thrown when an array with the wrong number of dimensions is passed to a method.
`StackOverflowException`	The exception that is thrown when the execution stack overflows by having too many pending method calls. This class cannot be inherited.
`SystemException`	Defines the base class for predefined exceptions in the `System` namespace.
`TypeInitializationException`	The exception that is thrown as a wrapper around the exception thrown by the class initializer. This class cannot be inherited.
`TypeLoadException`	The exception that is thrown when type-loading failures occur.
`TypeUnloadedException`	The exception that is thrown when there is an attempt to access an unloaded class.
`UnauthorizedAccessException`	The exception that is thrown when the operating system denies access because of an I/O error or a specific type of security error.
`UriFormatException`	The exception that is thrown when an invalid uniform resource identifier (URI) is detected.

Listing 5.8

```
using System;
class TryCatchExample {
    static void Main() {

      //Set up loop control variable
      bool OKToStop=false;

      while (!OKToStop) {

            //Assume the user will enter nonzero denominator
            OKToStop=true;
```

(continued)

```
            try {

                  //Prompt user
                  Console.Write("Enter an integer: ");
                  int num=Int32.Parse(Console.ReadLine());
                  Console.Write("Enter another integer: ");
                  int den=Int32.Parse(Console.ReadLine());

                  //Do the division
                  Console.WriteLine(num+"/"+den+"="+num/den);

            //If division by zero occurs, control transfers here
            } catch (DivideByZeroException dbze) {

                  //Display the exception
                  Console.WriteLine(dbze.ToString());

                  //Force another iteration
                  OKToStop=false;
            }

      //Control transfers here after catch block
      //Program does not return to the offending statement
      }
    }
}

Enter an integer: 27
Enter another integer: 4
27/4=6

Enter an integer: -38
Enter another integer: 0
System.DivideByZeroException: Attempted to divide by zero.
   at TryCatchExample.Main()
Enter an integer: 55
Enter another integer: 0
System.DivideByZeroException: Attempted to divide by zero.
   at TryCatchExample.Main()
Enter an integer: 0
Enter another integer: 0
System.DivideByZeroException: Attempted to divide by zero.
   at TryCatchExample.Main()
Enter an integer: 0
Enter another integer: -23
0/-23=0
```

Of course, division by zero is certainly not the only thing that can go wrong with this program. For example, when the user is prompted to enter an integer, he or she may enter some garbage that cannot be parsed as an integer. This particular type of exception is called a `FormatException`. We can add this to our `catch` blocks, as in Listing 5.9.

Listing 5.9

```
using System;
class TryCatchExample {
    static void Main() {

      //Set up loop control variable
      bool OKToStop=false;

      while (!OKToStop) {

            //Assume the user will enter nonzero denominator
            OKToStop=true;

            try {

                  //Prompt user
                  Console.Write("Enter an integer: ");
                  int num=Int32.Parse(Console.ReadLine());
                  Console.Write("Enter another integer: ");
                  int den=Int32.Parse(Console.ReadLine());

                  //Do the division
                  Console.WriteLine(num+"/"+den+"="+num/den);

            //If division by zero occurs, control transfers here
            } catch (DivideByZeroException dbze) {

                  //Display the exception
                  Console.WriteLine(dbze.ToString());

                  //Force another iteration
                  OKToStop=false;
            } catch (FormatException fe) {

                  //Display the exception
                  Console.WriteLine(fe.ToString());

                  //Force another iteration
                  OKToStop=false;
            }
```

(continued)

```
        //Control transfers here after catch block
        //Program does not return to the offending statement
        }
    }
}
```

Now our program catches either type of exception, and will continue to prompt the user until he or she enters valid integers.

```
Enter an integer: q
System.FormatException: Input string was not in a correct
format.
   at System.Number.ParseInt32(String s, NumberStyles style,
NumberFormatInfo info)
   at TryCatchExample.Main()
Enter an integer: 98
Enter another integer: three
System.FormatException: Input string was not in a correct
format.
   at System.Number.ParseInt32(String s, NumberStyles style,
NumberFormatInfo info)
   at TryCatchExample.Main()
Enter an integer: 98
Enter another integer: 0
System.DivideByZeroException: Attempted to divide by zero.
   at TryCatchExample.Main()
Enter an integer: 98
Enter another integer: 3
98/3=32
```

The problem, of course, with designing robust applications is trying to figure out in advance all the possible things that could go wrong, and to set up mechanisms to handle them.

chapter 

Arrays

There are many programs you will write in which you will want to manipulate large amounts of data of the same type. For example, you may wish to store a series of any of the following in memory

- Student grades
- Customer names
- Addresses
- Character codes
- Boolean values

If we had to create a separate variable for each value, the programming would be, for lack of a better word, strenuous. Arrays allow us to create multiple memory locations of the same type under a shared name. We can access individual locations in an array by using an index, or in the case of multidimensional arrays, indices.

■ DECLARING ONE-DIMENSIONAL ARRAYS

Declaring a one-dimensional array in C# creates a series of memory locations, each containing a value of the same type. This is done in the following manner:

```
<typeName>[] <arrayName> = new <typeName>[numLocations];
```

This simply creates `"numLocations"` memory cells, each of type `"typeName"`, under the common name `"arrayName"`. The following is an example that creates an array of 10 `int`s called `scores`:

```
int[] scores = new int[10];
```

Figure 6.1

An array is stored by reference; that is, the array name contains a reference to the location of the values in memory. In this example, the array scores might look something like Figure 6.1.

Notice that all of the memory locations have the value zero. This is C#'s default initialization behavior. If you want the locations to have different values, you must do the assignment yourself, or in the case of the simple types and strings, you can assign the values in the code. Here is how you would create an array and provide values for its memory locations at the same time:

```
<typeName>[] <arrayName> = {value1, value2, . . . , valueN};
```

The values `value1` through `valueN` must of course be of the type `"typeName"`. Here is an example of creating an array and providing it with initial values:

```
char[] vowels = {'A','E','I','O','U'};
```

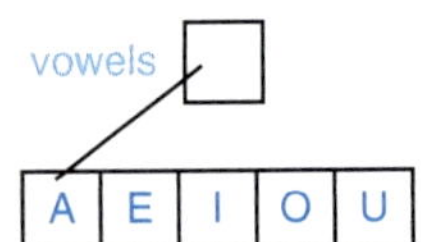

Figure 6.2

This produces the array in Figure 6.2.

Notice that if we declare an array in this way, we need not specify the number of memory locations to create, because the compiler counts the values and creates an array of the appropriate size.

Because an array is stored by reference, it is certainly possible to declare an array but allocate no memory locations for it. Here is an example:

```
double[] nada;
```

Figure 6.3

In this case, the array simply contains null, and points at nothing (see Figure 6.3).

☐ Indices

Accessing individual elements in a one-dimensional array is done by using an index. C# numbers the elements in an *n*-element array from 0 through *n*-1, the same way it numbers the characters in a string. Consider again the array

```
char[] vowels = {'A','E','I','O','U'};
```

In this array,

`vowels[0]` is the character `'A'`
`vowels[1]` is the character `'E'`

`vowels[2]` is the character `'I'`
`vowels[3]` is the character `'O'`
`vowels[4]` is the character `'U'`

Any particular array element can be treated as though it were of its declared type. In the case of the array vowels, each of `vowels[0]` through `vowels[4]` is of type `char`.

There is no reason that the index cannot be a variable; in fact, this is how we do the bulk of array processing. We write a loop that uses an `int` variable to pass through the individual elements in an array.

☐ Program: FibonacciArray

As an example of using variables as indices, Listing 6.1 is a program that creates an array containing the first 20 Fibonacci numbers. The Fibonacci sequence begins with two integers, 1 and 1. Each subsequent number is the sum of the two numbers preceding it. Thus, the first 10 Fibonacci numbers are

1, 1, 2, 3, 5, 8, 13, 21, 34, 55

Writing a program to calculate and store the numbers in this sequence simply means creating a large enough array of `ints` (or `longs`), setting the first two locations to the value 1, then setting each subsequent location equal to the sum of the two locations preceding it. This is most easily done in a loop, as you can see if you inspect the code.

Listing 6.1

```
using System;
class FibonacciArray {
    static void Main() {
      //Create an array of ints
      int[] fib = new int[25];

      //Set the first two locations to 1
      fib[0]=1;
      fib[1]=1;

      //Set each subsequent location in a loop
      for (int i=2;i<fib.Length;i++)
            fib[i]=fib[i-1]+fib[i-2];

      //Display the elements after computed
      Console.Write("The first "+fib.Length+" Fibonacci numbers are:");
      for (int i=0;i<fib.Length;i++) Console.Write(" "+fib[i]);
    }
}
```

```
The first 25 Fibonacci numbers are: 1 1 2 3 5 8 13 21 34 55 89
144 233 377 610 987 1597 2584 4181 6765 10946 17711 28657 46368
75025
```

As you can see, the Fibonacci numbers start to get large relatively quickly. You will notice that we used a property called `Length` in the `for` loop of this program:

```
for (int i=2;i<fib.Length;i++)
      fib[i]=fib[i-1]+fib[i-2];
```

In this case, `fib.Length` returns the value 10, the number of memory locations set aside for the elements it contains. If you read on, you will see that arrays have many properties and methods.

□ The `Array` Class

It turns out that all arrays are indeed objects of a class type, and there is an `Array` class in the `System` namespace that provides a great number of properties and methods for use with arrays. Table 6.1 shows these.

■ MULTIDIMENSIONAL ARRAYS

It is possible to declare an array with more than one dimension; for example, we could declare a two-dimensional array to represent a table of values, like in Table 6.2.

The numeric values in the table will be the values we wish to store. To access a particular value in a table, we must specify two indices; that is, a row and a column value. For example, the average temperature for Wednesday is in row 2, column 3 (if we number the rows and columns starting with zero, of course).

There are two approaches to creating multidimensional arrays in C#. We can create a perfectly rectangular array or a jagged array. We will discuss rectangular arrays first.

□ Rectangular Arrays

To declare a two-dimensional rectangular array, we simply indicate to the compiler the extra set of indices separated by a comma, as in the following example:

```
int[,] multTable = new int[10,10];
```

This creates a rectangular array with $4 \times 4 = 16$ elements, all initialized to the default value of zero. Accessing a particular element in the array requires two indices. For example, setting the element in row 2, column 0, to the value 7 in the previous array would be done in this way:

```
multTable[2,0] = 7;
```

TABLE 6.1

Public Properties	
`IsFixedSize`	Gets a value indicating whether the array has a fixed size.
`IsReadOnly`	Gets a value indicating whether the array is read-only.
`IsSynchronized`	Gets a value indicating whether access to the array is synchronized (thread-safe).
`Length`	Gets the total number of elements in all the dimensions of the array.
`Rank`	Gets the rank (number of dimensions) of the array.
`SyncRoot`	Gets an object that can be used to synchronize access to the array.
Public Methods	
`BinarySearch`	Overloaded. Searches a one-dimensional sorted array for a value, using a binary search algorithm.
`Clear`	Sets a range of elements in the array to zero, to false, or to a null reference, depending on the element type.
`Clone`	Creates a shallow copy of the array.
`Copy`	Overloaded. Copies a section of one array to another array and performs type casting and boxing as required.
`CopyTo`	Copies all the elements of the current one-dimensional array to the specified one-dimensional array, starting at the specified destination array index.
`CreateInstance`	Overloaded. Initializes a new instance of the `Array` class.
`GetEnumerator`	Returns an `IEnumerator` for the array.
`GetLength`	Gets the number of elements in the specified dimension of the array.
`GetLowerBound`	Gets the lower bound of the specified dimension in the array.
`GetUpperBound`	Gets the upper bound of the specified dimension in the array.
`GetValue`	Overloaded. Gets the value of the specified element in the current array.
`IndexOf`	Overloaded. Returns the index of the first occurrence of a value in a one-dimensional array or in a portion of the array.
`Initialize`	Initializes every element of the value-type array by calling the default constructor of the value type.
`LastIndexOf`	Overloaded. Returns the index of the last occurrence of a value in a one-dimensional array or in a portion of the array.
`Reverse`	Overloaded. Reverses the order of the elements in a one-dimensional array or in a portion of the array.
`SetValue`	Overloaded. Sets the specified element in the current array to the specified value.
`Sort`	Overloaded. Sorts the elements in one-dimensional array objects.

TABLE 6.2 Weekly Temperature Chart

	Sunday	Monday	Tuesday	Wednesday	Thursday	Friday	Saturday
Max	83	85	88	91	87	85	84
Min	71	68	70	78	73	71	71
Avg	74	75	77	83	78	76	75

☐ Program: MultiplicationTable

For the previous array, we will initialize the elements to the values in an elementary school multiplication table. To do this, we must remember that arrays begin their indices with 0, but a multiplication table begins with 1. To rectify this disparity, we can simply set the element in row i, column j, to the value $(i + 1) \times (j + 1)$. See Listing 6.2 to see how we do this.

Listing 6.2

```
using System;
class MultiplicationTable {
    static void Main() {
      //Create a 10 by 10 rectangular array
      int[,] multTable=new int[10,10];

      //Display the table Header
      Console.WriteLine("Multiplication table of 1 thru 10");

      //Traverse the rows in the table
      for (int row=0;row<10;row++)

          //Traverse the columns in the table
          for (int column=0;column<10;column++) {

            //Set element to row+1 times column+1
            //Remember, indices start with 0, but
            //Multiplication tables start with 1
            multTable[row,column]=(row+1)*(column+1);

            //Display value after computing it
            Console.Write(multTable[row,column]);

            //If not last column, issue a tab
            if (column<9) Console.Write("\t");
            //otherwise send cursor to next line
            else Console.WriteLine();
          }
    }
}
```

Here is a run of the program:

```
Multiplication table of 1 thru 10
1       2       3       4       5       6       7       8       9       10
2       4       6       8       10      12      14      16      18      20
3       6       9       12      15      18      21      24      27      30
4       8       12      16      20      24      28      32      36      40
5       10      15      20      25      30      35      40      45      50
6       12      18      24      30      36      42      48      54      60
7       14      21      28      35      42      49      56      63      70
8       16      24      32      40      48      56      64      72      80
9       18      27      36      45      54      63      72      81      90
10      20      30      40      50      60      70      80      90      100
```

There is no limit to the number of dimensions we can create for an array; for example, here are the definitions of rectangular arrays of three dimensions and higher:

```
float[,,] cube = new float[7,7,7];
double[,,,] hypercube = new double[12,12,12,12];
bool[,,,,,,,,,] bogglesTheMind =
new bool[1,2,3,4,5,6,7,8,9,10];
```

We can initialize multidimensional arrays at compile time. We do this by "nesting" the brackets. In the case of rectangular arrays, we must ensure that the number of values for each dimension is identical; for example, the following declaration, which creates a 3 × 2 array, is OK.

```
float[,] rectangle = {{1.1f,2.2f},{7.4f,6.1f},{2.6f,8.31f}};
```

However, the following declaration will not work, because the array is not rectangular. There is an extra value in the second group.

```
float[,] bogus = {{1.1f,2.2f},{7.4f,6.1f,9.77f},{2.6f,8.31f}};
```

How do we know bogus is a 3 × 2 array, and not a 2 × 3 array? C# uses the most deeply nested values for the rightmost index, and the outermost level for the leftmost index. So, because the array

```
float[,] rectangle = {{1.1f,2.2f},{7.4f,6.1f},{2.6f,8.31f}};
```

contains three groups, each containing two elements, it is a 3 × 2 array; that is, the leftmost index extends from 0 through 2, while the rightmost index can take the values 0 and 1. A slightly more complex example follows:

```
using System;
class CodeTester {
    static void Main() {
      int[,,] ia = {
            {{1,2,1,2},{3,4,3,4}},
            {{5,6,5,6},{7,8,7,8}},
            {{9,10,9,10},{11,12,11,12}}
            //A 3 by 2 by 4 array
            //3 groups of group pairs, each containing 4 elements
      };

      //Display the elements
      for (int i=0;i<3;i++) {//i leftmost index<3

          for (int j=0;j<2;j++) {//j middle index<2

            //Display one row of values
            for (int k=0;k<4;k++)//k rightmost index<4
                Console.Write(ia[i,j,k]+"\t");
            //Go to next line
            Console.WriteLine();
          }

          //Display a marker to separate 2D tables
          Console.WriteLine("---");
      }

    }
}
```

```
1       2       1       2
3       4       3       4
---
5       6       5       6
7       8       7       8
---
9       10      9       10
11      12      11      12
---
```

Jagged Arrays

Rectangular arrays demand that the number of values along any particular dimension be equal. A jagged array does not insist on this. Actually, a jagged array can be viewed as an array of arrays, and each subarray need not have the same number of elements. To declare a jagged array, we "stack" the indices in the form

```
[][][]...
```

rather than use the form

```
[,,]...
```

used for rectangular arrays. We create a jagged array in the next example:

```
float[][] nar = new float[2][];
```

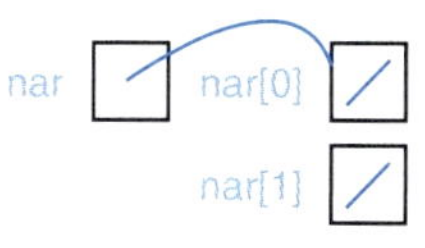

Figure 6.4

This says to create an array named `nar`, which contains two elements. Each of these elements, in turn, is a one-dimensional array. We do not yet know how many elements each subarray contains, because we have not yet produced them (see Figure 6.4).

We create the subarrays separately in the same way we create any other array. We can do this in a loop, or not; the arrays need not have the same length.

```
nar[0] = new float[4];
nar[1] = new float[3];
```

Figure 6.5 shows a representation of these newly created arrays.

Accessing individual elements in this jagged array is done by specifying in which subarray it resides with the first index, and its position in the subarray with the second index.

```
nar[0][2] = 7.2f;
nar[1][0] = 3.4f;
```

These two statements have the effect on the array shown in Figure 6.6.

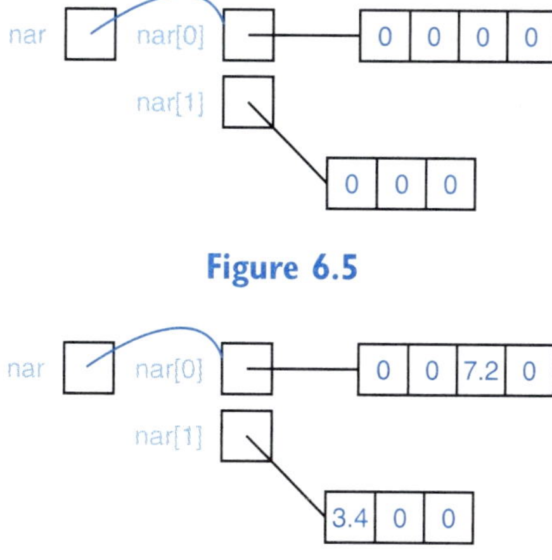

Figure 6.5

Figure 6.6

This logic of having arrays of arrays can be extended as far as desired. We can have arrays of arrays of arrays, ad infinitum simply by using more indices.

It is important to note that you cannot initialize a jagged array at compile time using brackets. Though it seems reasonable, you may not do the following:

```
float[][] arr = {{1.1f,2.2f},{7.4f,6.1f,9.77f},{2.6f,8.31f}};
```

Program: PascalsTriangle

Pascal's triangle is an interesting mathematical object. It is often useful when presenting the theory of permutations and combinations. Though we will not discuss these interesting properties, we will at least discuss its appearance.

The first two rows of Pascal's triangle look like this:

```
  1
1   1
```

The next row contains three elements. The two endpoints are both 1, whereas the middle point is 2—the sum of the two elements above it, to the left and right (both are 1).

```
    1
  1   1
1   2   1
```

The next row has four elements, and this row obeys the same rules: The two endpoints are 1, and the interior elements are the sum of the two elements to the left and right in the higher row. In this case, the interior elements are 3 = 1 + 2 and 3 = 2 + 1.

```
      1
    1   1
  1   2   1
1   3   3   1
```

Continuing in this manner, we can produce as many levels of Pascal's triangle as desired. Here, we go eight levels deep:

```
                     1
                  1     1
               1     2     1
            1     3     3     1
         1     4     6     4     1
      1     5    10    10     5     1
   1     6    15    20    15     6     1
1     7    21    35    35    21     7     1
```

If we were to write a program to compute the elements of Pascal's triangle and display them, let us allow ourselves some leeway and tilt the triangle so all of its leftmost endpoints line up on the left:

```
1
1       1
1       2       1
1       3       3       1
1       4       6       4       1
1       5       10      10      5       1
1       6       15      20      15      6       1
1       7       21      35      35      21      7       1
```

This clearly looks like it could be well represented using a jagged array. It can be an array of arrays, where the first subarray (row) has one element, and each subsequent subarray has one more element than the one preceding it. With the triangle tilted this way, we can compute non-endpoints in any row of the triangle by taking the sum of the element above it, and the element above and to the left. Listing 6.3 is a program that creates the triangle (10 levels deep), and computes and displays each element in it.

Listing 6.3

```
using System;
class PascalsTriangle {
    static void Main() {
      //Create a jagged array with 10 rows
      int[][] triangle = new int[10][];

      //Traverse thru the rows
      for (int row=0;row<triangle.Length;row++) {

          //Each row is a subarray of length 1 greater than row number
          triangle[row]=new int[row+1];

          //Set the values in a row
          for (int k=0;k<triangle[row].Length;k++) {

            //If not first or last element in the row
            if (k>0&&k<triangle[row].Length-1)
                //set it to sum of the element above it
                //and the one above and to the left
                triangle[row][k]=triangle[row-1][k-1]
                  +triangle[row-1][k];
            //otherwise, this is an endpoint; set it to 1
            else triangle[row][k]=1;
```

(continued)

```
            //Display the value
            Console.Write(triangle[row][k]+"\t");

          }

          //Finished processing row-send cursor to next line
          Console.WriteLine();

        }

      }
  }
```

The output of Pascal's triangle is shown here:

```
1
1       1
1       2       1
1       3       3       1
1       4       6       4       1
1       5       10      10      5       1
1       6       15      20      15      6       1
1       7       21      35      35      21      7       1
1       8       28      56      70      56      28      8
1
1       9       36      84      126     126     84      36
9       1
```

■ THE `foreach` STATEMENT

C# has what is called a "collection." We will discuss the general concept of a collection later, but for now it will suffice to know that an array is a collection. All collections can use the `foreach` statement, which is an alternative manner of traversing its elements.

The format of the `foreach` statement is

```
foreach (<type> <value> in <collection>) {
      <C# statements>
}
```

If the foreach block contains only a single statement, the brackets are unnecessary.

To see how this statement traverses the elements of an array, see the following example:

```
using System;
class CodeTester {
    static void Main() {
      int[] squares = new int[10];

      //Use a for loop to calculate first 10 squares
      for (int j=0;j<squares.Length;j++) squares[j]=j*j;

      //Use a foreach loop to display them
      foreach (int i in squares) Console.Write(i+" ");
    }
}
```

```
0 1 4 9 16 25 36 49 64 81
```

Which loops you use to iterate over arrays is largely a matter of choice. As you can see from the example, sometimes the index of an array is a useful value for calculation, and sometimes it is completely unnecessary.

☐ Program: CountCharsWordsLines

The following program prompts the user to enter some text. It counts the number of words, characters, and lines the user entered. For simplicity, a character will be any non-space character, and a word will be any group of characters not including the space (group may mean a single character). When the user enters an empty line, or a line consisting of only blanks, the program displays its results and terminates. The final blank line is not counted in the total number of lines.

The program demonstrates the foreach statement, as well as the Split() method from the String class.

```
public string[] Split(
   params char[] separator
);
```

This method is called by a String object. It accepts an array of characters as a parameter. The characters in this array are used as the delimiting characters upon which the string will be split into an array of strings. This array is returned to the calling method. The substrings in the array do not include the delimiting characters.

It is possible that two or more delimiting characters will be next to each other; when this happens, an empty string is returned as one of the array elements. Also, if a delimiting character is the last character in the string, the last element in the array will be the empty string.

The code for CountCharsWordsLines is in Listing 6.4.

Listing 6.4

```
using System;
class CountCharsWordsLines {
    static void Main() {

        //Variables to record #lines, words, chars (nonblanks)
        int numWords=0, numChars=0, numLines=0;

        //Split string on the space character
        char[] delimiter={' '};

        //Prompt the user
        Console.WriteLine("Enter some text.");
        Console.WriteLine("Hit return on a line by itself to stop.");
        bool allBlank=false;

        //Loop will terminate when all substrings are blank
        do {

            //Read in a line
            //Split the string into an array, separated by blank
            String[] words=Console.ReadLine().Split(delimiter);

            //A line was read in
            numLines++;

            //Assume all are blank
            allBlank=true;

            //Pass thru the array
            foreach (String word in words) {

                //Add length of each word (length may be 0)
                numChars+=word.Length;

                //If nonblank word found, increment numWords
                //Must read another line
                if (word.Length>0) {numWords++; allBlank=false;}
            }

        } while (!allBlank);

        //Final line was all blanks-decrement numLines
  numLines--;
```

(continued)

```
        Console.WriteLine("You entered "+numChars+" characters, "
              +numWords+" words, and "+numLines+" lines.");
    }
}
```

Here is a sample run of CountCharsWordsLines:

```
Enter some text.
Hit return on a line by itself to stop.
To be or not to be,
that is the question.
Whether it is nobler in the mind
to suffer the slings and arrows of outrageous fortune,
or to take arms against a sea of troubles,
and by opposing,
END THEM.

You entered 159 characters, 40 words, and 7 lines.
```

■ THE `Random` CLASS

A computer is very good at running simulations. It can simulate random events by using a random number generator. Of course, most computers do not generate true random numbers; the correct term is pseudo-random number generator. However, for most purposes, pseudo-random is just fine.

C# provides a `Random` class in the `System` namespace. Table 6.3 lists its members. The class provides a number of interesting methods, such as

- `Next()`, which returns a random positive integer.
- `NextBytes()`, which can be used to fill up an array of bytes with random bits.
- `NextDouble()`, which returns a random double x such that $0 \le x < 1$.

Here is a simple program to show how these methods are used:

```
using System;
class CodeTester {
    static void Main() {
      Random r=new Random();
      int ri = r.Next();
      double rd = r.NextDouble();
      byte[] rba = new byte[10];
      r.NextBytes(rba);
      Console.WriteLine("A random integer: "+ri);
      Console.WriteLine("A random double: "+rd);
      Console.Write("A random array of bytes: ");
      foreach (byte b in rba) Console.Write(b+" ");
      Console.WriteLine();
    }
}
```

Here are some sample runs:

```
A random integer: 2054063746
A random double: 0.0488436790410633
A random array of bytes: 198 53 158 250 105 25 238 210 180 11

A random integer: 1824078281
A random double: 0.537853137374787
A random array of bytes: 188 60 167 204 241 212 94 97 64 191
```

TABLE 6.3

Public Constructors	
`Random` Constructor	Overloaded. Initializes a new instance of the `Random` class.
Public Methods	
`Next`	Overloaded. Returns a random number.
`NextBytes`	Fills the elements of a specified array of bytes with random numbers.
`NextDouble`	Returns a random number between 0.0 and 1.0.
Protected Methods	
`Sample`	Returns a random number between 0.0 and 1.0.

```
A random integer: 409769079
A random double: 0.895234947509707
A random array of bytes: 173 136 184 24 110 152 71 79 137 16

A random integer: 882527396
A random double: 0.581685878141637
A random array of bytes: 170 39 54 178 133 70 1 206 252 88

A random integer: 1355285713
A random double: 0.268136808773566
A random array of bytes: 168 199 180 77 155 245 186 77 111 160
```

Using these methods, we can simulate many different kinds of random activity, like say, rolling dice.

□ Program: DiceFrequencies

Consider rolling a pair of dice over and over again. On each throw, take the total of the two dice, and record it. Repeat this for every throw. What would you expect the most frequent total to be? You would probably answer seven, because there are more ways to roll a seven than any other total.

$7 = 1 + 6 = 6 + 1 = 2 + 5 = 3 + 4 = 4 + 3 = 5 + 2 = 6 + 1$

But what if you rolled three dice at a time? Or four? Or 400? Using arrays and a `Random` object, we should be able to write a program to simulate and record these frequencies.

Suppose we are throwing n dice in a single throw. How big should the array be to record every possible sum? Well, the minimum sum is clearly n (each die comes up 1), and the maximum sum must be $6 \times n$ (each die comes up 6). We could make the array with $6n - n = 5n$ slots. However, it would be more convenient (and readable) if the sums matched up perfectly with the indices; that is, a sum of k causes the k-th element of the array to be incremented (see Figure 6.7).

With this in mind, we need to make an array of $6n + 1$ slots, because C# arrays start indexing at 0. The first n slots (0 through $n - 1$) will simply not be used. The `DiceFrequencies` class in Listing 6.5 demonstrates our use of such an array to simulate rolling dice.

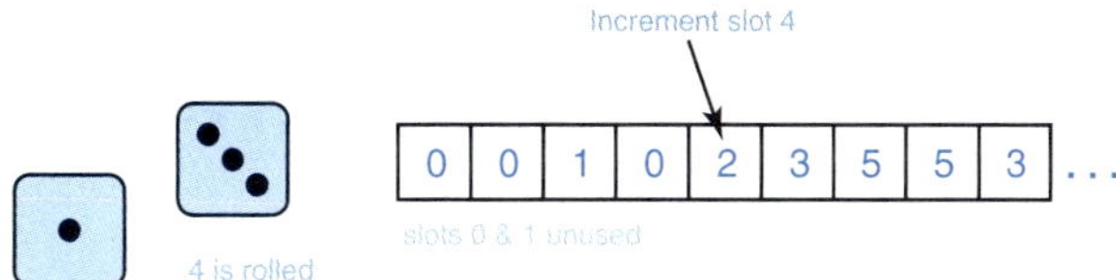

Figure 6.7

Listing 6.5

```
using System;
class DiceFrequencies {
      static void Main() {

          //Create a random object to generate random integers
            Random simulator=new Random();

          //User specifies # dice to throw in each throw
            Console.Write("Enter # of dice: ");
            int numdice=Int32.Parse(Console.ReadLine());

          //User specifies total number of throws
            Console.Write("Enter # of times to throw the dice: ");
            int numThrows=Int32.Parse(Console.ReadLine());

          //Minimum sum of spots = number of dice thrown
            int MINSPOTS=numdice;
          //Maximum sum of spots = number of dice thrown*6
            int MAXSPOTS=numdice*6;
          //Create an array to record occurrence of sums
            int[] spots=new int[MAXSPOTS+1];

          //Outer loop represents the throws
            for (int theThrow=1; theThrow<=numThrows; theThrow++) {
                //Number of spots starts at 0
                int numberOfSpots=0;
                //Inner loop represents the individual dice
                for (int die=1;die<=numdice;die++)
                //Add number of spots for this die to the total
                    numberOfSpots+=simulator.Next(1,7);
                //The total number of spots
                //is between MINSPOTS and MAXSPOTS
                //Increment that slot in the array
                spots[numberOfSpots]++;
            }

          //Display the output
            Console.WriteLine(
          "The approximate relative frequencies:");
            Console.WriteLine("Each '*' represents 1%");

          //Table should range from MINSPOTS to MAXSPOTS
            for (int spot=MINSPOTS;spot<=MAXSPOTS;spot++) {
                //Divide total # times this total occurred
                //by the number of throws-relative frequency
                double relativeFreq=(double)spots[spot]/numThrows;
```

(continued)

```
                //Display the number of spots
                Console.Write(spot+":\t");
                //Multiply relative frequency by 100
                //this is a percentage
                //display that many asterisks
                for (int i=1;i<=100*relativeFreq;i++)
                Console.Write("*");
                Console.WriteLine();
            }
        }
}
```

In this program, we used a slightly different form of the `Next()` method, which accepts two `int`s, `x` and `y`, as parameters, and returns a random integer `r` such that

$x \le r < y$

Now we test the program. We'll simulate rolling three dice. First, roll them 100 times, then 1000 times, then 100,000 times. Note how smooth the curve gets as the number of throws increases.

```
Enter # of dice: 3
Enter # of times to throw the dice: 100
The approximate relative frequencies:
Each '*' represents 1%
3:      **
4:      **
5:      ***
6:      ***
7:      ********
8:      *********
9:      ***********
10:     *************
11:     **************
12:     *********************
13:     ***
14:     ***
15:     ****
16:     *
17:     ***
18:
```

```
Enter # of dice: 3
Enter # of times to throw the dice: 1000
The approximate relative frequencies:
Each '*' represents 1%
3:
4:      *
5:      **
6:      ****
7:      ******
8:      *********
9:      *************
10:     *************
11:     **********
12:     *************
13:     *********
14:     ******
15:     *****
16:     **
17:     *
18:

Enter # of dice: 3
Enter # of times to throw the dice: 100000
The approximate relative frequencies:
Each '*' represents 1%
3:
4:      *
5:      **
6:      ****
7:      *******
8:      *********
9:      ***********
10:     ************
11:     ************
12:     ***********
13:     *********
14:     ******
15:     ****
16:     **
17:     *
18:
```

Using a little imagination, we can use random number generators to simulate a wide range of phenomena.

ARRAYS ARE FIXED IN SIZE

A disadvantage of using arrays is that they are fixed in size; that is, they cannot grow or shrink once created. This can be a problem, because:

1. If we have fewer elements to store than the size of the array, this may mean unnecessary wasted space.
2. If we have more elements than can be held in the array, our only alternatives are to
   a. Create a larger array, and copy the values into it, meaning extra processing time.
   b. Find some other way to store the data.

In Chapter 13 we will see more flexible data structures.

chapter 7

Static Methods

If you have worked in procedural languages before, static methods are much like the procedures and functions you defined in those languages. Both procedures and functions could accept values from a calling program; functions would typically return a value, whereas a procedure would not. In C#, a method that does not return a value is called "void."

A simplified syntax of a static method is

```
static <return-type> methodName(parameter-type1
                                parameter-name1,...) {
      <C# statements>
}
```

The return type can be any C# data type, and if the method returns no value, the return type is void. The parameters are separated by commas.

▪ THE `return` STATEMENT

If the method returns a value, at some point in the execution of the method the `return` statement must appear. Its format is

```
return <return-value>;
```

The value being returned by the method must be of the type specified in the method declaration. If the method is void, execution will return to the calling method after the last statement in the called method is executed; however, you may cause a return to the calling method at any point by using

```
return;
```

As an example of a static method, consider writing a method that accepts the positive radius of a circle, and returns the circumference of that circle. The mathematical formula for computing the circumference could be stated using functional notation as

$$C = f(r) = \pi r^2$$

where $\pi \approx 3.1415927$. The function f represents the method; r represents the radius, which is the incoming parameter (say, a `double`); and C represents the circumference, or the returned value (say, also a `double`). By using the format specification given earlier, we can write a method to compute and return the circumference of a circle with a given radius:

```
static double Circumference(double radius) {
  return 2*Math.PI*radius;
}
```

Here, of course, we get the approximate (but quite close) value of π from `Math.PI` in the `System` namespace.

☐ Program: CircleCircumferenceAndArea

Now, let us see how such a method would be called. For now, we will place our methods in the same class as the `Main()` method. Listing 7.1 is a program that prompts the user to enter a positive radius, then calls and displays the results of both a `Circumference()` method and an `Area()` method.

Listing 7.1

```
using System;
class CircleCircumferenceAndArea {
    static void Main() {

      //Prompt the user
      Console.Write("Enter the positive radius of a circle: ");

      //read radius in from console, parse to a double
      double r = Double.Parse(Console.ReadLine());

      //Call the Circumference() method
      Console.WriteLine("The circumference of a circle with radius "
            +r+" is "+Circumference(r));

      //Call the Area() method
      Console.WriteLine("The area of a circle with radius "
            +r+" is "+Area(r));
    }

    static double Circumference(double radius) {
      return 2*Math.PI*radius;
    }

    static double Area(double radius) {
      return Math.PI*radius*radius;
    }

}
```

Here are some sample runs of the program:

```
Enter the positive radius of a circle: 1
The circumference of a circle with radius 1 is 6.28318530717959
The area of a circle with radius 1 is 3.14159265358979

Enter the positive radius of a circle: 0
The circumference of a circle with radius 0 is 0
The area of a circle with radius 0 is 0

Enter the positive radius of a circle: 2
The circumference of a circle with radius 2 is 12.5663706143592
The area of a circle with radius 2 is 12.5663706143592

Enter the positive radius of a circle: 3
The circumference of a circle with radius 3 is 18.8495559215388
The area of a circle with radius 3 is 28.2743338823081
```

```
Enter the positive radius of a circle: -1
The circumference of a circle with radius -1 is -6.28318530717959
The area of a circle with radius −1 is 3.14159265358979
```

Let us step through the execution of this program. First, the `Main()` method is called. The `Main()` method is the point of entry to a program; thus, it doesn't matter if you define other methods before or after the `Main()` method.

Next, a prompt is displayed, and we read in a series of characters from the console, and parse it into a `double`; this is stored in the variable *r*.

```
Console.Write("Enter the positive radius of a circle: ");
double r = Double.Parse(Console.ReadLine());
```

r 1

Figure 7.1

Let us suppose the user entered the value 1 (see Figure 7.1).

The next line calls the `WriteLine()` method from `Console`:

```
Console.WriteLine("The circumference of a circle with radius "
     +r+" is "+Circumference(r));
```

In order to display the `double` value returned by `Circumference(r)`, it must call the method, which calculates the value. In the method call, `r` is known as the actual parameter. In the method definition

```
static double Circumference(double radius) {
  return 2*Math.PI*radius;
}
```

the variable `radius` is known as the formal parameter. The type of the actual parameter must be compatible with the type of the formal parameter, according to data conversion rules. In this case, they are the same type.

r 1 radius 1

Figure 7.2

When the method is called, a copy of the variable *r* is made, and assigned to radius, as can be seen in Figure 7.2.

This is called passing a parameter by value, and it is C#'s default behavior. The advantage of passing parameters by value is that the called method can change its local copy of the variable without changing the variable in the calling method. This often helps in preventing bugs and other unwanted side effects.

Within the `Circumference()` method, the value must use its local name, `radius`. Likewise, the `Main()` method must refer to it as `r`, because neither variable is visible outside the method in which it is created. Note that it is entirely irrelevant that "`r`" and "`radius`" are different names. They could both have the same name, in fact. If this were the case, any reference to that name inside `Circumference()` would still refer to its local copy, and likewise for the calling method.

Finally, the value to be returned is calculated:

```
return 2*Math.PI*radius;
```

This value is a `double`, as it should be. The value returned must be compatible with the return type defined in the method declaration, again according to C#'s data conversion rules. The value is returned to the point from which it was requested; that is, the

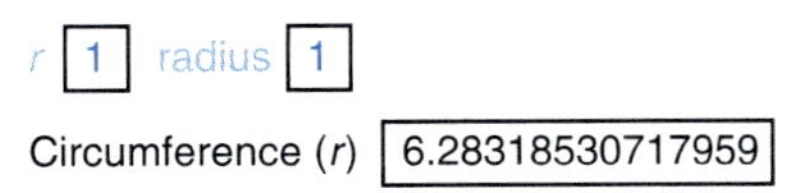

Figure 7.3

method call in the `WriteLine()` statement. Because the value returned is a `double`, it is treated the same way as any `double` (see Figure 7.3).

Much the same thing happens when we call the `Area()` method in the last line of the `Main()` method.

■ REFERENCE TYPES PASSED BY VALUE

When reference types are passed into a method by value, it is important to note that only a copy of the reference is made, not a copy of the object to which it refers. This can produce side effects, so care should be taken. Of course, this effect may be exactly what is desired.

As an example of passing by value, view the following program:

```
using System;
class CodeTester {
    static void Main() {

      int[] iWillChange = {1,2,3};

      //Call the ArrayChanger method
      //it returns nothing (is void)
      ArrayChanger(iWillChange);

      //Display the array elements
      foreach (int k in iWillChange)
            Console.WriteLine(k);

    }

    //This method accepts a referenced array
    static void ArrayChanger(int[] i) {
      //Change one of its elements
      i[1] = 9;
    }

}
```

As you can see, the array `iWillChange` begins with the values 1, 2, and 3.

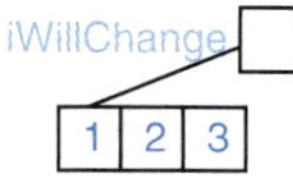

Figure 7.4

```
int[] iWillChange = {1,2,3};
```

This array, of course, is stored by reference (see Figure 7.4).

The next line of the program calls the `ArrayChanger()` method, passing to it the array of integers.

```
ArrayChanger(iWillChange);
```

This method accepts an array of integers; the local name for the array is `i`.

```
static void ArrayChanger(int[] i) {
  i[1] = 9;
}
```

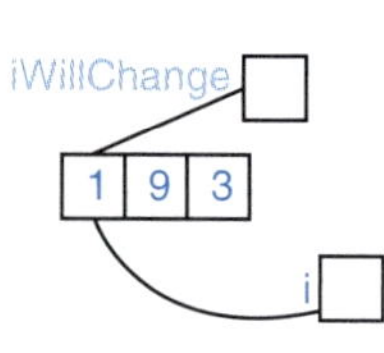

Figure 7.5

When the copy of the calling variable is made, however, only the reference is copied. This has the effect that both `iWillChange` and `i` refer to the same array! Thus, when the program changes `i[1]` to the value 9, the array in the `Main()` method is, of course, also changed, for it is, in fact, the same array (see Figure 7.5).

The proof occurs when we display the array, and see that it indeed has changed.

```
      foreach (int k in iWillChange)
            Console.WriteLine(k);
```

```
1
9
3
```

▪ PASSING PARAMETERS BY REFERENCE

C# allows you to pass variables by reference into a method. If the variable is stored by value—that is, a value type—C# will create a reference to it, and this reference is copied into the called method. The effect is, of course, that the two variables actually represent the same memory location. Thus, if you change the variable in the called method, you are in fact changing it in the calling method as well. Variables are passed by reference using the `ref` keyword.

As an example of passing by reference, consider the following method, which swaps two characters:

```
static void swap(ref char a,ref char b) {
  char temp=a;
  a=b;
  b=temp;
}
```

Suppose we set up the following character variables:

```
char first='Q';
char second='Z';
```

Figure 7.6

Figure 7.6 shows these assignments.

Now, we call the swap method, and pass in the two variables by reference:

```
swap(ref first,ref second);
```

Note that the `ref` keyword is necessary for both the calling method and the called method. For each variable, this sets up two references to the same memory location (see Figure 7.7).

Thus, when the two variables `a` and `b` exchange values, `first` and `second` exchange values as well (see Figure 7.8).

To verify the truth in this, view the following program and note that `first` and `second` have indeed exchanged values.

```
using System;
class CodeTester {
    static void Main() {

      char first='Q';
      char second='Z';

      Console.WriteLine("first: "+first);
      Console.WriteLine("second "+second);

      swap(ref first,ref second);

      Console.WriteLine("first: "+first);
      Console.WriteLine("second "+second);

    }

    static void swap(ref char a,ref char b) {
      char temp=a;
      a=b;
      b=temp;
    }

}
```

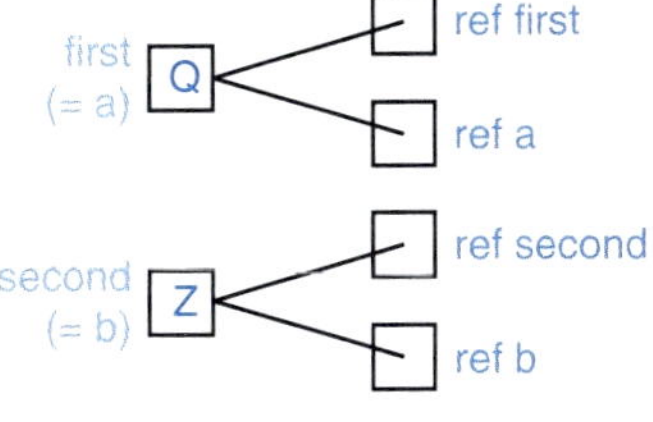

Figure 7.7

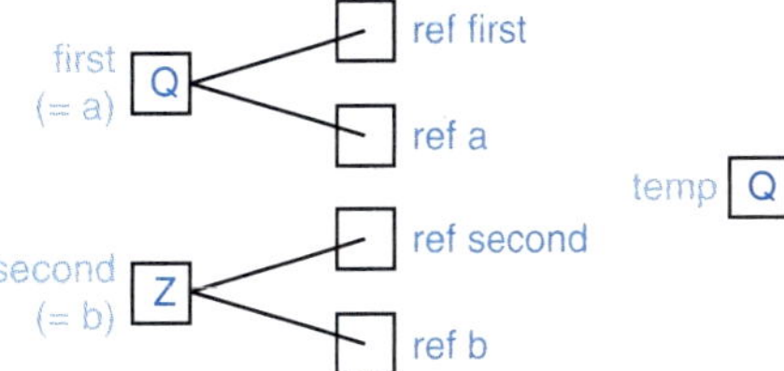

Figure 7.8

```
first: Q
second Z
first: Z
second Q
```

□ Program: BubbleSortChars

The program in Listing 7.2 makes extensive use of the `swap()` method we just developed. It is a program containing a `BubbleSort()` method, which sorts the characters in an array of characters. Sorting is central to the concept of data structures, because it is quicker to find items in sorted data.

The bubble sort is the simplest (and slowest) of sorting routines. Suppose we have a list of characters we wish to sort:

```
T    X    A    B    D
```

Begin by comparing the first two elements, and if they are out of order, swap them; otherwise, leave them alone.

```
T    X    A    B    D
```

Repeat this with the next pair of letters.

```
T    A    X    B    D
```

Continue this process with successive pairs until you have processed the last pair.

```
T    A    B    X    D
T    A    B    D    X
```

After one pass through this list you know that the largest item must be at the end. Thus, the next time you pass through the list, you do not need to check the last item. Every time you pass through the list, the number of items you need to check decreases by one.

Second pass:

```
A    T    B    D    X
A    B    T    D    X
A    B    D    T    X
```

Third pass:

```
A    B    D    T    X
A    B    D    T    X
```

Note that this pass did not require that we swap any items, and that can only mean that the list is already sorted, and no further passes are required.

```
A    B    D    T    X
```

Of course, even if this situation does not occur, the bubble sort will eventually terminate when the remaining list to sort has only one element in it.

Listing 7.2

```
using System;
class BubbleSortChars {

    static void BubbleSort(char[] array) {

      //top is end of the array
      int top=array.Length-1;

      //done will be set to true if array becomes sorted "early"
      bool done=false;

      while (!done) {

      //Assume array is sorted
         done=true;

      //Go to the end of array in one pass
         for (int i=0;i<top;i++) {

            //If two adjacent items are out of order
            if (array[i+1]<array[i]) {
            //The array is not sorted-must make another pass
               done=false;
            //Swap the two offending items
               swap(ref array[i],ref array[i+1]);
            }

         }

      //After one pass, largest item must be at top
      //Next pass does not need to go as far-decrement top
         top--;

      }

    }

    static void Main() {
      //Prompt the user
      Console.WriteLine("Enter some text: ");

      //Read in as a string, then convert to char[]
      char[] ca=Console.ReadLine().ToCharArray();

      //Pass the array to BubbleSort
      //Arrays stored by reference-changes in the method affect ca
      BubbleSort(ca);
```

(continued)

```
        //Display the array of sorted characters
        Console.WriteLine("The sorted characters in the text are:");
        Console.WriteLine(ca);

    }

    //Method to exchange two characters
    static void swap(ref char a,ref char b) {
        //Temporary location temp
        char temp=a;
        a=b;
        b=temp;
    }

}

Enter some text:
Since by man came death, by man comes also the resurrection of the dead.
The sorted characters in the text are:
             ,.Saaaaaabbccccdddeeeeeeeeefhhhiilmmmmnnnnooooorrrssstttttuyy
```

■ PASSING PARAMETERS OUTWARD

Passing parameters by value is basically the calling method communicating a value to the called method. In cases where it matters most, this value in the called method does not survive to affect its partner in the calling method. Passing by reference, on the other hand, allows a two-way communication of values between the caller and the called.

We will now cover a method specifically intended to pass values outward from a called method to the caller. Of course, a method can always return values through the normal mechanism (i.e., return), but if a method needs to return multiple values, this can be awkward.

We communicate values outward from a method by using the `out` keyword. The program MidPointFinder in Listing 7.3 shows how this is done.

☐ Program: MidPointFinder

Consider the problem of computing the midpoint of two points in the plane. If you recall from algebra, we can represent such a point as an (x,y) coordinate pair, where x represents the distance of the point from the origin along the x-axis, and y represents the distance from the origin along the y-axis, as shown in Figure 7.9.

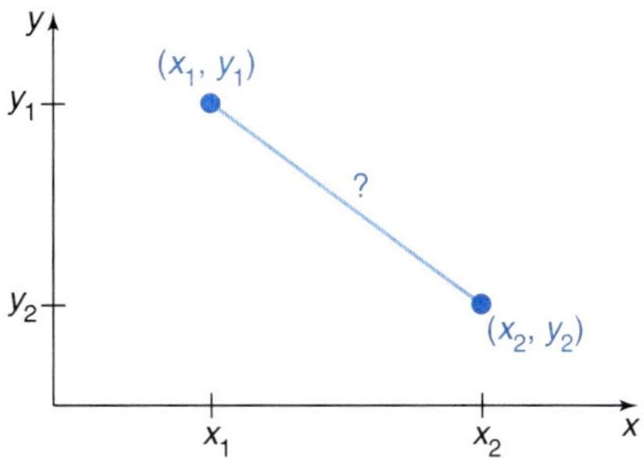

Figure 7.9

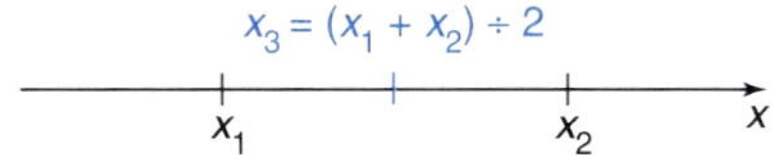

Figure 7.10

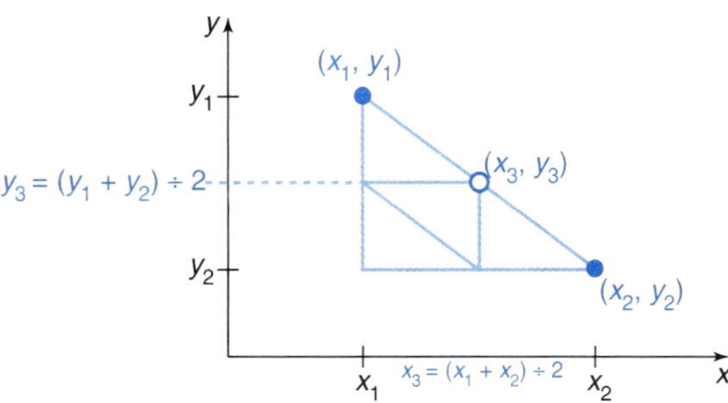

Figure 7.11

If we want to find the midpoint (x3,y3) of the segment joining the points (x1,y1) and (x2,y2), we can begin by first considering only the x-axis. Calculating the midpoint of x1 and x2 is simple; merely take the average (see Figure 7.10).

We can similarly find the midpoint along the y-axis by taking the average of y1 and y2. With a little geometry, you can easily prove that (x3,y3) is indeed the midpoint of the line segment joining (x1,y1) and (x2,y2) in the plane (see Figure 7.11).

We will define a `MidPoint()` method, which accepts the x and y coordinates (say, `doubles`) of two points, and returns the x and y coordinates of their midpoint. Because it would be awkward for the method to return these two `doubles`, we will return them through the parameter list using the `out` keyword.

```
static void MidPoint(double x1, double y1,
  double x2, double y2,
  out double midx, out double midy) {
        midx=(x2+x1)/2;
```

```
        midy=(y2+y1)/2;
}
```

If we write a `Main()` method to test `MidPoint()`, we will see that the last two parameters will receive values from the `MidPoint()` method.

Listing 7.3

```
using System;
class MidPointFinder {
    static void Main() {

      //Prompt user for coordinates
      Console.Write("Enter the x-coordinate of a planar point: ");
      double x1=Double.Parse(Console.ReadLine());
      Console.Write("Enter the y-coordinate of a planar point: ");
      double y1=Double.Parse(Console.ReadLine());
      Console.Write("Enter the x-coordinate of a 2nd planar point: ");
      double x2=Double.Parse(Console.ReadLine());
      Console.Write("Enter the y-coordinate of a 2nd planar point: ");
      double y2=Double.Parse(Console.ReadLine());

      //Declare the two receiving values
      //Note they are not explicitly initialized
      double x3,y3;

      //Call MidPoint() method
      //keyword out must be present for x3 and y3
      MidPoint(x1,y1,x2,y2,out x3,out y3);

      //Display all the points
      Console.WriteLine("The midpoint of the line segment joining ("
            +x1+","+y1+") and ("
            +x2+","+y2+") is ("
            +x3+","+y3+").");
    }

    static void MidPoint(double x1, double y1,
      double x2, double y2,
      out double midx, out double midy) {
            //Last two parameters must be assigned values
            //x and y coords of midpoint between (x1,y1) & (x2,y2)
            midx=(x2+x1)/2;
            midy=(y2+y1)/2;
    }

}
```

Note that, as with the `ref` parameter, the keyword `out` must be specified in both the called method and the calling method.

```
MidPoint(x1,y1,x2,y2,out x3,out y3);
```

Here are some sample runs of the program:

```
Enter the x-coordinate of a planar point: 23
Enter the y-coordinate of a planar point: -12
Enter the x-coordinate of a 2nd planar point: 0
Enter the y-coordinate of a 2nd planar point: 82
The midpoint of the line segment joining (23,-12) and (0,82) is
(11.5,35).

Enter the x-coordinate of a planar point: -1
Enter the y-coordinate of a planar point: -2
Enter the x-coordinate of a 2nd planar point: -3
Enter the y-coordinate of a 2nd planar point: -4
The midpoint of the line segment joining (-1,-2) and (-3,-4) is
(-2,-3).
```

▪ THE `params` MODIFIER

It is often the case that we need to send in a variable number of parameters to a method. This can actually be done using the `params` modifier. With it, we can call the same method using a different number of parameters on different calls. For example, consider the following method called `JoinWSpace()`, which accepts an arbitrary number of strings as arguments, joins them (with a space between each), and returns the joined string.

```
using System;
class CodeTester {

    //Method allows an arbitrary number of strings be passed to it
    static String JoinWSpace(params String[] seq) {

      String result=String.Empty;

      //Join the incoming strings, with space between each
      foreach (String s in seq) result+=(s+" ");

      return result;

    }
```

```
    static void Main() {

      //Call JoinWSpace() method passing in a few strings
      //Note we are NOT passing in an array of strings,
      //but multiple arguments
      Console.WriteLine(JoinWSpace("Hello,","I","love","you,",
            "don\'t","tell","me","your","name!"));

    }
}
```

Note that we are not passing in the strings as an array, but each string is a separate argument. Here is the output of this program:

```
Hello, I love you, don't tell me your name!
```

You should note that if you use the `params` modifier with other parameters in a method signature, the one using `params` must be the last parameter. For example, here is a similar method that allows you to specify the delimiting character between the strings. This `char` parameter must precede the one using the `params` modifier.

```
using System;
class CodeTester {
    //Method allows an arbitrary number of strings be passed to it
    static String Join(char delimiter, params String[] seq) {

      String result=String.Empty;

      //Join the incoming strings, with space between each
      foreach (String s in seq) result+=(s+delimiter);

      return result;
    }
    static void Main() {

      //Call Join() method passing in first a char,
      //then a few strings
      //Note we are NOT passing in an array of strings,
      //but multiple arguments
      Console.WriteLine(Join('-',"Hello,","I","love","you,",
            "don\'t","tell","me","your","name!"));

    }
}
```

```
Hello,-I-love-you,-don't-tell-me-your-name!-
```

▪ STATIC METHODS CALLED BY CLASS NAME

If you recall from an earlier discussion, static methods are typically called in the following way:

```
ClassName.MethodName()
```

Of course, you can see from the examples in this chapter that we left the class name out. Why? Simply because the methods were declared in the same class from which they were called. In this case, preceding the method with the class name would be redundant, and is not required in C#.

As an example, consider again the CircleCircumferenceAndArea program in Listing 7.4. When calling the `Circumference()` and `Area()` methods, one could have preceded the calls with the class name. However, because the methods are being called from the very same class in which they are defined, it isn't necessary.

Listing 7.4

```
using System;
class CircleCircumferenceAndArea {
    static void Main() {
      //Prompt the user
      Console.Write("Enter the positive radius of a circle: ");
      //read radius in from console, parse to a double
      double r = Double.Parse(Console.ReadLine());

      //Call the Circumference() method
      Console.WriteLine("The circumference of a circle with radius "
            +r+" is "+CircleCircumferenceAndArea.Circumference(r));

      //Call the Area() method
      Console.WriteLine("The area of a circle with radius "
            +r+" is "+CircleCircumferenceAndArea.Area(r));
    }

    static double Circumference(double radius) {
      return 2*Math.PI*radius;
    }

    static double Area(double radius) {
      return Math.PI*radius*radius;
    }
}
```

Later in this chapter we will discuss writing methods that normally reside in a different class than the `Main()` method. In fact, they usually are in a different file, namespace, and directory.

▪ METHOD SIGNATURES

The appearance of a method (i.e., its modifiers, name, and list of parameters) is known as its signature. For example, the signature of the `Circumference` method is

```
static double Circumference(double radius);
```

No other method defined in this class can have this same signature, for obvious reasons; namely, the runtime environment would not know which method to call if they looked identical to each other! However, it is possible for two methods in the same class to have the same name, but different signatures (usually the parameters are different). This is known as method overloading.

☐ Method Overloading

It is certainly possible for multiple methods in the same class to have the same name, as long as something in their respective signatures differ. For example, Listing 7.5 shows a class containing two static `Divide()` methods. One accepts two `doubles`, and returns a `double`; the other is `void` and accepts four `longs`, the last two having the `out` modifier.

Listing 7.5

```
using System;
class DivideOverload {

      //Two Divide() methods have same name
      //But different signatures

    static double Divide(double dividend, double divisor) {
      //Return results of real division
      return dividend/divisor;
    }

    static void Divide(long dividend, long divisor,
            out long quotient, out long remainder) {
      //Results of integer division returned thru parameters
      quotient=dividend/divisor;
      remainder=dividend%divisor;
    }

    static void Main() {
      //Prompt the user
      Console.Write("Enter a long dividend: ");
      long top=Int64.Parse(Console.ReadLine());
      Console.Write("Enter a long divisor: ");
      long bottom=Int64.Parse(Console.ReadLine());
```

(continued)

```
        //Call first Divide() method
        //Not necessary to cast longs to doubles-automatic
        Console.WriteLine("The results of real division are: "
              +top+"/"+bottom+" = "+Divide(top,bottom));

        long q,r;
        //Call second Divide() method
        //q and r capture the results
        Divide(top,bottom,out q,out r);
        Console.WriteLine("The results of integer division are: "
              +top+"/"+bottom+" = "+q+" R "+r);

    }
}
```

Here are some runs of the test program:

```
Enter a long dividend: 21784
Enter a long divisor: 2345
The results of real division are: 21784/2345 = 9.28955223880597
The results of integer division are: 21784/2345 = 9 R 679

Enter a long dividend: 92311111
Enter a long divisor: -12
The results of real division are: 92311111/-12 = -7692592.58333333
The results of integer division are: 92311111/-12 = -7692592 R 7

Enter a long dividend: 2
Enter a long divisor: 100
The results of real division are: 2/100 = 0.02
The results of integer division are: 2/100 = 0 R 2
```

▪ THE throw STATEMENT

Note that the CircleCircumferenceAndArea program will allow you to enter a nonpositive radius.

```
Enter the positive radius of a circle: -1
The circumference of a circle with radius -1 is -6.28318530717959
The area of a circle with radius -1 is 3.14159265358979
```

Although we could check for erroneous input in the `Main()` method, it is a better idea to check within the methods, and throw an exception if necessary. This is because the classes you develop will eventually be used by other programmers; because you have a better idea of the things that could go wrong in your class, you should have mechanisms in place to handle them, or to report them in an established manner. In C#, this manner means throwing exceptions.

You already know how to catch exceptions using `try ... catch`. Now, you can also throw them using the `throw` statement. The format is

```
throw <exception-type-object>;
```

To signal that a negative radius has been passed into the `Circumference()` and `Area()` methods, we can change them thus:

```
static double Circumference(double radius) {
  if (radius<=0) throw new ArgumentException(
        "Circles must have a positive radius");
  return 2*Math.PI*radius;
}
static double Area(double radius) {
  if (radius<=0) throw new ArgumentException(
        "Circles must have a positive radius");
  return Math.PI*radius*radius;
}
```

The choice of the type of exception to throw is entirely yours, but if you are choosing a predefined exception, pick one with a name that at least indicates the problem. Here, we throw a `new ArgumentException` object, using the `ArgumentException(String)` constructor. (Look in the `System` namespace and verify that this constructor exists.) The string that you pass to this constructor becomes the message displayed on the console when the system handles the exception, or if you decide to display the exception in a `catch` block. Listing 7.6 shows the `Main()` method modified to continue prompting until the user enters a positive radius.

Listing 7.6

```
using System;
class CircleCircumferenceAndArea {
    static void Main() {
      double r=0; bool okeedokee=false;
      while (!okeedokee) {
          try {
            okeedokee=true;
            //Prompt the user
            Console.Write("Enter the positive radius of a circle: ");
            //read radius in from console, parse to a double
            r = Double.Parse(Console.ReadLine());
          } catch (FormatException fe) {
            Console.WriteLine(fe);
            okeedokee=false;
          }
          try {
          //Call the Circumference() method
            Console.WriteLine(
            "The circumference of a circle with radius "+r+
            " is "+CircleCircumferenceAndArea.Circumference(r));
          //Call the Area() method
            Console.WriteLine(
            "The area of a circle with radius "+r+
            " is "+CircleCircumferenceAndArea.Area(r));
          } catch (ArgumentException ae) {
            Console.WriteLine(ae);
            okeedokee=false;
          }
      }
    }
    static double Circumference(double radius) {
      if (radius<=0) throw new ArgumentException(
            "Circles must have a positive radius");
      return 2*Math.PI*radius;
    }
    static double Area(double radius) {
      if (radius<=0) throw new ArgumentException(
            "Circles must have a positive radius");
      return Math.PI*radius*radius;
    }
}
```

The program also will catch a `FormatException` if the user enters some bogus text when prompted for the radius. Here is a sample run:

```
Enter the positive radius of a circle: -3
System.ArgumentException: Circles must have a positive radius
   at CircleCircumferenceAndArea.Circumference(Double radius)
   at CircleCircumferenceAndArea.Main()
Enter the positive radius of a circle: 0
System.ArgumentException: Circles must have a positive radius
   at CircleCircumferenceAndArea.Circumference(Double radius)
   at CircleCircumferenceAndArea.Main()
Enter the positive radius of a circle: q
System.FormatException: Input string was not in a correct format.
   at System.Number.ParseDouble(String s, NumberStyles style, NumberFormatInfo
                                info)
   at System.Double.Parse(String s, NumberStyles style, IFormatProvider
                          provider)
   at CircleCircumferenceAndArea.Main()
System.ArgumentException: Circles must have a positive radius
   at CircleCircumferenceAndArea.Circumference(Double radius)
   at CircleCircumferenceAndArea.Main()
Enter the positive radius of a circle: 2.1
The circumference of a circle with radius 2.1 is 13.1946891450771
The area of a circle with radius 2.1 is 13.854423602331
```

You are certainly not required to use the predefined exception classes. If none of them have a name that seems to indicate the type of exception that occurred, you are free to define your own exception classes. This is a simple thing to do, but we will defer discussion of it until Chapter 9.

■ RECURSION

A method is allowed to call itself in C#. This concept is known as recursion. Some functions are naturally defined recursively; for example, consider again the Fibonacci sequence:

```
1, 1, 2, 3, 5, 8, 13, 21, ...
```

The first two terms are 1, and subsequent terms are the sum of the two terms preceding it. Suppose we want to define a function $f(n)$ that computes the n-th value in the Fibonacci sequence. We could define the function as follows:

f(n) =	1	if n = 1 or n = 2
	f(n − 1) + f(n − 2)	if n = 3, 4, 5, . . .
	undefined	otherwise

Using this definition, we can find, say, the fifth term in the Fibonacci sequence by adding together the fourth and the third terms. Of course, finding these may require additional computation, and the process continues:

f(5) =				
f(4) +			f(3) =	
f(3) +		f(2) +	f(2) +	f(1) =
f(2) +	f(1) + 1 +		1 +	1 =
1 +	1 +	1 +	1 +	1 =
5				

The process cannot go on indefinitely of course, because we subtract a 1 or 2 each time we call the function, so the parameters eventually reach the value of 1 or 2, in which case the function value is 1.

☐ Program: FibonacciRecursion

Writing a static recursive method to compute Fibonacci terms is actually quite easy. In Listing 7.7, we'll put a `Main()` method with a recursive `Fibonacci` method for testing.

Listing 7.7

```
using System;
class FibonacciRecursion {
    static void Main() {
      Console.Write("Enter the index of the Fibonacci term: ");
      int n = Int32.Parse(Console.ReadLine());
      Console.WriteLine(
            "The "+n+"-th Fibonacci number is: "+Fibonacci(n));
    }
    static long Fibonacci(int n) {
      if (n<1) throw new ArgumentException(
            "Fibonacci function not defined for "+n);
      if (n==1||n==2) return 1;
      return Fibonacci(n-2)+Fibonacci(n-1);
    }
}
```

Here are example runs of the program:

```
Enter the index of the Fibonacci term: 40
The 40-th Fibonacci number is: 102334155

Enter the index of the Fibonacci term: 45
The 45-th Fibonacci number is: 1134903170

Enter the index of the Fibonacci term: 0

Unhandled Exception: System.ArgumentException: Fibonacci
function not defined for 0
   at FibonacciRecursion.Fibonacci(Int32 n)
   at FibonacciRecursion.Main()

Enter the index of the Fibonacci term: -12

Unhandled Exception: System.ArgumentException: Fibonacci
function not defined for -12
   at FibonacciRecursion.Fibonacci(Int32 n)
   at FibonacciRecursion.Main()
```

Note that the system handles the exceptions; we do not catch them in the `Main()` method.

☐ Efficiency of Recursion

Recursion can be very wasteful in terms of memory usage. Each time a recursive method calls itself, it needs to make copies of all its incoming parameters. This can mean an enormous number of method calls. For example, let us add a counter to the `Fibonacci` method (see Listing 7.8), and display the number of times the method calls itself.

Listing 7.8

```
using System;
class FibonacciRecursion {
    //Global var counts # of calls
    static long numCalls=0;
    static void Main() {
      Console.Write("Enter the index of the Fibonacci term: ");
      int n = Int32.Parse(Console.ReadLine());
      Console.WriteLine(
            "The "+n+"-th Fibonacci number is: "+Fibonacci(n));
      Console.WriteLine("This required "+numCalls+" method calls");
    }
```

(continued)

```
    static long Fibonacci(int n) {
      //Entered method-increment the counter
      numCalls++;
      if (n<1) throw new ArgumentException(
            "Fibonacci function not defined for "+n);
      if (n==1||n==2) return 1;
      return Fibonacci(n-2)+Fibonacci(n-1);
    }
}
```

Here is a sample run:

```
Enter the index of the Fibonacci term: 45
The 45-th Fibonacci number is: 1134903170
This required 2269806339 method calls
```

Wow! Finding the 45th Fibonacci number required over 2 billion method calls! This particular value of $n = 45$ required over a minute to compute on my PC. This is clearly unacceptable if a better alternative exists, and it turns out we can easily rewrite the `Fibonacci` method without recursion. We do this in Listing 7.9 in the FibonacciLoop program.

Listing 7.9

```
using System;
class FibonacciLoop {
    static void Main() {
      Console.Write("Enter the index of the Fibonacci term: ");
      int n = Int32.Parse(Console.ReadLine());
      Console.WriteLine(
            "The "+n+"-th Fibonacci number is: "+Fibonacci(n));
    }
    static long Fibonacci(int n) {
      if (n<1) throw new ArgumentException(
            "Fibonacci function not defined for "+n);
      if(n==1||n==2) return 1;
      long prevTerm=1, prevPrevTerm=1, answer=0;
      for (int index=3;index<=n;index++) {
            //Compute sum of 2 previous terms
            answer=prevTerm+prevPrevTerm;
            //Move the previous terms up the sequence
            prevPrevTerm=prevTerm;
            prevTerm=answer;
      }
      return answer;
    }
}
```

Running the program a few times should convince you that we get the same answers:

```
Enter the index of the Fibonacci term: 5
The 5-th Fibonacci number is: 5

Enter the index of the Fibonacci term: 6
The 6-th Fibonacci number is: 8

Enter the index of the Fibonacci term: 30
The 30-th Fibonacci number is: 832040

Enter the index of the Fibonacci term: 40
The 40-th Fibonacci number is: 102334155

Enter the index of the Fibonacci term: 45
The 45-th Fibonacci number is: 1134903170
```

In terms of efficiency, the loop is far preferable. Even computing the 45th Fibonacci number took a negligible amount of time, and it's easy to see why: The `for` loop will execute only $n - 2$ times for any value of n. Compare this to over 2 billion method calls for $n = 45$ in the recursive version. Each of these calls takes time, and each also takes more memory. The iterative version, on the other hand, requires only enough memory for one method call and its local variables.

This is not to say recursion should be avoided at any cost; in general, it's OK if it does not present a performance problem. Recursive methods that call themselves multiple times in each call are particularly suspect, however.

☐ Program: FactorialRecursion

As an example of a recursive function that does not cause an explosive number of method calls, consider the factorial function; this function `f(n)` (denoted in math as $n!$) is defined for nonnegative integers thus:

$$n! = \begin{cases} n \times (n-1) \times (n-2) \times \ldots \times 3 \times 2 \times 1 & \text{if } n > 1 \\ 1 & \text{if } n = 1 \text{ or } n = 0 \\ \text{undefined} & \text{otherwise} \end{cases}$$

As an example, compute 6!:

$$6! = 5 \times 4 \times 3 \times 2 \times 1 = 120$$

We can also define the factorial function recursively:

$$n! = \begin{cases} n \times (n-1)! & \text{if } n > 1 \\ 1 & \text{if } n = 1 \text{ or } n = 0 \\ \text{undefined} & \text{otherwise} \end{cases}$$

In order to compute 6! recursively, we do this:

$$6! = 5 \times 4! = 5 \times 4 \times 3! = 20 \times 3 \times 2! = 60 \times 2 \times 1! = 120 \times 1 = 1$$

A recursive Factorial() method is a snap, as you can see in Listing 7.10.

Listing 7.10

```
using System;
class FactorialRecursion {
    static void Main() {
      Console.Write("Enter a nonnegative integer: ");
      int n = Int32.Parse(Console.ReadLine());
      Console.WriteLine(n+"! is: "+Factorial(n));
    }
    static double Factorial(int n) {
      if (n<0) throw new ArgumentException(
            "Factorial function not defined for "+n);
      if(n==1||n==0) return 1;
      return n*Factorial(n-1);
    }
}
```

Note that Factorial() returns a double. Although a factorial is clearly an integer, you will see from the following test runs that the factorials become huge very quickly, and would soon even exhaust the storage capacity of a long.

```
Enter a nonnegative integer: 100
100! is: 9.33262154439441E+157

Enter a nonnegative integer: 200
200! is: Infinity

Enter a nonnegative integer: 10
10! is: 3628800

Enter a nonnegative integer: 1
1! is: 1

Enter a nonnegative integer: 0
0! is: 1

Enter a nonnegative integer: -1

Unhandled Exception: System.ArgumentException: Factorial
function not defined for -1
   at FactorialRecursion.Factorial(Int32 n)
   at FactorialRecursion.Main()
```

(Note the interesting way in which C# handles floating point overflow for $n = 200$.)

The recursive `Factorial()` method is not nearly as wasteful as the recursive `Fibonacci` method. In fact, for any value of n, `Factorial()` will call itself no more than n times. A loop to do the same task would also iterate no more than n times, however, and requires only one method call. In cases where recursive methods and iterative methods have about the same level of performance, you could choose

- The iterative method for the slight advantage in speed and memory usage
- The recursive method for "clarity"

An interesting exercise for you would be to write an iterative version of the `Factorial()` method

☐ Program: TowersOfHanoi

Sometimes it is quite difficult to conceive of an iterative solution to a problem; in such cases, recursion appears to be our only alternative. Consider, for example, the classic problem known as the "Towers of Hanoi."

Suppose you have three pegs, labeled "1," "2," and "3" (see Figure 7.12). Peg 1 holds n disks of decreasing size, with the largest on the bottom. The task is to move all n disks from peg 1 to peg 3, moving only one disk at a time, and never placing a larger disk upon a smaller one.

If you attempt an iterative solution to this problem (especially when n is "large"), you will probably find yourself dealing with a massive migraine. However, if you consider a recursive solution, the answer practically bites you.

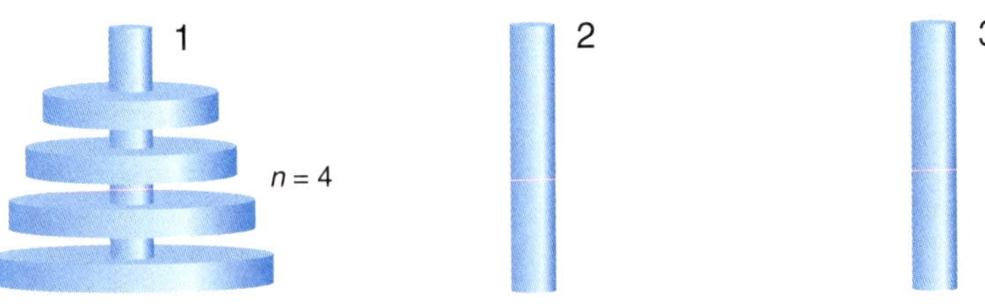

Figure 7.12

Step 1: Solve the Towers of Hanoi problem for $n - 1$ disks, and move the $n - 1$ disks above the largest disk (the one on the bottom) from peg 1 (the "source peg") to peg 2 (the "temporary holding peg").

Step 2: Move the bottom disk from peg 1 (source peg) to peg 3 (the "destination peg").

Step 3: Solve the Towers of Hanoi problem for $n - 1$ disks, and move the $n - 1$ disks in step 1 from peg 2 (temporary peg) to peg 3 (destination peg).

Solving the n disk Towers of Hanoi problem means first solving the $n - 1$ disk problem in Step 1 (with a different destination peg arrangement), then again in Step 2 (again with a different destination peg arrangement). Of course, we then solve the $n - 1$ disk problem by solving the n-2 disk problem, and so on.

Note that solving the smaller problem will never entail placing a larger disk on a smaller one, because the disk on the "bottom" moved in Step 2 is always the largest of that group of disks. As long as each call observes the same rules, you cannot place a larger disk on a smaller one.

The only things that change in solving successively smaller Towers of Hanoi problems are the number of disks, the source peg, the destination peg, and the temporary holding peg. Thus, these can be represented as variables. It is a simple matter to convert the algorithm just described into a recursive method, as is done in Listing 7.11.

Listing 7.11

```
using System;
class TowersOfHanoi {
      static void MoveDisks(int source, int dest,
                  int temp, int numDisks) {
            //Solve the n-1 problem with different peg arrangement
            if (numDisks>1) MoveDisks(source,temp,dest,numDisks-1);
            //Move the disk on the "bottom"
            Console.Write(source+" to "+dest+".\t");
            //Solve the n-1 problem with different peg arrangement
            if (numDisks>1) MoveDisks(temp,dest,source,numDisks-1);
      }
      static void Main() {
            Console.Write("Enter # of disks: ");
            int n =Int32.Parse(Console.ReadLine());
            Console.WriteLine(
                  "Moving "+n+" disks from peg 1 to peg 3:");
            //Move n disks from peg 1 to peg 3, temporary holding peg 2
            MoveDisks(1,3,2,n);
      }
}
```

The middle line in the `MoveDisks()` method is simply a `WriteLine()`, declaring the movement of a disk. Here are some sample runs, using different values of n:

```
Enter # of disks: 3
Moving 3 disks from peg 1 to peg 3:
1 to 3. 1 to 2. 3 to 2. 1 to 3. 2 to 1. 2 to 3. 1 to 3.
Enter # of disks: 6
Moving 6 disks from peg 1 to peg 3:
1 to 2. 1 to 3. 2 to 3. 1 to 2. 3 to 1. 3 to 2. 1 to 2. 1 to 3. 2 to 3. 2 to 1.
3 to 1. 2 to 3. 1 to 2. 1 to 3. 2 to 3. 1 to 2. 3 to 1. 3 to 2. 1 to 2. 3 to 1.
2 to 3. 2 to 1. 3 to 1. 3 to 2. 1 to 2. 1 to 3. 2 to 3. 1 to 2. 3 to 1. 3 to 2.
1 to 2. 1 to 3. 2 to 3. 2 to 1. 3 to 1. 2 to 3. 1 to 2. 1 to 3. 2 to 3. 2 to 1.
3 to 1. 3 to 2. 1 to 2. 3 to 1. 2 to 3. 2 to 1. 3 to 1. 2 to 3. 1 to 2. 1 to 3.
2 to 3. 1 to 2. 3 to 1. 3 to 2. 1 to 2. 1 to 3. 2 to 3. 2 to 1. 3 to 1. 2 to 3.
1 to 2. 1 to 3. 2 to 3.
Enter # of disks: 9
Moving 9 disks from peg 1 to peg 3:
1 to 3. 1 to 2. 3 to 2. 1 to 3. 2 to 1. 2 to 3. 1 to 3. 1 to 2. 3 to 2. 3 to 1.
2 to 1. 3 to 2. 1 to 3. 1 to 2. 3 to 2. 1 to 3. 2 to 1. 2 to 3. 1 to 3. 2 to 1.
3 to 2. 3 to 1. 2 to 1. 2 to 3. 1 to 3. 1 to 2. 3 to 2. 1 to 3. 2 to 1. 2 to 3.
1 to 3. 1 to 2. 3 to 2. 3 to 1. 2 to 1. 3 to 2. 1 to 3. 1 to 2. 3 to 2. 3 to 1.
2 to 1. 2 to 3. 1 to 3. 2 to 1. 3 to 2. 3 to 1. 2 to 1. 3 to 2. 1 to 3. 1 to 2.
3 to 2. 1 to 3. 2 to 1. 2 to 3. 1 to 3. 1 to 2. 3 to 2. 3 to 1. 2 to 1. 3 to 2.
1 to 3. 1 to 2. 3 to 2. 1 to 3. 2 to 1. 2 to 3. 1 to 3. 2 to 1. 3 to 2. 3 to 1.
2 to 1. 2 to 3. 1 to 3. 1 to 2. 3 to 2. 1 to 3. 2 to 1. 2 to 3. 1 to 3. 2 to 1.
3 to 2. 3 to 1. 2 to 1. 3 to 2. 1 to 3. 1 to 2. 3 to 2. 3 to 1. 2 to 1. 2 to 3.
1 to 3. 2 to 1. 3 to 2. 3 to 1. 2 to 1. 2 to 3. 1 to 3. 1 to 2. 3 to 2. 1 to 3.
2 to 1. 2 to 3. 1 to 3. 1 to 2. 3 to 2. 3 to 1. 2 to 1. 3 to 2. 1 to 3. 1 to 2.
3 to 2. 1 to 3. 2 to 1. 2 to 3. 1 to 3. 2 to 1. 3 to 2. 3 to 1. 2 to 1. 2 to 3.
1 to 3. 1 to 2. 3 to 2. 1 to 3. 2 to 1. 2 to 3. 1 to 3. 1 to 2. 3 to 2. 3 to 1.
2 to 1. 3 to 2. 1 to 3. 1 to 2. 3 to 2. 3 to 1. 2 to 1. 2 to 3. 1 to 3. 2 to 1.
3 to 2. 3 to 1. 2 to 1. 3 to 2. 1 to 3. 1 to 2. 3 to 2. 1 to 3. 2 to 1. 2 to 3.
1 to 3. 1 to 2. 3 to 2. 3 to 1. 2 to 1. 3 to 2. 1 to 3. 1 to 2. 3 to 2. 3 to 1.
2 to 1. 2 to 3. 1 to 3. 2 to 1. 3 to 2. 3 to 1. 2 to 1. 2 to 3. 1 to 3. 1 to 2.
3 to 2. 1 to 3. 2 to 1. 2 to 3. 1 to 3. 2 to 1. 3 to 2. 3 to 1. 2 to 1. 3 to 2.
1 to 3. 1 to 2. 3 to 2. 3 to 1. 2 to 1. 2 to 3. 1 to 3. 2 to 1. 3 to 2. 3 to 1.
2 to 1. 3 to 2. 1 to 3. 1 to 2. 3 to 2. 1 to 3. 2 to 1. 2 to 3. 1 to 3. 1 to 2.
3 to 2. 3 to 1. 2 to 1. 3 to 2. 1 to 3. 1 to 2. 3 to 2. 1 to 3. 2 to 1. 2 to 3.
1 to 3. 2 to 1. 3 to 2. 3 to 1. 2 to 1. 2 to 3. 1 to 3. 1 to 2. 3 to 2. 1 to 3.
2 to 1. 2 to 3. 1 to 3. 1 to 2. 3 to 2. 3 to 1. 2 to 1. 3 to 2. 1 to 3. 1 to 2.
3 to 2. 3 to 1. 2 to 1. 2 to 3. 1 to 3. 2 to 1. 3 to 2. 3 to 1. 2 to 1. 3 to 2.
1 to 3. 1 to 2. 3 to 2. 1 to 3. 2 to 1. 2 to 3. 1 to 3. 1 to 2. 3 to 2. 3 to 1.
2 to 1. 3 to 2. 1 to 3. 1 to 2. 3 to 2. 1 to 3. 2 to 1. 2 to 3. 1 to 3. 2 to 1.
```

```
3 to 2. 3 to 1. 2 to 1. 2 to 3. 1 to 3. 1 to 2. 3 to 2. 1 to 3. 2 to 1. 2 to 3.
1 to 3. 2 to 1. 3 to 2. 3 to 1. 2 to 1. 3 to 2. 1 to 3. 1 to 2. 3 to 2. 3 to 1.
2 to 1. 2 to 3. 1 to 3. 2 to 1. 3 to 2. 3 to 1. 2 to 1. 2 to 3. 1 to 3. 1 to 2.
3 to 2. 1 to 3. 2 to 1. 2 to 3. 1 to 3. 1 to 2. 3 to 2. 3 to 1. 2 to 1. 3 to 2.
1 to 3. 1 to 2. 3 to 2. 1 to 3. 2 to 1. 2 to 3. 1 to 3. 2 to 1. 3 to 2. 3 to 1.
2 to 1. 2 to 3. 1 to 3. 1 to 2. 3 to 2. 1 to 3. 2 to 1. 2 to 3. 1 to 3. 2 to 1.
3 to 2. 3 to 1. 2 to 1. 3 to 2. 1 to 3. 1 to 2. 3 to 2. 3 to 1. 2 to 1. 2 to 3.
1 to 3. 2 to 1. 3 to 2. 3 to 1. 2 to 1. 3 to 2. 1 to 3. 1 to 2. 3 to 2. 1 to 3.
2 to 1. 2 to 3. 1 to 3. 1 to 2. 3 to 2. 3 to 1. 2 to 1. 3 to 2. 1 to 3. 1 to 2.
3 to 2. 3 to 1. 2 to 1. 2 to 3. 1 to 3. 2 to 1. 3 to 2. 3 to 1. 2 to 1. 2 to 3.
1 to 3. 1 to 2. 3 to 2. 1 to 3. 2 to 1. 2 to 3. 1 to 3. 2 to 1. 3 to 2. 3 to 1.
2 to 1. 3 to 2. 1 to 3. 1 to 2. 3 to 2. 3 to 1. 2 to 1. 2 to 3. 1 to 3. 2 to 1.
3 to 2. 3 to 1. 2 to 1. 2 to 3. 1 to 3. 1 to 2. 3 to 2. 1 to 3. 2 to 1. 2 to 3.
1 to 3. 1 to 2. 3 to 2. 3 to 1. 2 to 1. 3 to 2. 1 to 3. 1 to 2. 3 to 2. 1 to 3.
2 to 1. 2 to 3. 1 to 3. 2 to 1. 3 to 2. 3 to 1. 2 to 1. 2 to 3. 1 to 3. 1 to 2.
3 to 2. 1 to 3. 2 to 1. 2 to 3. 1 to 3. 1 to 2. 3 to 2. 3 to 1. 2 to 1. 3 to 2.
1 to 3. 1 to 2. 3 to 2. 3 to 1. 2 to 1. 2 to 3. 1 to 3. 2 to 1. 3 to 2. 3 to 1.
2 to 1. 3 to 2. 1 to 3. 1 to 2. 3 to 2. 1 to 3. 2 to 1. 2 to 3. 1 to 3. 1 to 2.
3 to 2. 3 to 1. 2 to 1. 3 to 2. 1 to 3. 1 to 2. 3 to 2. 1 to 3. 2 to 1. 2 to 3.
1 to 3. 2 to 1. 3 to 2. 3 to 1. 2 to 1. 2 to 3. 1 to 3. 1 to 2. 3 to 2. 1 to 3.
2 to 1. 2 to 3. 1 to 3. 2 to 1. 3 to 2. 3 to 1. 2 to 1. 3 to 2. 1 to 3. 1 to 2.
3 to 2. 3 to 1. 2 to 1. 2 to 3. 1 to 3. 2 to 1. 3 to 2. 3 to 1. 2 to 1. 2 to 3.
1 to 3. 1 to 2. 3 to 2. 1 to 3. 2 to 1. 2 to 3. 1 to 3. 1 to 2. 3 to 2. 3 to 1.
2 to 1. 3 to 2. 1 to 3. 1 to 2. 3 to 2. 1 to 3. 2 to 1. 2 to 3. 1 to 3. 2 to 1.
3 to 2. 3 to 1. 2 to 1. 2 to 3. 1 to 3. 1 to 2. 3 to 2. 1 to 3. 2 to 1. 2 to 3.
1 to 3.
```

The most amazing thing about this program is that it works. If you care to make yourself crazy, verify the moves for $n = 9$. An interesting exercise for you would be to attempt an iterative solution to this problem. Good luck!

☐ The Eight Queens Problem

Let us examine one more classic problem before we go on. The Eight Queens Problem is expressed thus:

Given eight queens and an 8×8 chessboard, how is it possible to place the queens on the board so that no two queens are in the same column, the same row, or the same diagonal?

Figure 7.13 is a solution to the problem.

Now that you know there is a solution, are there others? Can you find them, or can you write a program to find them? Well, you won't have to, if you check out the NQueens program in Listing 7.12.

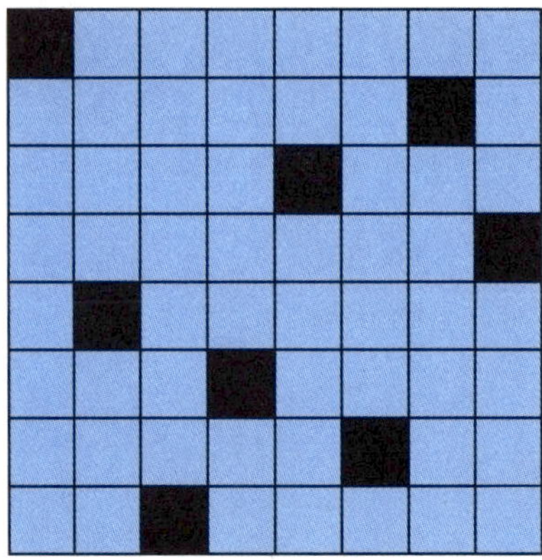

Figure 7.13

Figure 7.14

Program: NQueens

The Eight Queens Problem generalizes to the NQueens problem:

Given N queens and an $N \times N$ chessboard, how is it possible to place the queens on the board so that no two queens are in the same column, the same row, or the same diagonal?

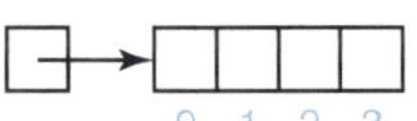

Figure 7.15

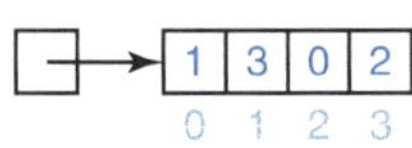

Figure 7.16

Depending on the value of N, there may be no solutions, as you can see in Figure 7.14, which shows there is no solution to the Three Queens Problem.

First we should decide on the most convenient/efficient way of representing a solution. This representation should be easily verifiable as a solution; that is, it should be easy to determine whether two queens lie in the same column, row, or diagonal.

We could represent a queen configuration using a one-dimensional array (see Figure 7.15). Suppose we are trying to solve the Four Queens Problem, and we construct a one-dimensional array of `int`s with four elements; the indices of the array represent the column numbers (numbered 0 through 3).

Inside the array is some permutation of 0, 1, 2, 3, as in Figure 7.16.

This particular configuration says there is a queen in each of the following places:

- Column 0, Row 1
- Column 1, Row 3
- Column 2, Row 0
- Column 3, Row 2

It remains to determine whether or not this is a solution. Of course, if you map this one out as in Figure 7.17, you will see that it is.

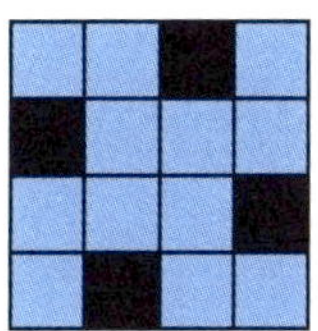

Figure 7.17

But how can the program determine this from the way it is represented?

First of all, note that the representation does not allow any two queens to be in the same column, because the indices of the array represent the columns, and they are unique.

To determine whether two queens are in the same row, you must simply ensure that there are no duplicate values in the array, because the values represent the rows. (Thus, a solution must be a permutation of 0, 1, 2, 3.)

To determine whether two queens lie in the same diagonal, we can do a trick with the indices. Suppose the array representing the possible solution is A. Note that if a queen in column x and a queen in column y lie along the same diagonal, one of the following is true:

- A[x] − x = A[y] − y
- A[x] + x = A[y] + y

Which of these is true depends on whether it is a left diagonal (\ ), or right diagonal (/). For example, consider the proposed solution to the Four Queens Problem:

```
3        1        2        0
```

This configuration looks like Figure 7.18.

Figure 7.18

As you can see, the queen in column 0 collides with the queen in column 3, and the queen in column 1 collides with the queen in column 2. But the program can determine this also, by checking that

A[0] + 0 = 3 + 0 = 3 = 0 + 3 = A[3] + 3   (right diagonal check fails)

and

A[1] − 1 = 1 − 1 = 0 = 2 − 2 = A[2] − 2   (left diagonal check fails)

Writing the program now simply becomes a matter of checking all possibilities; we can run values sequentially up in each column, check each configuration to see if it is a solution, and display it if it is. The NQueens program in Listing 7.12 does exactly that; check out how it places the queens recursively.

Listing 7.12

```
using System;
public class NQueens {

        //board will be a permutation of 0,1,2,3,4,5,6,7
        //if the permutation is a solution, it is displayed
    static int[] board;
    static int size;
```

(continued)

```
public static void Main() {

   Console.Write("Enter the number of rows/columns: ");
   size=Int32.Parse(Console.ReadLine());
   board=new int[size];

   //Display the header for the solutions
   Console.WriteLine("Column");
   for (int i=0;i<size;i++) Console.Write((i+1)+"\t");
   Console.WriteLine();
   for (int i=0;i<size;i++) Console.Write("---\t");
   Console.WriteLine();

   //Place a queen in column 0
   PlaceQueen(0);

}

public static void PlaceQueen(int column) {

   //if column reaches size, we successfully placed
   //queens in columns 0 thru size-1.
   //This is a solution; display it.
   if (column==size) {
        for (int index=0;index<size;index++)
         Console.Write((board[index]+1)+"\t");
         Console.WriteLine();
   }

   for (int row=0;row<size;row++)
         //If there are no collisions placing a queen
         //in this column, move to next column and
         //place a queen there
         if (NoCollisions(column,row)) {
               board[column]=row;
               PlaceQueen(column+1);
         }
         //If the recursion does not occur, there was a
         //collision.  The for loop continues with this
         //column, trying higher values for the row
         //If unable to place the queen, the program
         //backs up even further in the recursion

}
```

(continued)

```
    public static bool NoCollisions(int c, int r) {

        //Test that no two queens are in same row,
        //or in same right/left diagonal
        //No need to test same column; this will not happen
        //due to the way we conceived the program.
        for (int prevcol=0;prevcol<c;prevcol++)
        if (r==board[prevcol]||c-r==prevcol-board[prevcol]
               ||c+r==prevcol+board[prevcol]) return false;
        return true;

    }

}
```

For the benefit of the user, the columns are numbered 1, 2, . . . , N when displayed.

```
Enter the number of rows/columns: 1
Column
1
---
1

Enter the number of rows/columns: 2
Column
1       2
--- ---

Enter the number of rows/columns: 3
Column
1       2       3
--- --- ---

Enter the number of rows/columns: 4
Column
1       2       3       4
--- --- --- ---
2       4       1       3
3       1       4       2

Enter the number of rows/columns: 5
Column
1       2       3       4       5
--- --- --- --- ---
```

```
1       3       5       2       4
1       4       2       5       3
2       4       1       3       5
2       5       3       1       4
3       1       4       2       5
3       5       2       4       1
4       1       3       5       2
4       2       5       3       1
5       2       4       1       3
5       3       1       4       2

Enter the number of rows/columns: 6
Column
1       2       3       4       5       6
--- --- --- --- --- ---
2       4       6       1       3       5
3       6       2       5       1       4
4       1       5       2       6       3
5       3       1       6       4       2

Enter the number of rows/columns: 8
Column
1       2       3       4       5       6       7       8
--- --- --- --- --- --- --- ---
1       5       8       6       3       7       2       4
1       6       8       3       7       4       2       5
1       7       4       6       8       2       5       3
1       7       5       8       2       4       6       3
2       4       6       8       3       1       7       5
2       5       7       1       3       8       6       4
2       5       7       4       1       8       6       3
2       6       1       7       4       8       3       5
2       6       8       3       1       4       7       5
2       7       3       6       8       5       1       4
2       7       5       8       1       4       6       3
2       8       6       1       3       5       7       4
3       1       7       5       8       2       4       6
3       5       2       8       1       7       4       6
3       5       2       8       6       4       7       1
3       5       7       1       4       2       8       6
3       5       8       4       1       7       2       6
3       6       2       5       8       1       7       4
3       6       2       7       1       4       8       5
3       6       2       7       5       1       8       4
```

3	6	4	1	8	5	7	2
3	6	4	2	8	5	7	1
3	6	8	1	4	7	5	2
3	6	8	1	5	7	2	4
3	6	8	2	4	1	7	5
3	7	2	8	5	1	4	6
3	7	2	8	6	4	1	5
3	8	4	7	1	6	2	5
4	1	5	8	2	7	3	6
4	1	5	8	6	3	7	2
4	2	5	8	6	1	3	7
4	2	7	3	6	8	1	5
4	2	7	3	6	8	5	1
4	2	7	5	1	8	6	3
4	2	8	5	7	1	3	6
4	2	8	6	1	3	5	7
4	6	1	5	2	8	3	7
4	6	8	2	7	1	3	5
4	6	8	3	1	7	5	2
4	7	1	8	5	2	6	3
4	7	3	8	2	5	1	6
4	7	5	2	6	1	3	8
4	7	5	3	1	6	8	2
4	8	1	3	6	2	7	5
4	8	1	5	7	2	6	3
4	8	5	3	1	7	2	6
5	1	4	6	8	2	7	3
5	1	8	4	2	7	3	6
5	1	8	6	3	7	2	4
5	2	4	6	8	3	1	7
5	2	4	7	3	8	6	1
5	2	6	1	7	4	8	3
5	2	8	1	4	7	3	6
5	3	1	6	8	2	4	7
5	3	1	7	2	8	6	4
5	3	8	4	7	1	6	2
5	7	1	3	8	6	4	2
5	7	1	4	2	8	6	3
5	7	2	4	8	1	3	6
5	7	2	6	3	1	4	8
5	7	2	6	3	1	8	4
5	7	4	1	3	8	6	2
5	8	4	1	3	6	2	7
5	8	4	1	7	2	6	3

```
6    1    5    2    8    3    7    4
6    2    7    1    3    5    8    4
6    2    7    1    4    8    5    3
6    3    1    7    5    8    2    4
6    3    1    8    4    2    7    5
6    3    1    8    5    2    4    7
6    3    5    7    1    4    2    8
6    3    5    8    1    4    2    7
6    3    7    2    4    8    1    5
6    3    7    2    8    5    1    4
6    3    7    4    1    8    2    5
6    4    1    5    8    2    7    3
6    4    2    8    5    7    1    3
6    4    7    1    3    5    2    8
6    4    7    1    8    2    5    3
6    8    2    4    1    7    5    3
7    1    3    8    6    4    2    5
7    2    4    1    8    5    3    6
7    2    6    3    1    4    8    5
7    3    1    6    8    5    2    4
7    3    8    2    5    1    6    4
7    4    2    5    8    1    3    6
7    4    2    8    6    1    3    5
7    5    3    1    6    8    2    4
8    2    4    1    7    5    3    6
8    2    5    3    1    7    4    6
8    3    1    6    2    5    7    4
8    4    1    3    6    2    7    5
```

■ COMMAND LINE PARAMETERS

It is possible to pass parameters into the `Main()` method, but it must be a one-dimensional array of strings. When you execute the program, these parameters follow the program name and come in from the command line, separated by white space. There can be as few or as many values as you like, because the array will adjust to accommodate the incoming values.

Listing 7.13 is a simple example; the following program accepts an array of strings from the command line, and then writes each argument back to the console.

Listing 7.13

```
using System;
public class Repeat {
    static void Main(String[] args) {
      for (int i=0;i<args.Length;i++)
            Console.Write(args[i]+" ");
    }
}

C:\C#>Repeat Stop repeating everything I say!
Stop repeating everything I say!
C:\C#>Repeat I mean it!
I mean it!
C:\C#>Repeat Quit it!
Quit it!
C:\C#>Repeat Spaces          are      not          part          of
the          arguments.
Spaces are not part of the arguments.
```

Of course, this program does nothing with the arguments but send them back to the console, but command line arguments may have whatever meaning you give them, and your programs may process them in any way desired.

chapter 8

Defining Classes and Structures

C# allows us to define our own classes. We have the ability to define our own data types, with functionality surpassing those provided with the C# language. If you recall, there are many things a class may contain:

- *Constructors*—Create and initialize objects of the class
- *Fields*—Data fields containing information about the object
- *Properties*—Return specialized information for objects using a "get," and can sometimes be manipulated using a "set"
- *Indexers*—Provide a way to index elements in certain data structures
- *Methods*—Procedures/functions that manipulate/return objects
- *Operators*—Symbolic operators customized to work with objects

We will eventually discuss each of these.

■ CLASS: COMPLEX

As an introduction to building a class, let us build a new data type called `Complex`. A complex number is of the form $a + bi$, where a and b are real numbers, and i is called the "imaginary unit." It is a quantity with the property that $i^2 = -1$. The quantity a is known as the real part of the complex number $a + bi$, and bi is known as the imaginary part. Note that the symbol + in $a + bi$ cannot mean addition as we normally view it. We can simply regard it as a placeholder, separating the real and imaginary parts.

Now it makes a real difference what we decide to call our classes, because they will exist apart from the main program. Also, because the class must now be accessible from methods in other classes, we will use the access modifier `public`.

Listing 8.1 shows the complete class.

Listing 8.1

```
using System;
public class Complex {

      //Instance Fields-private by default

      double real;
      double imaginary;

      //Static fields

      //Complex.ZERO is readonly; i.e., value cannot be changed
      public static readonly Complex ZERO;

      //Properties

      public double RealPart {
            get { return real; }
            set { real=value; }
      }

      public double ImaginaryPart {
            get { return imaginary; }
            set { imaginary=value; }
      }

      //Instance Constructors

      public Complex() {
            real=0;
            imaginary=0;
      }
```

(continued)

```
public Complex(double real, double imaginary) {
      this.real=real;
      this.imaginary=imaginary;
}

public Complex(String z) {
      char[] delim={'+','i'};
      //Split incoming string on + and i
      String[] tokens=z.Split(delim);
      //Two vars record if real and imaginary part done
      bool realDone=false,imDone=false;
      //Traverse the array of tokens
      for (int index=0;index<tokens.Length;index++) {
            //Only last token should be empty
            if (tokens[index].Length==0
                  &&index<tokens.Length-1)
                  throw new FormatException(
                  "Complex number not in proper form");
            //If real part not done yet, do it,
            //and mark it done
            else if (!realDone) {
                  real=Double.Parse(tokens[index]);
                  realDone=true;
            //If imaginary part not done yet, do it,
            //and mark it done
            } else if (!imDone) {
                  imaginary=Double.Parse(tokens[index]);
                  imDone=true;
            }
      }
      //If either real part or imaginary part left
      //unassigned, this is a problem
      if (!realDone||!imDone) throw new FormatException(
            "Complex number not in proper form");
}

//Static constructor

static Complex() {
      ZERO = new Complex();
}

//Instance Methods

//To compare Complex objects
public bool Equals(Complex other) {
      return this.real==other.real
            &&this.imaginary==other.imaginary;
}
```

(continued)

```
//Returns Complex object a-bi for Complex a+bi
public Complex Conjugate() {
      return new Complex(real,-imaginary);
}

//Methods for Complex arithmetic - private by default
Complex Add(Complex z) {
      return new Complex(real+z.real,
            imaginary+z.imaginary);
}

Complex Subtract(Complex z) {
      return new Complex(real-z.real,
            imaginary-z.imaginary);
}

Complex Multiply(Complex z) {
      return new Complex(real*z.real-imaginary*z.imaginary,
            real*z.imaginary+z.real*imaginary);
}

Complex Divide(Complex z) {
      double den=z.real*z.real+z.imaginary*z.imaginary;
      Complex answer=this.Multiply(z.Conjugate());
      answer.real/=den;
      answer.imaginary/=den;
      return answer;
}

//Method to produce complex string "a+bi"
public override String ToString() {
      return real+"+"+imaginary+"i";
}

//Static Methods

//Parses a string as a Complex; just calls
public static Complex Parse(String z) {
      return new Complex(z);
}

//Overloaded operators

//Equality test ==
public static bool operator ==(Complex z1,Complex z2) {
      return z1.Equals(z2);
}
```

(continued)

```
    //Nonequality test != must be defined if == defined
    public static bool operator !=(Complex z1,Complex z2) {
          return !z1.Equals(z2);
    }

    //Overload arithmetic operators +,-,*,/
    //Just call the methods Add,Subtract,Multiply,Divide
    public static Complex operator +(Complex z1, Complex z2) {
          return z1.Add(z2);
    }

    public static Complex operator -(Complex z1, Complex z2) {
          return z1.Subtract(z2);
    }

    public static Complex operator *(Complex z1, Complex z2) {
          return z1.Multiply(z2);
    }

    public static Complex operator /(Complex z1, Complex z2) {
          return z1.Divide(z2);
    }

}
```

The modifier `public` means that the class is accessible from any other class. Recall that the default for classes and structures is `private`, and can be omitted in such cases. The `Complex` class, however, needs public access. An appendix in the back of the text lists the access modifiers, their meanings, and the defaults for types and their members. Access modifiers can be applied to classes and structures, and any members they contain. They can also be applied to enumerations; `public` is the default for `enums`.

■ FIELDS

First we need to consider how a complex number should be represented in our class. Because we can conveniently store `doubles`, perhaps we can use two `doubles` to store the values for a and b in the complex number $a + bi$:

```
public class Complex {
      double real;
      double imaginary;
//...
}
```

The two parts of the complex number $a + bi$ really should have meaningful names, so we have called them `real` and `imaginary` here.

▪ CONSTRUCTORS

The next task is creating a complex number and initializing its values. This means creating a constructor. Recall that a constructor is intended to initialize the data fields of an object. When we create a `Complex` object, we must be able to provide initial values for the `real` and `imaginary` parts. We can provide more than one constructor; in fact, we can provide as many as we like. This is called "overloading the constructor." As with methods, no two may have the same signature; that is, their parameter lists must be different.

First, create a parameterless constructor that creates the complex number zero, or $0 + 0i$:

```
public Complex() {
        real=0;
        imaginary=0;
}
```

Using this constructor, we can create a `Complex` object whose `real` and `imaginary` parts are both zero. Suppose some program makes the following declaration:

```
Complex zippo = new Complex();
```

This produces a `Complex` object called `zippo`, which references its data fields `real` and `imaginary`. Both of these fields are initialized to zero, as directed by the `Complex()` constructor (see Figure 8.1).

Note that this is entirely different from what the next declaration produces:

```
Complex nada;
```

This produces no object at all, because no constructor is called. We merely have a reference called `nada`, which points (by default) to null, or nothing (see Figure 8.2).

The next logical step is to provide a constructor that initializes the `real` and `imaginary` fields based on two incoming `doubles`:

```
public Complex(double real, double imaginary) {
        this.real=real;
        this.imaginary=imaginary;
}
```

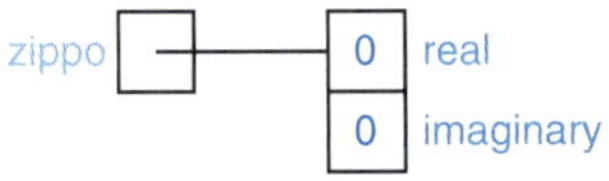

Figure 8.1

Figure 8.2

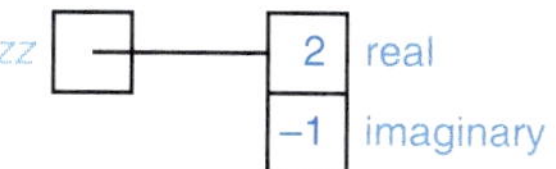

Figure 8.3

Note the usage of the keyword `this`. The term `this` refers to the object upon which the constructor is working. The terms `this.real` and `this.imaginary` refer to the field `real` and the field `imaginary` of this object. In most cases, we do not need to refer to fields and methods by preceding them with the keyword `this`; in fact, it is assumed, and redundant. However, in this case the incoming parameters `real` and `imaginary` have the same names as their counterpart data fields. To resolve the naming conflict, we use `this.real` and `this.imaginary` to distinguish them from the incoming parameters.

To create the complex number $2 + -1i = 2 - i$, we could use this constructor to do it:

```
Complex zz = new Complex(2,-1);
```

Figure 8.3 shows the effect this has on the `Complex` object `zz`.

Another constructor might be one that directly parses strings of the form $a + bi$ into `Complex` objects. For example, we want to parse all of the following strings

```
"2.75 + 3i"
"5.6 + 0i"
"0 + 2.33i"
"1 + -1i"
```

into their respective `Complex` counterparts; that is, we need to separate the `double` values from the markers "+" and "i". Note that, for simplicity's sake, the values for a and b must be present, even if redundant; for example,

```
"1 + 1i"
```

is correct, but

```
"1 + i"
```

is not. An interesting exercise for you would be to modify this method so it could also parse "nonstandard" strings like

```
"i"
"3.6-i"
"2.3"
```

into `Complex` objects. The `Split()` method from the `String` class can help us with our task; we can split using `'+'` and `'i'` as the delimiting characters.

```
public Complex(String z) {
      char[] delim={'+','i'};

      //Split incoming string on + and i
      String[] tokens=z.Split(delim);

      //Two vars record if real and imaginary part completed
      bool realDone=false,imDone=false;

      //Traverse the array of tokens
      for (int index=0;index<tokens.Length;index++) {

            //Only last token should be empty
            if (tokens[index].Length==0&&index<tokens.Length-1)
                  throw new FormatException(
                     Complex number not in proper form");

            //If real part not done yet, do it, and mark it done
            else if (!realDone) {
                  real=Double.Parse(tokens[index]);
                  realDone=true;

            //If imaginary part not done yet, do it, and mark it done
            } else if (!imDone) {
                  imaginary=Double.Parse(tokens[index]);
                  imDone=true;
            }
      }

      //If either real part or imaginary part left unassigned
      if (!realDone||!imDone) throw new FormatException(
            "Complex number not in proper form");

}
```

This constructor could probably use some explaining. Suppose we want to make the following call:

```
Complex z = new Complex("5+-2i");
```

Of course, we have created a new `Complex` object, so the first thing we have is an object `z`, as in Figure 8.4.

Now the job is to separate the 5 and the -2 from the symbols "+" and "i", and parse the numbers as `double`s. We split the string `"5+-2i"` here:

```
char[] delim={'+','i'};
String[] tokens=z.Split(delim);
```

Figure 8.4

Figure 8.5

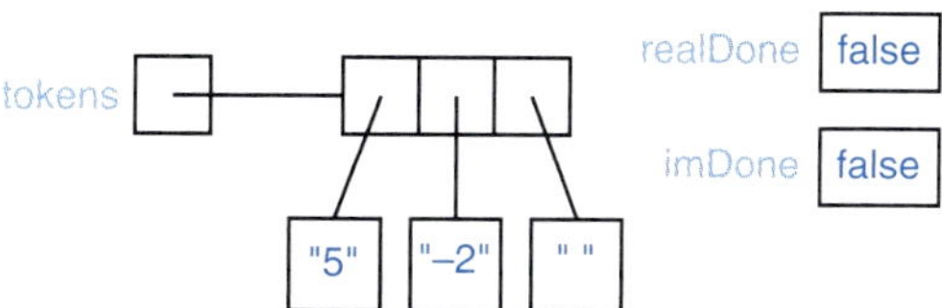

Figure 8.6

In this case, an array containing exactly three strings is created (see Figure 8.5).

The reason the last string is empty is because the last character was `'i'`, one of the delimiting symbols.

We set up a couple of Boolean variables to record whether both the real and imaginary fields are assigned values:

```
bool realDone=false,imDone=false;
```

The effects of this assignment are seen in Figure 8.6.

We then begin traversing through the tokens in a `for` loop. We first check that only the last string is empty; if it is not, this implies that two of the delimiting characters are adjacent to each other, like in `"3++2i"`. This clearly should not happen, so we throw a `FormatException` if we encounter it:

```
if (tokens[index].Length==0&&index<tokens.Length-1)
      throw new FormatException(
         Complex number not in proper form");
```

In this example, you can see that this does not happen. When `index=2` in the `for` loop, `tokens[2]` is a blank token, but it is the last token, because a `FormatException` is not thrown. We then have an `else` associated with this `if`:

```
else if (!realDone) {
      real=Double.Parse(tokens[index]);
      realDone=true;
```

To execute this `else`, we must have a nonempty token that is not the last token, and the `real` field can not have been assigned. This happens when `index=0`, and so the assignment is made (assuming the token can be parsed as a `double`), and `realDone` is set to `true`. If the token cannot be parsed as a `double`, the `Parse()` method will throw a `FormatException`. See Figure 8.7 for a representation of object `z` at this point.

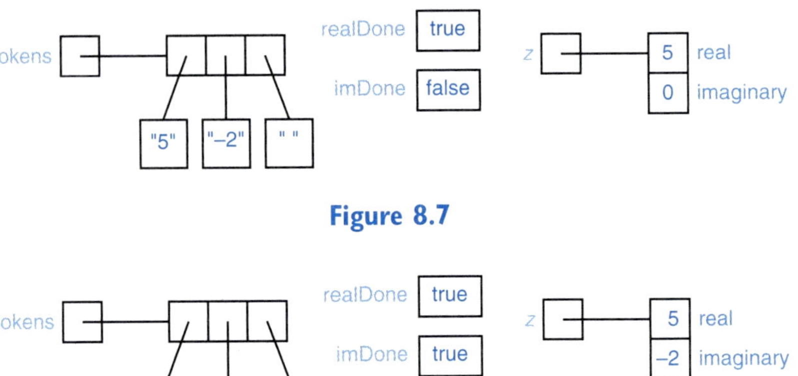

Figure 8.7

Figure 8.8

When `realDone` has been set to `true` and we have a nonempty nonfinal token, the next `else` in the `if-else` chain is executed. If the imaginary part has not been set, we do the assignment, and mark `imDone` as true. This happens when `index=1`.

```
} else if (!imDone) {
      imaginary=Double.Parse(tokens[index]);
      imDone=true;
}
```

Figure 8.8 shows our progress up to this point.

One final check is done after the loop to ensure that both the `real` and `imaginary` fields are assigned.

```
if (!realDone||!imDone) throw new FormatException(
      "Complex number not in proper form");
```

Without this check, it is possible to get out of the loop by splitting a string like `"7i"`. This code will erroneously set the `real` part to 7 and exit the loop, leaving the `imaginary` part with its default value 0.

□ Read-Only Fields

It would be nice to declare a constant called `ZERO` for this class, to represent the complex number 0 + 0*i*. Declaring constants with the `const` keyword can be done only with the simple types, however, like `char`, `int`, and `double`. Thus, we cannot use `const` for a `Complex` object. C# provides the `readonly` keyword for this very purpose, however. We declare the `readonly Complex` value of `ZERO` thus:

```
public class Complex {
      double real;
```

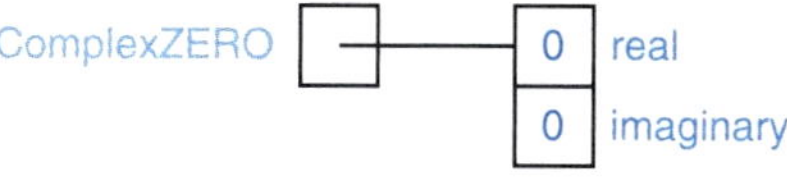

Figure 8.9

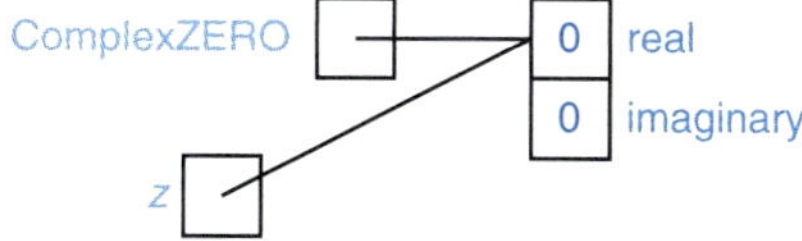

Figure 8.10

```
        double imaginary;
        static readonly Complex ZERO = new Complex();
//...
}
```

ZERO becomes initialized through the use of a Complex constructor. It simply initializes the real and imaginary parts of ZERO to 0. We also declared the data field ZERO static, meaning it belongs to the class, and is called by the class name. Figure 8.9 shows a representation of Complex.ZERO.

Thus, for any program in which the Complex value ZERO is desired, it can be created thus:

```
Complex z = Complex.ZERO;
```

This merely points the z reference to Complex.ZERO, as shown in Figure 8.10.

Note that this assignment is merely an assignment of a reference; thus, z and Complex.ZERO are referencing the same object. Because this object is readonly, there is no chance of changing one as a side effect of changing the other. In fact, static fields are often declared readonly.

☐ Static Fields

It is important to be mindful of static members, and in particular, static fields. All static members belong to the class, and not to any object that instantiates the class. Consider the class in Listing 8.2, which declares both a static field and an instance field. Neither is constant, and both are public, so both can be changed directly. The class also contains a Main() method, so we can test the differing behavior of static data and instance data.

Listing 8.2

```
using System;
public class StaticFields {

      //x is static-it belongs to class
      //shared by all objects that instantiate the class
      static int x=0;

      //y is instance-it belongs to a particular object
      int y=0;

      //Instance Constructor, which takes no arguments
      public StaticFields() {}

      static void Main() {
            //Make a StaticFields object
            StaticFields sf1=new StaticFields();

            //Increment its static data and instance data
            StaticFields.x++;
            sf1.y++;

            //Display results
            Console.WriteLine("StaticFields.x: "+StaticFields.x
                  +" sf1.y: "+sf1.y);

            //Make another StaticFields object
            StaticFields sf2=new StaticFields();

            //Increment its static data and instance data
            StaticFields.x++;
            sf2.y++;

            //Display results
            Console.WriteLine("StaticFields.x: "+StaticFields.x
                  +" sf2.y: "+sf2.y);
      }
}
```

The `Main()` method begins executing, and it first creates the `StaticFields` object `sf1`, by calling the `StaticFields()` constructor.

```
StaticFields sf1=new StaticFields();
```

The constructor doesn't seem to do anything, because `x` and `y` are already initialized, but we need it to create a `StaticFields` object.

```
public StaticFields() {}
```

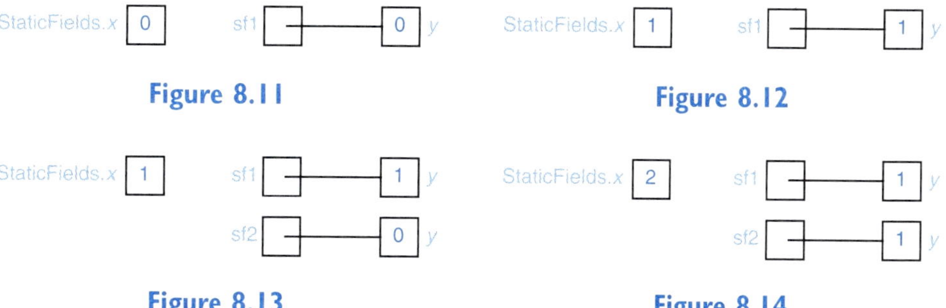

Figure 8.11

Figure 8.12

Figure 8.13

Figure 8.14

The effect is something like in Figure 8.11.

Then we increment the static and instance data of `sf1`:

```
StaticFields.x++;
sf1.y++;
```

This, of course, adds 1 to both `x` and `y`, as in Figure 8.12.

The program then displays its results; no surprises here:

```
StaticFields.x: 1 sf1.y: 1
```

Next, we create another `StaticFields` object called `sf2`. We call the constructor again, which, remember, doesn't seem to initialize anything.

```
StaticFields sf2=new StaticFields();
```

The effect is the creation of another `StaticFields` object, referencing a new set of instance data, shown in Figure 8.13.

When we increment the fields again, we see that the static field is incremented to 2, and the instance field `y` of `sf2` is incremented to 1:

```
StaticFields.x++;
sf2.y++;
```

The effect of this is shown in Figure 8.14.

The program displays its final results, which agree with our development:

```
StaticFields.x: 1 sf1.y: 1
StaticFields.x: 2 sf2.y: 1
```

☐ Static Constructors

C# also allows a single parameterless static constructor. The purpose of a static constructor is to initialize static fields of a class. In the `Complex` class, we have such a constructor to initialize the `Complex` value `ZERO`.

```
static Complex() {
      ZERO = new Complex();
}
```

The static constructor may have no access modifiers. In this case, we could have initialized `ZERO` in the following way:

```
public static readonly Complex ZERO = new Complex();
```

However, the initialization code when creating a class may be more complicated than simple assignments; thus, this type constructor exists.

▪ PROPERTIES

Properties can be viewed as object-oriented fields. To the user, getting a property looks much the same as getting the value of a field; for example, if the `real` field of `Complex` were public, we could retrieve its value by saying something like

```
Complex c = new Complex(1.3,2.1);
double r = c.real;        //r assigned value 1.3
```

We could also set the field by using an assignment:

```
c.real = 9.22;
```

However, fields are usually not public (they are private by default). This is so that the users of a class cannot freely change the data fields, except by the properties and methods the class designer provides for them.

The `Complex` class contains two properties, `RealPart` and `ImaginaryPart`. Using them, you can `get` and/or `set` the values of the real and imaginary fields of a `Complex` object.

```
public double RealPart {
      get { return real; }
      set { real=value; }
}

public double ImaginaryPart {
      get { return imaginary; }
      set { imaginary=value; }
}
```

Defining a property involves defining a `get` block, whose purpose is to execute some code and eventually return some value, and a `set` block, which executes code and usually assigns at least one field a value.

Consider the `get` block of the `RealPart` property. If the user codes something like the following,

```
Complex z = new Complex(3,4);
double rp = z.RealPart//Assigned value real=3.0 thru RealPart property
```

Figure 8.15

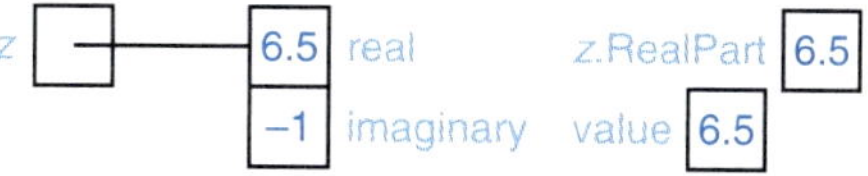

Figure 8.16

the effect is that the `get` block of the `RealPart` property is invoked. It executes only a single statement, to return the value of the `real` field (see Figure 8.15).

You should note that the `get` block can do much more than a simple return; it can execute a series of C# statements before returning the value. The point is that all this activity is hidden from the users; it simply appears to them as an assignment.

A `set` block accepts some value, either by assignment or perhaps by capturing it through a formal parameter, and uses that value to change the state of the object. Consider the `set` block of the `RealPart` property, and the following code:

```
Complex z = new Complex(4,-1);
z.RealPart = 6.5;//real field of z assigned value 6.5, replacing 4.0
```

The `set` block of the `RealPart` property is called, which captures the value and assigns it to the `real` field (see Figure 8.16).

The `set` block must be able to refer in some way to the value it is using; C# provides the `value` keyword for this purpose.

```
public double RealPart {
      get { return real; }
      set { real=value; }//Using keyword "value"
}
```

Again, the code in a `set` block need not be a simple assignment, but could possibly be a series of C# statements. The user, however, simply sees an assignment.

It is not necessary to define a `set` block for a property; the effect is that the property is read-only. For example, if you leave out the `set` blocks of `RealPart` and `ImaginaryPart`, you cannot change the values of the `real` and `imaginary` fields by using those properties. Sometimes, this is exactly what you want.

■ ARITHMETIC WITH COMPLEX NUMBERS

We would like to have methods to compare `Complex` objects and to perform arithmetic with them. To do this, we must discuss how to compare complex numbers, and how to add, subtract, multiply, and divide with them.

For the following, let us consider two arbitrary complex numbers

$$z = a + bi$$
$$w = c + di$$

To add z and w, we simply add their real parts and their imaginary parts separately; that is,

$$\begin{aligned} z + w &= (a + bi) + (c + di) \\ &= (a + c) + (b + d)i \end{aligned}$$

This sum has a real part, namely $a + b$, and an imaginary part, $(c + d)i$, and so is a complex number.

Example:

$$\begin{aligned} &(4 - i) + (6 + 7i) \\ &= (4 + 6) + (-1 + 7)i \\ &= 10 + 6i \end{aligned}$$

Subtracting w from z is just as direct:

$$\begin{aligned} z - w &= (a + bi) - (c + di) \\ &= (a - c) + (b - d)i \end{aligned}$$

The real part of $z - w$ is $a - b$, and the imaginary part is $(c - d)i$.

Example:

$$\begin{aligned} &(3 + 2i) - (1 + 5i) \\ &= (3 - 1) + (2 - 5)i \\ &= 2 - 3i \end{aligned}$$

Multiplying z and w is a little trickier, and it makes use of the fact that $i^2 = -1$. First we cross-multiply all the terms of the two complex numbers:

$$\begin{aligned} zw &= (a + bi)(c + di) \\ &= ac + adi + bci + bdi^2 \end{aligned}$$

Then we take note of the fact that $i^2 = -1$, and thus, the last term is actually a real number:

$$\begin{aligned} &= ac + adi + bci + bd(-1) \\ &= ac + adi + bci - bd \end{aligned}$$

By rearranging the terms, we get a complex number in standard form:

$$zw = (ac - bd) + (ad + bc)i$$

This complex number is the product of the two complex numbers z and w.

Example:

$(6 + 2i)(3 - i)$
$= 18 - 6i + 6i - 2i^2$
$= 18 + 0i + 2$
$= 20$

In order to perform complex division, we should first talk about the conjugate of a complex number. If $w = c + di$, then the conjugate of w is $c - di$. Note that if we multiply a complex number by its conjugate, we get a real number; that is, the product has no imaginary part:

$(c + di)(c - di)$
$= c^2 - cdi + cdi - (di)^2$
$= c^2 - (di)^2$ (middle terms cancel out)
$= c^2 - d^2(-1)^2$ ($i^2 = -1$)
$= c^2 + d^2$ (surprise! a real number!)

The conjugate is quite useful in complex division. Dividing complex z by complex w can be done, if we can just turn the denominator of

$z/w = (a + bi)/(c + di)$

into a real number, because we know how to divide by real numbers. This turns out not to be so hard; in fact, we simply multiply the numerator and denominator by the conjugate of the complex denominator. (We can always multiply the numerator and denominator of a fraction by the same nonzero number without changing the value of the fraction.) Doing this yields the following:

$z/w = (a + bi) / (c + di)$
$= (a + bi)(c - di) / [(c + di)(c - di)]$
$= (ac + bci - adi - (bdi)^2) / (c^2 + d^2)$
$= (ac + bci - adi + (bd)^2) / (c^2 + d^2)$(since $i^2 = -1$)
$= [(ac + bd) + (bc - ad)i] / (c^2 + d^2)$

Note that the last expression is just a complex number divided by a real number. We can separate these into a real and imaginary part, and get a complex number in standard form:

$z/w = [(ac + bd) + (bc - ad)i] / (c^2 + d^2)$
$= [(ac+bd) / (c^2 + d^2)] + [(bc - ad) / (c^2 + d^2)]i$

This rather ugly expression is, in fact, z divided by w.

Example:

$(3 + 2i)/(2 - i)$
$= (3 + 2i)(2 + i) / [(2 - i)(2 + i)]$
$= (6 + 3i + 4i + 2i^2) / (4 + 1)$
$= (6 + 3i + 4i - 2) / 5$
$= (4 + 7i) / 5$
$= 4/5 + (7/5)i$

Complex numbers are considered equal if both their real parts are equal and their imaginary parts are equal. This seems trivial:

$3 + 5i$	$=$	$3 + 5i$	(because $3 = 3$ and $5i = 5i$)
$6.3 + \pi i$	$\neq$	$-6.3 + \pi i$	(because $6.3 \neq -6.3$)
$9.1 + 3.001i$	$\neq$	$9.1 + 3i$	(because $3.001i \neq 3i$)

Now, we will see C# methods to perform all these operations.

▪ METHODS

Given the previous development, it should be easy to write methods to perform arithmetic with `Complex` objects. Let's call the methods `Add`, `Subtract`, `Multiply`, and `Divide`. Each will accept a `Complex` object as a parameter, and return a new `Complex` object.

```
//Methods for Complex arithmetic - private by default
Complex Add(Complex z) {
      return new Complex(real+z.real,
            imaginary+z.imaginary);
}

Complex Subtract(Complex z) {
      return new Complex(real-z.real,
            imaginary-z.imaginary);
}

Complex Multiply(Complex z) {
      return new Complex(real*z.real-imaginary*z.imaginary,
            real*z.imaginary+z.real*imaginary);
}
```

```
Complex Divide(Complex z) {
      double den=z.real*z.real+z.imaginary*z.imaginary;
      Complex answer=this.Multiply(z.Conjugate());
      answer.real/=den;
      answer.imaginary/=den;
      return answer;
}

//Returns Complex object a-bi for Complex a+bi
public Complex Conjugate() {
      return new Complex(real,-imaginary);
}
```

To aid the `Divide()` method, it is convenient to also define a `Conjugate()` method, which returns the conjugate of a `Complex` object. Note that each method just follows the development done earlier, with

- `real` used in place of `a`
- `z.real` used in place of `b`
- `imaginary` used in place of `c`
- `z.imaginary` used in place of `d`

Note that because these methods are called by an object, the names `real` and `imaginary` refer to those fields in the object calling the method; that is, "`this`" object. One could just as easily use

- `this.numerator` instead of `numerator`
- `this.denominator` instead of `denominator`

However, the `this` keyword is assumed, and unless ambiguity is present, is not necessary. Note also that the methods `Add()`, `Subtract()`, `Multiply()`, and `Divide()` do not have an access modifier, and so are private by default; that is, they cannot be called from outside the `Complex` class. This is OK, because we will later overload the +, –, *, and / operators to work with `Complex` objects. Each operator will call its respective method.

Example:

Because `Conjugate()` is the only public method in this group, let's discuss how it might be called. Suppose we have the following code, which has access to the `Complex` class:

```
Complex z = new Complex(2.3,1);
Complex zc = z.Conjugate();
```

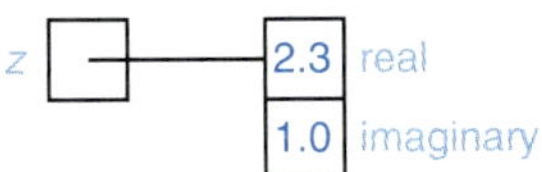

Figure 8.17

Figure 8.18

For the first line, we have already seen how this constructor produces and initializes a `Complex` object (see Figure 8.17).

The next line creates a `Complex` reference `zc`, made to point at a `Complex` object, and this is exactly what `Conjugate()` produces. Here is the `Conjugate()` code again:

```
public Complex Conjugate() {
      return new Complex(real,-imaginary);
}
```

The call `z.Conjugate()` returns a new `Complex` object, formed by passing in `z.real` and the negative of `z.imaginary` as the two parameters. This new object returns from whence it was called, and is assigned (by reference) to `zc` (see Figure 8.18).

If we want to write a method to test for equality of `Complex` objects, it seems to be a simple matter of comparing their real parts and imaginary parts separately. Only if both are equal do we declare the two `Complex` objects equal; otherwise, we declare them unequal.

Writing an instance method (i.e., a method called by an object) is much like writing a static method, except, of course, you leave the keyword `static` out of the definition. Here is an `Equals` method in the `Complex` class:

```
public bool Equals(Complex other) {
      return this.real==other.real
            &&this.imaginary==other.imaginary;
}
```

Here you can see that the keyword `this` is used. In this case, and most others, it can be left out, but it never hurts to provide clarity. Calling this method is a simple task:

```
Complex z1 = new Complex(2,1);
Complex z2 = new Complex(2,-1);
```

```
Complex z3 = new Complex(2,1);
Console.WriteLine(z1.Equals(z2)?"z1==z2":"z1!=z2");
Console.WriteLine(z1.Equals(z3)?"z1==z3":"z1!=z3");
```

It should be clear that the real and imaginary parts of z1 and z3 are equal, but this is not the case for z1 and z2. Thus, the output would be

```
z1!=z2
z1==z3
```

Suppose you want to output a Complex object:

```
Complex z = new Complex(3.7,2);
Console.WriteLine("This is the complex number "+z);
```

The variable z is a Complex object. We would like the output to be something like this:

```
This is the complex number 3.7+2i
```

How in the world do we get the WriteLine() method to display a Complex object as something of the form a + bi? If you recall, when an object is encountered in an output statement or is concatenated to a string using the string concatenation operator +, a search ensues for a ToString() method in the class to which the object belongs. In this case, the search for a ToString() method begins in the Complex class, and there in fact is such a method:

```
public override String ToString() {
      return real+"+"+imaginary+"i";
}
```

This method returns a string, and accepts no parameters. It is an instance method (i.e., not static) and so is called by a Complex object. The string it returns is the real part, followed by a "+", then the imaginary part, followed by "i".

The use of the word override here means that there is already a ToString() method in the Object class, from which Complex is a descendant by default. To distinguish the ToString() method in Complex from the one in Object, the word "override" must be present. We will discuss overriding methods in Chapter 9, when we cover inheritance.

Another interesting exercise for you would be to modify the ToString() method to leave out either the real or imaginary part if it is zero; for example, to display $0 + 3i$ as $3i$, and $7.1 + 0i$ as 7.1. Also, if the imaginary part is negative, it would be nice to use − instead of + to separate the real and imaginary parts, like to display $3.5 + -7.75i$ as $3.5 - 7.75i$. Finally, if the coefficient of i is exactly 1 or −1, it would be nice if it were omitted, like displaying $3 + 1i$ as $3 + i$. Whatever rules you decide to follow here, make sure the constructor that parses strings into Complex objects obeys the same rules!

■ OPERATORS

C# allows us to overload some operators. This is very convenient if you want these operators to function in a meaningful way with other types. The `String` class overloads the + operator, for instance; its behavior is of course quite different from numerical addition in this context.

Operators are static; thus, because they are not called by objects, all arguments must be passed in through a parameter list. Overloading an operator is much like declaring a static method; we use the keyword `operator`, followed by the operator symbol and the parameters. The number of parameters required depends, of course, on the operator you are trying to overload. Here we overload the +, –, *, and / operators to perform complex arithmetic, and we overload the == and != operators to test the equality of `Complex` objects.

```
//Equality test ==
public static bool operator ==(Complex z1,Complex z2) {
      return z1.Equals(z2);
}

//Nonequality test != must be defined if == defined
public static bool operator !=(Complex z1,Complex z2) {
      return !z1.Equals(z2);
}

//Overload arithmetic operators +,-,*,/
//Just call the methods Add,Subtract,Multiply,Divide
public static Complex operator +(Complex z1, Complex z2) {
      return z1.Add(z2);
}

public static Complex operator -(Complex z1, Complex z2) {
      return z1.Subtract(z2);
}

public static Complex operator *(Complex z1, Complex z2) {
      return z1.Multiply(z2);
}

public static Complex operator /(Complex z1, Complex z2) {
      return z1.Divide(z2);
}
```

Note that == and != accept two `Complex` parameters, and return a `bool`. Given the expression

```
a==b
```

the first parameter represents `a`, the operand on the left, and the second parameter represents `b`, the parameter on the right. This left to right order also is respected with other operators that have multiple operands.

Note that the == operator simply calls the `Equals()` method, passing in the two arguments (one is being used as the object calling the `Equals()` method) and returns the same result. If you are satisfied that `Equals()` works for `Complex` objects, you can be satisfied that == works also.

The != operator for `Complex` objects simply returns the logical negative of the `Equals` method. You should note that if you overload either == or != for a class, you must also overload the other, as is done here.

Consider the following code, which calls the overloaded `Complex` == and != operators:

```
Complex z1 = new Complex(2,1);
Complex z2 = new Complex(2,-1);
Complex z3 = new Complex(2,1);
Console.WriteLine(z1==z2);
Console.WriteLine(z1!=z3);
```

Note that the operands on the left and right are `Complex` objects, and because the operators are overloaded they return true or false based on whether the real and imaginary parts of the operands are equal. The output of the previous code would be

```
False
False
```

Note that even if you did not overload == and != for `Complex` objects, the previous code will still function! This is because == and != are defined for objects; when comparing objects with these operators, the default behavior would be to compare only their references. Because `z1`, `z2`, and `z3` all reference different objects in memory, they are all considered unequal if compared in this fashion!

To prove this, modify the code slightly:

```
Complex z1 = new Complex(2,1);
Complex z2 = new Complex(2,-1);
Complex z3 = new Complex(2,1);
Console.WriteLine((Object)z1==(Object)z2);//False-different objects
Console.WriteLine((Object)z1!=(Object)z3);//True-different objects!
```

Here we use the `cast` operator to cast `Complex` objects into Objects. (We will cover object casting in detail later.) The effect is that they are compared using the behavior defined by == and != in the `Object` class. The output is indeed

```
False
True
```

Now we consider the arithmetic operators +, –, *, and /. Each operator returns a `Complex` object, and each simply calls its private method counterpart `Add`, `Subtract`, `Multiply`, or `Divide`. If you are satisfied that those methods work, then you should be confident in these operators as well.

We use the overloaded operators for `Complex` objects in the same way we would use them for simple types:

```
Complex z1 = new Complex(1,1);
Complex z2 = new Complex(2,-1);
Console.WriteLine("z1+z2: "+(z1+z2));
Console.WriteLine("z1-z2: "+(z1-z2));
Console.WriteLine("z1*z2: "+z1*z2);
Console.WriteLine("z1/z2: "+z1/z2);
```

The output of this code is

```
z1+z2: 3+0i
z1-z2: -1+2i
z1*z2: 3+1i
z1/z2: 0.2+0.6i
```

▪ COMPILING TO A DLL

The `Complex` class has no point of entry; that is, no `Main()` method. Such a class will not compile to an executable program (.exe file). However, we can compile it to a dynamic link library, or DLL (.dll file). To do this, we set the `/t` (target) compiler option to the value `library`:

```
C:\C#>csc /t:library Complex.cs
Microsoft (R) Visual C# .NET Compiler version 7.00.9466
for Microsoft (R) .NET Framework version 1.0.3705
Copyright (C) Microsoft Corporation 2001. All rights reserved.
Complex.cs(2,14): warning CS0660: 'Complex' defines operator ==
or operator != but does not override Object.Equals(object o)
Complex.cs(2,14): warning CS0661: 'Complex' defines operator ==
or operator != but does not override Object.GetHashCode()
```

This particular compilation generates a couple of warnings, but we need not be concerned with them. It is not necessary to override the `Object.GetHashCode()` or the

`Object.Equals` method in this case. This compilation produces a .dll file in the same directory in which it was compiled.

```
C:\C#>dir Complex.dll
 Volume in drive C has no label.
 Volume Serial Number is 156F-1503

 Directory of C:\C#

07/31/2002  06:39 PM               5,120 Complex.dll
               1 File(s)            5,120 bytes
               0 Dir(s)   3,174,350,848 bytes free
```

We will use Complex.dll in our next program. To view a complete list of compiler options, see the Appendix. They can also be viewed by typing

```
csc /?
```

or

```
csc /help
```

☐ Program: TestComplex

The TestComplex program in Listing 8.3 tests most of the properties, constructors, and methods of the `Complex` class. It prompts the user to enter a couple of complex numbers, then manipulates them in various ways.

Listing 8.3

```
using System;
class TestComplex {
  static void Main() {
    bool goodUser=false;
    //Loop til user follows directions
    while (!goodUser) {
      try{

      //Assume input is good
      goodUser=true;

      //Prompt user to enter complex z1=a+bi
      Console.Write("Enter a complex number z1: ");

      //Use the constructor that parses a string to Complex
      Complex z1=new Complex(Console.ReadLine());
```

(continued)

```
        //Test the gets for the properties
        Console.WriteLine("The real part: "+z1.RealPart);
        Console.WriteLine("The imaginary part: "+z1.ImaginaryPart);

        //Test conjugate method (and ToString)
        Console.WriteLine("The conjugate: "+z1.Conjugate());

        //Create z2=0+0i
        Complex z2=new Complex();

        //Prompt user for new real/imaginary parts for z2
        Console.Write("Enter the real part of complex number z2: ");
        double rz2=Double.Parse(Console.ReadLine());
        //Set it
        z2.RealPart=rz2;
        Console.Write("Enter the coefficient of i for z2: ");
        double iz2=Double.Parse(Console.ReadLine());
        //Set it
        z2.ImaginaryPart=iz2;

        //Test the gets for the properties
        Console.WriteLine("The real part: "+z2.RealPart);
        Console.WriteLine("The imaginary part: "+z2.ImaginaryPart);

        //Test conjugate method (and ToString)
        Console.WriteLine("The conjugate: "+z2.Conjugate());

        //Test the equality and arithmetic operators
        Console.WriteLine("z1==z2: "+(z1==z2));
        Console.WriteLine("z1+z2: "+(z1+z2));
        Console.WriteLine("z1-z2: "+(z1-z2));
        Console.WriteLine("z1*z2: "+z1*z2);
        Console.WriteLine("z1/z2: "+z1/z2);

        //Whoops!
        } catch (FormatException fe) {
        Console.WriteLine(fe+"\n\rYou screwed up!");
        //Force another iteration
        goodUser=false;
        }
      }
    }
  }
```

■ REFERENCING A DLL

In order to compile TestComplex.cs to TestComplex.exe, the compiler needs to know where the `Complex` class is. This will be easy, because we are still placing everything in the same directory, which we specify by using the `/r` (reference) compiler option:

```
C:\C#>csc /r:Complex.dll TestComplex.cs
Microsoft (R) Visual C# .NET Compiler version 7.00.9466
for Microsoft (R) .NET Framework version 1.0.3705
Copyright (C) Microsoft Corporation 2001. All rights reserved.
```

This produces the file TestComplex.exe:

```
C:\C#>dir TestComplex.*
 Volume in drive C has no label.
 Volume Serial Number is 156F-1503

 Directory of C:\C#

07/31/2002  06:33 PM             1,705 TestComplex.cs
07/31/2002  06:55 PM             4,096 TestComplex.exe
               2 File(s)          5,801 bytes
               0 Dir(s)   3,173,507,072 bytes free
```

This executable runs like any other:

```
C:\C#>TestComplex
Enter a complex number z1: 3+i
System.FormatException: Complex number not in proper form
   at Complex..ctor(String z)
   at TestComplex.Main()
You screwed up!
Enter a complex number z1: 3+1i
The real part: 3
The imaginary part: 1
The conjugate: 3+-1i
Enter the real part of complex number z2: three
System.FormatException: Input string was not in a correct
format.
   at System.Number.ParseDouble(String s, NumberStyles style,
NumberFormatInfo info)
   at System.Double.Parse(String s, NumberStyles style,
IFormatProvider provider)
   at TestComplex.Main()
You screwed up!
```

```
Enter a complex number z1: 3+1i
The real part: 3
The imaginary part: 1
The conjugate: 3+-1i
Enter the real part of complex number z2: 3
Enter the coefficient of i for z2: -2
The real part: 3
The imaginary part: -2
The conjugate: 3+2i
z1==z2: False
z1+z2: 6+-1i
z1-z2: 0+3i
z1*z2: 11+-3i
z1/z2: 0.538461538461538+0.692307692307692i
```

■ DESTRUCTORS

Destructors are the natural complement to constructors. A constructor creates and then initializes object data, whereas a destructor performs any cleanup code on an object before the garbage collector hauls it off.

A class can have only one parameterless destructor. Its name must be the name of the class preceded by the symbol "~". In any class with a destructor defined, the destructor's code will be executed for objects of that type before the garbage collector returns their space to the operating system.

□ Program: TestDestructor

As an example of a destructor and how it functions, take a look at the program in Listing 8.4. The `TestDestructor` class has a constructor that initializes a `String` instance field, and the destructor merely displays a message. The destructor is not called by the program, but is called automatically before a `TestDestructor` object is returned to the operating system.

In the program we create two `TestDestructor` objects, then move a reference away from one of the `TestDestructor` objects to the other. This has the effect of two references pointing at the same object, while nothing points at the other. The "dangling" object is a candidate for garbage collection. Even if the garbage collector does not run during a test run of this program, the destructors will certainly be called before the program terminates. At that point the garbage collector must return all of the application's resources to the system.

Listing 8.4

```
using System;
public class TestDestructor {

      //Instance field
      String identifier=null;

      //Constructor
      public TestDestructor(String ident) {
            //initialize the field
            identifier=ident;
      }

      //Destructor
      ~TestDestructor() {
            //This executes before a TestDestructor object
            //is reclaimed by OS
            Console.WriteLine(this.ToString()
                  +": Yeow!  The garbage collector got me!");
      }

      //Method to turn TestDestructor object into a String
      //This is useful for the user to distinguish
      //the objects when output
      public override String ToString() {
            return identifier;
      }

      static void Main(String[] args) {

            //Make two TestDestructor objects
            //and announce their presence
            //Names of the objects captured from command line
            TestDestructor td1=new TestDestructor(args[0]);
            Console.WriteLine(td1+": I am here.");
            TestDestructor td2=new TestDestructor(args[1]);
            Console.WriteLine(td2+": I am here.");

            //Move a reference away from an object
            Console.WriteLine("Moving reference away from "+td1);
            //object td1 "was" pointing at is now a candidate
            //for garbage collection
            td1=td2;

            //Run the garbage collector; you normally let it
            //run itself, but we need to see the destructor run
            GC.Collect();
```

(continued)

```
            Console.WriteLine("Program paused-hit return");
            Console.ReadLine();
            Console.WriteLine(td2+": I'm still here.");

            //The destructor for 2nd object will run
            //before the OS kills this program
      }

}

C:\C#>TestDestructor David Gie-Gie
David: I am here.
Gie-Gie: I am here.
Moving reference away from David
Program paused-hit return
David: Yeow!  The garbage collector got me!

Gie-Gie: I'm still here.
Gie-Gie: Yeow!  The garbage collector got me!
```

In summary, and in addition, here are some rules for destructors of which you should take note:

- Destructors cannot be used with structures. They are used only with classes.
- A class can have only one destructor.
- Destructors cannot be inherited or overloaded.
- Destructors cannot be called; they are invoked automatically.
- A destructor does not take modifiers or have parameters.

■ STRUCTURES

Objects of a structure type are stored by value, whereas objects that instantiate a class are stored by reference. If the object is relatively "small," declaring it as a structure can be more efficient, because a structure object doesn't carry with it all the excess baggage of a reference type. If necessary, structures can be cast or "boxed" into a corresponding reference type, and back again.

Defining a structure is similar to defining a class, but there are some differences. A `struct` can contain

- Constructors
- Constants
- Fields

- Methods
- Properties
- Indexers
- Operators

It is an error to declare a parameterless constructor for a `struct`, because a default constructor is always provided to initialize the `struct` members to their default values. It is also an error to initialize an instance field in a `struct`; for example, you may not do the following:

```
public struct MyStructure {
//      int field1 = 0;      Can't do this
      double myDouble;
      char myChar;
      String myString;
}
```

Another important difference is that because a structure object is stored by value, it is not necessary to use the keyword `new` in a constructor to initialize one. For example, you may create a `MyStructure` object without ever calling a constructor:

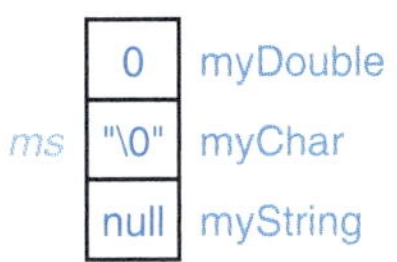

Figure 8.19

```
MyStructure ms;
```

The fields are all initialized to their default values (zero, basically), including any fields that are reference types (see Figure 8.19).

Of course, you certainly couldn't get away with this if you were dealing with a class; such an object does not even exist until a constructor is called with the keyword `new`. Only the reference to the object exists without a constructor call.

☐ Structures Are Stored by Value

Although it's been mentioned numerous times before, all structures are stored by value. This means, for one thing, that when they are passed into a method (by value, by default) a copy of the structure object is made. Any modifications made to this copy will not affect the corresponding object outside the method. To illustrate this, consider the Sphere structure, which follows.

☐ Structure: Sphere

The Sphere structure in Listing 8.5 has only one field, `radius`. It has a `Radius` property, with the ability to set the `radius` field. It also has a couple of methods to compute and return the surface area and/or volume of this sphere.

Listing 8.5

```
using System;
public struct Sphere {

      //Instance field
      double radius;

      //Constructor
      public Sphere(double radius) {
            this.radius=radius;
      }

      //Radius property with get/set
      public double Radius {
            get {return radius;}
            set {radius=Math.Abs(value);}
      }

      //Methods
      public double SurfaceArea() {
            return 4*Math.PI*radius*radius;
      }

      public double Volume() {
            return 4*Math.PI*radius*radius*radius/3;
      }

}
```

The test program in Listing 8.6 creates a `Sphere` object with a radius captured from an incoming parameter on the command line. It displays the information about the sphere, then passes it to a method. This method modifies the `Sphere` object and displays the results, but because the `Sphere` is a copy, the `Sphere` object in the `Main()` method remains the same. The program verifies this by displaying the radius on the `Main() Sphere` object after executing the method.

Listing 8.6

```
using System;
public class TestSphere {
    static void Main(String[] incoming) {
      //Create a Sphere using command line argument
      Sphere s=new Sphere(Double.Parse(incoming[0]));

      //Show the radius, surface area, and volume
      Console.WriteLine("Outside, radius of circle: "+s.Radius);
      Console.WriteLine("SurfaceArea: "+s.SurfaceArea());
      Console.WriteLine("Volume: "+s.Volume());

      //We will change the radius of the sphere inside the method
      //The Sphere s is passed by value; a copy is made
      TryToMessWithTheSphere(s);

      //Show the radius again; it remains undisturbed
      Console.WriteLine("Outside, radius of circle: "+s.Radius);
    }

    //Accepts a Sphere structure object (by value)
    static void TryToMessWithTheSphere(Sphere s) {
      //Double the radius of the local copy of the Sphere
      s.Radius=2*s.Radius;
      //Display effects on the copy
      Console.WriteLine("Inside, radius of circle: "+s.Radius);
      Console.WriteLine("SurfaceArea: "+s.SurfaceArea());
      Console.WriteLine("Volume: "+s.Volume());
    }
}
```

If you run this, you should be convinced that structures are indeed stored by value:

```
C:\C#>TestSphere 10
Outside, radius of circle: 10
SurfaceArea: 1256.63706143592
Volume: 4188.79020478639
Inside, radius of circle: 20
SurfaceArea: 5026.54824574367
Volume: 33510.3216382911
Outside, radius of circle: 10
```

☐ Boxing and Unboxing Structures

A value type can be converted back and forth to its corresponding reference type. Turning a value type into a reference type is known as boxing, whereas the reverse is called "unboxing." This is done by casting.

Boxing can be quite useful if you are passing a value type into a method that expects a reference type. Boxing allows a value type to be treated the same way as any referenced object.

Listing 8.7 contains an example of boxing some doubles to objects. Note the differences in how they are treated depending on whether they are reference types or value types at the time. Note that boxing to an object is automatic, whereas unboxing requires an explicit cast.

Listing 8.7

```
using System;
public class TestBoxing {
    static void Main() {
      double d1=5;
      double d2=5;

      //double values are compared-5=5
      Console.WriteLine(d1==d2);

      //Object references are compared-
      //different objects, not equal
      Console.WriteLine(CompareAsObjects(d1,d2));

      //Box d1, then unbox it; it is a value type again
      double d3=(double)UnboxMe(d1);

      //double values are compared-5=5
      Console.WriteLine(d2==d3);
    }

      //any structures are automatically "boxed"
      //to reference type Object-they become reference types
    static bool CompareAsObjects(Object first,Object second) {
      return first==second;
    }
```

(continued)

```
      //Automatically boxed to Object
      //Sends back an Object, which we "unbox"
      //to double using a cast
    static Object UnboxMe(Object o) {
      return o;
    }
}


True
False
True
```

We are not free to cast structures to any type we wish. You will observe these restrictions shortly when we cover inheritance in Chapter 9.

chapter 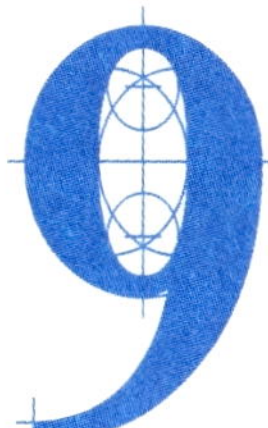

Object-Oriented Programming

Constructing objects and using them is the backbone of object-oriented programming. This is opposed to defining a program with a `Main()` method and a series of procedures to manipulate data, which, by comparison, is relatively disorganized. By defining classes, we naturally group the data for an object with the methods that manipulate them. But there is more to it than that, as you will see.

■ INHERITANCE

C# classes can inherit all of the members of another class. We call this inheritance, or derivation. In the literature, a class that inherits from another class can be called a "subclass," "derived class," or "child class"; a class that is inherited from can be called the "superclass," "base class," or "parent class." A derived class D has all the functionality of the base class B, plus whatever capabilities the programmer has added to D. This can greatly enhance programming, because it allows one to add considerable power to a class simply by subclassing another class.

▪ THE `Object` CLASS

The truth is, with one exception, all C# classes are derived from another class. The `Object` class is the base class for all other classes, and every class is either directly derived from `Object` or indirectly derived through some other class. This means that all objects that instantiate classes have access to the public members of `Object`. For the curious, Table 9.1 lists the members of the `Object` class.

Every class has access to these public members, and some have access to the protected members. In fact, every class we have written so far is a derived class of `Object` by default, and has access to its public members.

The cardinal rule of inheritance in C# is that no class can have more than one parent. (In fact, except for `Object`, every class has exactly one parent!) Allowing a class to have more than one parent is called "multiple inheritance," and is not allowed in C#. This concept of single inheritance creates a hierarchy among the classes, with `Object` at the top (see Figure 9.1).

Note that some classes do not directly inherit from `Object`, but from other classes; however, their line of ancestry always eventually leads back to `Object`.

TABLE 9.1

Public Constructors	
`Object` Constructor	Initializes a new instance of the `Object` class.
Public Methods	
`Equals`	Overloaded. Determines whether two `Object` instances are equal.
`GetHashCode`	Serves as a hash function for a particular type, suitable for use in hashing algorithms and data structures like a hash table.
`GetType`	Gets the `Type` of the current instance.
`ReferenceEquals`	Determines whether the specified `Object` instances are the same instance.
`ToString`	Returns a string that represents the current `Object`.
Protected Methods	
`Finalize`	Overridden. Allows an `Object` to attempt to free resources and perform other cleanup operations before the `Object` is reclaimed by garbage collection. In C#, finalizers are expressed using destructor syntax.
`MemberwiseClone`	Creates a shallow copy of the current `Object`.

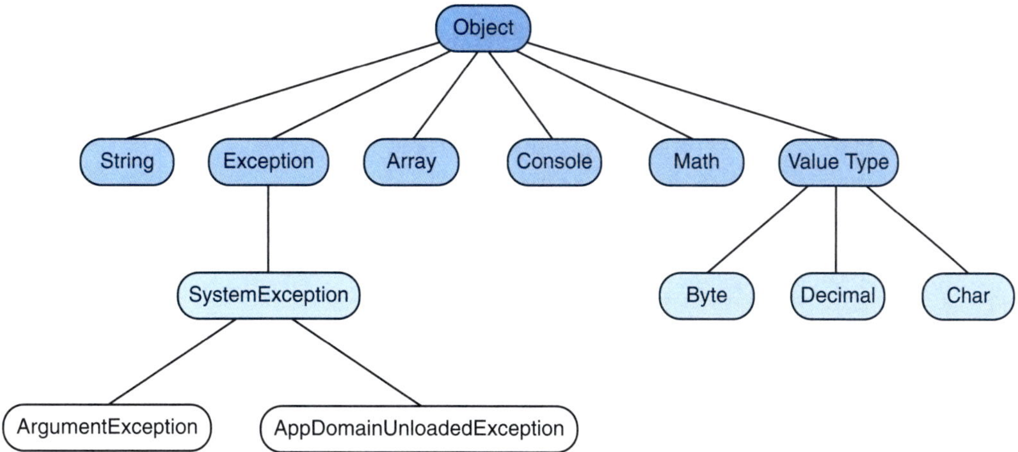

Figure 9.1

In C#, we create a derived class by using the derivation symbol ":" in the class definition. For example, consider the class called `Parallelogram`, which is derived from `Object`, shown in Listing 9.1.

Listing 9.1

```
using System;
public class Parallelogram:Object {
  //Parallelogram inherits from Object by default
  //Doesn't hurt to say it though

  //Fields of a parallelogram
  protected double bottom=0,
              side=0,
              lowerLeftAngle=0;

  //Properties
  public double Height {
      get {return side*Math.Sin(lowerLeftAngle);}
  }

  //Instance Constructors

  //This does something; it calls Object()
  public Parallelogram() {}
```

(continued)

```
    public Parallelogram(double bottom,double side,
            double lowerLeftAngle) {
            this.bottom=bottom;
            this.side=side;
            this.lowerLeftAngle=lowerLeftAngle;
    }

    //Methods

    public virtual double Perimeter() {
            return 2*bottom+2*side;
    }

    public virtual double Area() {
            return bottom*Height;
    }

}
```

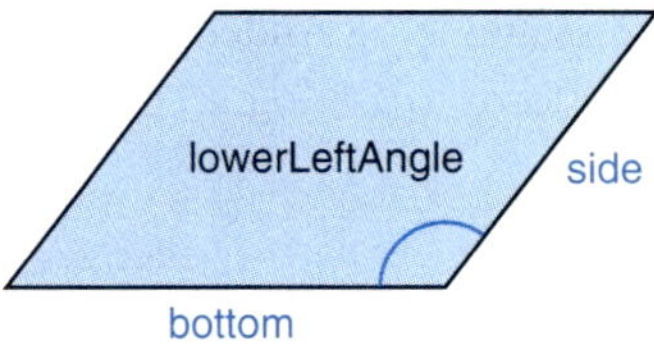

Figure 9.2

This class represents a parallelogram. Here we explicitly declare `Parallelogram` to derive from `Object`; this is actually redundant because unless a class specifies some other class, it is a subclass of `Object` by default.

Of course, `Parallelogram` declares the `double` fields `bottom`, `side`, and `lowerLeftAngle` to represent its spatial characteristics (see Figure 9.2).

☐ Protected Members

Note that the fields `bottom`, `side`, and `lowerLeftAngle` in the `Parallelogram` class are declared protected. Members declared protected are not accessible everywhere; they are accessible only within the class, and within any class that is derived from it.

☐ Base Class Constructors

The `Parallelogram` class has a constructor to initialize the fields. The manner in which fields are initialized in a class is significant, because now that we know all classes except `Object` inherit the members of another class, the initialization of all the super-

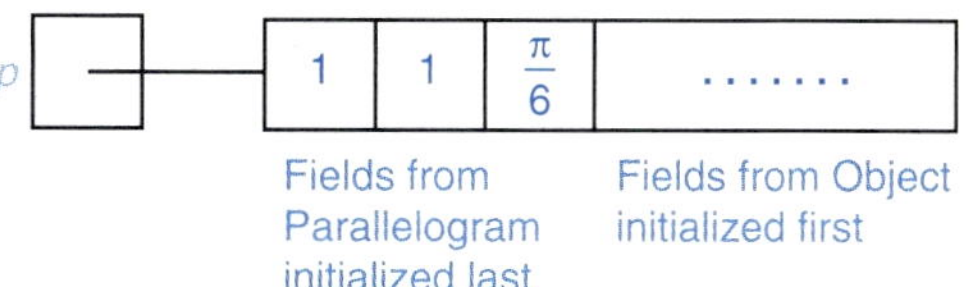

Figure 9.3

class data must be performed as well. The first initializations that take place are those in the field declarations; in the case of `Parallelogram`, these:

```
protected double bottom=0,
                 side=0,
                 lowerLeftAngle=0;
```

Then, when you make a constructor call like

```
Parallelogram p = new Parallelogram(1,1,Math.PI/3);
```

The object `p` must initialize all of the fields in `Parallelogram`, but because it is also an `Object` by inheritance, it must initialize the `Object` fields as well. How is this done? The first thing a constructor does is call a base class constructor. If you do not specify which base constructor or "superconstructor" to call, it will call the parameterless constructor. So, before the `Parallelogram(double, double, double)` constructor initializes the fields of `Parallelogram`, it calls the `Object()` constructor, and there is such a constructor in the `Object` class. (If there is no such constructor in the base class, you cannot call it by default, and must specify which base constructor to call. We will demonstrate this in an example in Listing 9.2.) This guarantees that the fields in the base class are also initialized. Of course, if the base class is not `Object`, a call to a constructor may entail calls to many superconstructors, all the way up to the `Object` class. In the case of the `Parallelogram` constructor call, we have something like Figure 9.3.

Notice that we don't know what the inherited fields are initialized to; after all, we didn't write the `Object` class. It isn't our business to know anyway; it is sufficient to know that it is done.

`Parallelogram` has a property `Height` that returns the height of the parallelogram. This is an example of a property that does more than just return a field value. With a little trig, you can see that

$$\sin(\text{lowerLeftAngle}) = \sin(\pi - \text{lowerLeftAngle}) = \text{Height} / \text{side}$$

So calculating the `Height` means calculating

$$\text{side} \times \sin(\text{lowerLeftAngle})$$

which, as you can see from the class, is exactly what the `Height` property does (see Figure 9.4).

Figure 9.4

☐ Virtual Members

The class also has two methods, `Perimeter()` and `Area()`, which calculate the perimeter and area of the parallelogram. Notice that they are declared with the keyword `virtual`. This allows any subclasses of `Parallelogram` to override these methods; that is, to provide their own implementations of the same method. We have already seen overriding by periodically providing a `ToString()` method for our classes. This implies that in the `Object` class, `ToString()` is declared virtual. Any member of a class can be virtual; not just methods.

Here is a test program for the `Parallelogram` class:

```
using System;
class CodeTester {
    static void Main() {
      //Create 2 parallelograms of identical dimension
      Parallelogram p = new Parallelogram(12,10,Math.PI/6);
      Parallelogram q = new Parallelogram(12,10,Math.PI/6);

      //Display Parallelogram properties and method results of p
      Console.WriteLine("p-Height: "+p.Height);
      Console.WriteLine("p-Perimeter: "+p.Perimeter());
      Console.WriteLine("p-Area: "+p.Area());

      //Display Object method results of p
      Console.WriteLine("p-HashCode: "+p.GetHashCode());
      Console.WriteLine("p-Type: "+p.GetType());

      //Display Parallelogram properties and method results of q
      Console.WriteLine("q-Height: "+q.Height);
      Console.WriteLine("q-perimeter: "+q.Perimeter());
      Console.WriteLine("q-Area: "+q.Area());

      //Display Object method results of q
      Console.WriteLine("q-HashCode: "+q.GetHashCode());
      Console.WriteLine("q-Type: "+q.GetType());

      //Are the two parallelograms equal?
```

```
    //No, they have different references/hash codes
    //Must override Equals in Parallelogram class
    //if something other than reference comparison is desired
    Console.WriteLine("Equals: "+p.Equals(q));
  }
}
```

Note that the program calls the `Parallelogram` properties and methods, but it also calls some methods from the `Object` class. This is fine, because a `Parallelogram` is also an `Object` by inheritance.

```
p-Height: 5
p-Perimeter: 44
p-Area: 60
p-HashCode: 71
p-Type: Parallelogram
q-Height: 5
q-perimeter: 44
q-Area: 60
q-HashCode: 72
q-Type: Parallelogram
Equals: False
```

Note that the two `Parallelograms` were declared with identical dimensions, but at least one of their characteristics differ, namely, the hash codes. What is a hash code? C# stores all objects in a hash table; their locations in the table are specified by the hash code. The "reference" for reference types is actually this hash code.

As we have seen, two objects are considered equal in C# only if they reference the same object. The equality test == by default does comparisons this way, as does the `Equals()` method in `Object`. Because the two objects `p` and `q` are stored in different places in the object hash table, they are not considered equal. Of course, if we want == or `Equals()` to mean something else, we are free to redefine these in any way we wish. Because there is no `Equals()` method defined in the `Parallelogram` class,

```
p.Equals(q);
```

calls the method `Equals()` from the `Object` class. This is the way method calls work in the object hierarchy; if the method with the proper signature does not exist in the class, the method is sought in the base class. If it doesn't exist there either, a search up the object's line of ancestry ensues, possibly leading all the way up to the `Object` class. The first method found (the deepest in the line) that has the proper signature is used.

The previous program calls a `GetType()` method for an `Object`, and returns a `Type` object. `Type` is a direct descendant of `Object` that contains much more and highly specialized information about objects. Using the properties provided by the `Type` class, you can determine much about the nature and state of an object.

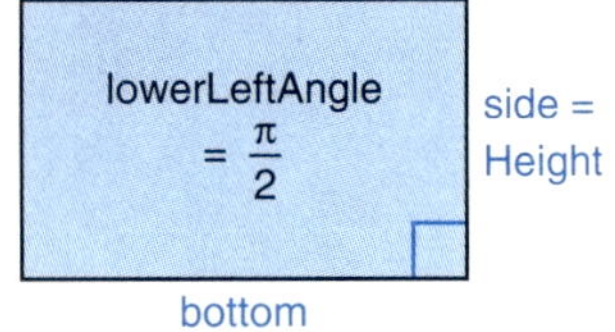

Figure 9.5

☐ Base Constructors

Recall that the first task of a constructor is to call a base class constructor. You have seen the default behavior of calling the parameterless base class constructor from the `Parallelogram` class. Now, we will examine specifying the base constructor in a constructor declaration.

Consider a rectangle, which has the same spatial characteristics as a parallelogram, except all its interior angles are $\pi/2 = 90°$ (see Figure 9.5).

Thus, if we were to construct a `Rectangle` class, it is natural for it to extend `Parallelogram`. Listing 9.2 is such a `Rectangle` class.

Listing 9.2

```
using System;
public class Rectangle:Parallelogram {
  //No fields-all inherited from Parallelogram and Object

  //Constructors
 //Call the base constructor using pi/2.
  public Rectangle(double bottom,double height)
      :base(bottom,height,Math.PI/2) {
      //This class has no fields, so nothing to do here!
  }

  //Override the area method from the Parallelogram class.
  public override double Area() {
    return bottom*side;
  }
}
```

There doesn't seem to be much in this class. First of all there are no fields declared; however, a `Rectangle` inherits all the members from `Parallelogram` (and `Object`). With `bottom`, `side`, and `lowerLeftAngle` already present, there is no need to redefine them. These base class fields are initialized when the `Rectangle(double,double)` constructor is called, because it specifies to first call the `Parallelogram(double,double,double)` constructor. The call to the base

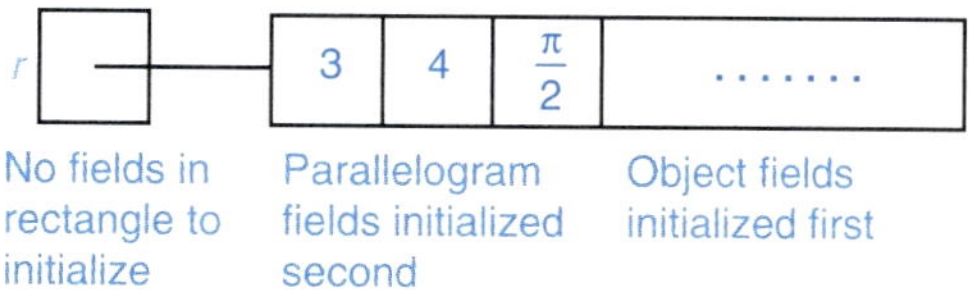

Figure 9.6

constructor passes in `Math.PI/2`, so the object created has the characteristics of a rectangle. So, when making the call

```
Rectangle r = new Rectangle(3,4);
```

we have something like Figure 9.6.

Overriding Members

It is often the case that a base class member is not appropriate for the subclass you are defining, or the member isn't efficient enough, or the like. There could be any number of reasons to want to provide a member in your subclass to be used instead of the one with the same signature in a superclass. For example, consider the `Area()` method in `Parallelogram`:

```
public virtual double Area() {
        return bottom*Height;
}
```

In this case, the same method would work just as well in the `Rectangle` subclass, because a rectangle has interior angles of $\pi/2$ each, so computing the `Height` property (inherited from `Parallelogram`) would yield

Height = $\sin(\pi/2) \times$ side = $1 \times$ side = side

so computing `bottom` × `Height` is equivalent to computing `bottom` × `side` for a rectangle. It is not always the case that a superclass member is appropriate for a subclass, however. In this case, because we know `side` = `Height` for a rectangle, we could shave a little computation time and avoid invoking the `Height` property:

```
//Override the area method from the Parallelogram class.
public override double Area() {
  return bottom*side;
}
```

This returns the correct area, but in slightly less time than the same method in the `Parallelogram` class would. This is reason enough to override a method.

Let's carry this derivation a little further. We'll make a subclass `Square` of `Rectangle`. Of course, a square can be thought of as a special kind of rectangle whose sides are all the same length, as in Figure 9.7.

The `Square` class in Listing 9.3 doesn't seem to declare much of anything new; most of its characteristics come from `Object`, `Parallelogram`, and `Rectangle`.

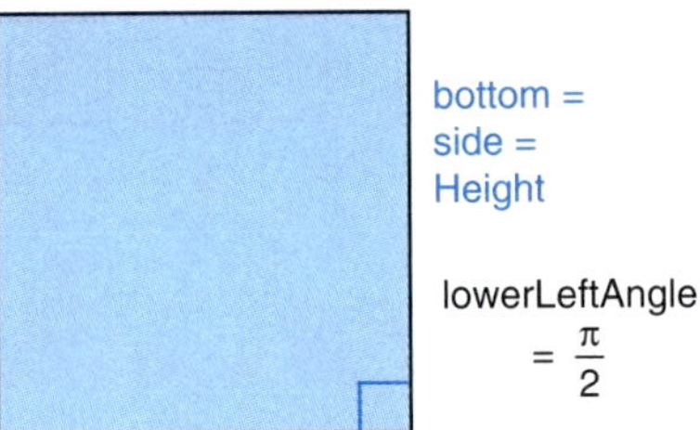

Figure 9.7

Listing 9.3

```
public class Square:Rectangle {
  //fields-all inherited from Parallelogram and Object

  //Constructors
  public Square(double s):base(s,s) {}

  //Override the perimeter method from Parallelogram
  public override double Perimeter() {
        return 4*side;
  }
}
```

The `Square` constructor accepts a single `double`, the length of a side. The constructor simply calls the `Rectangle(double, double)` constructor, which in turn calls the `Parallelogram(double, double, double)` constructor, which in turn calls the `Object()` constructor! Thus, the following call

```
Square s = new Square(5);
```

produces an object looking something like Figure 9.8.

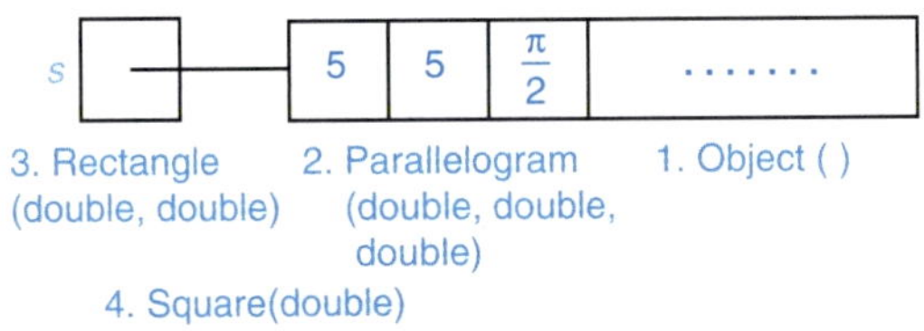

Figure 9.8

The `Perimeter()` method from `Parallelogram` is overridden in `Square`. Note that `Parallelogram` is the supersuperclass of `Square`. Again, this method was overridden for only a slight gain in efficiency (and to show you how it's done).

Listing 9.4 is a test program that creates `Squares`, `Rectangles`, and `Parallelograms`. If you are paying attention, what is interesting about the program is not the constructor and method calls, but rather

- The intricate initialization process occurring behind the scenes
- The actual class in which a method resides when called by an object

Listing 9.4

```
using System;
public class TestShapes {
       public static void Main() {
              Parallelogram p=new Parallelogram(10,4,Math.PI/6);
              Rectangle r=new Rectangle(10,4);
              Square s=new Square(3);
              Console.WriteLine(p.Perimeter());//From Parallelogram
              Console.WriteLine(r.Perimeter());//From Parallelogram
              Console.WriteLine(s.Perimeter());//From Square
              Console.WriteLine(p.Area());//From Parallelogram
              Console.WriteLine(r.Area());//From Rectangle
              Console.WriteLine(s.Area());//From Rectangle
       }
}

C:\C#>csc /r:Parallelogram.dll /r:Rectangle.dll /r:Square.dll
TestShapes.cs
Microsoft (R) Visual C# .NET Compiler version 7.00.9466
for Microsoft (R) .NET Framework version 1.0.3705
Copyright (C) Microsoft Corporation 2001. All rights reserved.

C:\C#>TestShapes
28
28
12
20
40
9
```

Note that the `TestShapes` class must reference all three of the DLLs for `Square`, `Rectangle`, and `Parallelogram`.

■ DEFINING EXCEPTIONS

`Exception` is a special type of class in C#. Only objects of type `Exception` (or one of its many subclasses) can be thrown using the `throw` statement. Table 9.2 is a table of `Exception` members. (We do not show members inherited from `Object`.)

If none of the predefined exceptions seems to indicate the particular exception you want to describe, you may subclass `Exception` or one of its many subclasses. You derive such a class pretty much the same way you do any other.

If all of the characteristics of the exception from which you are deriving are OK (usually the case with exceptions), the only thing you need to worry about is providing constructors for your derived class. Exceptions typically contain only two public constructors:

```
public Exception();
public Exception(String);
```

To subclass `Exception`, merely provide two constructors—one that accepts string and the other, parameterless. Here we derive `NegativeRadiusException` from `Exception`:

```
using System;
public class NegativeRadiusException:Exception {
      public NegativeRadiusException() {}//Implicitly calls
base()
      public NegativeRadiusException(String s):base(s) {}
}
```

The deceptively simple appearance of this class belies the truly complicated nature of the `Exception` class, and the fact that its is hidden from the programmer is not a bad thing. Rebuilding the wheel is a common expression, and rebuilding the `Exception` wheel would be quite a task.

Listing 9.5 is the `Circle` class, which makes use of this new `Exception` type.

Listing 9.5

```
using System;
public class Circle {
      private double radius;

      public Circle(double r) {
            if (r<0) throw new NegativeRadiusException(
                  "Radius must be nonnegative!");
            radius=r;
      }
```

(continued)

TABLE 9.2

Public Constructors	
`Exception` Constructor	Overloaded. Initializes a new instance of the `Exception` class.
Public Properties	
`HelpLink`	Gets or sets a link to the help file associated with this exception.
`InnerException`	Gets the `Exception` instance that caused the current exception.
`Message`	Gets a message that describes the current exception.
`Source`	Gets or sets the name of the application or the object that causes the error.
`StackTrace`	Gets a string representation of the frames on the call stack at the time the current exception was thrown.
`TargetSite`	Gets the method that throws the current exception.
Public Methods	
`GetBaseException`	When overridden in a derived class, returns the `Exception` that is the root cause of one or more subsequent exceptions.
`GetObjectData`	When overridden in a derived class, sets the `SerializationInfo` with information about the exception.
`ToString`	Overridden. Creates and returns a string representation of the current exception.
Protected Constructors	
`Exception` Constructor	Overloaded. Initializes a new instance of the `Exception` class.
Protected Properties	
`HResult`	Gets or sets `HRESULT`, a coded numerical value that is assigned to a specific exception.

(continued from page 210)

```
        public double Radius {
            get {return radius;}
            set {
              if (value<0) throw new NegativeRadiusException(
                    "Radius must be nonnegative!");
              radius=value;
            }
        }

        public double Perimeter() {
              return 2*Math.PI*radius;
        }

        public double Area() {
              return Math.PI*radius*radius;
        }
  }
```

Creating a `Circle` object with a negative radius or trying to set the radius of a `Circle` to a negative value will cause a `NegativeRadiusException` to be thrown. Listing 9.6 shows a class that tests this claim.

Listing 9.6

```
using System;
public class TestCircle {
  public static void Main() {

    Circle c=null;
    bool userIsIdiot;

    do {
          userIsIdiot=false;
      Console.Write("Enter radius of a circle: ");

      try {

            c=new Circle(Double.Parse(Console.ReadLine()));

      } catch (FormatException fe) {
            Console.WriteLine(fe+"\n\r"+fe.StackTrace);
            userIsIdiot=true;
```

(continued)

```
        } catch (NegativeRadiusException nre) {
            Console.WriteLine(nre+"\n\r"+nre.StackTrace);
            userIsIdiot=true;

        } catch (Exception) {
            Console.WriteLine("Something went horribly wrong!");
        }

    } while (userIsIdiot);

    Console.WriteLine("Circumference: "+c.Perimeter());
    Console.WriteLine("Area: "+c.Area());

  }
}
```

If we run the program, we see that the program will allow us to enter only a positive radius:

```
Enter radius of a circle: -1
NegativeRadiusException: Radius must be nonnegative!
   at Circle..ctor(Double r)
   at TestCircle.Main()
   at Circle..ctor(Double r)
   at TestCircle.Main()
Enter radius of a circle: One
System.FormatException: Input string was not in a correct
format.
   at System.Number.ParseDouble(String s, NumberStyles style,
NumberFormatInfo info)
   at System.Double.Parse(String s, NumberStyles style,
IFormatProvider provider)
   at TestCircle.Main()
   at System.Number.ParseDouble(String s, NumberStyles style,
NumberFormatInfo info)
   at System.Double.Parse(String s, NumberStyles style,
IFormatProvider provider)
   at TestCircle.Main()
Enter radius of a circle: 1
Circumference: 6.28318530717959
Area: 3.14159265358979
```

This program also uses the `StackTrace` property from `Exception`. This property returns a `String` representation of the path the `Exception` took as it was thrown out from deep within the code. This allows us to identify the particular place where the error occurred, and helps us to determine exactly why it occurred.

```
//...
      } catch (FormatException fe) {
            Console.WriteLine(fe+"\n\r"+fe.StackTrace);
//...
```

☐ Order of `catch` Blocks

The order in which `catch` blocks appear is significant. When an exception is thrown, the first `catch` block that handles the exception will be used. Because `Exception` is the base class for `NegativeRadiusException`, a `NegativeRadiusException` object is an `Exception` object by inheritance.

In the previous program, if `Exception` precedes `NegativeRadiusException` in the `catch` blocks, the `Exception` block will handle the `NegativeRadiusException`. If you attempt to place it before `FormatException`, it will handle those as well. The purpose of defining our own subclasses of `Exception` is for handling specialized problems; thus, C# forces you to place subclasses before superclasses in `catch` blocks. To see this, note the compiler errors from compiling Listing 9.7.

Listing 9.7

```
using System;
public class TestCircle {
  public static void Main() {
    Circle c=null;
    bool userIsIdiot;
    do {
          userIsIdiot=false;
      Console.Write("Enter radius of a circle: ");
      try {
            c=new Circle(Double.Parse(Console.ReadLine()));
      } catch (Exception) {
            Console.WriteLine("Something went horribly wrong!");
      } catch (FormatException fe) {
            Console.WriteLine(fe+"\n\r"+fe.StackTrace);
            userIsIdiot=true;
      } catch (NegativeRadiusException nre) {
            Console.WriteLine(nre+"\n\r"+nre.StackTrace);
            userIsIdiot=true;
      }
```

(continued)

```
    } while (userIsIdiot);
    Console.WriteLine("Circumference: "+c.Perimeter());
    Console.WriteLine("Area: "+c.Area());
  }
}

C:\C#>csc /r:NegativeradiusException.dll /r:Circle.dll TestCircle.cs
Microsoft (R) Visual C# .NET Compiler version 7.00.9466
for Microsoft (R) .NET Framework version 1.0.3705
Copyright (C) Microsoft Corporation 2001. All rights reserved.

TestCircle.cs(13,11): error CS0160: A previous catch clause already
catches all exceptions of this or a super type ('system.Exception')
TestCircle.cs(16,11): error CS0160: A previous catch clause already
catches all exceptions of this or a super type ('system.Exception')
```

▪ CASTING OBJECTS

It is possible in C# to use the `cast()` operator to cast objects from one type to another, subject to these rules:

- An object can only be cast upward (towards its ancestors), and this cast is automatic.
- An object can be cast downward, as long as the object is actually of the type cast to, or a subclass of that type. This kind of cast must be done manually.

Listing 9.8 shows some casts, some of which are legal and some not. The illegal ones are commented out, and the program will not compile if the comments are removed. (If you selectively remove certain comments, the program will compile, but the invalid casts will still be caught at runtime.)

Listing 9.8

```
using System;
class TestObjectCasting {
    static void Main() {

      //OK - a String is an Object
      Object obj="Hi!";

      //Wrong - Object has no ToUpper() method
      //Even though its really a String
```

(continued)

```
//      Console.WriteLine(obj.ToUpper());

     //OK if you manually cast it to a String
     Console.WriteLine(((String)obj).ToUpper());

     //Nope - Cannot assign an Object to a String
     //Even though it really IS a String!
//      String r=obj;

     //This is OK if you manually cast it back down
     String s=(String) obj;

     Object o2 = new Object();

     //No way
//      String t = o2;

     //Even a cast won't help this one
     //o2 is NOT a String, and you can't make it be one!
//      String u=(String) o2;

     //OK
     displayHash(obj);

     //OK-automatically casted up
     displayHash(s);

     displayString(s);

     //No-Method expects a String
//      displayString(obj);

     //That's better
     displayString((String)obj);

     //Don't-can't cast o2 to a String because it isn't one
//      displayString((String)o2);

   }

   static void displayHash(Object o) {
     Console.WriteLine(o.GetHashCode());
   }
```

(continued)

```
    static void displayString(String s) {
      Console.WriteLine(s);
    }

}

Hi!
193458245
193458245
Hi!
Hi!
```

■ ABSTRACT METHODS AND CLASSES

Sometimes we can group the common functionality of certain classes into a superclass, but that superclass is too general to clearly specify all of the characteristics of its subclasses. For example, suppose you create a `Shape2D` class, knowing that every `Shape2D` object has an area and a perimeter. However, you cannot specify how the perimeter and area will be calculated until you create more concrete subclasses, like `Parallelogram` or `Circle`.

In C#, we call a member that leaves its behavior unspecified an "abstract member." An abstract member is declared using the keyword `abstract`. Any class that contains at least one abstract member is called an "abstract class," and is also declared with the keyword `abstract`.

As an example of this, we will create another subtree in the `Object` hierarchy, as shown in Figure 9.9.

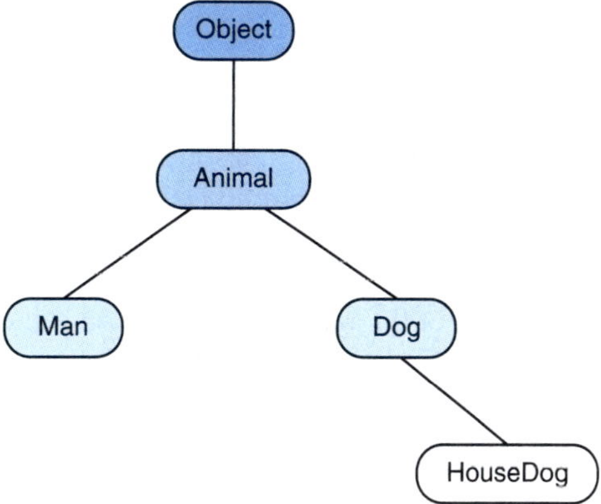

Figure 9.9

We will begin with the `Animal` class in Listing 9.9.

Listing 9.9

```
using System;
public abstract class Animal {

      //Fields
      protected bool fourLegged;
      protected int cuteness;
      protected int combativeness;

      //This property is virtual-can be overridden
      //Measures an animal's "adorability"
      public virtual int Adorability {
            get {
                  int difference=cuteness-combativeness;
                  if (fourLegged) return difference;
                  return 10*difference;
            }
      }

      //Methods
      //This method can be overridden
      public virtual String Misc() {
            return "Extinct, or soon to be";
      }

      //An abstract method
      //Sound an animal makes cannot be determined here
      public abstract String Sound();

}
```

The `Animal` class is abstract because it contains an "abstract method," `Sound()`. Note that an abstract method terminates with a semicolon:

```
public abstract String Sound();
```

The use of {} for an abstract method is incorrect, because there is a difference between an abstract method and a method that simply does nothing.

The method is abstract because we don't know what kind of sound an animal makes until we know what kind of animal we are talking about. However, there are other things we feel all animals have in common, and by which they should be grouped together. Thus, it is natural to place such items in an abstract class. This makes it a simple matter to branch off from Animal in many directions, with each subtree sharing these common characteristics.

It is important to note that you cannot instantiate objects of an abstract class type; for example, you cannot say

```
Animal me = new Animal();
```

for an obvious reason; how could you possibly make the call

```
String s = me.Sound();
```

when Sound() is not defined for an Animal?

A class that derives from an abstract class must override all of its abstract methods, or the subclass must also be abstract. This is, of course, because of inheritance. A subclass of an abstract class has abstract methods by inheritance.

Listing 9.10 is a class called Man, which implements the Sound() method it inherits from Animal.

Listing 9.10

```
using System;
public class Man:Animal {

      public Man() {
            fourLegged=false;
            cuteness=2;
            combativeness=10;
      }

      public override String Sound() {
            return "BLAH BLAH BLAH BLAH";
      }
}
```

The Man() constructor initializes the fields it inherits from Animal to appropriate values. Listing 9.11 is another class called Dog, which implements Sound in a different way.

Listing 9.11

```
using System;
public class Dog:Animal {

      public Dog() {
            fourLegged=true;
            cuteness=10;
```

(continued)

```
                combativeness=5;
        }

        public override String Misc() {
                return "Will inherit the Earth";
        }

        public override String Sound() {
                return "WOOF!";
        }
}
```

▪ ACCESSING BASE CLASS MEMBERS

Sometimes we may want to access members of a particular class's superclass. In the case of constructors this is always done, and always in the same way. However, we can access any members in a superclass by using the keyword `base`.

To see this in action, consider the `HouseDog` class in Listing 9.12, which is derived from `Dog`. It also implements the abstract method `Sound()`, but it is not required to do so, because the method is already implemented in the `Dog` superclass.

Listing 9.12

```
using System;
public class HouseDog:Dog {

        bool protectingHouse;

        public HouseDog(bool wellTrained) {
                protectingHouse=wellTrained;
        }

        public override int Adorability {
                get {return protectingHouse
                        ?-1000000000
                        :base.Adorability+5;}
        }

        public override String Misc() {
                if (!protectingHouse) return "Untrained";
                return "Well trained";
```

(continued)

```
        }

        public override String Sound() {
              return protectingHouse?"GRRR!":base.Sound();
        }
  }
```

Here, we see `HouseDog` members accessing `Dog` members in two places (besides the implicit base call in the constructor); namely, here:

```
public override int Adorability {
      get {return protectingHouse
            ?-1000000000
            :base.Adorability+5;}
}
```

where a `HouseDog` returns an `Adorability` value by getting the corresponding `Adorability` value from `Dog`, and adding 5 to it. The other occurrence is here:

```
public override String Sound() {
      return protectingHouse?"GRRR!":base.Sound();
}
```

Based on a condition, either "`GRRR!`" or "`WOOF!`" will be returned.

Using these classes, we can create different types of animal objects and see information about them. Listing 9.13 is a test program.

Listing 9.13

```
using System;
class TestAnimals {
    static void Main() {
      //Create some Animals
      Man m = new Man();
      Dog d = new Dog();
      HouseDog pup = new HouseDog(false);
      HouseDog rex = new HouseDog(true);

      //What are these animals like?
      Console.WriteLine("List of common animal characteristics:");
      Console.WriteLine("Category: "+m.GetType()
            +". Adorability: "+m.Adorability+". Sound: "
            +m.Sound()+". Other: "+m.Misc()+".");
```

(continued)

```
        Console.WriteLine("Category: "+d.GetType()
              +". Adorability: "+d.Adorability+". Sound: "
              +d.Sound()+". Other: "+d.Misc()+".");
        Console.WriteLine("Category: "+pup.GetType()
              +". Adorability: "+pup.Adorability+". Sound: "
              +pup.Sound()+". Other: "+pup.Misc()+".");
        Console.WriteLine("Category: "+rex.GetType()
              +". Adorability: "+rex.Adorability+". Sound: "
              +rex.Sound()+". Other: "+rex.Misc()+".");
    }
}
```

Here is sample output:

```
List of common animal characteristics:
Category: Man. Adorability: -80. Sound: BLAH BLAH BLAH BLAH.
Other: Extinct, or soon to be.
Category: Dog. Adorability: 5. Sound: WOOF!. Other: Will
inherit the Earth.
Category: HouseDog. Adorability: 10. Sound: WOOF!. Other:
Untrained.
Category: HouseDog. Adorability: -1000000000. Sound: GRRR!.
Other: Well trained.
```

■ POLYMORPHISM

Consider the program in Listing 9.14, where the user is prompted to enter his or her choice of `Animal`. Based on the choice, an `Animal` of a certain type is created. We then call a method to display that animal's characteristics.

Listing 9.14

```
using System;
class TestAnimalPolymorphism {
    static void Main() {
      //Create an Animal
      Console.WriteLine("Enter a character: ");
      Console.WriteLine("M = Create a Man");
      Console.WriteLine("D = Create a Dog");
      Console.WriteLine("H = Create a House Dog");
      Console.Write("==>");
```

(continued)

```
        char choice= (char)Console.Read();

        Animal animal=null;
        bool screwedUp=false;

        switch(choice) {
              case 'M':animal=new Man();
                    break;
              case 'D':animal=new Dog();
                    break;
              case 'H':animal=new HouseDog(true);
                    break;
              default: screwedUp=true;
                    break;
        }

        if (!screwedUp) displayAnimalCharacteristics(animal);
        else Console.WriteLine("You screwed up.");

      }

      static void displayAnimalCharacteristics(Animal a) {
        Console.WriteLine("Category: "+a.GetType());
        Console.WriteLine("Adorability: "+a.Adorability);
        Console.WriteLine("Sound: "+a.Sound());
        Console.WriteLine("Other: "+a.Misc());
      }
  }
```

Note that we cannot instantiate an `Animal` object. There is certainly nothing wrong with assigning a `Man` object, for instance, to an `Animal` reference:

```
Animal animal;
...
animal = new Man();
```

What may strike you as odd about the program is this: Because the user does not determine the Animal `type` until runtime, how could the compiler possibly know what kind of `Animal` the variable `animal` refers to? How could it know, for example, whether `animal.Adorability` refers to the `Adorability` property of `Man`, `Dog`, or `HouseDog`?

The answer is that the compiler doesn't know. The runtime environment has the responsibility of checking the class to which an object belongs at execution time, and selecting the correct method to call based on that determination. This ability is known as polymorphism; without it, object-oriented programs could not function properly, or at least would be far more difficult to write.

To help you see why this is so, reexamine the displayAnimalCharacteristics() method in the previous program:

```
static void displayAnimalCharacteristics(Animal a) {
  Console.WriteLine("Category: "+a.GetType());
  Console.WriteLine("Adorability: "+a.Adorability);
  Console.WriteLine("Sound: "+a.Sound());
  Console.WriteLine("Other: "+a.Misc());
}
```

This method accepts an Animal object and displays its characteristics. Without the aid of polymorphism, you would have to write three different methods, one to accept each parameter of type Man, Dog, and HouseDog!

Also, do you now see the necessity of abstract methods and classes? In the case of Animal, the Sound() method is not implemented, but the call

```
Animal a = new Dog();
String sound = a.Sound();
```

gets past the compiler. Grouping all these properties together in a type called Animal is not simply a natural way to program (though that is reason enough); with the aid of C#'s polymorphic ability, it makes your programs far more powerful, flexible, and easy to write.

▪ HIDING MEMBERS

The override keyword causes a member in a subclass to override the corresponding member in the base class. This effectively causes a replacement in the derived class. We are able to hide a member of a base class rather than overriding it by using the new keyword. This is useful for polymorphism and object casting.

Consider the following class, which contains only a virtual method:

```
using System;
public class ParentWMethod {
      public virtual void Method() {
            Console.WriteLine("I'm still here!");
      }
}
```

Now, derive a class from it and override the method:

```
using System;
public class ChildWOverride:ParentWMethod {
      public override void Method() {
            Console.WriteLine("I'm taking over!");
      }
}
```

Derive a different class that does not override the method, but simply hides it:

```
using System;
public class ChildWNew:ParentWMethod {
      public new void Method() {
            Console.WriteLine("I'm not taking over!");
      }
}
```

ChildWNew objects can access the parent method via casting and polymorphism, because ChildWNew objects have both methods, whereas ChildWOverride cannot, because the parent method simply doesn't exist in ChildWOverride; it has been replaced. To see this, note the following test program in Listing 9.15.

Listing 9.15

```
using System;
class TestOverrideNew {
    static void Main() {
      ChildWOverride cwo=new ChildWOverride();
      ChildWNew cwn=new ChildWNew();
      cwo.Method();
      ((ParentWMethod)cwo).Method();
      cwn.Method();
      ((ParentWMethod)cwn).Method();
    }
}

I'm taking over!
I'm taking over!
I'm not taking over!
I'm still here!
```

As you can see, hiding a member can provide more flexibility than overriding one. There is some additional overhead in maintaining both members in the derived class object, and if the superclass member is not appropriate for the subclass, you should certainly override it. Consider carefully which you would like (or need) to do.

■ INTERFACES

To carry abstract classes to the extreme, consider the concept of an interface, which can contain only abstract methods and nothing else. A class can be derived from ("implement") an interface, in the same way in which it is derived from a class. Here is an example of an interface; it is a predefined interface in the `System` namespace called `IComparable`:

```
public interface IComparable {
      public int CompareTo(Object other);
}
```

This interface contains only one method: `CompareTo()`. Although it isn't clear from any documentation you will find, an implementation of `CompareTo(Object other)` should return

a negative `int` if `this` < `other`
a positive `int` if `this` > `other`
0 if `this` = `other`

Note that neither an interface nor any of its methods need be declared abstract; this is assumed. Also, the methods (as are any abstract methods) are implicitly virtual. All interfaces begin by convention with the capital letter "I". It is wise for you to adopt this convention.

There doesn't seem to be much to this interface, or to any interface. This is deceptive; because a class C can implement an interface I, any object of type C can be cast to type I. As you will see, this gives polymorphism even more of the incredible leverage it has.

A big motivation for the existence of interfaces is the fact that C# does not allow multiple inheritance. That is, a class cannot inherit properties from more than one class. The reason is simple: If a class inherits multiple methods with the same signature from multiple parents or grandparents, which method does it use? Although this issue can be resolved by setting up some rather complicated rules, it simply isn't worth the trouble. This is especially true if you consider that determining an object's class must be deferred until runtime. If the rules specifying which method to choose are complicated, the program will be slowed down, perhaps considerably.

C# allows you to derive a class from another class, but you may implement as many interfaces as desired. Note that even if multiple interfaces share a method with the same signature, there is no trouble in determining which method to choose, because all the methods in an interface are abstract! That is to say, none of them can be used. By simply implementing the troublesome method(s), you determine the method to use.

A class should implement every method of every interface it implements, unless the class is intended to be abstract.

☐ Class: `Rational`

We will develop a class called `Rational` that implements the `IComparable` interface. Thus, it must provide the code for a `CompareTo()` method. This will allow `Rational` objects to be passed into any methods requiring `IComparable` objects.

Rational numbers are of the form m/n, where m and n are both integers and n is nonzero. Rational numbers have an order among them; that is, for any two rational numbers a/b and c/d, exactly one of the following must be true:

$a/b < c/d$

$a/b > c/d$

$a/b = c/d$

Thus, it is natural for the `Rational` class to implement `IComparable`. But how do we compare `Rational` objects? For example, how do we know that 2/3 > 3/5? We determine this, of course, by giving both fractions a common denominator. The easiest way to do this is by multiplying the numerator and denominator of one fraction by the denominator of the other; for example,

$$2/3 = (2 \times 5)/(3 \times 5) = 10/15 > 9/15 = (3 \times 3)/(5 \times 3) = 3/5$$

(Actually, once you determine what to multiply by, you can simply do it to the numerators, and compare them as integers; disregard multiplying the denominators.)

It may be possible to multiply by a smaller number; we could first divide the multiplier by the greatest common divisor of the two denominators. For example, compare the fractions 13/24 and 5/9. The GCD of 24 and 9 is 3; thus, we do the following:

$$13/24 = (13 \times 9/3)/(24 \times 9/3) = 39/72 < (40/72) = (5 \times 24/3)/(9 \times 24/3)$$

By multiplying by the smallest possible number, we can reduce the probability of an overflow when we get around to writing the `Equals()` and `CompareTo()` methods.

By convention, we reduce rational numbers to lowest common terms by extracting the greatest common divisor from the numerator and denominator; for example, the rational number

$$24/54 = (4 \times 6)/(9 \times 6) = 4/9$$

We all learned how to find the GCD in school, but probably not the quick way, known as the Euclidean algorithm. It works like this: Let GCD(a,b) be a function that computes the GCD of positive integers a and b. It is true that

$$\gcd(a,b) = \gcd(b,r_1)$$

where r_1 is the remainder of a divided by b. If $b < a$, then $r_1 = (a \bmod b) < a$. We can continue this process until the remainder eventually becomes zero for some r_n. Because the GCD of any integer i and 0 is i, this means that the gcd(a,b) is r_{n-1}, the last nonzero remainder.

$\gcd(a,b)$

$= \gcd(b,r_1)$

$= \gcd(r_1,r_2) \leftarrow (r_2 = b \bmod r_1 < r_1)$

$= \gcd(r_2,r_3) \leftarrow (r_3 = r_1 \bmod r_2 < r_2)$

...

$=\gcd(r_{n-2},r_{n-1}) \leftarrow (r_{n-1} = r_{n-3} \bmod r_{n-2} < r_{n-2})$

$= \gcd(r_{n-1},r_n) \leftarrow (r_n = r_{n-2} \bmod r_{n-1} < r_{n-1})$

$= \gcd(r_{n-1},0) \leftarrow (r_n = 0 \text{ for some } n, \text{ since } r_1 > r_2 > r_3 \ldots)$

$= r_{n-1}$

Example:
Find the GCD of 21 and 96:

gcd(96, 21)
= gcd(21, 96 mod 21) = gcd(21, 12)
= gcd(12, 21 mod 12) = gcd(12, 9)
= gcd(9, 12 mod 9) = gcd(9, 3)
= gcd(3, 9 mod 3) = gcd(3, 0) = 3

The greatest common divisor of 96 and 21 is 3.

Note that it doesn't matter if we begin with the largest value on the left, because even if we don't, they simply switch places:

gcd(21, 96)
= gcd(96, 21 mod 96) = gcd(96, 21) ← (The remainder of 21 divided by 96 is 21)
= ... ← (From here on it's the same)
= 3

Also, if you allow negative remainders, it doesn't matter if either integer is negative. Just make sure to take the absolute value of the last nonnegative remainder to get the GCD. Prove this fact to yourself. For convenience, we also define gcd(0,0) = 0.

Now we can define a method to find the GCD of two integers (actually `longs`). It is clearly recursive, a natural choice considering the previous development. The method is private, and exists in the `Rational` class.

```
private static long gcd(long a,long b) {
      if (b==0) return a;
      return gcd(b,a%b);
}
```

This method can actually return the negative of the GCD, so care is taken to always get the absolute value of the result.

The least common multiple of two integers is easily computed given the GCD. It is simply

lcm(a,b) = ab/gcd(a,b)

Example:

lcm(96,21) = 96 × 21/gcd(96,21) = 2016/3 = 672

We could discuss arithmetic with rational numbers, but you should already be quite familiar with such computations from school. Review the `Add()`, `Subtract()`, `Multiply()`, and `Divide()` methods in the `Rational` class and determine how they work.

Listing 9.16 displays the `Rational` class in its entirety. We will not discuss what you already know about class members; rather, we will discuss how this class represents a rational number, and how it implements the `IComparable` interface.

Listing 9.16

```
using System;
public class Rational:IComparable {

	//Instance fields

	long numerator;
	long denominator;

	//Static fields

	public static readonly Rational ZERO;

	//Properties

	public long Numerator {
		get {return numerator;}
	}

	public long Denominator {
		get {return denominator;}
	}

	//Instance constructors

	//Creates a fraction of form n/1
	public Rational(long numerator) {
		this.numerator=numerator;
		denominator=1;
	}

	//Creates m/n in lowest terms
	public Rational(long numerator,long denominator) {
		//Cannot have 0 denominator
		if (denominator==0) throw new DivideByZeroException(
			"Rational may not have zero denominator");

		//If denominator negative, invert signs
		if (denominator<0) {
			denominator=-denominator;
			numerator=-numerator;
		}
```

(continued)

```
        //Find gcd of numerator and denominator
        long g=Math.Abs(gcd(numerator,denominator));

        //Divide it out
        this.numerator=numerator/g;
        this.denominator=denominator/g;
    }

    //Creates a Rational from a string
    //String may be an integer; i.e., no denominator
    public Rational(String s) {

        //Split on the / character
        char[] delim={'/'};
        String[] numDen=s.Split(delim);

        //Should be only 1 or 2 terms in this array
        if (numDen.Length<1||numDen.Length>2)
            throw new FormatException(
            "Rational number not in proper m/n format");

        //If there is a denominator, assign both
        if (numDen.Length!=1) {
            numerator=Int64.Parse(numDen[0]);
            denominator=Int64.Parse(numDen[1]);
        //No denominator specified; set to 1
        } else {
            numerator=Int64.Parse(numDen[0]);
            denominator=1;
        }

        //Put in lowest terms
        if (denominator==0) throw new DivideByZeroException(
            "Rational may not have zero denominator");
        if (denominator<0) {
            denominator=-denominator;
            numerator=-numerator;
        }
        long g=Math.Abs(gcd(numerator,denominator));
        numerator=numerator/g;
        denominator=denominator/g;
    }
```

(continued)

```
//Static constructor

//Initialize the static field
static Rational() {
      ZERO=new Rational(0,1);
}

//Methods

//Method to find gcd-Euclidean algorithm
private static long gcd(long a,long b) {
      if (b==0) return a;
      return gcd(b,a%b);
}

//Find the least common multiple
private static long lcm(long a,long b) {
      return a*b/gcd(a,b);
}

//Test for equality
public bool Equals(Rational r) {
      return numerator==r.numerator
            &&denominator==r.denominator;
}

//Compares two Objects-implements CompareTo in IComparable
public int CompareTo(Object o) {
      Rational r=(Rational)o;

      //Compute gcd of the 2 denominators
      long g=gcd(denominator,r.denominator);

      //Cross-multiply by smallest value
      long n1=numerator*r.denominator/g;
      long n2=denominator*r.numerator/g;

      //Compare the two values
      //this is smaller
      if (n1<n2) return -1;
      //o is smaller
      if (n1>n2) return 1;
```

(continued)

```
            //this and o are equal
            return 0;
      }

      //Methods to perform Rational arithmetic
      private Rational Add(Rational r) {
            //Give two fractions common denominator
            //by cross-multiplying denominators
            //Add the numerators
            //Reduce to lowest terms using constructor
            return new Rational(numerator*r.denominator
                  +r.numerator*denominator,
                  denominator*r.denominator);
      }

      private Rational Subtract(Rational r) {
            //Works like Add, but numerators subtracted
            return new Rational(numerator*r.denominator
                  -r.numerator*denominator,
                  denominator*r.denominator);
      }

      private Rational Multiply(Rational r) {
            //Multiply the numerators and denominators
            return new Rational(numerator*r.numerator,
                  denominator*r.denominator);
      }

      private Rational Divide(Rational r) {
            //Flip 2nd fraction and multiply
            return new Rational(numerator*r.denominator,
                  denominator*r.numerator);
      }

      //Parses a string into a Rational
      //Just calls Rational(String) constructor
      public static Rational Parse(String s) {
            return new Rational(s);
      }

      //Converts a Rational to a string
      //Overrides ToString() from Object
```

(continued)

```
public override String ToString() {
      if (denominator==1) return numerator.ToString();
      else return numerator+"/"+denominator;
}

//Operators

//Relational Operators
//Just call CompareTo or Equals

public static bool operator <(Rational r, Rational s) {
      return (r.CompareTo(s)<0);
}

public static bool operator >(Rational r, Rational s) {
      return (r.CompareTo(s)>0);
}

public static bool operator <=(Rational r, Rational s) {
      return !(r.CompareTo(s)>0);
}

public static bool operator >=(Rational r, Rational s) {
      return !(r.CompareTo(s)<0);
}

public static bool operator ==(Rational r, Rational s) {
      return r.Equals(s);
}

public static bool operator !=(Rational r, Rational s) {
      return !r.Equals(s);
}

//Arithmetic operators
//Just call Add,Subtract,Multiply,Divide

public static Rational operator +(Rational r, Rational s) {
      return r.Add(s);
}
```

(continued)

```
    public static Rational operator -(Rational r, Rational s) {
          return r.Subtract(s);
    }

    public static Rational operator *(Rational r, Rational s) {
          return r.Multiply(s);
    }

    public static Rational operator /(Rational r, Rational s) {
          return r.Divide(s);
    }

}
```

As you can see, the Rational class has two instance fields, numerator and denominator. It has two properties, Numerator and Denominator, to get their respective fields. Note that neither property allows you to set the field values once the Rational object has been created. Thus, you could say that Rational objects are immutable.

There are various instance constructors; of note is the one that parses a String as a Rational object. Note that it also will parse integers as Rational objects.

```
public Rational(String s) {

      //Split on the / character
      char[] delim={'/'};
      String[] numDen=s.Split(delim);

      //Should be only 1 or 2 terms in this array
      if (numDen.Length<1||numDen.Length>2)
            throw new FormatException(
            "Rational number not in proper m/n format");

      //If there is a denominator, assign both
      if (numDen.Length!=1) {
            numerator=Int64.Parse(numDen[0]);
            denominator=Int64.Parse(numDen[1]);
      //No denominator specified; set to 1
      } else {
            numerator=Int64.Parse(numDen[0]);
            denominator=1;
      }
```

```
        //Put in lowest terms
        if (denominator==0) throw new DivideByZeroException(
              "Rational may not have zero denominator");
        if (denominator<0) {
              denominator=-denominator;
              numerator=-numerator;
        }
        long g=Math.Abs(gcd(numerator,denominator));
        numerator=numerator/g;
        denominator=denominator/g;
}
```

There is a `ToString()` method of course, which outputs `Rational` objects in the form `m/n`, unless `n = 1`, in which case it simply outputs the numerator.

```
public override String ToString() {
      if (denominator==1) return numerator.ToString();
      else return numerator+"/"+denominator;
}
```

Of particular importance is the `CompareTo()` method, which `Rational` must implement from the `IComparable` interface. Suppose `r` and `s` are `Rational` objects. In order to work as it should, `CompareTo` should return:

a negative `int` if `r` < `s`
a positive `int` if `r` > `s`
0 if `r` = `s`

If you review the earlier discussion about comparing fractions, you should see easily how this works:

```
public int CompareTo(Object o) {
      Rational r=(Rational)o;

      //Compute gcd of the 2 denominators
      long g=gcd(denominator,r.denominator);
      //Denominators always positive

      //Cross-multiply by smallest value
      long n1=numerator*r.denominator/g;
      long n2=denominator*r.numerator/g;

      //Compare the two values
      //this is smaller
      if (n1<n2) return -1;
      //o is smaller
```

```
        if (n1>n2) return 1;
        //this and o are equal
        return 0;
}
```

Note that CompareTo() takes an object as a parameter. We must cast it into a Rational in order to access its numerator and denominator fields.

Based on the CompareTo() method, we can overload all of the following operators: ==, !=, <, >, <=, and >=. Each one simply calls either the Equals() method or the CompareTo() method, and returns a Boolean value based on the result.

```
public static bool operator <(Rational r, Rational s) {
        return (r.CompareTo(s)<0);
}

public static bool operator >(Rational r, Rational s) {
        return (r.CompareTo(s)>0);
}

public static bool operator <=(Rational r, Rational s) {
        return !(r.CompareTo(s)>0);
}

public static bool operator >=(Rational r, Rational s) {
        return !(r.CompareTo(s)<0);
}

public static bool operator ==(Rational r, Rational s) {
        return r.Equals(s);
}

public static bool operator !=(Rational r, Rational s) {
        return !r.Equals(s);
}
```

□ Program: TestRational

Listing 9.17 is a test program for the Rational class.

Listing 9.17

```
using System;
class TestRational {
    static void Main() {
```

(continued)

```
        Console.Write("Enter a rational number r: ");
        Rational r=new Rational(Console.ReadLine());
        Console.WriteLine("r: "+r);
        Console.Write("Enter a rational number s: ");
        Rational s=new Rational(Console.ReadLine());
        Console.WriteLine("s: "+s);
        Console.WriteLine("r==s: "+(r==s));
        Console.WriteLine("r<s: "+(r<s));
        Console.WriteLine("r>s: "+(r>s));
        Console.WriteLine("r+s: "+(r+s));
        Console.WriteLine("r-s: "+(r-s));
        Console.WriteLine("r*s: "+r*s);
        Console.WriteLine("r/s: "+r/s);
    }
}
```

Here are sample runs of `Testrational`:

```
Enter a rational number r: 18/-54
r: -1/3
Enter a rational number s: 121/33
s: 11/3
r==s: False
r<s: True
r>s: False
r+s: 10/3
r-s: -4
r*s: -11/9
r/s: -1/11

Enter a rational number r: -35/-14
r: 5/2
Enter a rational number s: 100/-25
s: -4
r==s: False
r<s: False
r>s: True
r+s: -3/2
r-s: 13/2
r*s: -10
r/s: -5/8

Enter a rational number r: 0
r: 0
```

```
Enter a rational number s: 10/4
s: 5/2
r==s: False
r<s: True
r>s: False
r+s: 5/2
r-s: -5/2
r*s: 0
r/s: 0

Enter a rational number r: 12/-15
r: -4/5
Enter a rational number s: 0/3
s: 0
r==s: False
r<s: True
r>s: False
r+s: -4/5
r-s: -4/5
r*s: 0

Unhandled Exception: System.DivideByZeroException: Rational may
not have zero denominator
   at Rational..ctor(Int64 numerator, Int64 denominator)
   at Rational.Divide(Rational r)
   at Rational.op_Division(Rational r, Rational s)
   at TestRational.Main()
```

You'll notice the test program doesn't attempt to catch any of the exceptions that can be thrown. Modify the program to catch these exceptions.

Note that the `Rational` class contains only two fields; likewise for the `Complex` class. Given this, it could be well argued that both of these classes would be better written as structures. It may be interesting for you to do this.

☐ Program: SelectionSorter

One activity requiring large amounts of comparisons is sorting. In Chapter 7, we saw a bubble sort program to sort a sequence of characters. That sorting program would have been more useful if it simply were able to work with more than one type. Now that we know about interfaces (in particular, the `IComparable` interface) and polymorphism, we can make this happen.

Rather than redo the bubble sort, let's consider a somewhat different method of sorting known as the selection sort.

The selection sort passes through a list of n elements indexed 0 through $n - 1$, and identifies the largest element. (Largest, of course, depends entirely on what kind of items

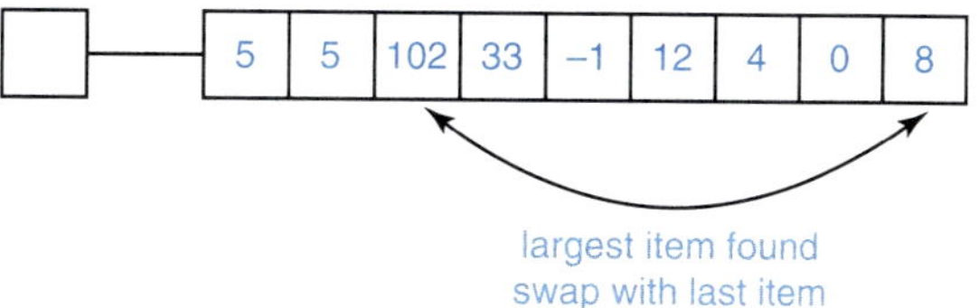

Figure 9.10

you are comparing.) It then swaps this item with the item at the end of the list (see Figure 9.10).

Now that you know the largest item is at the end of the list, the next pass needs to check only up to position $n - 2$. This is repeated until the end of the list reaches 0.

This is similar to the bubble sort, except only one swap per pass occurs, whereas many swaps can occur before the largest item reaches the end of the list in a bubble sort.

The `SelectionSorter` class in Listing 9.18 contains a static `SelectionSort` method, which accepts an array of `IComparable` as a parameter. Therefore, *any* data type that implements the `IComparable` interface can be sorted using this method. This is infinitely preferable to writing a new sorting routine every time you create a new type!

To demonstrate this polymorphic wonder, the `Main()` method in Listing 9.18 creates an array of `Strings`, and an array of random `Rationals`. Both of these classes implement `IComparable`. The array items are displayed, sorted, and then displayed again.

Listing 9.18

```
using System;
public class SelectionSorter {
   public static void SelectionSort(IComparable[] array) {
      //Top of array comes down on each pass
      int top=array.Length-1;
      //Var to record pos of largest element
      int indexOfLargest;
      do {
      //Assume largest item at bottom of array
         indexOfLargest=0;
         for (int i=1;i<=top;i++)
            //if you find a larger item, record its position
            //Comparisons done using CompareTo,
            //and this depends on type passed in
            if (array[indexOfLargest].CompareTo(array[i])<0)
               indexOfLargest=i;
      //After loop over, swap largest item with item at "top"
         IComparable temp=array[top];
```

(continued)

```
            array[top]=array[indexOfLargest];
            array[indexOfLargest]=temp;
         //Top of the list is one less on next pass
            top--;
         } while (top>0);
      }

      static void Main()  {

         //Make array of strings, and random Rationals
         String[] sa={"Since","by","man","came","death"};
         Rational[] ra=new Rational[10];
         Random rand=new Random();
         for (int i=0;i<ra.Length;i++)
               ra[i]=new Rational(rand.Next(),rand.Next());

         //Display contents of each array
         Console.WriteLine("Unsorted strings:");
         foreach (String s in sa) Console.WriteLine(s);
         Console.WriteLine("Unsorted rationals:");
         foreach (Rational r in ra) Console.WriteLine(r);

         //Sort the two arrays
         //Both strings and Rationals can be cast to IComparable
         SelectionSort((IComparable[])sa);
         SelectionSort((IComparable[])ra);

         //Display contents of each sorted array
         Console.WriteLine("Sorted strings:");
         foreach (String s in sa) Console.WriteLine(s);
         Console.WriteLine("Sorted rationals:");
         foreach (Rational r in ra) Console.WriteLine(r);
      }

   }
```

Here is the program running:

```
Unsorted strings:
Since
by
man
came
death
```

```
Unsorted rationals:
148869971/206311977
605513826/718548131
519419737/1327144897
710167103/748176291
847885329/956935586
195029711/1140446573
47094575/91080542
2138367883/210839141
135961431/155052322
17954623/40165799
Sorted strings:
by
came
death
man
Since
Sorted rationals:
195029711/1140446573
519419737/1327144897
17954623/40165799
47094575/91080542
148869971/206311977
605513826/718548131
135961431/155052322
847885329/956935586
710167103/748176291
2138367883/210839141
```

■ SEALED CLASSES

The sealed modifier in a class declaration disallows any other classes to derive from it, making it sort of a "constant" class. For example:

```
public sealed class NoKids {
...
}

public class Surprisc:NoKids {//Cannot derive from sealed
NoKids class
...
}
```

Structures, by contrast, are inherently sealed; you cannot derive from a structure.

■ DELEGATION

When object-oriented programming was in its infancy, there were two fundamental OOP paradigms. One approach was to use inheritance and polymorphism to determine how objects were created and how members were invoked. The other approach was known as delegation. Modern OO languages like C# use both mechanisms to accomplish their tasks.

Delegation is a process by which one object sends information to another. In C#, this is done by way of a delegate. A delegate is a special type that references a method rather than an object. Here is a delegate declaration:

```
using System;
//This delegate Extractor is made to point to a method
//This method must accept a String, and return a String
public delegate String Extractor(String s);
```

`Extractor` is a new delegate class type. However, objects of type `Extractor` will not point to data, but to a function. Said function must accept and return a string, as demanded by the `Extractor` declaration. Here is how we create an `Extractor` object, and point it at a method:

```
//Extractor e1 points to GetDigits method
Extractor e1=new Extractor(GetDigits);
```

Extractor `e1` references a method called `GetDigits`, which must accept and return a String (see Figure 9.11).

Elsewhere in the class we provide the code for the `GetDigits()` method:

```
  //This method extracts digits from a String and returns them
static String GetDigits(String s) {
  StringBuilder result=new StringBuilder("");
  for (int index=0;index<s.Length;index++)
        if (Char.IsDigit(s[index]))
              result.Append(s[index].ToString());
  return result.ToString();
}
```

Figure 9.11

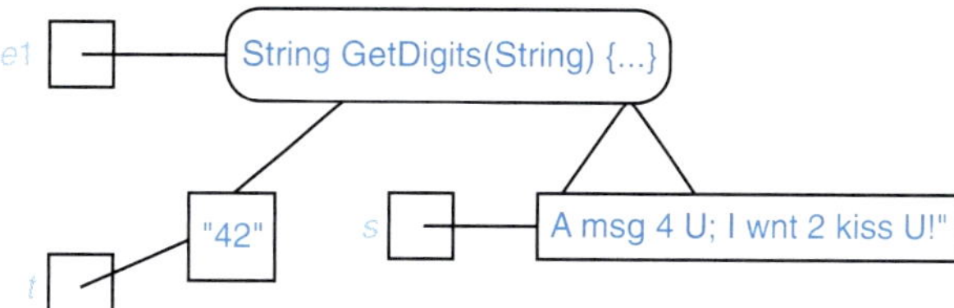

Figure 9.12

Calling this method can be done through the delegate; that is, making the call

```
String s = "A msg 4 U; I wnt 2 kiss U!";
String t = e1.(s);
```

will call the `GetDigits()` method through the `Extractor` object `e1` and assign the string `"42"` to `t`. The effect is shown in Figure 9.12.

Listing 9.19 is a test program that creates a couple of `Extractor` objects; one points to a `GetDigits()` method, as described here, while another references a `GetUpperCaseLetters()` method.

Listing 9.19

```
using System;
using System;
using System.Text;
public class TestExtractorDelegate {
    static void Main() {
      Console.WriteLine("Enter a string: ");
      String s=Console.ReadLine();

      //Create two Extractor objects; Extractor objects are
      //delegates, and reference methods
      //Extractor e1 points to GetDigits method
      Extractor e1=new Extractor(GetDigits);
      //Extractor e2 points to GetUpperCaseLetters method
      Extractor e2=new Extractor(GetUpperCaseLetters);

      //Call the methods THRU the delegate objects
      Console.WriteLine("Digits extracted from string: "
            +e1(s));
      Console.WriteLine("Upper case letters from string: "
            +e2(s));
    }
```

(continued)

```
    //This method extracts digits from a String and returns them
  static String GetDigits(String s) {
    StringBuilder result=new StringBuilder("");
    for (int index=0;index<s.Length;index++)
          if (Char.IsDigit(s[index]))
                result.Append(s[index].ToString());
    return result.ToString();
  }

    //This is a comment; you can edit me
    //Extracts uppercase letters from a String and returns them
  static String GetUpperCaseLetters(String s) {
    StringBuilder result=new StringBuilder("");
    for (int index=0;index<s.Length;index++)
          if (Char.IsUpper(s[index]))
                result.Append(s[index].ToString());
    return result.ToString();
  }

}
```

Here is the program running:

```
Enter a string:
This is THX-1138 wishing you a MERRY XMAS this December 25!
Digits extracted from string: 113825
Uppercase letters from string: TTHXMERRYXMASD
```

☐ The `StringBuilder` Class

You will notice the use of the `StringBuilder` class in the previous program. Strings are immutable; that is, their values cannot be changed once they are created. Although this helps to prevent certain mistakes, it also means strings are very inefficient for certain operations, like concatenation.

When you concatenate one string to another, the result is an entirely new `String` object. If this occurs repetitively and frequently, as is the case with certain tasks, it can mean a lot of derelict strings hanging around for the garbage collector. A `StringBuilder` object, on the other hand, is a memory-saving alternative, because its value can be modified. Using the `Append()` method on a `StringBuilder` object allows it to grow without creating a new object.

As an example of this, consider the program in Listing 9.20.

Listing 9.20

```
using System;
using System.Text;
class TestStringBuilder {
    static void Main() {

      //Create a string
      String wasteful="";
      //Create a StringBuilder object
      StringBuilder notWasteful=new StringBuilder("");

      //Create arrays of object references
      Object[] objects=new Object[10];
      Object[] objects2=new Object[10];

      for (int i=0;i<objects.Length;i++) {
            //Point an array element at old string
            objects[i]=wasteful;
            //Create a new string by concatenating to old
            wasteful+="Blah";
            //Point a reference to "old" StringBuilder object
            objects2[i]=notWasteful;
            //Append a string to the StringBuilder
            notWasteful.Append("Blah");
      }
      //These are all unique strings
      Console.WriteLine("Multiple strings follow:");
      foreach (Object o in objects) Console.WriteLine(o);

      //All these objects are referencing the same StringBuilder
      Console.WriteLine("Single StringBuilder referenced many times:");
      foreach (Object o in objects2) Console.WriteLine(o);
    }
}
```

The program starts with an empty string and an empty `StringBulder`; it concatenates the string `"Blah"` to the string 10 times in a loop, and makes a reference to each one. It also appends `"Blah"` to the `StringBuilder` 10 times, and points a reference to the `StringBuilder` object within each loop. The difference between the two is that there are multiple strings created, but only one `StringBuilder` exists throughout. You can see this in the output:

```
Multiple strings follow:

Blah
BlahBlah
BlahBlahBlah
BlahBlahBlahBlah
BlahBlahBlahBlahBlah
BlahBlahBlahBlahBlahBlah
BlahBlahBlahBlahBlahBlahBlah
BlahBlahBlahBlahBlahBlahBlahBlah
BlahBlahBlahBlahBlahBlahBlahBlahBlah
Single StringBuilder referenced many times:
BlahBlahBlahBlahBlahBlahBlahBlahBlahBlah
BlahBlahBlahBlahBlahBlahBlahBlahBlahBlah
BlahBlahBlahBlahBlahBlahBlahBlahBlahBlah
BlahBlahBlahBlahBlahBlahBlahBlahBlahBlah
BlahBlahBlahBlahBlahBlahBlahBlahBlahBlah
BlahBlahBlahBlahBlahBlahBlahBlahBlahBlah
BlahBlahBlahBlahBlahBlahBlahBlahBlahBlah
BlahBlahBlahBlahBlahBlahBlahBlahBlahBlah
BlahBlahBlahBlahBlahBlahBlahBlahBlahBlah
BlahBlahBlahBlahBlahBlahBlahBlahBlahBlah
```

`StringBuilders` are obviously quite useful for tasks involving frequent modification of strings.

■ MULTICAST DELEGATES

The real power of delegation isn't noticeable until you see a multicast delegate, which in C# is a delegate declared `void`. Such a delegate can be made to point at multiple methods, with each one being invoked when called via the delegate. Thus, a multicast delegate can spawn numerous activities.

Listing 9.21 is an example of a multicast delegate, called `TrainSound`.

Listing 9.21

```
//This delegate accepts an int, returns nothing
//This multicast delegate can invoke multiple methods when called
public delegate void TrainSound(int repeat);
```

TrainSound delegates will point to methods that accept an int as an incoming parameter, and return nothing. Now, create a TrainSound object, and point it at a method:

```
TrainSound ts=new TrainSound(BuildSteam);
```

Here is the BuildSteam() method, which is void, and accepts an int:

```
static void BuildSteam(int repeat) {
      for (int i=0;i<repeat;i++)
            Console.Write("Chug chug chug chug... ");
}
```

But now, add another TrainSound object to the reference.

```
ts+=new TrainSound(BlowWhistle);
```

What in the world does "+=" mean when adding to a reference? The + operator is overloaded to allow such a reference to point at more than one method. A multicast delegate reference basically maintains a "list" of all the methods it points to. This list is called its invocation list. Delegates can also be removed from an invocation list by using the –= operator.

Here is the BlowWhistle() method:

```
static void BlowWhistle(int repeat) {
      for (int i=0;i<repeat;i++)
            Console.Write("Choo Choo! ");
}
```

Thus, by calling the delegate, in effect one calls all of the methods it points to

```
ts(10);//Display Chug chug chug chug... & Choo choo! ten times
each
```

Listing 9.22 is a test program for the TrainSound delegate. Just for chuckles, I threw in a couple more methods to the multicast delegate.

Listing 9.22

```
using System;
public class TestTrainSoundDelegate {
      static void Main(String[] args) {

            //Create a TrainSound delegate reference
            TrainSound ts=null;
```

(continued)

```
        //Add new delegate objects
        //+ is overloaded for delegates
        //basically produces a list of method references
        //All these method must be void, & accept an int
        ts+=new TrainSound(BuildSteam);
        ts+=new TrainSound(BlowWhistle);
        ts+=new TrainSound(HitBrakes);
        ts+=new TrainSound(Derail);

        //Call the TrainSound delegate,
        //and watch the sparks fly!
        //int comes in thru command line
        if (args.Length==1) ts(Int32.Parse(args[0]));
    }
    static void BuildSteam(int repeat) {
        for (int i=0;i<repeat;i++)
            Console.Write("Chug chug chug chug... ");
    }
    static void BlowWhistle(int repeat) {
        for (int i=0;i<repeat;i++)
            Console.Write("Choo Choo! ");
    }
    static void HitBrakes(int repeat) {
        for (int i=0;i<repeat;i++)
            Console.Write("SCRREEEEEEECH!!!!! ");
    }
    static void Derail(int repeat) {
        for (int i=0;i<repeat;i++)
            Console.Write("BOOM!!!!!!!!!! ");
    }
}
```

Here are the program results for a couple of test runs:

```
C:\C#>TestTrainSoundDelegate 3
Chug chug chug chug... Chug chug chug chug... Chug chug chug chug... Choo
Choo! Choo Choo! Choo Choo! SCRREEEEEEECH!!!!! SCRREEEEEEECH!!!!!
SCRREEEEEEECH!!!!! BOOM!!!!!!!!!! BOOM!!!!!!!!!! BOOM!!!!!!!!!!
C:\C#>TestTrainSoundDelegate 10
Chug chug chug chug... Chug chug chug chug... Chug chug chug chug... Chug chug
chug chug... Chug chug chug chug... Chug chug chug chug... Chug chug chug
```

```
chug... Chug chug chug chug... Chug chug chug chug... Chug chug chug chug...
Choo Choo! Choo Choo! Choo Choo! Choo Choo! Choo Choo! Choo Choo! Choo Choo!
Choo Choo! Choo Choo! Choo Choo! SCRREEEEEEECH!!!!! SCRREEEEEEECH!!!!!
SCRREEEEEEECH!!!!! SCRREEEEEEECH!!!!! SCRREEEEEEECH!!!!! SCRREEEEEEECH!!!!!
SCRREEEEEEECH!!!!! SCRREEEEEEECH!!!!! SCRREEEEEEECH!!!!! SCRREEEEEEECH!!!!!
BOOM!!!!!!!!!! BOOM!!!!!!!!!!
BOOM!!!!!!!!!! BOOM!!!!!!!!!! BOOM!!!!!!!!!! BOOM!!!!!!!!!! BOOM!!!!!!!!!!
BOOM!!!!!!!!!! BOOM!!!!!!!!!! BOOM!!!!!!!!!!
```

Note that the parameter comes in by way of a command line argument (`args[0]`).

▪ EVENTS

Later on, when we cover graphical user interfaces (GUIs) in Chapter 10, we will discuss event processing. GUIs are said to be event driven; that is, action is taken when various events occur, like the mouse moving, the mouse clicking on a button, the Enter key being pressed when a button has focus, and so on. However, the concept of events is independent of GUIs; events are handled using multicast delegates.

Typically, a delegate that is invoked to handle an event accepts two parameters:

- The object that generated the event
- The parameters describing the event, encapsulated together in an object of type `System.EventArgs`, or a class derived from the same

Thus, to define an event, our first task is to derive from `EventArgs`. Table 9.3 shows members of this class.

From viewing its public and protected members, there doesn't seem to be much to this class, but of course we know by now that a good portion of a class can be hidden from us.

Suppose we want to create a `PrimalityTester` class. This class accepts integers and fires an event when the integer is prime. We begin by making a subclass of `EventArgs` in Listing 9.23.

TABLE 9.3

Name	Description
Public Constructors	
`EventArgs` Constructor	Initializes a new instance of the `EventArgs` class.
Public Fields	
`Empty`	Represents an event with no event data.

Listing 9.23

```
using System;
public class PrimeEventArgs:EventArgs {

      //This field will be tested for primality
      public int theInteger;

      //Constructor sets the field
      //Default parameterless base constructor called first
      public PrimeEventArgs(int anInteger) {
            theInteger=anInteger;
      }

}
```

Event Handlers

Once we have defined our derived class of `EventArgs`, we produce a multicast delegate that signifies what methods to call should this event occur. By convention, the arguments are the source of the event and an object of type `EventArgs` or a subclass of the same (see Listing 9.24).

Listing 9.24

```
using System;
//The handler for a "Prime Event" is a multicast delegate

public delegate void PrimeEventHandler
      (Object source, PrimeEventArgs pea);

//The parameters are:
//1.      The source of the event
//2.      An object of type PrimeEventArgs (subclass of EventArgs)
//All event handlers have this format by convention
```

The methods that we point the delegate to are called the "event handlers" for the event.

We must then specify under what conditions the event occurs; that is, we define the event itself. In this case, we create a `PrimalityTester` class in Listing 9.25.

Listing 9.25

```
using System;
public class PrimalityTester {
      //The number being tested for primality
      int theNumber;

      //Declare an event for this class called Primality
      //It is of type PrimeEventHandler; that is, it is a delegate
      public event PrimeEventHandler Primality;

      //Integer property gets and sets the field
      //The set property sets the field and fires the event
      //if the number is prime
      public int Integer {

            get {
                  return theNumber;
            }

            set {
                  //Set the value
                  theNumber=value;
                  //Test if the number is prime
                  if (IsPrime(value))
                        //Ensure Primality has handlers to call
                        if (Primality!=null) {
                              PrimeEventArgs pea=
                              new PrimeEventArgs(value);
                              //Fire the event
                              //delegate is set in motion
                              Primality(this,pea);
                        }
            }
      }

      //private method to attempt factoring
      private static bool IsPrime(int val) {
            //All primes >= 2
            if (val<2) return false;
            //Assume number is prime
            bool isprime=true;
```

(continued)

```
            //Test all divisors under square root of number
            for (int divisor=2;divisor<=Math.Sqrt(val);divisor++)
                  //If one divides evenly, not prime
                  if (val%divisor==0) {
                        isprime=false;
                        break;
                  }
            //True if prime, false o.w.
            return isprime;
      }
}
```

The following line

```
public event PrimeEventHandler Primality;
```

creates an event named `Primality` of type `PrimeEventHandler`. The `event` keyword simply ensures that only the += and −= operations can be performed on the delegate (otherwise, you could treat it as freely as any object). `Primality` represents the delegate that will call the event handlers for this event.

The event occurs if the number being tested turns out to be prime; in our code, that occurs here:

```
if (IsPrime(value))
      if (Primality!=null) {
            PrimeEventArgs pea=
            new PrimeEventArgs(value);
            Primality(this,pea);
      }
```

The method `IsPrime()` is a private helper method that returns true or false based on whether its argument is prime. Before the delegate is started, however, we first check whether some event handlers are actually in the invocation list. This check should always be present before firing an event. Of course, we often cannot determine whether these handlers exist until runtime!

The `TestPrimalityTester` class in Listing 9.26 tests this event by providing a handler for it called `FoundaPrime()`. This method is added to the invocation list of the `Primality` event for a `PrimalityTester` object. The program generates a series of random integers, and sets the `Integer` property of the `PrimalityTester` object to each one. If the number is prime, the event will be fired, and subsequently handled by the `FoundaPrime()` method. In this case, it merely reports that the number is prime.

Listing 9.26

```
using System;
public class TestPrimalityTester {

      //Create a new PrimalityTester object
      static PrimalityTester pt=new PrimalityTester();

      //Prepare to generate random integers
      static Random r=new Random();

      static void Main(String[] args) {
            //Default number of random integers=100
            int numInts=100;
            //If there is incoming parameter from command line
            //this should be the number of integers to produce
            if (args.Length!=0) numInts=Int32.Parse(args[0]);

            //Add FoundaPrime() to the invocation list
            pt.Primality+=new PrimeEventHandler(FoundaPrime);

            Console.WriteLine("Generating "+numInts+" integers.");

            //Setting the integer property will fire the event
            //IF the number is prime
            for (int i=0;i<numInts;i++) pt.Integer=r.Next();
      }

      //The prime event happened
      static void FoundaPrime(Object source,PrimeEventArgs e) {
            Console.WriteLine
                ("Alert the media! "+pt.Integer+" is prime!");
      }

}
```

Note that only certain integers fire the event; namely, the prime ones.

```
C:\C#>TestPrimalityTester
Generating 100 integers.
Alert the media! 1069783703 is prime!
Alert the media! 761022337 is prime!
Alert the media! 118672889 is prime!
Alert the media! 691104647 is prime!
```

```
Alert the media! 1003115909 is prime!
Alert the media! 164016317 is prime!

C:\C#>TestPrimalityTester 300
Generating 300 integers.
Alert the media! 2089096769 is prime!
Alert the media! 1665805727 is prime!
Alert the media! 298037543 is prime!
Alert the media! 1305690553 is prime!
Alert the media! 1003161611 is prime!
Alert the media! 1716764957 is prime!
Alert the media! 1658532179 is prime!
Alert the media! 1377924683 is prime!
Alert the media! 1979124347 is prime!
Alert the media! 532948909 is prime!
Alert the media! 1519292381 is prime!
Alert the media! 906280033 is prime!
Alert the media! 1492113079 is prime!
Alert the media! 1250552207 is prime!
Alert the media! 1729740251 is prime!
Alert the media! 380645149 is prime!
Alert the media! 857063693 is prime!
Alert the media! 890931421 is prime!
Alert the media! 77644477 is prime!
Alert the media! 1454915107 is prime!
Alert the media! 202453687 is prime!
```

This program sets up only a single event handler for the "prime event." Because events are fired using a multicast delegate, you are free to make and call as many handlers as you wish. This program also creates and uses only one `PrimalityTester` object. You can create many, and each one can call its own custom-made set of event handlers.

chapter 10

Graphical User Interfaces (GUIs)

Designing an application with an interface in C# is easy, because all GUI components are represented as objects. Thus, throwing a window (or a `Form` object) on the screen and adding controls to it simply is a matter of becoming familiar with the GUI classes. Figure 10.1 is a diagram of some of the GUI classes.

The `Form` class represents a window, and most objects placed on a form are derived from the `Control` class; some, however, are derived from `Component`.

C# is really intended to be used with an advanced editor that allows you to design forms by dragging and dropping components on the screen (like Visual Studio). However, if you are willing to do all the coding by yourself, you can create a GUI without the help of a fancy development environment. You certainly learn more about GUI object properties and methods, and it's much cheaper, too!

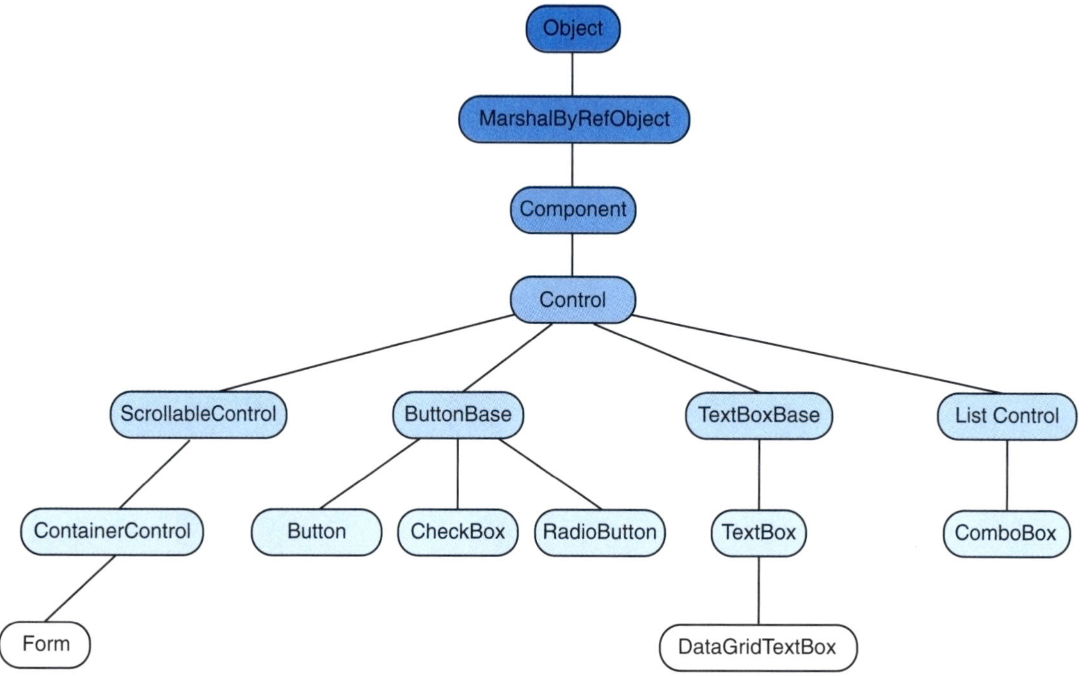

Figure 10.1

▪ CLASS: FIRSTFORM

To demonstrate how easy it is to create a form, note the program in Listing 10.1.

Listing 10.1

```
using System.Windows.Forms;
public class FirstForm:Form {
    //FirstForm() constructor created automatically
    static void Main() {
      //Windows app runs by calling Application.Run(Form)
      Application.Run(new FirstForm());
    }
}
```

The `Form` and `Application` classes are in `System.Windows.Forms`. We create custom forms by subclassing `Form`. Displaying this form means calling the static `Run()` method of `Application`, and passing in a `Form` object. Note that we did not provide the `Form()` constructor; C# provides this for you if you do not write it, and it sets all members to default values.

▪ COMPILING TO A WINDOWS EXECUTABLE

Because this is a windowed application, and it has a `Main()` method, you should compile it with the /t:winexe option. You can then run it from the command line, or by clicking on the executable file.

```
C:\C#>csc /t:winexe FirstForm.cs
Microsoft (R) Visual C# .NET Compiler version 7.00.9466
for Microsoft (R) .NET Framework version 1.0.3705
Copyright (C) Microsoft Corporation 2001. All rights reserved.

C:\C#>FirstForm

C:\C#>
```

Running this application produces the fully functional window shown in Figure 10.2.

The window has no title, takes a default size of 300 × 300 pixels, and has a default icon in the upper left corner. Changing these things, and a million other things, means learning the members of `Form` and its base classes in the hierarchy. The window is fully functional. It can be moved/resized; it has the standard working menu that comes up when you click the icon; and the minimize/maximize/restore/close buttons work.

▪ CONTROL AND FORM MEMBERS

We can change the appearance of any `Form` (or any other `Control`) by changing properties and calling methods from `Form` or `Control`.

□ Class: SecondForm

Listing 10.2 is a program that dresses up a form. It also adds a `Label`, which is a subclass of `Control`.

Figure 10.2

Listing 10.2

```
using System.Windows.Forms;
using System.Drawing;//Contains Icon, Color, Bitmap
public class SecondForm:Form {
    public SecondForm() {

      //Change some form properties
      this.Height=100;
      this.Width=200;
      this.Icon=new Icon("C#Icon.ico");

      this.BackColor=Color.DarkBlue;
      this.ForeColor=Color.Yellow;

      this.BackgroundImage=new Bitmap("Dufus.bmp");
      this.Text="Dressed Up Window";

      //Create a label
      Label warning=new Label();
      warning.Width=150;
      warning.Text="Do not try this at home!";

      //Add the label to the form
      this.Controls.Add(warning);
    }

    static void Main() {
      //Windows app runs by calling Application.Run(Form)
      Application.Run(new SecondForm());
    }
}
```

Figure 10.3 shows what the window looks like.

For readability, we use the keyword "`this`" to make it clear when we're referring to the `Form` object.

- The `Height` and `Width` properties are set to 100 × 200 pixels.
- The `Icon` property is set to a new `Icon` object. The `Icon(String)` constructor accepts a file name of an icon (.ico) file and creates an `Icon` object.
- The foreground and background colors are set. Color values can be found in `System.Drawing.Color`.
- The `BackgroundImage` property is set to `Bitmap`, which is a subclass of `Image`. The `Bitmap(String)` constructor accepts a bitmap file name, and creates a `Bitmap` object. The background image is tiled.
- The `Text` of this control (`Form`) is set to a string. In the case of `Forms`, the text is displayed in the window's title bar.

Figure 10.3

- A `Label` object (also a `Control`) is created, and its `Width` and `Text` properties are set. The default width of a `Label` is 100 pixels.
- The `Label` is added to the form by calling the `Add()` method of the Controls property of the form. In this way we can add any control to a form.

All of the following properties are actually inherited from the `Control` class: `Height`, `Width`, `BackgroundImage`, `ForeColor`, and `Text`. `Control` also has a `BackColor` property, but it is overridden in `Form`.

■ THE `Button` AND `TextBox` CLASSES

The next program in Listing 10.3, `AddScrollableTextForm` will do something besides look pretty. The form will have two text boxes and a button on it. One text box will be a single line box in which you may type characters. When the button is pressed, the text will be captured from the box, and appended to the text in a multiline text box (initially empty). The multiline box will not be editable by the user. To do this, we'll use the `Button` and `TextBox` classes, which are `Controls` by inheritance.

Listing 10.3

```
using System;//Contains Object & EventHandler
using System.Windows.Forms;
using System.Drawing;//Contains Rectangle
public class AddScrollableTextForm:Form {

    TextBox inBox=new TextBox();
    Button addButton=new Button();
    TextBox outBox=new TextBox();

    public AddScrollableTextForm() {

      //Set some form properties
      int h=this.Height=200;
      int w=this.Width-200;
      this.Text=this.GetType().ToString();
```

(continued)

```
        //w and y will help position controls
        w-=10;
        int y=10;

        //Set positions of the controls
        inBox.Bounds=new Rectangle(0,y,w,20);
        addButton.Bounds=new Rectangle(0,y+=20,w,20);
        outBox.Bounds=new Rectangle(0,y+=20,w,h-y-30);

        //Put text on button face
        addButton.Text="Add text";

        //Multiple lines can be entered in outBox
        outBox.Multiline=true;
        //User cannot type in outBox
        outBox.ReadOnly=true;
        //Give the TextBox a scrollbar
        outBox.ScrollBars=ScrollBars.Vertical;

        //Add the controls
        this.Controls.Add(inBox);
        this.Controls.Add(addButton);
        this.Controls.Add(outBox);

        //Set up method to call when addButton is clicked
        addButton.Click+=new EventHandler(this.addButton_Click);

      }

      private void addButton_Click(Object Sender,System.EventArgs e) {
        outBox.Text+=inBox.Text;
        inBox.Text="";
      }

      static void Main() {
        //Windows app runs by calling Application.Run(Form)
        Application.Run(new AddScrollableTextForm());
      }
  }
```

The controls here are defined outside the constructor, so they will be accessible outside of it. For each control, we set its position on the form by setting the `Bounds` property (from `Control`). The `Bounds` property takes a `Rectangle` (from `System.Drawing`) object, where the arguments in the

```
Rectangle(int x, int y, int width, int height);
```

constructor represent the *x*-coordinate and *y*-coordinate of the upper left corner of the control relative to the item on which it is placed, and the width and height of the control. When the controls are added to the form, the `Bounds` property will be used to place them in position.

A `TextBox` is made multiline by setting its `Multiline` property to `true` (the default is `false`). We disable the box, that is, make it so the user cannot interact with it, by setting the `Enabled` property (from `Control`) to `false`.

☐ The `Click` Event

When the button is pressed—in fact, when any activity occurs on a form—an event occurs. In C#, events, like everything else, are modeled as objects. To enable this particular event to do something, we add an `EventHandler` to the `Click` event (from `Control`) of the `Button`.

```
addButton.Click+=new EventHandler(this.addButton_Click);
```

Note that we are passing to `EventHandler` the name of a method. `EventHandler` is a delegate (from the `System` namespace). So, in the `AddScrollableTextForm` class, we must write such a method, which takes the sender of the event (an `Object`) as the first parameter, and the event arguments (`EventArgs` from `System`) as the second.

```
private void addButton_Click(Object Sender,System.EventArgs e)
{
  outBox.Text+=inBox.Text;
  inBox.Text="";
}
```

You will notice that all this is accomplished by using a multicast delegate, because the handler is void; this allows many event handlers to exist and be called for any event. This is how event processing is handled for GUIs. It is easily the most prevalent use of delegates in C#.

To get a look at this GUI, see Figure 10.4.

Note that the `TextBox` has a vertical scrollbar. We do this by setting its `ScrollBars` property:

```
outBox.ScrollBars=ScrollBars.Vertical;
```

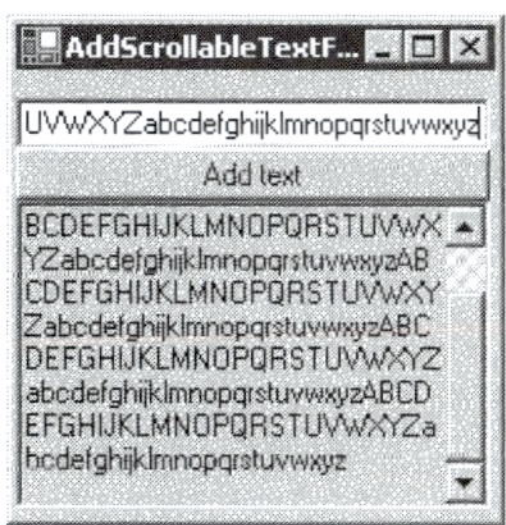

Figure 10.4

`ScrollBars` is an enumeration. Its valid values are

- ScrollBars.None
- ScrollBars.Vertical
- ScrollBars.Horizontal
- ScrollBars.Both

Revisited: TestBitwiseLogicalForm

Earlier we saw a GUI that demonstrated the `Bitwise` logical operators. Its controls were placed on specific positions on the form. Here we created an event handler for each of the buttons. The source is in Listing 10.4.

Listing 10.4

```
using System;
using System.Windows.Forms;
using System.Drawing;
public class TestBitwiseLogicalForm:Form {

    //Text boxes for input
    TextBox entryBox=new TextBox();
    TextBox entryBox2=new TextBox();

    //Buttons to perform &,|,^
    Button andButton=new Button();
    Button orButton=new Button();
    Button uorButton=new Button();

    //Box for the output
    TextBox outBox=new TextBox();

    TestBitwiseLogicalForm() {

      //Define dimensions of the form
      Bounds=new Rectangle(0,0,200,175);
      //Title bar of form
      Text="Enter 2 ints";

      //All controls as wide as client portion of form
      entryBox.Width=ClientSize.Width;
      entryBox2.Width=ClientSize.Width;
      andButton.Width=ClientSize.Width;
      orButton.Width=ClientSize.Width;
      uorButton.Width=ClientSize.Width;
      outBox.Width=ClientSize.Width;
```

(continued)

```
    //Each control is 25 pixels under control above it
    entryBox.Top=0;
    entryBox2.Top=25;
    andButton.Top=50;
    orButton.Top=75;
    uorButton.Top=100;
    outBox.Top=125;

    //Place text on the buttons
    andButton.Text="AND";
    orButton.Text="OR";
    uorButton.Text="XOR";

    //Output cannot be manipulated by user
    outBox.ReadOnly=true;

    //Add the controls to the form
    //Positions have already been determined
    Controls.Add(entryBox);
    Controls.Add(entryBox2);
    Controls.Add(andButton);
    Controls.Add(orButton);
    Controls.Add(uorButton);
    Controls.Add(outBox);

    //Add an event handler for each button
    andButton.Click+=new EventHandler(DoAnd);
    orButton.Click+=new EventHandler(DoOr);
    uorButton.Click+=new EventHandler(DoXor);
  }

  void DoAnd(Object sender,EventArgs ea) {
    //Capture and parse ints from the entry boxes,
    //do the & bitwise logical operation,
    //put output in outbox
    try {
          outBox.Text=(
          Int32.Parse(entryBox.Text)
          &
          Int32.Parse(entryBox2.Text)
          ).ToString();
    } catch (FormatException) {
          outBox.Text="Invalid input!";
    } catch (OverflowException) {
          entryBox.Text="Out of range!";
    }
  }
```

(continued)

```
    void DoOr(Object sender,EventArgs ea) {
      //Capture and parse ints from the entry boxes,
      //do the | bitwise logical operation,
      //put output in outbox
      try {
            outBox.Text=(
            Int32.Parse(entryBox.Text)
            |
            Int32.Parse(entryBox2.Text)
            ).ToString();
      } catch (FormatException) {
            outBox.Text="Invalid input!";
      } catch (OverflowException) {
            entryBox.Text="Out of range!";
      }
    }

    void DoXor(Object sender,EventArgs ea) {
      //Capture and parse ints from the entry boxes,
      //do the ^ bitwise logical operation,
      //put output in outbox
      try {
            outBox.Text=(
            Int32.Parse(entryBox.Text)
            ^
            Int32.Parse(entryBox2.Text)
            ).ToString();
      } catch (FormatException) {
            outBox.Text="Invalid input!";
      } catch (OverflowException) {
            entryBox.Text="Out of range!";
      }
    }

    static void Main(String[] args) {
      Application.Run(new TestBitwiseLogicalForm());
    }
}
```

In Figure 10.5 you can see how the form is used.

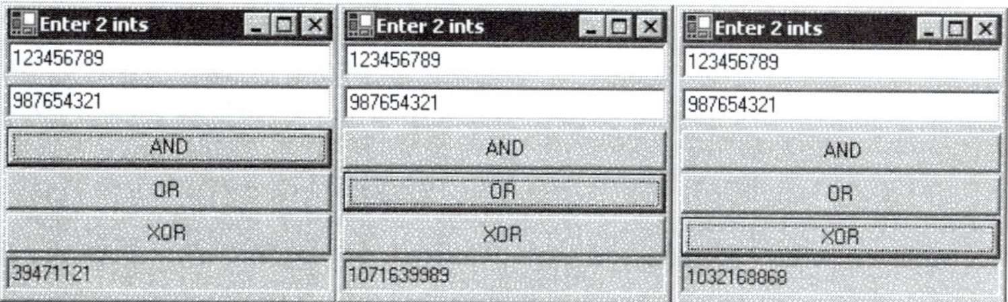

Figure 10.5

■ DOCKING AND ANCHORING CONTROLS

Up to now, we have been placing controls on forms by specifically determining their size and position. If such a form is resized, however, the controls on that form do not stretch or move. We can force controls to do this by anchoring or docking them to different places on the form.

A control can be anchored to the top, bottom, left, or right side of a container, or any combination of these. The `AnchorStyles` enumeration defines the acceptable values:

- `AnchorStyles.None`
- `AnchorStyles.Top`
- `AnchorStyles.Bottom`
- `AnchorStyles.Left`
- `AnchorStyles.Right`

To anchor a control to the top of a container, say, a `TextBox` to the top of a `Form`, we set its `Anchor` property:

```
TextBox tb = new TextBox();
tb.Anchor = AnchorStyles.Top;
this.Controls.Add(tb);//this is a Form
```

If this `Form` is resized, the text box maintains the same distance from the top. You may also anchor a control to more than one side, possibly all four.

```
TextBox tb = new TextBox();
tb.Anchor = AnchorStyles.Top|AnchorStyles.Bottom
      |AnchorStyles.Left|AnchorStyles.Right;
this.Controls.Add(tb);//this is a Form
```

We use the bitwise or operator to combine the values; each value sets a bit in the `Anchor` property.

Sometimes you may wish to dock a control to a single side of a container. A docked control stretches to occupy the side to which it is docked, and stretches or shrinks as the container is resized. The `DockStyles` enumeration specifies acceptable values:

- `DockStyles.None`
- `DockStyles.Top`
- `DockStyles.Bottom`
- `DockStyles.Left`
- `DockStyles.Right`
- `DockStyles.Fill`

A control may also be docked to fill a container. We dock a control by setting its `Dock` property:

```
TextBox tb = new TextBox();
tb.Dock = DockStyles.Bottom;
this.Controls.Add(tb);//this is a Form
```

Our next example shows docking a control on a form.

☐ Revisited: TestShiftOperatorForm

In Chapter 2 we saw a form that demonstrated the shift operators on the `int` type. Figure 10.6 is another look at it.

The `TextBox` is docked to the top of the form; if we stretch/shrink the form sideways, the text box stretches/shrinks along the top as well, as you can see in Figure 10.7.

The source code for the `TestShiftOperatorForm` is in Listing 10.5. Notice where the dock is set for the text box.

Listing 10.5

```
using System;
using System.Windows.Forms;
using System.Drawing;
public class TestShiftOperatorForm:Form {

    TextBox entryBox=new TextBox();
    Button leftShiftButton=new Button();
    Button rightShiftButton=new Button();
    Button urightShiftButton=new Button();
```

(continued)

Figure 10.6

Figure 10.7

```
TestShiftOperatorForm() {

  Bounds=new Rectangle(0,0,300,80);
  Text="Enter an int";

  entryBox.Dock=DockStyle.Top;

  leftShiftButton.Top=25;
  leftShiftButton.Text="Left shift";

  rightShiftButton.Top=25;
  rightShiftButton.Left=100;
  rightShiftButton.Text="Right shift";

  urightShiftButton.Top=25;
  urightShiftButton.Left=200;
  urightShiftButton.Text="URight shift";

  Controls.Add(entryBox);
  Controls.Add(leftShiftButton);
  Controls.Add(rightShiftButton);
  Controls.Add(urightShiftButton);

  leftShiftButton.Click+=new EventHandler(DoLeft);
  rightShiftButton.Click+=new EventHandler(DoRight);
  urightShiftButton.Click+=new EventHandler(DoURight);
}

void DoLeft(Object sender,EventArgs ea) {
  try {
        entryBox.Text=(Int32.Parse(
              entryBox.Text)<<1).ToString();
  } catch (FormatException) {
        entryBox.Text="Not an int!";
  }
}

void DoRight(Object sender,EventArgs ea) {
  try {
        entryBox.Text=(Int32.Parse(
              entryBox.Text)>>1).ToString();
  } catch (FormatException) {
        entryBox.Text="Not an int!";
  }
}

void DoURight(Object sender,EventArgs ea) {
  try {
        int temp=Int32.Parse(entryBox.Text);
        uint utemp=(uint)temp;
```

(continued)

```
            entryBox.Text=(utemp>>1).ToString();
        } catch (FormatException) {
            entryBox.Text="Not an int!";
        }
    }

    static void Main(String[] args) {
        Application.Run(new TestShiftOperatorForm());
    }
}
```

The next example shows how to anchor controls.

■ THE Panel, CheckBox, AND RadioButton CLASSES

Here we will introduce some other controls; we will place panels, check boxes, and radio buttons on a form. Each of these is represented by a class, of course: Panel, CheckBox, and RadioButton. Because they are controls similar to any other control, they share many common properties and methods. In particular, a Panel object is a ScrollableControl object; controls can be placed on a Panel in much the same way they are placed on a Form.

Here is some code that creates a CheckBox object and places it on a Form (this refers to a Form object here):

```
CheckBox c=new CheckBox();
c.Text="Check me!;
c.Top=20;
c.Width=20;
c.Anchor=AnchorStyles.Left|AnchorStyles.Top;
this.Controls.Add(c);
c.CheckedChanged+=new EventHandler(ProcessCheck);
```

The CheckBox will appear thus on the form:

- The caption is "Check me!"
- The check box is 20 pixels down from the top of the form.
- The checkbox is 20 pixels from the left side of the form.

- The check box is anchored to the upper left corner of the form.
- `ProcessCheck` is a multicast delegate called to handle a `CheckChanged` event for this check box.

A `CheckedChanged` event is generated every time a `CheckBox` is checked or unchecked. This event also occurs when a `RadioButton` is checked (note that a radio button is never unchecked). In the case of a `CheckBox`, we note whether it has been checked or unchecked by testing its `Checked` property: true if checked, false if unchecked. Here is how we check the state of `CheckBox c`:

```
private void ProcessCheck(Object sender,EventArgs ea) {
      if (c.Checked);//Do Whatever
}
```

Radio buttons are similar to check boxes, but only one may be selected at any time. A group of radio buttons are defined by the component on which they are placed. If you wish to have multiple groups of radio buttons on a form, place multiple `Panel` objects on the form, the place the radio buttons on the `Panels`. We will show this in an example later in Listing 10.6. Here is an example of placing a `RadioButton` on a form (`this`):

```
RadioButton r=new RadioButton();
r.Text="Select me!";
r.Top=20;
r.Width=20;
r.Anchor=AnchorStyles.Right|AnchorStyles.Top;
r.CheckedChanged+=new EventHandler(ProcessRadio);
this.Controls.Add(r);
```

`ProcessRadio` is the multicast delegate that is called whenever the `CheckedChanged` event for `RadioButton r` occurs:

```
private void ProcessRadio(Object sender,EventArgs ea) {
            if (sender==r);//Do whatever
}
```

Again, we need not examine the `Checked` property here; the `CheckedChanged` event is fired for a `RadioButton` only when it is selected.

☐ Class: CheckForm

The example in Listing 10.6 creates a form that has

- A group of check boxes on a panel anchored to the upper left corner
- A group of radio buttons on another panel anchored to the upper right corner
- A text box docked to the bottom

Listing 10.6

```
using System;
using System.Windows.Forms;
public class CheckForm:Form {

      static String[] s={"Beautiful","Sexy","Irresistable"};
      static String[] s2={"Male","Female","Neither"};
      CheckBox[] b=new CheckBox[s.Length];
      RadioButton[] rb=new RadioButton[s2.Length];
      TextBox outArea=new TextBox();
      Panel upperLeft=new Panel();
      Panel upperRight=new Panel();

      public CheckForm() {

            Text="Personal Profile Form";
            Height=120;
            Width=180;

            upperLeft.Width=Width/2;
            upperLeft.Height=Height/2;
            upperLeft.Anchor=AnchorStyles.Left|AnchorStyles.Top;

            upperRight.Width=Width/2;
            upperRight.Height=Height/2;
            upperRight.Left=Width/2;
            upperRight.Anchor=AnchorStyles.Right
                  |AnchorStyles.Top;

            for (int i=0;i<s.Length;i++) {
                  b[i]=new CheckBox();
                  b[i].Text=s[i];
                  b[i].Top=i*20;
                  b[i].Width=Width/2;
                  upperLeft.Controls.Add(b[i]);
                  b[i].CheckedChanged+=new EventHandler
                        (ProcessCheck);
                  rb[i]=new RadioButton();
                  rb[i].Text=s2[i];
                  rb[i].Top=i*20;
                  rb[i].Width=Width/2;
                  rb[i].CheckedChanged+=new EventHandler
                        (ProcessRadio);
                  upperRight.Controls.Add(rb[i]);
            }

            outArea.Dock=DockStyle.Bottom;
            outArea.ReadOnly=true;
```

(continued)

```
        Controls.Add(upperLeft);
        Controls.Add(upperRight);
        Controls.Add(outArea);

    }

    private void ProcessCheck(Object sender,EventArgs ea) {
        for (int i=0;i<b.Length;i++)
            if (sender==b[i])
                if (b[i].Checked)
                    outArea.Text=b[i].Text
                        +"? YEAH RIGHT!";
                else outArea.Text="Okay then.";

    }

    private void ProcessRadio(Object sender,EventArgs ea) {
        for (int i=0;i<rb.Length;i++)
            if (sender==rb[i])
                outArea.Text=rb[i].Text+"? G"
                    +new String('R',2*(i+1))
                    +new String('!',2*(i+1));
    }

    public static void Main() {
        Application.Run(new CheckForm());
    }
}
```

Figure 10.8 shows the form reacting to the user's input.

NOTE

- The check boxes are situated on the upper left panel, which is anchored to the top and left of the form.
- The radio buttons are situated on the upper right panel, which is anchored to the top and right of the form.
- The text box is docked to the bottom of the form.

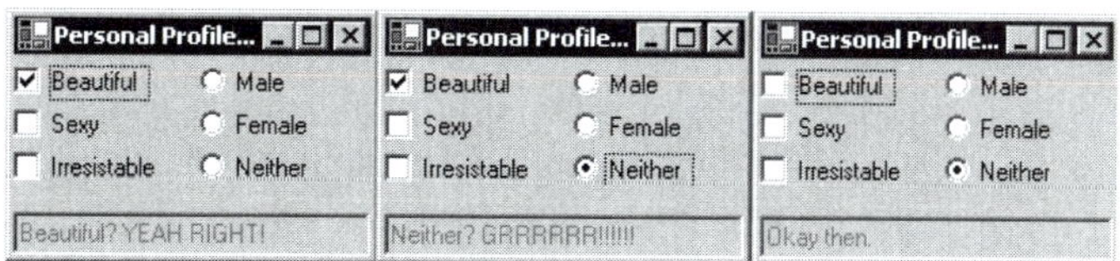

Figure 10.8

Figure 10.9

Thus, you will see that if we drag the corners of the form out, the anchored controls follow the corner they are anchored to, while the docked control stretches out along the bottom (see Figure 10.9).

Note that the panels are not visible. This is because they have no border defined for them. You can easily put borders on a `Panel` object by changing its `BorderStyle` property to one of the `BorderStyle` enumeration values:

- `BorderStyle.None` (default for Panel.BorderStyle)
- `BorderStyle.Fixed3D`
- `BorderStyle.FixedSingle`

MENUS

Unless your form is designed for a simple and specific task, it won't be much good without a menu. In C#, menu items are represented by the `MenuItem` class, whereas the menu itself is either a `MainMenu` or `ContextMenu` object.

A `MainMenu` is placed on a form, whereas a `ContextMenu` appears when an item is right-clicked.

In order for a `MenuItem` to be displayed, you must add it to a `MainMenu` or `ContextMenu` using its `MenuItems` property. To create submenus, you can add `MenuItem` objects to the `MenuItems` property of the parent `MenuItem`.

Class: MenuForm

`MenuForm` is a derivation of `Form`. It has a main menu and a multiline editable text box that fills the `Form`. Figure 10.10 shows what it looks like when we first bring it up (resized a little).

Now, type some text in the text box, as in Figure 10.11.

If we select Options, it expands into a menu with two options, Clear and Upper. Clicking on the Upper option converts the text in the box to uppercase, as you can see in Figure 10.12 and Figure 10.13.

Clicking on Clear empties the text box (see Figure 10.14 and Figure 10.15).

Clicking on the About option throws up a message box, as in Figure 10.16.

Figure 10.10

Figure 10.11

Figure 10.12

Figure 10.13

Figure 10.14

Figure 10.15

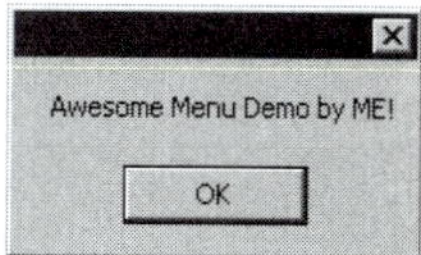

Figure 10.16

To create this menu, we first create all the controls for the `MenuForm`.

```
//Create some menu items
MenuItem options = new MenuItem();
MenuItem about = new MenuItem();
MenuItem clear = new MenuItem();
MenuItem upper = new MenuItem();
//Create a main menu
MainMenu mm=new MainMenu();
//For will have a multi-line editable text box
TextBox tb=new TextBox();
```

We set the text for all the menu items in the `MenuForm` constructor, and add them either to the main menu or as a submenu of another menu item. This is the case with Options, which has Clear and Upper as its menu items. We also bind the main menu to the form.

```
//Add Options and Exit to main menu
options.Text="Options";
mm.MenuItems.Add(options);
about.Text="About";
mm.MenuItems.Add(about);

//Put Clear and Upper as menu items of Options
clear.Text="Clear";
options.MenuItems.Add(clear);
upper.Text="Upper";
options.MenuItems.Add(upper);

//Bind the main menu to the form
this.Menu=mm;
```

To give functionality to Upper, Clear, and About, we add an `EventHandler` to the `Click` event of these `MenuItem` objects.

```
//Add Click event handlers for Clear, Upper, and About
clear.Click+=new EventHandler(DoClear);
upper.Click+=new EventHandler(DoUpper);
about.Click+=new EventHandler(DoShamelessPlug);
```

Here are the handlers for these events:

```
private void DoClear(Object sender,EventArgs ea) {
  //Clear the text box
  tb.Text="";
}

private void DoUpper(Object Sender,EventArgs ea) {
  //Shift contents of text box to upper case
  tb.Text=tb.Text.ToUpper();
}

private void DoShamelessPlug(Object Sender,EventArgs ea) {
  //Throw a message box on screen
  MessageBox.Show("Awesome Menu Demo by ME!");
}
```

The entire `MenuForm` class can be seen in Listing 10.7.

Listing 10.7

```
using System;
using System.Windows.Forms;
public class MenuForm:Form {

    //Create some menu items
    MenuItem options = new MenuItem();
    MenuItem about = new MenuItem();
    MenuItem clear = new MenuItem();
    MenuItem upper = new MenuItem();
    //Create a main menu
    MainMenu mm=new MainMenu();
    //For will have a multi-line editable text box
    TextBox tb=new TextBox();

    public MenuForm() {
      this.Text="Menu Form";

      //Add Options and Exit to main menu
      options.Text="Options";
      mm.MenuItems.Add(options);
      about.Text="About";
      mm.MenuItems.Add(about);

      //Put Clear and Upper as menu items of Options
      clear.Text="Clear";
      options.MenuItems.Add(clear);
      upper.Text="Upper";
      options.MenuItems.Add(upper);

      //Bind the main menu to the form
      this.Menu=mm;

      tb.Multiline=true;
      tb.Dock=DockStyle.Fill;
      this.Controls.Add(tb);

      //Add Click event handlers for Clear, Upper, and About
      clear.Click+=new EventHandler(DoClear);
      upper.Click+=new EventHandler(DoUpper);
      about.Click+=new EventHandler(DoShamelessPlug);
    }

    private void DoClear(Object sender,EventArgs ea) {
      //Clear the text box
      tb.Text="";
    }
```

(continued)

```
    private void DoUpper(Object Sender,EventArgs ea) {
      //Shift contents of text box to uppercase
      tb.Text=tb.Text.ToUpper();
    }

    private void DoShamelessPlug(Object Sender,EventArgs ea) {
      //Throw a message box on screen
      MessageBox.Show("Awesome Menu Demo by ME!");
    }

    static void Main(String[] args) {
      Application.Run(new MenuForm());
    }
}
```

The `MessageBox` Class

Note our use of a message box in our previous program.

```
MessageBox.Show("Awesome Menu Demo by ME!");
```

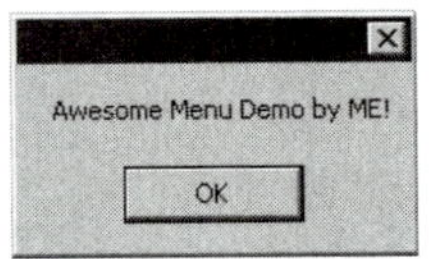

Figure 10.17

This produces the window shown in Figure 10.17.

The `MessageBox` class represents a simple window with a message on it and an OK button. This kind of box is called "modal"; when it has the focus, you must respond to it before you can return to the application that spawned it. `MessageBox` is derived from `Object`, and adds only one new method, `Show`, which is overloaded. Here are some versions:

- Displays a message box with specified text:

  ```
  public static DialogResult Show(string);
  ```

- Displays a message box with specified text and caption:

  ```
  public static DialogResult Show(string, string);
  ```

- Displays a message box with specified text, caption, and buttons:

  ```
  public static DialogResult Show(string, string,
  MessageBoxButtons);
  ```

- Displays a message box with specified text, caption, buttons, and icon:

  ```
  public static DialogResult Show(string, string,
  MessageBoxButtons, MessageBoxIcon);
  ```

- Displays a message box with the specified text, caption, buttons, icon, and default button:

```
public static DialogResult Show(string, string,
MessageBoxButtons, MessageBoxIcon,
MessageBoxDefaultButton);
```

- Displays a message box with the specified text, caption, buttons, icon, default button, and options:

```
public static DialogResult Show(string, string,
MessageBoxButtons, MessageBoxIcon,
MessageBoxDefaultButton, MessageBoxOptions);
```

Depending on which version of `Show` we use, we can display message boxes that vary widely in appearance and functionality. Note that `MessageBox` objects return a `DialogResult`, which is an enumeration having the following values:

- `DialogResult.Yes`
- `DialogResult.No`
- `DialogResult.Cancel`
- `DialogResult.Abort`
- `DialogResult.Ignore`
- `DialogResult.None`
- `DialogResult.Retry`
- `DialogResult.OK`

These `DialogResult` values will depend on the actual message box being displayed. This is determined by the `MessageBoxButtons` enumeration, whose values are shown in Table 10.1.

`MessageBoxIcon` is an enumeration (see Table 10.2), which when used with the appropriate `MessageBox` constructor, determines the type of icon to display on the message box.

If a message box has more than one button on it, we can specify which button (numbered 1, 2, and 3) is the default by applying the proper `MessageBoxDefaultButton` value in a `MessageBox` constructor. The default button, of course, is the one that is

TABLE 10.1

`MessageBoxButtons.AbortRetryIgnore`	Box has Abort, Retry, and Ignore buttons.
`MessageBoxButtons.OK`	Has an OK button. This is the default.
`MessageBoxButtons.OKCancel`	Has OK and Cancel buttons.
`MessageBoxButtons.RetryCancel`	Has Retry and Cancel buttons.
`MessageBoxButtons.YesNo`	Has Yes and No buttons.
`MessageBoxButtons.YesNoCancel`	Has Yes, No, and Cancel buttons.

TABLE 10.2

`MessageBoxIcon.Asterisk`	Icon is a symbol consisting of a lowercase letter *i* in a circle.
`MessageBoxIcon.Error`	Icon is a symbol consisting of a white X in a circle with a red background.
`MessageBoxIcon.Exclamation`	Icon is a symbol consisting of an exclamation point in a triangle with a yellow background.
`MessageBoxIcon.Hand`	Icon is a symbol consisting of a hand in a circle with a red background.
`MessageBoxIcon.Information`	Icon is a symbol consisting of a lowercase letter *i* in a circle.
`MessageBoxIcon.None`	The message box contain no icon.
`MessageBoxIcon.Question`	Icon is a symbol consisting of a question mark in a circle.
`MessageBoxIcon.Stop`	Icon is a symbol consisting of a white X in a circle with a red background.
`MessageBoxIcon.Warning`	Icon is a symbol consisting of an exclamation point in a triangle with a yellow background.

activated if the user simply presses the Enter key. The values for the `MessageBoxDefaultButton` enumeration are

- `MessageBoxDefaultButton.Button1`
- `MessageBoxDefaultButton.Button2`
- `MessageBoxDefaultButton.Button3`

The program in Listing 10.8 is an example that produces and displays a customized `MessageBox` object.

☐ Program: ShowFancyMessageBox

Here, we use a `MessageBox` constructor, which determines the text, caption, icon, button types, and default button on a message box.

Listing 10.8

```
using System;
using System.Windows.Forms;
public class ShowFancyMessageBox {
    static void Main(String[] args) {
      DialogResult cliffHangerResolved=MessageBox.Show(
            "Are you sure you want to destroy the universe?",
            "Armageddon Confirmation",
```

(continued)

```
            MessageBoxButtons.YesNoCancel,
            MessageBoxIcon.Question,
            MessageBoxDefaultButton.Button3
        );
        if (cliffHangerResolved==DialogResult.Yes)
            MessageBox.Show("Commencing des....AAAARRRGGHHHH!!!");
        else if (cliffHangerResolved==DialogResult.No)
            MessageBox.Show("Perhaps further meditation is required.");
        else MessageBox.Show("Whew!");
    }
}
```

Specifically, it is a message box with Yes, No, and Cancel buttons, with a question mark icon. The Cancel button is made the default. If this option is taken, the value `DialogResult.Cancel` is returned, and another message box is shown (see Figure 10.18 and Figure 10.19).

Figure 10.20 and Figure 10.21 show the No option being chosen.

The result of choosing the Yes option is shown in Figure 10.22 and Figure 10.23.

Message boxes are quick and convenient ways to throw a simple message to the user, and allow them to respond in limited ways.

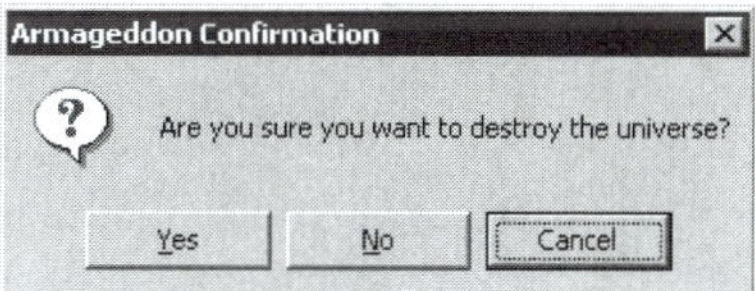

Figure 10.18

Figure 10.19

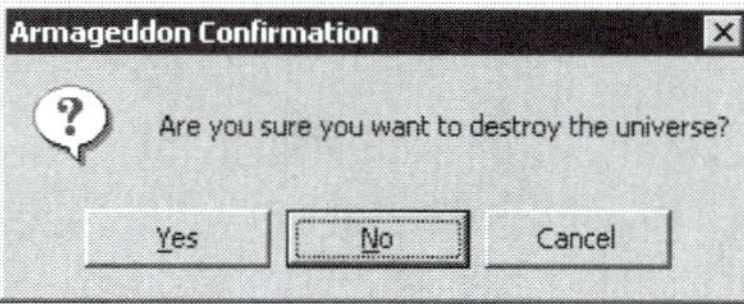

Figure 10.20

Figure 10.21

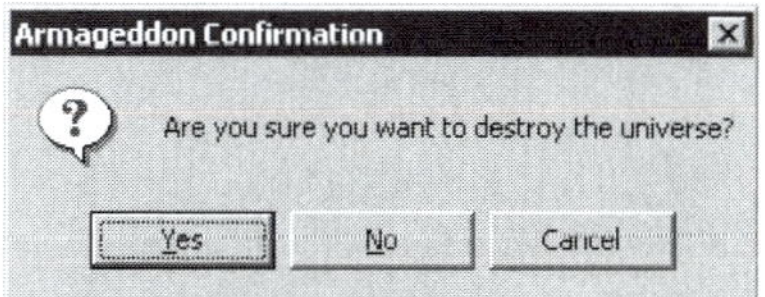

Figure 10.22

Figure 10.23

chapter 11

Algorithm Analysis

An essential element to programming is efficiency. Clearly, the faster an algorithm runs, the better. One facet of algorithm analysis is studying the speed of algorithms. To do this, we first represent the running time of algorithms as functions. (We'll discuss exactly how to do this in the section on analyzing code.) Let n be the number of elements in a data set, and let T_1, T_2, T_3, and T_4 be the running times of four algorithms depending on n, where

$T_1(n) = n + 1/2$

$T_2(n) = \log_2 n + 2$

$T_3(n) = (1/4)n^2 + (1/3)n + 1$

$T_4(n) = 1.9^n$

In Figure 11.1 we graph these functions, to get an idea of how they grow as n grows.

(Note that we graph the functions as continuous functions, even though they are really defined only for nonnegative integers.)

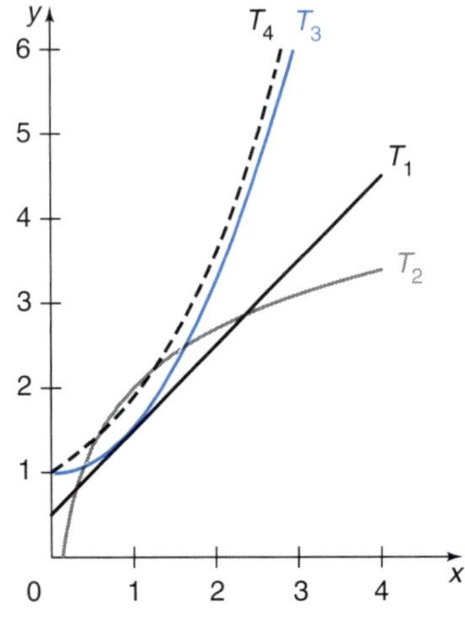

Figure 11.1

Note that T_1 is a linear function, whereas T_2 is a logarithmic function. T_1 grows faster than T_2, even though for a short time it is under T_2. T_3 is a quadratic function, and it grows faster than both T_1 and T_2. Finally, T_4 is an exponential function, and it grows faster than all the others. Can we make statements more general than these? For example, can we say that any linear function $f(n) = an + b$ will eventually dominate any logarithmic function $g(n) = \log_z n + c$ (where the base $z > 1$)? Big-O analysis is intended to give us these answers.

■ BIG-O NOTATION

Big-O is a mathematical notation used to describe the running time of algorithms. It allows us to classify algorithms based on their running times, where running time is expressed as a function of the data size n, say $T(n)$. It is reasonable to say that for most algorithms, the running time $T(n)$ grows as n grows. The formal definition of Big-O follows:

> Definition of Big O: A function $f(n)$ is said to be $O(g(n))$ if there exists $c > 0$ and $N > 0$ such that $f(n) \le cg(n)$ for all $n \ge N$.

As an example of how this is used, let us show the following:

$f(n) = 3n^2 + 2n + 5$ is $O(n^2)$.

To do this, we must find a positive constant c such that

$3n^2 + 2n + 5 \le cn^2$

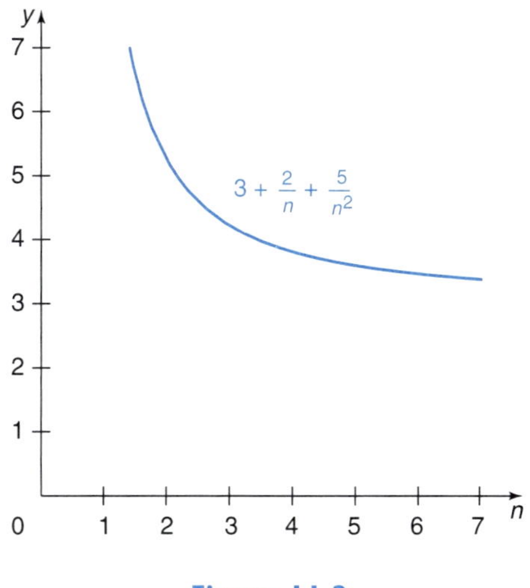

Figure 11.2

for a sufficiently large value of n. First, divide both sides by n^2. We get

$$3 + 2/n + 5/n^2 \leq c$$

Note from Figure 11.2 that the left-hand side of the previous equation is strictly decreasing.

So, we can choose $N = 1$ and $c = 10$, because this says

$$3 + 2/n + 5/n^2 \leq c \text{ for all } n \geq N, \text{ where } c = 10 \text{ and } N = 1$$

or equivalently,

$$3n^2 + 2n + 5 \leq cn^2 \text{ for all } n \geq N, \text{ where } c = 10 \text{ and } N = 1$$

Thus, by definition, $f(n)$ is $O(n^2)$.

Note that $N = 1$ and $c = 10$ is only one of infinitely many pairs we could have chosen. But what have we just done? We have established that the coefficients of all the terms, and in fact, all terms but the dominant term, can be ignored in Big-O analysis. Surely you can see that we could easily repeat the proof we just did if we replaced the coefficients of $f(n)$ with arbitrary values. In fact, you can easily do this proof:

Show that $f(n) = a_2n^2 + a_1n + a_0$ is $O(n^2)$.

The ability to ignore these coefficients and constant terms extends to all functions. Using the definition of Big-O analysis, we can establish all of the following propositions:

1. If $f(n)$ is $O(g(n))$ and $g(n)$ is $O(h(n))$, then $f(n)$ is $O(h(n))$.
2. If $f(n)$ and $g(n)$ are both $O(h(n))$, then $f(n) + g(n)$ is $O(h(n))$.
3. If $f(n)$ is $O(h_1(n))$ and $g(n)$ is $O(h_2(n))$, then $f(n)g(n)$ is $O(h_1(n)h_2(n))$.
4. $f(n) + k$ is $O(f(n))$.

TABLE 11.1

Category	Colloquial Reference Runs in "X" Time
O(1)	Constant
O(log$n$)	Logarithmic
O(n)	Linear
O($n$log$n$)	$n$log$n$
O(n^2)	Quadratic
O(n^3)	Cubic
O(n^k)	Polynomial, where $k > 3$
O(b^n)	Exponential

5. $kf(n)$ is $O(f(n))$.
6. $a_k n^k + a_{k-1} n^{k-1} + \ldots + a_1 n + a_0$ is $O(n^k)$.
7. a^n is $O(b^n)$ for all $a > 1$ and $b > 1$.
8. $\log_a n$ is $O(\log_b n)$ for all $a > 1$, $b > 1$.

Note that the last two propositions say that neither the base of an exponential function nor the base of a logarithmic function is significant in Big-O analysis. Thus, we often leave the base b unspecified, as long as it's understood that $b > 1$.

We can also establish that certain functions $f(n)$ are *not* O(g(n)). This is even more important, because it establishes boundaries for these functions, and allows us to categorize them.

Propositions:

1. b^n is *not* $O(n^k)$ for any integer k, where $b > 1$.
2. n^k is *not* $O(n^{k+1})$ for any integer $k > 0$.
3. n^2 is *not* O($n$log$n$).
4. $n$log$n$ is *not* O(n).
5. n is *not* O(log$n$).
6. log$n$ is *not* O(1).

All of these assertions tell us that certain types of algorithms are categorically faster than others. Table 11.1 lists the most common categories, from fastest to slowest.

▪ ANALYZING CODE

This now begs the question: How do we express the running time of an algorithm as a function? We do this by examining the code. As you will see, usually only the loops make a difference. We will do a series of examples.

☐ Example 1

```
int[] a=new int[n];
for (int i=0;i<n;i++) {
      for (int j=0,sum=a[0];j<n;j++)
            sum+=a[j];
}
```

Table 11.2 shows what happens.

First of all, we look at all the individual statements in the code; we create an array, create and initialize some integer variables, update the variables, and do some assignments. All of these occur in constant time; that is, the time these statements take to execute does not depend on n. This is not to suggest that these constants are all the same; only that they are constant.

If we group together the running time of all the statements that execute only once, and repeat this for all statements that occur n times and n^2 times, we can express the total running time $T(n)$ as a quadratic polynomial

$$T(n) = an^2 + bn + c$$

TABLE 11.2

Statement	Statement Runs in "X" Time	# of Times Statement Executes
An array of size n is created.	Constant	1
Variable i is created and initialized.	Constant	1
Outer Loop		
i is tested against n.	Constant	n
Variable j is created and initialized.	Constant	n
sum is initialized to a[0].	Constant	n
Inner Loop		
j is tested against n.	Constant	n^2
sum is incremented by a[j].	Constant	n^2
j is incremented by 1.	Constant	n^2
i is incremented by 1.	Constant	n

Of course, only the dominant term in $T(n)$ matters, so we can say

$T(n)$ is $O(n^2)$

To convince ourselves that this algorithm runs in quadratic time, we can time this program for various values of n. We do this by using the `DateTime` structure; that is, we get a `long` from the `Ticks` property of `DateTime.Now`, which is itself a `DateTime` instance:

```
long start = DateTime.Now.Ticks;
```

This `long` represents the number of "ticks" that have passed since midnight, January 1, in the year 0001. There are 10 million ticks per second. Then, we execute the algorithm, and after it is finished, we get the time (in "ticks") again.

```
long stop = DateTime.Now.Ticks;
```

The difference between `stop` and `start`, that is, `stop-start`, represents the number of ticks that passed while the algorithm was running. To convert this value to seconds, just divide it by 10 million. Here, I divide by 10 to get microseconds. Here is some code surrounding the algorithm to time it:

```
int n=Int32.Parse(args[0]);
long start=DateTime.Now.Ticks;

int[] a=new int[n];
for (int i=0;i<n;i++) {
      for (int j=0,sum=a[0];j<n;j++)
            sum+=a[j];
}

long stop=DateTime.Now.Ticks;
Console.WriteLine((stop-start)/10+" microseconds");
```

Note we also get the value of n from the command line, so we can easily test this code for different values of n.

```
C:\C#>CodeTester 10000
312506 microseconds

C:\C#>CodeTester 100000
30906843 microseconds
```

Note that when n is increased tenfold, $T(n)$ increases by a hundredfold, or by the square of ten. $T(n)$ is indeed $O(n^2)$.

☐ Example 2

Now, we'll do something a little trickier. We'll take the same code we had before, but now the inner loop executes `i` times for each execution on the outer loop:

```
int[] a=new int[n];
for (int i=0;i<n;i++) {
      for (int j=1,sum=a[0];j<=i;j++)
            sum+=a[j];
}
```

The number of times the inner loop executes is variable, from n times down to once for each execution of the outer loop. Because each statement in the body of the inner loop runs in constant time, say K, group them together and express the time it takes for the inner loop to execute as

$$t(n) = K(n + n - 1 + n - 2 + \dots + 1) = Kn(n + 1)/2$$

Now, we merely add the term for the statements in the outer loop and for those that execute only once to get

$$T(n) = Kn(n + 1)/2 + K'n + K''$$

If we multiply the terms out completely and regroup we get

$$T(n) = an^2 + bn + c$$

and $T(n)$ is again $O(n^2)$. To verify this, let us test this example for different values of n.

```
C:\C#>CodeTester 10000
156253 microseconds

C:\C#>CodeTester 100000
15203416 microseconds
```

Note that as n increases tenfold, the running time increases one hundredfold. Because 100 is 10^2, this confirms our claim that the algorithm runs in quadratic time.

□ Example 3

It is not necessarily true that a loop within a loop runs in quadratic time. Here is an example that does not:

```
int[] a=new int[n];
for (int i=4;i<n;i++) {
      for (int j=i-3,sum=a[i-4];j<=i;j++)
            sum+=a[j];
}
```

Here, the running time $T(n)$ of the algorithm is $O(n)$ because $T(n) = 4an + b$, where a and b are constant. This is because the inner loop executes exactly *four* times on each iteration of the outer loop; that is, the inner loop does not depend on n. To test this claim, time the algorithm for two large values of n:

```
C:\C#>CodeTester 1000000
46875 microseconds
```

```
C:\C#>CodeTester 10000000
421883 microseconds
```

Note that as the data size *n* increases tenfold, the running time correspondingly increases tenfold. This is clearly a linear relationship.

☐ Example 4

Here is a loop that exhibits logarithmic performance:

```
for (double d=1,i=0;d<n;d*=2) {
      i+=d;
}
```

This algorithm is O(log *n*) because `d` doubles during each iteration. The variable `d` will exceed `n` within $\log_2$`n` iterations. We can try to test this algorithm, but it is so fast we cannot record its passage! In the test program, we can even make `n` a `double` to vastly increase our range, but it doesn't help:

```
Double n=Double.Parse(args[0]);
long start=DateTime.Now.Ticks;

for (double d=1,i=0;d<n;d*=2) {
      i+=d;
}

long stop=DateTime.Now.Ticks;
Console.WriteLine((stop-start)/10+" microseconds");

C:\C#>CodeTester 1E100
0 microseconds

C:\C#>CodeTester 1E200
0 microseconds

C:\C#>CodeTester 1E300
0 microseconds
```

Even if `n` is as high as 3 googol, the algorithm takes less than a microsecond to execute! Clearly, logarithmic performance is highly desirable.

☐ Example 5

Consider the following code fragment:

```
for (int i=0,j=0; i<n; i++)
      for (double d=1; d<n; d*=2)
            j++;
```

This is $O(n\log n)$ because the outer loop executes n times, and each time the inner loop executes $\log n$ times. If we view the performance of this algorithm, note that the growth is super-linear, yet subquadratic, because a tenfold increase in n clearly produces more than a tenfold increase, but not nearly a hundredfold increase in the running time.

```
C:\C#>CodeTester 100000
15625 microseconds

C:\C#>CodeTester 1000000
140627 microseconds

C:\C#>CodeTester 10000000
1703157 microseconds

C:\C#>CodeTester 100000000
18844111 microseconds

C:\C#>CodeTester 1000000000
206628967 microseconds
```

■ ANALYZING RECURSIVE ALGORITHMS

Looping can also come about by recursion, and we should get some practice analyzing this as well. When analyzing recursion, we must note not only how deep the recursion goes, but also how many times a method calls itself in each level of the recursion.

□ Example 6

First, we examine a recursive function that computes $n!$

```
static double Factorial(int n) {
  if (n<0) throw new ArgumentException(
        "Factorial function not defined for "+n);
  if(n==1||n==0) return 1;
  return n*Factorial(n-1);
}
```

Each time `Factorial` calls itself, it does so only once, and with a value of `n` one less than the current call. Thus, this method calls itself about n times, then must pull out of the recursion to compute the answer. This backing up also has depth n. So $T(n) = an + bn$, and therefore $T(n)$ is $O(n)$.

```
static long Fibonacci(int n) {
  if (n<1) throw new ArgumentException(
        "Fibonacci function not defined for "+n);
```

```
  if (n==1||n==2) return 1;
  return Fibonacci(n-2)+Fibonacci(n-1);
}
```

☐ Example 7

Now, consider a recursive method that computes the `gcd` of two `long` positive integers `n` and `r`:

```
private static long gcd(long n,long r) {
      if (r==0) return n;
      return gcd(r,n%r);
}
```

Suppose `n` is the larger of `n` and `r`. Here, the recursive method calls itself only once in any particular level of the recursion, but the question is, how many calls does it take to reach the base case? You will see that this does not depend on `n`, but on the number of bits of `n`. To see this, take for example

101010B mod 100000B = 001010B

Note that the result has fewer significant bits than `r`, and is certainly smaller bitwise than `n`. Note that this is always the case because if `r` has the same number of significant bits as `n`, or if `r` is strictly smaller bitwise than `n`, either way `n` mod `r` has fewer significant bits than `r`, and hence, `n`. Thus, if `n` is `q` bits long, no more than `q` calls are required to reach the base case. Because $q \geq \log_2 n$, we have a running time not exceeding O(log*n*).

☐ Example 8

For our next example, let's take the Towers of Hanoi problem, and the recursive method `MoveDisks`.

```
static void MoveDisks(int source, int dest,
           int temp, int n) {
      //Solve the n-1 problem with different peg arrangement
      if (n>1) MoveDisks(source,temp,dest,n-1);
      //Move the disk on the "bottom"
      Console.Write(source+" to "+dest+".\t");
      //Solve the n-1 problem with different peg arrangement
      if (n>1) MoveDisks(temp,dest,source,n-1);
}
```

Note that this method calls itself twice—once before the output statement and once afterwards. Each of these calls is with a value of `n` one less than the current call. This might suggest linear time, but because there are two more calls to `MoveDisk` every time we call `MoveDisk`, this creates an explosion of method calls. Say $T(n)$ is the time required to move n disks, and t_n is the time required to move the nth disk; then,

$T(n)$

$= T(n-1) + t_n + T(n-1)$

$= T(n-2) + t_{n-1} + T(n-2) + t_n + T(n-2) + t_{n-1} + T(n-2)$

...

$= T(1) + t_2 + T(1) + t_3 + \ldots + t_3 + T(1) + t_2 + T(1)$

$= t_1 + t_2 + t_1 + t_3 + \ldots + t_3 + t_1 + t_2 + t_1$

By regrouping the t_i terms we get

$T(n) = t_n + 2t_{n-1} + 4t_{n-2} + \ldots + 2^{n-1}t_1$

Now, because all of the t_i are equal (i.e., in our algorithm we assume that it takes no longer to move any disk than to move any other), let $k = t_i$ for any i, and we have

$T(n) = k(1+2+4+\ldots+2^{n-1}) = k(2^n - 1) = 2^n k - k$

and so $T(n) = 2^n$. (We could also write $T(n) = b^n$, as some textbooks do.)

This is an algorithm that runs in exponential time. Such algorithms are excruciatingly slow for only moderate values of n. These are to be avoided if possible, although unfortunately their use is sometimes unavoidable.

The following test program times the algorithm for some relatively small values of n. I replaced the output statement in `MoveDisks` with a loop that just spins its wheels and wastes some time, simulating moving a disk. The output statement was removed because it can cause the program to be blocked until the output request is complete. During this time, other processes can run. This obviously invalidates any times reported; you must take care with output statements when testing for this reason.

```
static void Main(String[] args) {

  int n=Int32.Parse(args[0]);
  long start=DateTime.Now.Ticks;

  MoveDisks(1,3,2,n);

  long stop=DateTime.Now.Ticks;
  Console.WriteLine((stop-start)/10+" microseconds");

}

static void MoveDisks(int source, int dest, int temp, int n) {
  if (n>1) MoveDisks(source,temp,dest,n-1);
  //Simulate moving single disk
  for (int i=0;i<100;i++);
  if (n>1) MoveDisks(temp,dest,source,n-1);
}
```

Here are some test runs:

```
C:\C#>CodeTester 20
234379 microseconds
```

```
C:\C#>CodeTester 21
500009 microseconds

C:\C#>CodeTester 22
1000019 microseconds

C:\C#>CodeTester 23
2000038 microseconds

C:\C#>CodeTester 24
4031327 microseconds

C:\C#>CodeTester 25
8047029 microseconds
```

Note that as we increment n by one on each successive run, the running time effectively doubles, confirming our analysis that $T(n)$ is exponential. If you try only slightly larger values, waiting for the program to complete is nearly unendurable (if you are impatient like me). Larger values can also easily exhaust memory, because the recursion takes up so much memory as it makes each method call.

■ WORST CASE AND BEST CASE ANALYSIS

Generally, Big-O analysis deals with average cases. We often assume this when we do an analysis of this kind. However, there are sometimes cases when configuration of the data precipitates an improvement or a decline in the performance of an algorithm. A configuration that maximizes this improvement/decline is called a best/worst case, respectively. Sometimes a best/worst case can change the running time for $T(n)$ so drastically that $T(n)$ changes its asymptotic nature. Take, for example, the following algorithm:

```
for (int i=0,length=1;i<n-1;i++) {
      int i2=i,i1=i;
      for (int k=i;k<n-1&&a[k]<a[k+1];k++,i2++);
            if (length<i2-i1+1)
                  length=i2-i1+1;
}
```

These loops do the following:

1. The outer loop simply passes through the array `a`.
2. On each iteration of the outer loop, say iteration `i`, the inner loop does the following:
   a. It examines the sequence of numbers higher in the array than `a[k]` as long as the sequence `a[k]`, `a[k+1]`, `a[k+2]` . . . is an increasing sequence.

b. When it encounters a value `j` such that `a[j-1] ≥ a[j]`, the inner loop stops.

c. If the entire sequence `a[k], a[k+1], ..., a[n-1]` is increasing, the inner loop terminates at the end of the array.

Is there a particular configuration of the array that causes this program to run especially quickly? Obviously, if the array is in decreasing order, the inner loop will fail its test every time, and will never execute its body of statements. In this case, running time $T(n)$ will depend only on the outer loop, which is $O(n)$.

Now, consider an increasing sequence. Such a sequence will cause the inner loop to pass all the way from element `a[k]` through the last element on the `k`-th iteration of the outer loop. This will give a quadratic $O(n^2)$ running time. Thus, the best case and the worst case are categorically different.

What about the average case? $T(n)$ must lie between the worst case and the best case, so it could be no faster than $O(n)$, but no worse than $O(n^2)$. If we consider the average case to be an array of random elements, then we must determine the average length of a sequence of increasing elements in such a list. Let's consider this: We can argue that the average length of an increasing sequence in a random list must be short, by the following reasoning:

1. If we take two random elements, the odds that the second is larger than the first is 1/2.

2. If we add a random element in the third position, the odds that it is smaller than the second is also 1/2, and so the odds that a random sequence of length 3 is increasing is 1/2 times 1/2, or 25%.

3. In general, then, the odds that a random sequence of length n occurs is only $(1/2)^n$. This is a probability that vanishes very quickly.

By this reasoning, large increasing subsequences are highly unlikely in a random list, so the inner loop does *not* depend on n, and will run in constant time for long lists as well as short lists. This means that in the average case, $T(n)$ is $O(n)$.

We should note that determining the average case itself is often not elementary. Assuming that the average case is the "random" case may simply be wrong.

The following test program creates an array and runs it through the loop just described. The program allows you to enter a command line option to create

- `a`—An array of ascending values
- `d`—An array of descending values
- `otherwise`—An array of random values

```
int n=Int32.Parse(args[0]);
char option=args.Length>1?args[1][0]:'r';
Random r=new Random();
long start=DateTime.Now.Ticks;

int[] a=new int[n];
```

```
int value=0;
for (int i=0;i<n;i++) {
      if (option=='a') value++;
      else if (option=='a') value--;
      else value=r.Next(Int32.MaxValue);
      a[i]=value;
}

for (int i=0,length=1;i<n-1;i++) {
      int i2=i,i1=i;
      for (int k=i;k<n-1&&a[k]<a[k+1];k++,i2++);
            if (length<i2-i1+1)
                  length=i2-i1+1;
}

long stop=DateTime.Now.Ticks;
Console.WriteLine((stop-start)/10+" microseconds");
```

If you note the running times, you will see a clear linear relationship when the array has descending or random values, and runs in quadratic time when the array consists of increasing values.

```
C:\C#>CodeTester 100000
15625 microseconds

C:\C#>CodeTester 1000000
171878 microseconds

C:\C#>CodeTester 10000000
2000038 microseconds

C:\C#>CodeTester 100000 d
15625 microseconds

C:\C#>CodeTester 1000000 d
171878 microseconds

C:\C#>CodeTester 10000000 d
1765658 microseconds

C:\C#>CodeTester 10000 a
421883 microseconds

C:\C#>CodeTester 100000 a
83532853 microseconds
```

chapter 12

Sorting and Searching

We have seen only one data structure in C# so far; namely, the array. We can outline the advantages and disadvantages of arrays here:

- An array is quite efficient in terms of memory usage; it needs only enough space to hold its elements (plus a few bytes for its properties).
- If it is discovered that an array is not large enough to hold all the data, this presents a problem, because arrays are fixed in size.
- By using an index, we can immediately retrieve a particular element from the array.
- Even though you can jump immediately to an item, knowing where it is in the array is a different problem. You may have to search the array sequentially until you come across it. This kind of sequential search takes time.
- Sorting the array first will allow you to find an item much faster using a binary search. Sorting the array first, however, is an expensive operation, and has meaning only when the items stored have an order established among them. (How would you sort Objects, for example?)

- If the array must be sorted, inserting and deleting elements into/from the array can mean significant data movement each time this is done. If insertions and deletions occur frequently, the sorting routine may not be able to keep up.

Under the right conditions, an array might be entirely appropriate. Thus, it is worthwhile to talk about different sorting and searching techniques.

■ SORTING

You have seen the bubble sort and the selection sort earlier in the text. Both of these sorts are simple and direct in their manner of sorting, but neither can be considered nearly fast enough for a real application.

If we analyze bubble sort, we see it has $O(n^2)$ efficiency. To see this, review the following code:

```
public static void BubbleSort(IComparable[] array,int size) {
   int top=size-1;
   bool done=false;
   while (!done) {
      done=true;
      for (int i=0;i<top;i++) {
         if (array[i+1].CompareTo(array[i])<0) {
            done=false;
            swap(array,i,i+1);
         }
      }
      top--;
   }
}
```

If the array is in random order, the outer `while` loop will execute about `n` times, where `n` is the size of the array. Although the inner `for` loop passes through a shorter array on each pass (because the largest element in each pass finds it way to the end), we still get $O(n^2)$ efficiency, because if K is the time it takes to do a comparison and swap, we have

$$T(n) = nK + (n - 1)K + \ldots + 2K + K = K[n + (n - 1) + \ldots + 2 + 1] = Kn(n + 1)/2,$$

and so $T(n)$ is $O(n^2)$.

If we examine the selection sort, we can see it is also $O(n^2)$.

```
public static void SelectionSort(IComparable[] array,int size)
{
   if (size==0) return;
   int top=size-1;
```

```
    int indexOfLargest;
    do {
       indexOfLargest=0;
       for (int i=1;i<=top;i++)
          if (array[indexOfLargest].CompareTo(array[i])<0)
             indexOfLargest=i;
       swap(array,top,indexOfLargest);
       top--;
    } while (top>0);
}
```

Although the selection sort makes only a single swap on each pass, it still makes the same number of passes through an array as the bubble sort, and also makes the same number of comparisons of each pass. For this reason, we conclude that selection sort is $O(n^2)$.

We consider now some different methods of sorting.

□ The Insertion Sort

The insertion sort is another sort that runs in quadratic time, but in practice fares much better than bubble sort or selection sort for arrays that are not too large. It is also simple to conceive and to code.

To see how it works, examine this list of numbers:

4   1   7   5   6   0   3

First of all, if the list contains one or zero elements, there is nothing to do. This is not the case here, so we continue. We examine the second number—here, the 1 in the list—and begin with the assumption that the list to the left of the number we are examining is sorted. Initially, this left sublist contains only one element, namely, 4, and so is sorted. We note $1 < 4$, so we "insert" the 1 at the beginning.

1   4   7   5   6   0   3

We now examine the next number, 7. We note first that the sublist to the left of 7 is sorted, and we consider the 7's proper position in this left sublist. Because $7 > 4$, it is already in the proper position.

1   4   7   5   6   0   3

The 5 is then considered, which should be inserted between the 4 and the 7.

1   4   5   7   6   0   3

Now, we consider the 6, which should be inserted between the 5 and the 7.

1   4   5   6   7   0   3

The next value is 0, which should be inserted all the way at the head of the left sublist.

0 1 4 5 6 7 3

Finally, the last element 3 is considered, which should be placed between 1 and 4.

0 1 3 4 5 6 7

Note that at any point in this process, the left sublist of the element we are considering is always sorted.

Because we are sorting arrays at this point, note that inserting an item at some position may mean moving a considerable number of items out of the way first. For example, consider inserting the 0 into its proper position in the following list:

1 4 5 6 7 0 3

In order to fill the slot at the beginning, the 1, 4, 5, 6, and 7 all need to shift one position to the right.

0 1 4 5 6 7 3

Finally, 3 is inserted into its proper position, with the 4, 5, 6, and 7 shifting to the right.

0 1 3 4 5 6 7

The algorithm for the insertion sort follows:

```
public static void InsertionSort(IComparable[] array, int size)
{
   IComparable temp; int j;
   if (array.Length<2) return;
   for (int i=1; i<=size; i++) {
         temp=array[i];
         for (j=i; j>0 && temp.CompareTo(array[j-1])<0; j--)
              array[j]=array[j-1];
         array[j]=temp;
   }
}
```

Note that this sort consists of a `for` loop within a `for` loop. The outer loop passes through the array, examining each element to determine its insertion point, and the inner `for` loop moves the data out of the way for an item to be inserted. This inner `for` loop will move about half the items in the left sublist over on any pass. For the average case, this yields a running time of $O(n^2)$.

☐ The Shell Sort

The problem with the bubble sort and selection sort is that it takes so long for an item to get in proper position, or even close to its proper position. In fact, it takes an entire pass through the array just to get one item (the largest) in position. Items other than the largest after any pass can still be light years from their proper place.

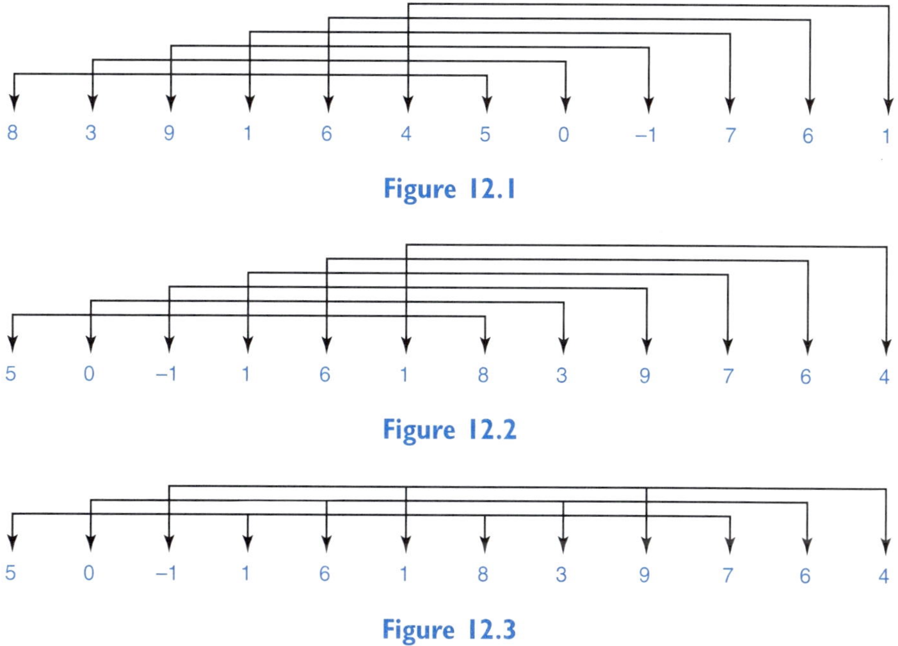

Figure 12.1

Figure 12.2

Figure 12.3

The shell sort attempts to get more items closer to their "spot" as early in the game as possible. It does this by creating a series of "sublists," each based on a "gap." The gap represents the distance between items in the sublists, and starts with the value

(Length of List) / 2

(Ignore any remainder.)

Each of these sublists is sorted separately. For example, suppose we have the following items to sort:

8 3 9 1 6 4 5 0 −1 7 6 1

There are 12 items here, so the gap starts at 12/2 = 6. This produces six sublists, each containing two elements (see Figure 12.1).

We sort each of these sublists separately. We can use whatever sort we wish for this—a bubble sort, selection sort, or whatever—as long as each sublist is completely sorted. This gives us the list in Figure 12.2.

Now, we repeat this, but use a smaller gap. On the next pass (and each subsequent pass) take

gap = gap/2

(Again ignore any remainder.)

In this case, gap = 6/2 = 3, and we get three sublists, each containing four elements. If it should turn out that the list doesn't divide evenly, don't worry about it; the sublists need not contain the same number of elements (see Figure 12.3).

Again, we sort each sublist, as in Figure 12.4.

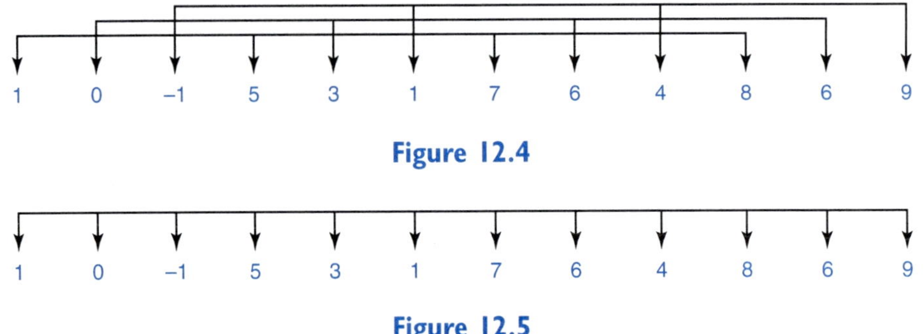

Figure 12.4

Figure 12.5

Now, we continue reducing the gap until gap = 1, as it is on this next pass in the example (see Figure 12.5). When gap = 1, we are sorting the entire list. Whatever sort we use at this point (or at any point when sorting the sublists) is up to us.

Thus, after sorting the list as a whole, we have

−1 0 1 1 3 4 5 6 6 7 8 9

The shell sort does not specify how to sort at each stage; it only specifies that you divide in this way, based on a decreasing sequence of gaps. Although this dividing of the list doesn't seem like a real time saver, you will indeed see a dramatic difference between the execution time of the shell sort and the selection sort, for instance.

The `ShellSort()` method follows:

```
public static void ShellSort(IComparable[] ca,int size) {
      int hi=size;
      for (int gap=hi/2;gap>0;gap=gap/2) {
          for (int i=gap;i<hi;i++) {
              IComparable temp=ca[i];
              int j=i;
              for (;j>=gap
                     &&temp.CompareTo(ca[j-gap])<0;j-=gap)
                     ca[j]=ca[j-gap];
              ca[j]=temp;
          }
      }
}
```

Note that the `gap` is divided by two each time in the outer `for` loop. In the inner loop, each sublist is sorted using a selection sort (but this one places the smallest element at the beginning of the list on each pass). When `gap` becomes 1, we eventually perform one final selection sort.

The `ShellSort` often calls a `swap()` method (also defined in this class) simply to swap array elements:

```
private static void swap(IComparable[] a,int f, int s) {
   IComparable temp=a[f];
```

```
        a[f]=a[s];
        a[s]=temp;
    }
```

Later you will see a test program of the shell sort, as well as other sorting methods.

An analysis of a shell sort is notoriously difficult. In fact, the analysis of the algorithm is not complete to this day. It is known to be subquadratic; that is, its performance is better than $O(n^2)$, but not as good as $O(n \times \log n)$.

Simply by choosing different methods of selecting the gap, we can alter the performance of the shell sort. For example, if we divide `gap` by 2.2 on each pass (truncating to make the gap an integer) instead of by 2, the algorithm runs noticeably faster. Why? Nobody knows! Of course, if we use any decreasing sequence of integers for the gap, we can prove that the shell sort eventually sorts the array, but some choices for this sequence are considerably better than others. We will not attempt to do an analysis of the shell sort; it is a perfect example of an apparently simple algorithm that remains not completely understood.

☐ The Merge Sort

Now we examine a sorting algorithm that runs significantly faster than the quadratic sorts, and somewhat faster than the shell sort. It is also easy to analyze.

The merge sort assumes that you begin with two sorted sublists, which you then "merge" together into a single sorted list. We can do this merging by making a single pass through each of the two sorted sublists. For example, suppose we have the two sublists

1 5 7 9

and

2 3 6 8

To merge them, we examine the leading element of each sublist, and choose the smaller. Here, we choose the 1 from the first sublist, place it in a third (let's call it the merged) list, and advance the index in the first sublist.

1 5 7 9   2 3 6 8

1

We now compare the 5 and 2; 2 is the smaller, so we place it in the merged list, and advance the index in the second list.

1 5 7 9   2 3 6 8

1 2

We continue in this way until we run out of elements in one of the sublists; then we copy any elements remaining in the other sublist over to the merged list. Here is the process for the remaining elements in our example:

1 5 7 9 2 3 6 8

1 2 3

Here, we have $3 < 5$:

1 5 7 9 2 3 6 8

1 2 3 5

Here, we have $5 < 6$:

1 5 7 9 2 3 6 8

1 2 3 5 6

Here, $6 < 7$:

1 5 7 9 2 3 6 8

1 2 3 5 6 7

Now, $7 < 8$:

1 5 7 9 2 3 6 8

1 2 3 5 6 7 8

We see that $8 < 9$, and we have exhausted all elements from the second sublist. The only task left is to copy the remaining elements over from the first sublist; in this example, only the 9 remains.

1 5 7 9 2 3 6 8

1 2 3 5 6 7 8 9

The question that now begs to be answered is, of course, "How do I sort the two sublists?" The answer is, of course, "The same way you sorted the larger list." Thus, a merge sort is easily defined recursively; that is, doing a merge sort on a list means dividing the list in half, doing a merge sort on each half, and then merging the halves together into a sorted list in the manner just described.

The merging process is shown in the following algorithm, which merges a left and right sublist of the array `a` into an array `ta`. These elements are then copied back into the original array `a`. The boundaries of the left and right sublists are defined by `leftPos`, `rightPos`, and `rightEnd`.

```
private static void Merge(IComparable[] a, IComparable[] ta,
```

```
            int leftPos, int rightPos, int rightEnd) {
    int leftEnd=rightPos-1;
    int tmpPos=leftPos;
    int numElements=rightEnd-leftPos+1;
    while(leftPos<=leftEnd&&rightPos<=rightEnd)
        if (a[leftPos].CompareTo(a[rightPos])<0)
            ta[tmpPos++]=a[leftPos++];
        else
            ta[tmpPos++]=a[rightPos++];
    while (leftPos<=leftEnd)
        ta[tmpPos++]=a[leftPos++];
    while (rightPos<=rightEnd)
        ta[tmpPos++]=a[rightPos++];
    for (int i=0;i<numElements;i++,rightEnd--)
        a[rightEnd]=ta[rightEnd];
}
```

Of course, once we know how to merge, doing the merge sort is easy. We proceed by first dividing the array and recursively calling merge sort for the left and right subarrays and then finally merging them. The merge sort is only four lines of code.

```
public static void MergeSort(IComparable[] a, int size) {
      IComparable[] ta = new IComparable[size];//Set up temporary array
      MergeSort(a,ta,0,size-1);
}

public static void MergeSort(IComparable[] a,IComparable[] ta,
               int left,int right) {
      if (left<right) {
            int center=(left+right)/2;//Compute the midpoint
            MergeSort(a,ta,left,center);//Do a merge sort on left
            MergeSort(a,ta,center+1,right);//Do a merge sort on right
            Merge(a,ta,left,center+1,right);//Merge left and right
      }
}
```

An analysis of merge sort is pretty straightforward. In order to do a merge sort, we first divide the list in half, then merge the two halves together. The merging obviously runs in linear time, but at each stage in the recursion the list is divided in half, so the merge sort deals with a list half the size of the original as we progress to deeper levels in the recursion. This halving of the work runs in logarithmic time, so the merge sort is $O(n \times \log n)$.

A drawback to the merge sort is that it appears necessary to create another array for the merging process. This may present a problem if memory is limited.

Figure 12.6

The Quick Sort

The quick sort may be the fastest general-purpose sorting algorithm known. It uses a recursive technique to divide the list into sublists, and then sorts the sublists in the same way a merge sort does. However, quick sort requires no extra memory, unlike the merge sort.

Here is how the quick sort is done; start with, say, the following list:

8 3 9 1 6 –12 30 3 102 7 5 1

Now, pick an item in this list. Any one will do, so choose the first: 8. This becomes the "partition point" or the "pivot point." We must rearrange the list so that everything smaller than the partition point falls to the left of it, and everything larger than it falls to the right of it (see Figure 12.6).

It doesn't matter if the items to the left are sorted, as long as they are all smaller than the partition point. Likewise, the only criteria for the items to the right is that each be larger than the partition point. Actually, the partition value may appear multiple times in the list; in this case, it doesn't matter if any one of these falls to the left or to the right of the partition point.

Without yet considering how this partitioning is to be done, do the following: Repeat the quick sort on the left sublist, and then the right sublist. If a sublist has zero or one items in it, it is sorted. This is clearly a recursive definition. Succinctly, to do a quick sort if the list has more than one item in it:

- Pick a pivot point in the list and partition the list so that everything less than the pivot point falls to the left of it (the left sublist), and everything larger than the pivot point falls to the right of it (the right sublist). Values equal to the pivot point can fall to the left or right.
- Do a quick sort on the left sublist.
- Do a quick sort on the right sublist.

Because you are continually dividing lists up into sublists, you will eventually encounter sublists with only one item in them; these sublists are already sorted, and we back up to a higher point in our recursion.

The Partition Stage

Partitioning the list in the quick sort isn't as hard as you might think. Take this example list:

<u>7</u> 3 9 1 6 4 5 0 –1 8 6 1

To move 7 into position, leave it where it is for the moment, and take note of the index just to the right of the partition point; we will call this the "swap pointer": The enlarged number is the number we are testing against the pivot; the underlined number is the number we will swap with the test number, if necessary. (These may be the same number.)

7 **3** 9 1 6 4 5 0 −1 8 6 1

Because 3 < 7, we will "swap it with itself." Now, advance the swap pointer to the next element, 9, and examine the element 9.

7 3 **9** 1 6 4 5 0 −1 8 6 1

Nine is larger than 7, so we don't do anything to it. Here we leave the swap pointer where it is, and advance to the next element.

7 3 9 **1** 6 4 5 0 −1 8 6 1

Note that 1 < 7, so we swap it with the element in the swap pointer position; here, the 9. After the swap, we advance the swap pointer, and examine the next element. Basically, the swap pointer is advanced only when a swap occurs.

7 3 1 9 **6** 4 5 0 −1 8 6 1

We continue in this way until we have examined and possibly swapped out the last element in the list:

7 3 1 6 9 **4** 5 0 −1 8 6 1

(6 < 7: swap occurs, advance swap pointer.)

7 3 1 6 4 9 **5** 0 −1 8 6 1

(4 < 7: swap occurs, advance swap pointer.)

7 3 1 6 4 5 9 **0** −1 8 6 1

(5 < 7: swap occurs, advance swap pointer.)

7 3 1 6 4 5 0 9 **−1** 8 6 1

(0 < 7: swap occurs, advance swap pointer.)

7 3 1 6 4 5 0 −1 9 **8** 6 1

(−1 < 7: swap occurs, advance swap pointer.)

7 3 1 6 4 5 0 −1 9 8 **6** 1

(8 > 7: swap does not occur, do not advance swap pointer.)

7 3 1 6 4 5 0 −1 6 8 9 **1**

(6 < 7: swap occurs, advance swap pointer.)

7 3 1 6 4 5 0 −1 6 1 9 8

(1 < 7: swap occurs, advance swap pointer.)

Here, the final 1 is just preceding the swap pointer position, and we do one last swap; we swap the pivot item with that item:

1 3 1 6 4 5 0 −1 6 **7** 9 8

This list is now partitioned at the 7. This partitioning can be modified to work on any sublist; we simply specify the starting and ending indices of the sublist. We know nothing about the order of the items in the left or right sublists, but doing a quick sort on each sublist will straighten them out.

Here is the `QuickSort()` method. You can see that it follows the algorithm described earlier. It also calls the `swap()` method to swap items.

```
public static void QuickSort(IComparable[] a, int size) {
   RecurseQuickSort(a,0,size-1);
}

private static void RecurseQuickSort(IComparable[] a,
   int lo, int hi) {
   int pivot;
   if (lo<hi) {
      pivot=partition(a,lo,hi);
      RecurseQuickSort(a,lo,pivot-1);
      RecurseQuickSort(a,pivot+1,hi);
   }
}

private static int partition(IComparable[] a, int lo, int hi) {
   int pivot=lo;
   IComparable pivotKey=a[lo];
   for (int i=lo+1;i<=hi;i++)
      if (a[i].CompareTo(pivotKey)<0)
         swap(a,++pivot,i);
   swap(a,lo,pivot);
   return pivot;
}
```

We will see the quick sort compared to the other sorts in a forthcoming test program. We should note that the quick sort has a serious drawback: Its worst case performance has $O(n^2)$ running time! What is the worst case? When the list is already sorted, or nearly sorted. Why? Consider the following argument:

1. If we consistently choose the first element as the partition element (as we have done here), the partitioning step consistently produces a small (possibly empty) left sublist, and a very long right sublist.

TABLE 12.1

Algorithm	Complexity
Bubble Sort	$O(n^2)$
Selection Sort	$O(n^2)$
Insertion Sort	$O(n^2)$
Shell Sort	Better than $O(n^2)$ but not as fast as $O(n \times \log n)$
Merge Sort	$O(n \times \log n)$
Quick Sort	$O(n \times \log n)$
Heap Sort	$O(n \times \log n)$

2. When we quick sort on these unbalanced sublists, the right sublist takes almost as long to process as the original list. Thus, we get linear, rather than logarithmic, performance at this stage.
3. The combination of linear efficiency at the partition stage and linear efficiency at the quick sort stage yields a quadratic worst case running time.

There are many ways to deal with this; first, do *not* choose the first (or last) element as the partition. Choosing the middle element, or even a random element from the list, is much better.

Analysis Summary of Sorting

To summarize, Table 12.1 compares the complexity of the sorts we have seen.

Included in this table is a heap sort, which we will cover in the section on heaps in Chapter 14.

Class: Sorter

In order to encapsulate sorting methods together you can use the `Sorter` class, which contains a set of static methods:

- `public static void Sort(IComparable[] array, int size, SortAlgorithm choice);`
- `public static void BubbleSort(IComparable[] array, int size);`
- `public static void SelectionSort(IComparable[] array, int size);`
- `public static void InsertionSort(IComparable[] array, int size);`
- `public static void ShellSort(IComparable[] array, int size);`

- `public static void MergeSort(IComparable[] array, int size);`
- `public static void QuickSort(IComparable[] array, int size);`
- `public static void HeapSort(IComparable[] array, int size);`

The `SortAlgorithm` is an enumeration type that represents the various choices of sorting. It is declared in the same file as the sorter class (Sorter.cs).

```
public enum SortAlgorithm {
        BubbleSort,
        SelectionSort,
        InsertionSort,
        ShellSort,
        MergeSort,
        QuickSort,
        HeapSort
}
```

This enumeration allows you to choose the sorting method when calling `Sort()`, as in:

```
String[] sortMe = {"I","am","unsorted?"};
Sorter.Sort(sortMe,sortMe.Length,SortAlgorithm.ShellSort);
```

Listing 12.1 contains the entire `Sorter` class, including the definitions of `BubbleSort()` and `SelectionSort()`.

Listing 12.1

```
using System;

public enum SortAlgorithm {
        BubbleSort,
        SelectionSort,
        InsertionSort,
        ShellSort,
        MergeSort,
        QuickSort,
        HeapSort
}

public class Sorter {
```

(continued)

```
public static void Sort(IComparable[] array,int numberOfElements,
        SortAlgorithm choice) {
   switch (choice) {
         case SortAlgorithm.BubbleSort:
               BubbleSort(array,numberOfElements);
               break;
         case SortAlgorithm.SelectionSort:
               SelectionSort(array,numberOfElements);
               break;
         case SortAlgorithm.InsertionSort:
               InsertionSort(array,numberOfElements);
               break;
         case SortAlgorithm.ShellSort:
               ShellSort(array,numberOfElements);
               break;
         case SortAlgorithm.MergeSort:
               MergeSort(array,numberOfElements);
               break;
         case SortAlgorithm.QuickSort:
               QuickSort(array,numberOfElements);
               break;
         case SortAlgorithm.HeapSort:
               HeapSort(array,numberOfElements);
               break;
         default:
               throw new ArgumentException
               ("Invalid algorithm choice");
   }
}

public static void BubbleSort(IComparable[] array,int size) {
   int top=size-1;
   bool done=false;
   while (!done) {
      done=true;
      for (int i=0;i<top;i++) {
         if (array[i+1].CompareTo(array[i])<0) {
            done=false;
            swap(array,i,i+1);
         }
      }
      top--;
   }
}

public static void HeapSort(IComparable[] a,int size) {
   Heap heap=new Heap(a.Length);
   foreach(IComparable item in a) heap.Insert(item);
   for(int index=0;index<a.Length;index++) {
         a[index]=heap.Peek();
```

(continued)

```
            heap.Remove();
        }
    }

    public static void SelectionSort(IComparable[] array,int size) {
        if (size==0) return;
        int top=size-1;
        int indexOfLargest;
        do {
            indexOfLargest=0;
            for (int i=1;i<=top;i++)
                if (array[indexOfLargest].CompareTo(array[i])<0)
                    indexOfLargest=i;
            swap(array,top,indexOfLargest);
            top--;
        } while (top>0);
    }

    public static void InsertionSort(IComparable[] array, int size) {
        IComparable temp; int j;
        if (array.Length<2) return;
        for (int i=1; i<size; i++) {
                temp=array[i];
                for (j=i; j>0 && temp.CompareTo(array[j-1])<0; j--)
                        array[j]=array[j-1];
                array[j]=temp;
        }
    }

    public static void ShellSort(IComparable[] ca,int size) {
            int hi=size;
            for (int gap=hi/2;gap>0;gap=gap/2) {
                for (int i=gap;i<hi;i++) {
                    IComparable temp=ca[i];
                    int j=i;
                    for (;j>=gap
                    &&temp.CompareTo(ca[j-gap])<0;j-=gap)
                    ca[j]=ca[j-gap];
                    ca[j]=temp;
                }
            }
    }

    public static void MergeSort(IComparable[] a, int size) {
           IComparable[] ta = new IComparable[size];
           MergeSort(a,ta,0,size-1);
    }

    public static void MergeSort(IComparable[] a,IComparable[] ta,
                    int left,int right) {
```

(continued)

```
        if (left<right) {
            int center=(left+right)/2;
            MergeSort(a,ta,left,center);
            MergeSort(a,ta,center+1,right);
            Merge(a,ta,left,center+1,right);
        }
    }

    private static void Merge(IComparable[] a,IComparable[] ta,
                int leftPos,int rightPos,int rightEnd) {
        int leftEnd=rightPos-1;
        int tmpPos=leftPos;
        int numElements=rightEnd-leftPos+1;
        while(leftPos<=leftEnd&&rightPos<=rightEnd)
            if (a[leftPos].CompareTo(a[rightPos])<0)
                ta[tmpPos++]=a[leftPos++];
            else
                ta[tmpPos++]=a[rightPos++];
        while (leftPos<=leftEnd)
            ta[tmpPos++]=a[leftPos++];
        while (rightPos<=rightEnd)
            ta[tmpPos++]=a[rightPos++];
        for (int i=0;i<numElements;i++,rightEnd--)
            a[rightEnd]=ta[rightEnd];
    }

    public static void QuickSort(IComparable[] a, int size) {
      RecurseQuickSort(a,0,size-1);
    }



    private static void RecurseQuickSort(IComparable[] a,
      int lo, int hi) {
      int pivot;
      if (lo<hi) {
         pivot=partition(a,lo,hi);
         RecurseQuickSort(a,lo,pivot-1);
         RecurseQuickSort(a,pivot+1,hi);
      }
    }

    private static int partition(IComparable[] a, int lo, int hi) {
      int pivot=lo;
      IComparable pivotKey=a[lo];
      for (int i=lo+1;i<=hi;i++)
         if (a[i].CompareTo(pivotKey)<0)
            swap(a,++pivot,i);
      swap(a,lo,pivot);
      return pivot;
    }
```

(continued)

```
   private static void swap(IComparable[] a,int f, int s) {
      IComparable temp=a[f];
      a[f]=a[s];
      a[s]=temp;
   }
}
```

Note that the `Sorter` class also has a `HeapSort()` method. We will discuss the heap sort after we cover heaps later in the text.

Listing 12.2 is a program to test the various sorting methods. It times each algorithm, using a timer.

Listing 12.2

```
using System;
public class TestSorter {
   static void Main() {

      //Make a Random object to produce random integers
      Random rnd=new Random();

      //The list of algorithms to test
      SortAlgorithm[] alg={SortAlgorithm.BubbleSort,
      SortAlgorithm.SelectionSort,
      SortAlgorithm.ShellSort,
      SortAlgorithm.QuickSort};

      //Prompt the user for the array size
      Console.Write("Enter # of random integers to sort: ");
      int numInts=Int32.Parse(Console.ReadLine());

      //One pass represents the test of a single sort algorithm
      for (int pass=0;pass<alg.Length;pass++) {

      //Create an array of random integers
      //int implements IComparable interface
      IComparable[] numbers=new IComparable[numInts];
      for (int index=0;index<numbers.Length;index++)
            numbers[index]=(IComparable)rnd.Next();
      //Done producing random ints

      //Start the timer
      //There are 10 million ticks per second
      long start=DateTime.Now.Ticks;
```

(continued)

```
      //Begin sorting-algorithm used is last parameter
      Sorter.Sort(numbers,numbers.Length,alg[pass]);
      //Sorting finished

      //Stop the timer
      long stop=DateTime.Now.Ticks;

      //# ticks expired is the difference of stop-start
      //Divide by 10 million (a floating point) to get seconds
      Console.WriteLine(alg[pass]+" took "
            +(stop-start)/10000000.0+" seconds.");

      }
   }
}
```

Here is the algorithm running a test on the four sorts; each sorts an array of 10,000 random integers.

```
Enter the # of random integers you want to sort: 10000
BubbleSort took 15.0216 seconds.
SelectionSort took 5.3777328 seconds.
ShellSort took 0.0801152 seconds.
QuickSort took 0.050072 seconds.
```

If you try 100,000 integers (on my PC), the bubble sort and selection sort will take around 1000 to 2000 seconds *each* to sort them, whereas the shell sort and selection sort will still take less than a second! If you try even larger quantities, this difference in performance becomes even more staggering.

▪ SEARCHING

Why sort? This should be obvious to anyone who has used the phone book. Finding someone's number would be much more difficult if the names in the phone book were not in any particular order!

When you traverse in sequence the elements in a list looking for a particular item, this is called a "sequential search." Such an algorithm clearly runs in linear time. If a list is large, this can be time consuming; for example, consider an unsorted list containing 1 billion items. On the average, it will take 500 million lookups to find some item. This number is prohibitive, even for modern machines.

We can consider a different type of search, called a "binary search." Suppose you have a list of items sorted from smallest to largest:

1. If the list has more than one item in it:
   - Divide the list into two halves (a left sublist and a right sublist), and examine the item in the middle. If the list has an even number of items, it has two items in the middle; choose the one to the left as the middle item.
   - If the item you are looking for is larger than this middle item, perform a binary search on the right sublist.
   - If the item you are looking for is smaller than this middle item, perform a binary search on the left sublist.
   - If the item you are looking for is this middle item, you're finished.
2. If the list has one item in it, the item is either what you are looking for or it isn't. Either way, you're finished.
3. If the list has zero items in it, the item you are looking for is not in the list.

This is clearly a recursive definition. Let's consider an example:

−3 0 1 4 6 8 9 22 35 44 107 222

Suppose we are looking for the integer 4 in this list; first, locate the middle element of this list. Because it has an even number of items, the two middle items are 8 and 9. Choose the left-hand item: 8. Because $4 < 8$, we can disregard the right half of this list (and the middle item 8 as well). We continue with a binary search of this sublist:

−3 0 1 4 6

The middle item is 1. Because $4 > 1$, we continue with a binary search of this sublist.

4 6

The middle item of this list is 4 (the one on the left of the two middle items). This is what we were looking for.

Now, take the same list, and look for an item that isn't in the list, say 5. We get the same sequence of sublists:

−3 0 1 4 6 8 9 22 35 44 107 222

−3 0 1 4 6

4 6

4 is the middle item of this sublist. Because $5 > 4$, we can disregard the left sublist (empty) and the middle point 4. This yields the sublist

6

This is a list with one item; it is either the item we are looking for or it isn't. In this case, it isn't.

From these tiny examples, the binary search doesn't seem to be much of a time saver. However, consider a sorted list with a billion items in it. Because you basically discard half of the list at every stage in a binary search, and because 1 billion < 2^{30}, a binary search would take *at most* 30 comparisons to either find an item or discover that it isn't in the list. Compare this to the average number of 500 *million* lookups for a sequential search!

Clearly, a binary search runs in logarithmic time because it is able to discard half of any sublist after it examines its middle element. This yields O(log*n*), or logarithmic performance.

Class: Searcher

Searcher (see Listing 12.4) is a class containing two static methods:

- `public static int SequentialSearch(Object target, Object[] array,int size);`
- `public static int BinarySearch(IComparable target, IComparable[] array, int lo, int hi);`

The `SequentialSearch()` method can search an array for any object. The `Equals()` method of `Object` should be overridden to provide value equality for the items as opposed to referential equality (if that is in fact what you wish).

The `BinarySearch()` method accepts an array of `IComparable` items; thus, the `BinarySearch()` can be used only on objects for which a `CompareTo()` method is defined. This method will not function properly on an unsorted array.

If the item we are looking for is not in the array, both sequential search and binary search throw a `NotFoundException`, which is defined in Listing 12.3.

Listing 12.3

```
using System;
public class NotFoundException:Exception {
      public NotFoundException() {}
      public NotFoundException(String s):base(s) {}
}
```

Listing 12.4

```
using System;
public class Searcher {

   public static int SequentialSearch(Object target,
      Object[] array,int size) {

      //Traverse the array sequentially
      for (int index=0;index<size;index++)
      //Use Equals-assumes subclass overrides
         if (target.Equals(array[index]))
            return index;

      //If you got all the way thru the for loop
      //The item wasn't in the array
      throw new NotFoundException
      ("Target not found by sequential search.");
   }

   public static int BinarySearch(IComparable target,
      IComparable[] array,int lo, int hi) {
      int answer=0;

      //Executes as long as lo index<=hi
      if (lo<=hi) {
      //Find the middle index between lo and hi

         int mid=(lo+hi)/2;

      //if this is it, great
         if (array[mid].CompareTo(target)==0) answer=mid;

      //if it's smaller than what you're looking for
      //continue search in lower half of sublist
         else if (array[mid].CompareTo(target)<0)
            answer=BinarySearch(target,array,mid+1,hi);

      //if it's larger than what you're looking for
      //continue search in upper half of sublist
         else answer=BinarySearch(target,array,lo,mid-1);

      //if lo>hi, you never found the item
      } else throw new NotFoundException
            ("Target not found by binary search.");

      //If you got out here, you found the item
      return answer;
   }

}
```

The test program in Listing 12.5 generates an array of random integers; the size of this array is determined by the user. It makes a second array identical to the first, and sorts the second array. It prompts the user to enter a target integer, and will then execute a sequential search for that integer in the unsorted array, and a binary search for the same item in the sorted array.

The program makes no attempt to compare the efficiency of the two searching methods. This would be an interesting exercise for you.

Listing 12.5

```
using System;
public class TestSearcher {
   public static void Main() {
      Random rnd=new Random();

      Console.Write("Enter # of ints to generate: ");
      int numInts=Int32.Parse(Console.ReadLine());
      IComparable[] array = new IComparable[numInts];
      IComparable[] array2 = new IComparable[numInts];

      for (int index=0;index<array.Length;index++) {
            array[index]=(IComparable)rnd.Next(array.Length);
            array2[index]=array[index];
      }

      Console.WriteLine("Sorting the array.");
      Sorter.QuickSort(array2,array2.Length);

      bool goAgain=true;

      while (goAgain) {

            goAgain=false;

            Console.Write("Enter target integer: ");
            int target=Int32.Parse(Console.ReadLine());

         try {
            int position=Searcher.SequentialSearch(
                  (IComparable)target,array,array.Length);
            Console.WriteLine(target+" found at index "
                  +position+" in the unsorted array.");

            position=Searcher.BinarySearch((IComparable)target,
                  array2,0,array2.Length-1);
            Console.WriteLine(target+" found at index "
                  +position+" in the sorted array.");
```

(continued)

```
            } catch (NotFoundException) {
              Console.WriteLine(target+" not in the array.");
              goAgain=true;
            }

        }//End while

    }
}

Enter # of ints to generate: 1000000
Sorting the array.
Enter target integer: 69
69 not in the array.
Enter target integer: 66
66 found at index 753618 in the unsorted array.
66 found at index 63 in the sorted array.
```

Is the binary search preferable to the sequential search? The short answer is "sometimes." Remember:

- A binary search can be done only on a sorted list, and the fastest general-purpose sorting algorithm is O(*n*log*n*). If items are added/deleted frequently, re-sorting the modified list can be a time-consuming step.
- A short list of items can be searched quickly using a sequential search; there is no appreciable difference between an O(*n*) search and an O(log*n*) search when *n* is small.

chapter 13

Linear Data Structures

The concept of data structures is central to good programming. A data structure is a particular representation of data. The purpose of a data structure varies; sometimes it exists to control access to the data, to provide more convenient access to the data, or to enhance performance by implementing efficient techniques in organizing the data. Often, a data structure is intended to do a combination of these things, stressing varying degrees of importance in each category.

■ SELF-REFERENCING CLASSES

The biggest limitation of an array is that it is fixed in size; it cannot "grow" if necessary. For this reason, we develop other data structures that have this capability. This is often done by using a class that references itself.

Consider the `Node` class, from Listing 13.1.

Listing 13.1

```
using System;
public class Node {

      //Fields
      Object datum;
      Node next;

      //Constructors
      public Node(Object item,Node link) {
            datum=item;
            next=link;
      }

      //Properties
      public Object Datum {
            get {return datum;}
      }

      public Node Next {
            get {return next;}
      }
}
```

This class has two fields:

- datum, which references an Object
- next, which references a Node type (the very name of the class!)

This circular definition might seem odd at first, but it allows us to build complicated and flexible data structures. Suppose, for example, we create something of type Node:

```
Node n = new Node("Hi!");
```

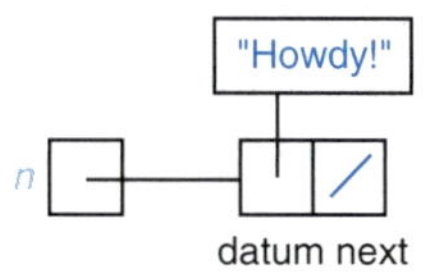

Figure 13.1

Note that a String is an Object, and totally suitable as an argument. This produces something like Figure 13.1.

The slash used in the drawing represents the null value for the field next. Now we can create another Node and attach it to the first just by assigning a reference:

```
Node n2 = new Node("This is cool!",n);
```

Here we pass in the value of n (which is just a reference) as the second argument to the Node constructor. This assigns the next field of n2 to reference the same object that n references (see Figure 13.2).

There is no reason why we can't continue forming such a chain and make it as long as we like. We can also traverse the elements in this chain, as long as we know where the head of the chain is. For example, we can display the two elements in this chain by doing something like this:

```
Node traveler = n2;
while (traveler!=null) {
Console.WriteLine(traveler.Datum);
traveler=traveler.Next;
}
```

This would produce the output:

```
This is cool!
Hello!
```

Why? The `Node` reference traveler begins by referencing the object pointed at by `n2` (see Figure 13.3).

We perform the test in the `while` loop; `traveler` is not null (it points at something), so we enter the loop. We first display `traveler.Datum`, which is, at this point, "This is cool!" (Note that we use the properties `Datum` and `Next`, because the fields `datum` and `next` are private—we could make these public if we want to.) We then execute the statement `traveler=traveler.Next;` which moves `traveler` to reference what `traveler.Next` references, namely, `n` (see Figure 13.4).

The variable `traveler` is still not null, so we enter the body of the `while` loop, display "Howdy!", and then execute `traveler=traveler.Next` again. This time, however, `traveler.Next` is null, so traveler becomes null, as seen in Figure 13.5.

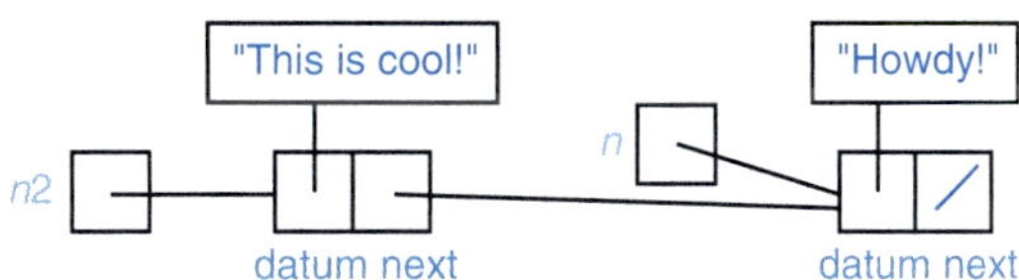

Figure 13.2

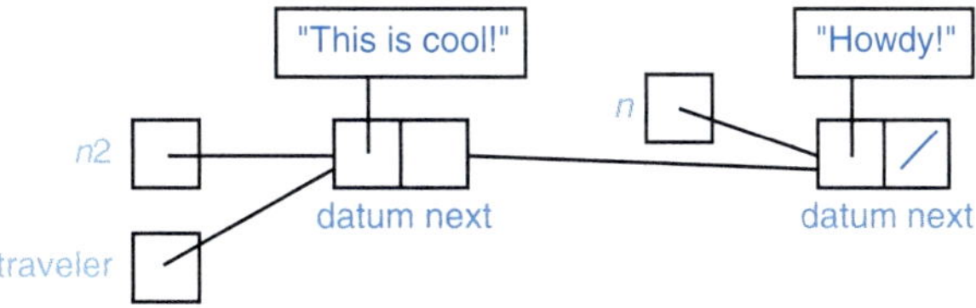

Figure 13.3

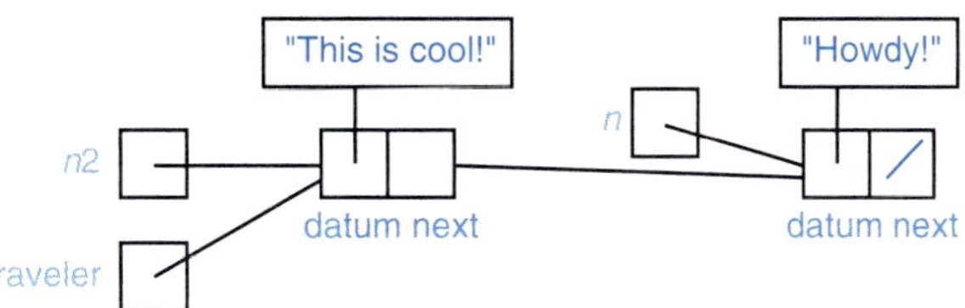

Figure 13.4

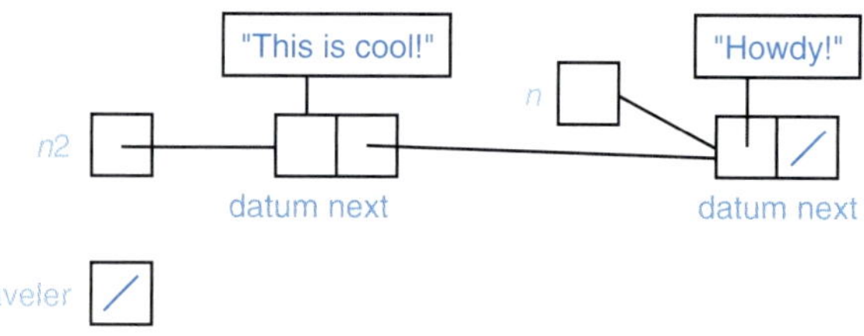

Figure 13.5

Now that `traveler` is null, it fails the test of the `while` loop, and the loop terminates. Note that we don't need to maintain a separate reference `n`, `n2`, `n3`, . . . for each node in the chain. In fact, we only need to know where the head of the chain is to traverse its entire length.

We now examine and design concrete classes that have this functionality.

■ STACKS

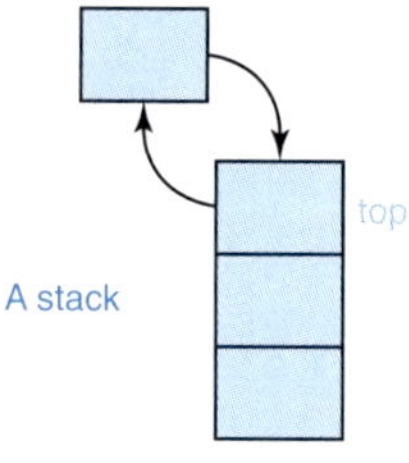

Figure 13.6

A stack is a data structure that works pretty much like it sounds: it represents a stack of items. If you place item X on a stack, then place more items on top of it, you cannot get to item X again until you have removed the items above it (see Figure 13.6).

This is the rule of the stack data structure; it should be a linear structure (i.e., a chain of items), but the only one you can look at and/or remove is the item on the "top." Also, items can only be placed on a stack at the top. Such a data structure is said to be a LIFO (last in-first out) structure.

A stack with no elements is said to be, amazingly, empty. If you attempt to remove an item from an empty stack or look at the top element of an empty stack, this should generate an error. Thus, for the `Stack` class (and for other classes) we will provide the definition for an `EmptyException`:

```
using System;
public class EmptyException:Exception {
      public EmptyException() {}
      public EmptyException(String s):base(s) {}
}
```

At the very least, a stack should be able to provide properties and/or methods to

- Tell whether or not the stack is empty
- Indicate how many items are on the stack
- Put an item on top of the stack (traditionally called a push)
- Look at the item on the top of the stack without removing it (peek)
- Remove the item on the top of the stack (pop)

- Clear the stack (remove all its items)
- Return a string representation of the items on the stack

Class: Stack

We will develop a `Stack` class with all the functionality required. To make it as flexible as possible, we will create a stack by chaining items together using the `Node` class. Here is the `Node` class again:

```
using System;
public class Node {
      Object datum;
      Node next;
      public Node(Object item,Node link) {
            datum=item;
            next=link;
      }
      public Object Datum {
            get {return datum;}
      }
      public Node Next {
            get {return next;}
      }
}
```

To build a stack chain, we really only need to know where the top is. This is perfect for using a linked chain. Thus, the fields in a stack could be the following:

```
public class Stack {
   Node top;
   int numElements;
//...
}
```

The field `top` will always point at the top of the stack, and `numElements` will keep a record of how many items are on the stack. We increment `numElements` every time we push something on the stack, and decrement it every time we pop something off. Note that without this field, getting the number of elements in a chain would mean traveling through them and counting as we go. This would be far too time consuming.

The `Stack()` constructor follows; it simply creates an empty `Stack`. Thus, `top` is null and `numElements` is 0 (their default values).

```
public Stack() {}
```

`Stack` implements `Empty` as a read-only property and `Size()` as a method:

```
public bool Empty {
   get {return top==null;}
}
```

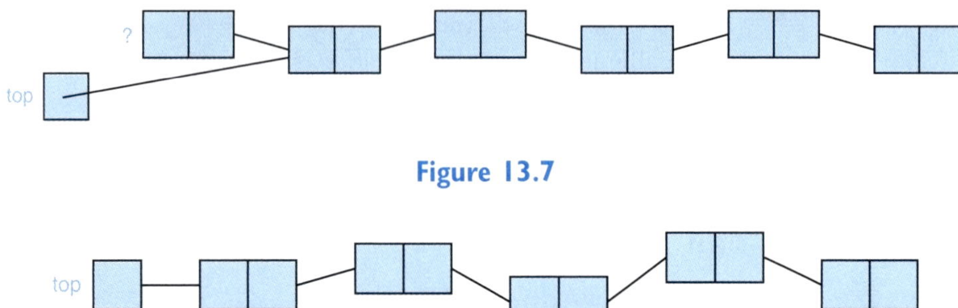

Figure 13.7

Figure 13.8

```
public int Size() {
   return numElements;
}
```

The Peek() method simply returns the Object on the top of the stack, but it can throw an EmptyException if the stack is empty.

```
public Object Peek() {
   if (Empty) throw new EmptyException("Stack is empty!");
   return top.Datum;
}
```

The Pop() method actually removes the item from the top of the stack. It does this simply by moving to reference the next node in the stack (i.e., top=top.Next).

```
public void Pop() {
   if (Empty) throw new EmptyException("Stack is empty!");
   top=top.Next;
   numElements--;
}
```

What happens to the old Node that used to be the top of the Stack (see Figure 13.7)?

When top moves to point at the next node, nothing remains pointing at the old top Node. The garbage collector will discover this Node is now inaccessible, and will return it to the operating system, as shown in Figure 13.8.

Pushing an item on the stack means creating a new node, pointing the next field of that node to the top of the stack, and then moving the top pointer to point at the new node (which is now the new top of the stack).

```
public void Push(Object item) {
   Node newNode=new Node(item,top);
   top=newNode;
   numElements++;
}
```

There is one more method here, added for convenience. We override the `ToString()` method inherited from `Object`. It simply traverses the stack from top to bottom, adding each item to a `String`, which is then returned. This is a handy way of seeing all the items on the stack. Of course, the type of the actual items that the stack is storing should override `ToString()` as well.

```
public override String ToString() {
   String outString="";
   Node traveler=top;
   while(traveler!=null) {
         outString=outString+" "+traveler.Datum.ToString();
         traveler=traveler.Next;
   }
   return outString;
}
```

The `Stack` class in Listing 13.2 restricts access to the data in the manner specified in our definition of a stack. It does everything we said a stack should do. Here is the `Stack` class in its entirety:

Listing 13.2

```
using System;
public class Stack {

   Node top;
   int numElements;

   public Stack() {}

   public bool Empty {
      get {return top==null;}
   }

   public Object Peek() {
      if (Empty) throw new EmptyException("Stack is empty!");
      return top.Datum;
   }

   public void Pop() {
      if (Empty) throw new EmptyException("Stack is empty!");
      top=top.Next;
      numElements--;
   }

   public void Push(Object item) {
      Node newNode=new Node(item,top);
      top=newNode;
```

(continued)

```
        numElements++;
    }

    public int Size() {
        return numElements;
    }

    public void Clear() {
            while (!Empty) Pop();
    }

    public override String ToString() {
        String outString="";
        Node traveler=top;
        while(traveler!=null) {
                outString=outString+" "+traveler.Datum.ToString();
                traveler=traveler.Next;
        }
        return outString;
    }
}
```

A stack is a very efficient data structure, simply because of the way you are limited in accessing its elements. In fact, the only element you can access is the top! For this reason, most of the `Stack` class methods/properties run in constant time, as you can see from Table 13.1.

Note that the `ToString` and `Clear` methods run in linear time. This is because both methods pass through each item on the stack. There may be a more efficient way to

TABLE 13.1

Constructor/Method/Property	***T*(*n*)**
`public Stack()`	O(1)
`public bool Empty;`	O(1)
`public Object Peek();`	O(1)
`public void Pop();`	O(1)
`public void Push(Object item);`	O(1)
`public int Size();`	O(1)
`public void Clear();`	O(*n*)
`public override String ToString();`	O(*n*)

clear the stack than by popping off each element, as this Clear method does. It may be an interesting exercise for you to consider this.

☐ Class: StackArray

There is no reason why we have to use a chain to implement a stack. In fact, the whole point of data structures, objects, and abstract data types (ADTs) is that you generally don't know what the underlying implementation is! You are usually given information for only the properties and methods you have access to.

We could use an array to implement a stack. Of course, because an array is fixed in size, any data structure using an array for its underpinnings could eventually "fill up." Because this is a possibility, we define a new Exception called FullException:

```
using System;
public class FullException:Exception {
      public FullException() {}
      public FullException(String s):base(s) {}
}
```

The fields in the StackArray class are these:

```
public class StackArray {
   int top;
   int maxSize;
   Object[] element;
//...
}
```

The StackArray has a maxSize field; this will be used by the constructor to create an array of Objects of the appropriate size, and it will also serve to tell us how many items can be placed on the stack before it becomes full.

An array can easily behave like a stack; the integer top will be an index, starting at −1. If top equals −1, this signifies an empty stack. If top equals maxSize-1, this is a full stack. Except when the stack is empty, top indexes the topmost item of the stack.

The array is indicated here in the field Object[] element. Only a reference to an array exists initially. We will not create the array until the constructor is called (for only then will we know how large the array should be).

The StackArray constructor follows; it accepts an int as a parameter. This int represents the maximum number of elements that can be placed on the stack (and the size of the array).

```
public StackArray(int max) {
   top=-1;
   maxSize=max;
   element=new Object[max];
}
```

The `Empty` and `Full` properties are read-only:

```
public bool Empty {
   get {return top==-1;}
}

   public bool Full {
      get {return top==maxSize-1;}
   }
```

The `Size` method returns how many items are on the stack. Because C# array indices start with 0, the method rightly returns the value `top+1`:

```
public int Size() {
   return top+1;
}
```

If the stack is not full, the `Push()` method increments the index `top`, then sets that slot in the array to the new element.

```
public void Push(Object item) {
   if (Full) throw new FullException("Stack is full!");
   element[++top]=item;
}
```

It is important to increment `top` before the insertion, or the new element will replace the element that is already there.

The `Peek` method simply returns the element indexed by `top`:

```
public Object Peek() {
   if (Empty) throw new EmptyException("Stack is empty!");
   return element[top];
}
```

The `Pop()` method simply decrements `top`, but it first sets `element[top]` to null. Whatever item `element[top]` was pointing at is no longer referenced, and the garbage collector will remove it. This is entirely appropriate; you should no longer have access to the item after it is popped. If you want to see it, peek before you pop.

```
public void Pop() {
   if (Empty) throw new EmptyException("Stack is empty!");
   element[top--]=null;
}
```

The `Clear()` method simply calls the `Pop()` method until the stack is empty:

```
public void Clear() {
   while (!Empty) Pop();
}
```

Of course, we provide a `ToString()` method for the `StackArray` class as well. It traverses the stack by using an index.

```
public override String ToString() {
   String ans="";
   int traveler=top;
   while (traveler!=0) {
         ans=ans+" "+element[traveler].ToString();
         traveler--;
   }
   return ans;
}
```

For completeness, Listing 13.3 shows the entire `StackArray` class.

Listing 13.3

```
using System;
public class StackArray {

   int top;
   int maxSize;
   Object[] element;

   public StackArray(int max) {
      top=-1;
      maxSize=max;
      element=new Object[max];
   }

   public bool Empty {
      get {return top==-1;}
   }

   public bool Full {
      get {return top==maxSize-1;}
   }

   public Object Peek() {
      if (Empty) throw new EmptyException("Stack is empty!");
      return element[top];
   }

   public void Pop() {
      if (Empty) throw new EmptyException("Stack is empty!");
      element[top--]=null;
   }
```

(continued)

```
   public void Push(Object item) {
      if (Full) throw new FullException("Stack is full!");
      element[++top]=item;
   }

   public int Size() {
      return top+1;
   }

   public void Clear() {
      while (!Empty) Pop();
   }

   public override String ToString() {
      String ans="";
      int traveler=top;
      while (traveler!=0) {
            ans=ans+" "+element[traveler].ToString();
            traveler--;
      }
      return ans;
   }
}
```

It's about time we take a look at how a stack behaves. The program in Listing 13.4 creates a stack (in this case, a `StackArray` object), and then gives the user the option of pushing, peeking, and popping items, displaying the contents of the stack, and clearing it. By modifying only one line in this program, you can test the chain implementation of a stack as well.

Listing 13.4

```
using System;
public class TestStackArray {
    static void Main() {
      StackArray stack=new StackArray(1000);
      String result="";

      DisplayHeader();
      char option = Console.ReadLine()[0];
      while (option!='Q') {
            switch (option) {
                  case 'U':
                  Console.Write("Enter item: ");
```

(continued)

```
                stack.Push(Console.ReadLine());
                break;

                case 'E':
                try {
                      result=(String)stack.Peek();
                } catch (EmptyException ne) {
                      Console.WriteLine(ne);
                }
                Console.WriteLine(result);
                break;

                case 'O':
                try {
                      stack.Pop();
                } catch (EmptyException ne) {
                      Console.WriteLine(ne);
                }
                break;

                case 'S':
                Console.WriteLine(stack.ToString());
                break;

                case 'X':
                stack.Clear();
                break;

                default:
                Console.WriteLine("Invalid option");
                break;
          }
          DisplayHeader();
          option = Console.ReadLine()[0];
      }
    }

    static void DisplayHeader() {
          Console.WriteLine("Enter one of the following:");
          Console.WriteLine("U - push");
          Console.WriteLine("E - peek");
          Console.WriteLine("O - pop");
          Console.WriteLine("S - show stack");
          Console.WriteLine("X - clear stack");
          Console.WriteLine("Q - quit");
          Console.Write("==> ");

    }

}
```

Here is a test run of the program:

```
Enter one of the following:
U - push
E - peek
O - pop
S - show stack
X - clear stack
Q - quit
==> U
Enter item: A
Enter one of the following:
U - push
E - peek
O - pop
S - show stack
X - clear stack
Q - quit
==> U
Enter item: B
Enter one of the following:
U - push
E - peek
O - pop
S - show stack
X - clear stack
Q - quit
==> U
Enter item: C
Enter one of the following:
U - push
E - peek
O - pop
S - show stack
X - clear stack
Q - quit
==> U
Enter item: D
Enter one of the following:
U - push
E - peek
O - pop
S - show stack
X - clear stack
```

```
Q - quit
==> S
D C B A
Enter one of the following:
U - push
E - peek
O - pop
S - show stack
X - clear stack
Q - quit
==> O
Enter one of the following:
U - push
E - peek
O - pop
S - show stack
X - clear stack
Q - quit
==> P
Invalid option
Enter one of the following:
U - push
E - peek
O - pop
S - show stack
X - clear stack
Q - quit
==> E
C
Enter one of the following:
U - push
E - peek
O - pop
S - show stack
X - clear stack
Q - quit
==> S
C B A
Enter one of the following:
U - push
E - peek
O - pop
S - show stack
X - clear stack
```

```
Q - quit
==> X
Enter one of the following:
U - push
E - peek
O - pop
S - show stack
X - clear stack
Q - quit
==> S

Enter one of the following:
U - push
E - peek
O - pop
S - show stack
X - clear stack
Q - quit
==> Q
```

■ QUEUES

A queue is a linear data structure with access at two ends, a front and a rear (see Figure 13.9). Insertions into the queue are always done at the rear, and removals are always from the front. A queue should be able to provide properties and/or methods to

- Tell whether or not the queue is empty
- Indicate how many items are in the queue
- Insert an item in the rear of the queue
- Look at the item in the front of the queue without removing it (peek)
- Remove the item in the front of the queue
- Clear the queue (remove all its items)
- Return a string representation of the items in the queue

Given this, how do we want to represent a queue? We can use some kind of self-referencing class, but in the case of queues, using an array may be more challenging.

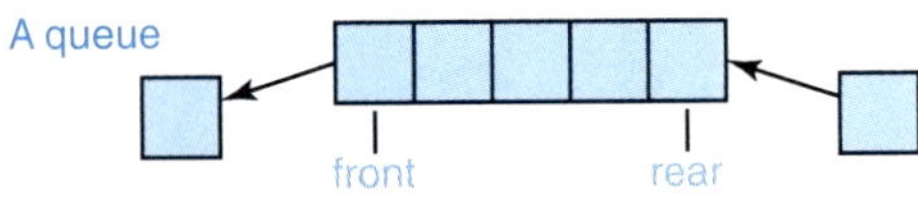

Figure 13.9

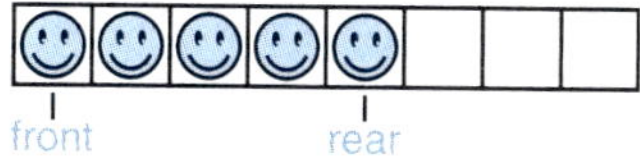

Figure 13.10

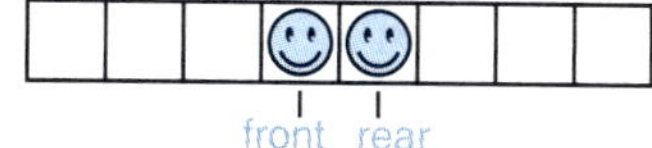

Figure 13.11

Figure 13.12

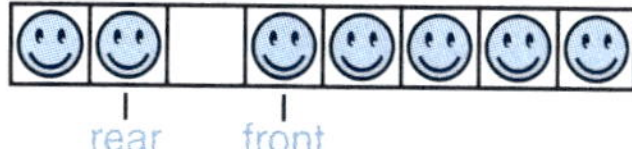

Figure 13.13

If we use an array, we must first take note of the important fact that both ends of a queue move (as opposed to a stack, where only the top moves and the other end stays fixed). Suppose we start with an array in which an index called `front` is set to 0 and another index called `rear` is set to −1.

Every time we insert something into the queue, we increment the `rear` index. When `rear` and `front` are equal, the queue has exactly one item in it. If we insert many items, `rear` advances far away from `front` (see Figure 13.10).

If we begin then to remove items, `front` approaches `rear` again, as seen in Figure 13.11.

Of course, we can continue to add and remove in this way, until `rear` gets to the end of the array, as in Figure 13.12.

The queue is not full, because we have empty slots from where items were removed earlier. We must allow `rear` to wrap around to 0 again to accommodate more insertions, as shown in Figure 13.13.

We must allow the `front` index to do the same thing. Thus, we cannot tell how many items are in the queue by examining the positions of the `front` and `rear` indices, but we can easily use another variable that keeps count of the items in the queue. We start this variable at 0, increment it every time an insertion is made, and decrement it every time a removal is done.

☐ Class: Queue

With this in mind, we are ready to prepare the Queue class. Here are the field declarations:

```
public class Queue {
      public int front;
      public int rear=-1;
      public int numElements;
      Object[] element;
      int maxSize;
//...
}
```

The array is represented by the field element, front and rear are indices representing the front and rear of the queue; maxSize represents the size of the array; and the field numElements records how many items are in the queue at any given time.

The constructor doesn't have to do much; it creates the array, and sets the maxSize field to the incoming value.

```
public Queue(int maxSize) {
      element=new Object[maxSize];
      this.maxSize=maxSize;
}
```

Here, we have the read-only properties Empty, Full, and Size. It should be clear what they provide:

```
public bool Empty { get{return numElements==0;}}
public bool Full { get{return numElements==maxSize;}}
public int Size { get{return numElements;}}
```

If the queue is not full, we insert an item into the queue using the Insert() method. It advances the rear pointer (with a possible wrap-around), inserts the item at that slot, and then increments numElements.

```
public void Insert(Object item) {
      if (Full) throw new FullException("Queue is full");
      rear=(rear+1)%maxSize;
      element[rear]=item;
      numElements++;
}
```

The `Peek()` method simply returns whatever the front pointer is pointing at (provided the queue isn't empty):

```
public Object Peek() {
      if (Empty) throw new EmptyException("Queue is empty");
      return element[front];
}
```

Removing from a nonempty queue means first setting the array reference of the `front` to null, rendering it inaccessible from that point on, and then incrementing `front` with a possible wrap-around. It is important to do these two things in the correct order! Finally, `numElements` is decremented. The `Remove()` method is void; if you want to see the item in the front of the queue before you delete it, peek at it first.

```
public void Remove() {
      if (Empty) throw new EmptyException("Queue is empty");
      element[front]=null;
      front=(front+1)%maxSize;
      numElements--;
}
```

Clearing the queue means removing until the queue is empty:

```
public void Clear() {while (!Empty) Remove();}
```

We can see a `String` representation of all the items in the queue by calling the `ToString()` method, given here. It traverses the array, starting at `front` and advancing with wrap-around until it has processed `numElements` items. All these are concatenated to a `String`, which is returned.

```
public override String ToString() {
      String ans="";
      int traveler=front;
      int count=0;
      while (count<numElements) {
            ans=ans+"  "+element[traveler].ToString();
            traveler=(traveler+1)%maxSize;
            count++;
      }
      return ans;
}
```

Listing 13.5 shows the entire `Queue` class.

Listing 13.5

```
using System;
public class Queue {

      public int front;
      public int rear=-1;
      public int numElements;
      Object[] element;
      int maxSize;

      public Queue(int maxSize) {
            element=new Object[maxSize];
            this.maxSize=maxSize;
      }

      public bool Empty { get{return numElements==0;}}
      public bool Full { get{return numElements==maxSize;}}
      public int Size { get{return numElements;}}

      public void Insert(Object item) {
            if (Full) throw new FullException("Queue is full");
            rear=(rear+1)%maxSize;
            element[rear]=item;
            numElements++;
      }

      public Object Peek() {
            if (Empty) throw new EmptyException("Queue is empty");
            return element[front];
      }

      public void Remove() {
            if (Empty) throw new EmptyException("Queue is empty");
            element[front]=null;
            front=(front+1)%maxSize;
            numElements--;
      }

      public void Clear() {while (!Empty) Remove();}

      public override String ToString() {
            String ans="";
            int traveler=front;
            int count=0;
            while (count<numElements) {
                  ans=ans+" "+element[traveler].ToString();
                  traveler=(traveler+1)%maxSize;
                  count++;
            }
            return ans;
      }

}
```

TABLE 13.2

Constructor/Property/Method	T(n)
`public Queue(int maxSize);`	O(1)
`public bool Empty;`	O(1)
`public void Insert(Object item);`	O(1)
`public Object Peek();`	O(1)
`public void Remove();`	O(1)
`public void Clear();`	O(n)
`public override String ToString();`	O(n)

A queue is also an efficient data structure timewise, because insertions and removals can be made only at the rear and the front, respectively. Thus, insertions and removals run in constant time, and this is true for most properties and methods of this `Queue` class, as you can see from Table 13.2.

Listing 13.6 is a program that will test the operations of a queue. It allows the reader to insert and remove items to/from a queue, peek at the item in front, clear the queue, and display its contents.

Listing 13.6

```
using System;
public class TestQueue {
    static void Main() {
      Queue queue=new Queue(1000);
      String result="";

      DisplayHeader();
      char option = Console.ReadLine()[0];
      while (option!='Q') {
            switch (option) {
                  case 'I':
                  Console.Write("Enter item: ");
                  queue.Insert(Console.ReadLine());
                  break;

                  case 'P':
                  try {
                        result=(String)queue.Peek();
                  } catch (EmptyException ne) {
                        Console.WriteLine(ne);
                  }
```

(continued)

```
                    Console.WriteLine(result);
                    break;

                    case 'R':
                    try {
                          queue.Remove();
                    } catch (EmptyException ne) {
                          Console.WriteLine(ne);
                    }
                    break;

                    case 'S':
                    Console.WriteLine(queue.ToString());
                    break;

                    case 'X':
                    queue.Clear();
                    break;

                    default:
                    Console.WriteLine("Invalid option");
                    break;
              }
              DisplayHeader();
              option = Console.ReadLine()[0];
        }
    }

    static void DisplayHeader() {
              Console.WriteLine("Enter one of the following:");
              Console.WriteLine("I - insert");
              Console.WriteLine("P - peek");
              Console.WriteLine("R - remove");
              Console.WriteLine("S - show queue");
              Console.WriteLine("X - clear queue");
              Console.WriteLine("Q - quit");
              Console.Write("==> ");

    }

}
```

Here is the test program running:

```
Enter one of the following:
I - insert
P - peek
R - remove
S - show queue
X - clear queue
Q - quit
==> I
Enter item: HELLO I HAVE A MESSAGE FOR YOU
Enter one of the following:
I - insert
P - peek
R - remove
S - show queue
X - clear queue
Q - quit
==> I
Enter item: YOU'RE NOT GOING TO LIKE IT
Enter one of the following:
I - insert
P - peek
R - remove
S - show queue
X - clear queue
Q - quit
==> P
HELLO I HAVE A MESSAGE FOR YOU
Enter one of the following:
I - insert
P - peek
R - remove
S - show queue
X - clear queue
Q - quit
==> S
 HELLO I HAVE A MESSAGE FOR YOU YOU'RE NOT GOING TO LIKE IT
Enter one of the following:
I - insert
P - peek
R - remove
S - show queue
X - clear queue
```

```
Q - quit
==> R
Enter one of the following:
I - insert
P - peek
R - remove
S - show queue
X - clear queue
Q - quit
==> I
Enter item: C# RULZ!
Enter one of the following:
I - insert
P - peek
R - remove
S - show queue
X - clear queue
Q - quit
==> S
 YOU'RE NOT GOING TO LIKE IT C# RULZ!
Enter one of the following:
I - insert
P - peek
R - remove
S - show queue
X - clear queue
Q - quit
==> X
Enter one of the following:
I - insert
P - peek
R - remove
S - show queue
X - clear queue
Q - quit
==> S

Enter one of the following:
I - insert
P - peek
R - remove
S - show queue
X - clear queue
Q - quit
==> Q
```

Of course, we need not necessarily use an array to implement a queue. A chain of nodes would also work for this purpose, as long as there are two node references—one pointing at the front of the chain and the other pointing at the rear. An interesting exercise would be for you to implement such a queue.

■ LINKED LISTS

Stacks and queues limit access to the nodes, for that is their nature; you should only access the top of a stack, for example. We would like a data structure in which we can access the internal nodes. We will call such a data structure a linked list, or a list. (Do not confuse this special usage of the word "list" with its colloquial meaning.)

You will notice that traversing a chain works well in one direction only; that is, in the direction of the links. For example, Figure 13.14 shows it is not easy to get from the last node to the first node in such a chain.

There are various ways around this; for one thing, you can connect the last node to the first and make a circular chain, as in Figure 13.15.

This, however, doesn't solve the problem of moving backwards through a chain. This is accomplished by having two sets of references—one to the next node and one to the previous node (see Figure 13.16).

Of course, each node still has a reference to the data it contains.

We will use such a doubly linked chain to implement a list. To navigate most easily through such a list, see Figure 13.17. It helps to have a reference to the front of the list, to the rear, and to an arbitrary point in the list called the "current position."

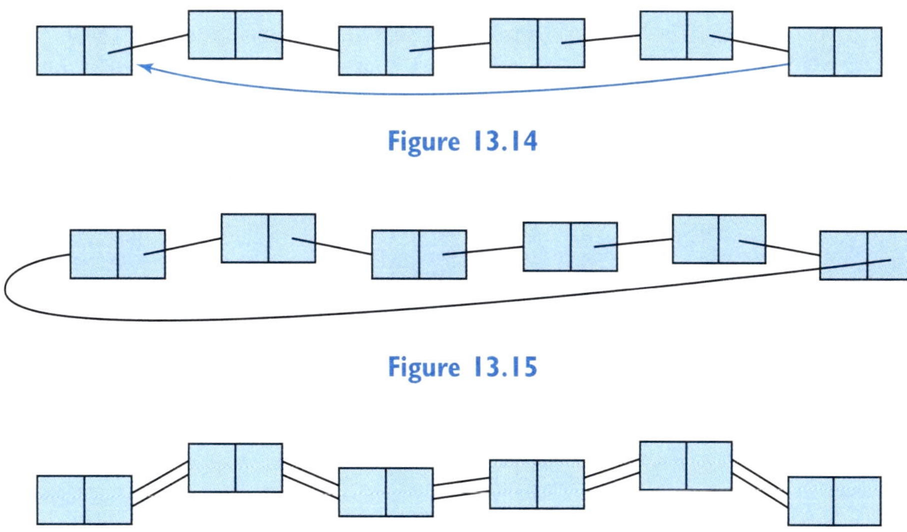

Figure 13.14

Figure 13.15

Figure 13.16

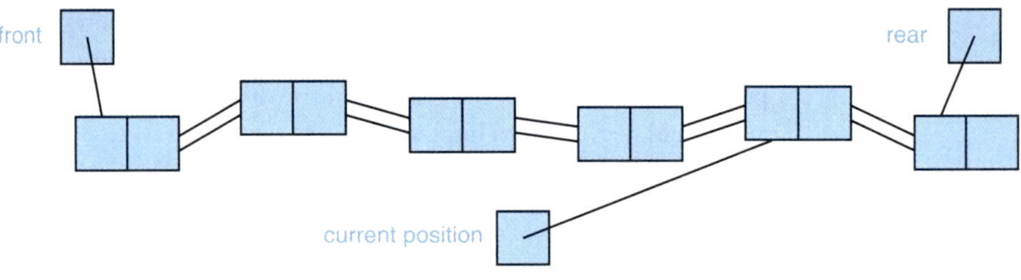

Figure 13.17

We can move the current position pointer back and forth along the list by supplying `Next()` and `Previous()` methods.

A list should provide properties and/or methods to

- Tell whether or not the list is empty
- Indicate how many items are in the list
- Move the current position back and forth along the list
- Insert an item just before the item in the current position of the list
- Look at the item in the current position of the list
- Remove the item in the current position of the list
- Clear the list (remove all its items)
- Return a string representation of the items on the list

If you recall the linked implementation of the stack, these methods practically write themselves.

☐ Class: List

The `List` class is doubly linked, so it makes use of a `ListNode` class, which provides dual `ListNode` references, `previous` and `next` (see Listing 13.7).

Listing 13.7

```
public class ListNode {

   public Object datum;
   public ListNode prev;
   public ListNode next;

   public ListNode(Object newdatum) {
      this.prev=null;
      this.datum=newdatum;
      this.next=null;
   }

}
```

A `List` will have three references—to the head, tail, and current position of the list. All begin with the value `null`, as the constructor shows.

```
public class List {

   ListNode head;
   ListNode tail;
   ListNode position;

   //Create an empty list
   public List() {
      head=null;
      tail=null;
      position=null;
   }
//...
}
```

The `Empty` property returns a Boolean, and the `Current` property returns the `Object` in the current position of the list. Both properties are read-only.

```
public bool Empty {get{return head==null;}}

public Object Current {
   get {
            if (position==null) throw new EmptyException
               ("List is empty");
            return position.datum;
   }
}
```

The `Insert()` method will insert an item just before the current item in the list. There are some special cases to consider; for example:

- The list is empty.
- The list contains only one item.
- The list contains multiple items.
- The current position is the head of the list.
- The current position is the tail of the list.
- The current position is neither the head nor the tail.

All these factors affect an insertion; thus, as an aid, two special private helper methods, `InsertBeforeHead()` and `InsertBeforeTail()`, are provided.

Note that because our list always inserts before the item in the current position, there is no way to insert anything after the tail end item in a list. You may wish to redefine our concept of a list to take this into account.

```
private void InsertBeforeHead(Object item) {
   ListNode newNode=new ListNode(item);
   head.prev=newNode;
   newNode.next=head;
   head=newNode;
}

private void InsertBeforeTail(Object item) {
   ListNode newNode=new ListNode(item);
   if (tail.prev!=null) {
         newNode.prev=tail.prev;
         tail.prev.next=newNode;
   }
   tail.prev=newNode;
   newNode.next=tail;
}

public void Insert(Object item) {
   if (position==null) {
         ListNode newNode=new ListNode(item);
         head=newNode;
         tail=newNode;
         position=newNode;
   } else if (head==tail) {
         InsertBeforeHead(item);
   } else if (position==head) {
         InsertBeforeHead(item);
   } else if (position==tail) {
         InsertBeforeTail(item);
   } else {
         ListNode newNode=new ListNode(item);
         newNode.next=position;
         position.prev.next=newNode;
         newNode.prev=position.prev;
         position.prev=newNode;
   }
}
```

Removing an item from the current position means adjusting the references on the `previous` and `next` nodes. Of course, there are special cases here as well; for example, there may be no `next` node (i.e., you are removing the tail):

```
public void Remove() {
   if (Empty) throw new EmptyException
         ("Can't remove from empty list");
```

```
    if (head==tail) {
          head=null;
          tail=null;
          position=null;
    } else if (position==head) {
          head.next.prev=null;
          head=head.next;
          position=head;
    } else if (position==tail) {
          tail.prev.next=null;
          tail=tail.prev;
          position=tail;
    } else {
          position.prev.next=position.next;
          position.next.prev=position.prev;
          position=position.next;
    }
}
```

The `Next()` and `Previous()` methods move the current position back and forth one node at a time along the list. If you are at the head of the list, `Previous()` does nothing; likewise, if you are at the tail, the `Next()` method has no effect on the current position.

```
public void Next() {
    if (position==null) throw new EmptyException
          ("Cannot call Next() on empty list");
    if (position.next!=null)
          position=position.next;
}

public void Previous() {
    if (position==null) throw new EmptyException
          ("Cannot call Previous() on empty list");
    if (position.prev!=null)
          position=position.prev;
}
```

The `Clear` method simply cuts off the reference points to the chain. Once they are cut off, the garbage collector can come and collect the nodes at its leisure.

```
public void Clear() {
    head=null;
    tail=null;
    position=null;
}
```

The ToString() method provides a string representation of all the items by simply traveling down the list and appending a string representation of the object referenced by each node. It returns these as a String.

```
public override String ToString() {
      StringBuilder result=new StringBuilder("");
      ListNode traveler=head;
      while (traveler!=null) {
            result.Append(" "+traveler.datum);
            traveler=traveler.next;
      }
      return result.ToString();
}
```

Listing 13.8 shows the entire List class.

Listing 13.8

```
using System;
using System.Text;
public class List {

   public class ListNode {

      public Object datum;
      public ListNode prev;
      public ListNode next;

      public ListNode(Object newdatum) {
         this.prev=null;
         this.datum=newdatum;
         this.next=null;
      }

   }

   ListNode head;
   ListNode tail;
   ListNode position;

   //Create an empty list
   public List() {
      head=null;
      tail=null;
      position=null;
   }

   public bool Empty {get{return head==null;}}
```

(continued)

```
public Object Current {
   get {
            if (position==null) throw new EmptyException
               ("List is empty");
            return position.datum;
   }
}

private void InsertBeforeHead(Object item) {
   ListNode newNode=new ListNode(item);
   head.prev=newNode;
   newNode.next=head;
   head=newNode;
}

private void InsertBeforeTail(Object item) {
   ListNode newNode=new ListNode(item);
   if (tail.prev!=null) {
         newNode.prev=tail.prev;
         tail.prev.next=newNode;
   }
   tail.prev=newNode;
   newNode.next=tail;
}

public void Insert(Object item) {
   if (position==null) {
         ListNode newNode=new ListNode(item);
         head=newNode;
         tail=newNode;
         position=newNode;
   } else if (head==tail) {
         InsertBeforeHead(item);
   } else if (position==head) {
         InsertBeforeHead(item);
   } else if (position==tail) {
         InsertBeforeTail(item);
   } else {
         ListNode newNode=new ListNode(item);
         newNode.next=position;
         position.prev.next=newNode;
         newNode.prev=position.prev;
         position.prev=newNode;
   }
}

public void Remove() {
   if (Empty) throw new EmptyException
         ("Can't remove from empty list");
   if (head==tail) {
         head=null;
```

(continued)

```
            tail=null;
            position=null;
        } else if (position==head) {
            head.next.prev=null;
            head=head.next;
            position=head;
        } else if (position==tail) {
            tail.prev.next=null;
            tail=tail.prev;
            position=tail;
        } else {
            position.prev.next=position.next;
            position.next.prev=position.prev;
            position=position.next;
        }
    }

    public void Clear() {
       head=null;
       tail=null;
       position=null;
    }

    public void Next() {
       if (position==null) throw new EmptyException
            ("Cannot call Next() on empty list");
       if (position.next!=null)
            position=position.next;
    }

    public void Previous() {
       if (position==null) throw new EmptyException
            ("Cannot call Previous() on empty list");
       if (position.prev!=null)
            position=position.prev;
    }

    public override String ToString() {
          StringBuilder result=new StringBuilder("");
          ListNode traveler=head;
          while (traveler!=null) {
                result.Append(" "+traveler.datum);
                traveler=traveler.next;
          }
          return result.ToString();
    }

 }
```

TABLE 13.3

Constructor/Property/Method	*T*(*n*)
`public List();`	O(1)
`public bool Empty;`	O(1)
`public Object Current;`	O(1)
`public void Insert(Object item);`	O(1)
`public void Remove();`	O(1)
`public void Clear();`	O(*n*)
`public void Next();`	O(1)
`public void Previous();`	O(1)
`public override String ToString();`	O(*n*)

The `List` members also execute quickly; only `Clear` and `ToString` execute in poorer than constant time, as shown in Table 13.3.

If the only item we are concerned with looking at is the one in the current position, lists would be fast indeed. However, this belies the nature of a list, which allows us access to the internal nodes (via `Current`, `Previous`, and `Next`), and hence is searchable. Of course, any search of a `List` is bound to be sequential, and hence will run in linear time.

Listing 13.9 is a test program for lists.

Listing 13.9

```
using System;
public class TestList {
    static void Main() {
      List list=new List();
      String result="";

      DisplayHeader();
      char option = Console.ReadLine()[0];
      while (option!='Q') {
            switch (option) {
                  case 'I':
                  Console.Write("Enter item: ");
```

(continued)

```
list.Insert(Console.ReadLine());
break;

case 'C':
try {
      result=(String)list.Current;
} catch (EmptyException ne) {
      Console.WriteLine(ne);
}
Console.WriteLine(result);
break;

case 'R':
try {
      list.Remove();
} catch (EmptyException ne) {
      Console.WriteLine(ne);
}
break;

case 'N':
try {
      list.Next();
} catch (EmptyException ne) {
      Console.WriteLine(ne);
}
break;

case 'P':
try {
      list.Previous();
} catch (EmptyException ne) {
      Console.WriteLine(ne);
}
break;

case 'S':
Console.WriteLine(list.ToString());
break;

case 'X':
list.Clear();
break;
```

(continued)

```
                default:
                Console.WriteLine("Invalid option");
                break;
            }
            DisplayHeader();
            option = Console.ReadLine()[0];
        }
    }

    static void DisplayHeader() {
            Console.WriteLine("Enter one of the following:");
            Console.WriteLine("I - insert");
            Console.WriteLine("C - current");
            Console.WriteLine("R - remove");
            Console.WriteLine("N - next");
            Console.WriteLine("P - previous");
            Console.WriteLine("C - current");
            Console.WriteLine("S - show list");
            Console.WriteLine("X - clear list");
            Console.WriteLine("Q - quit");
            Console.Write("==> ");

    }

}
```

Here is a sample run of the list testing program:

```
Enter one of the following:
I - insert
C - current
R - remove
N - next
P - previous
C - current
S - show list
X - clear list
Q - quit
==> I
Enter item: BILLY
Enter one of the following:
```

```
I - insert
C - current
R - remove
N - next
P - previous
C - current
S - show list
X - clear list
Q - quit
==> I
Enter item: GOAT's
Enter one of the following:
I - insert
C - current
R - remove
N - next
P - previous
C - current
S - show list
X - clear list
Q - quit
==> C
BILLY
Enter one of the following:
I - insert
C - current
R - remove
N - next
P - previous
C - current
S - show list
X - clear list
Q - quit
==> P
Enter one of the following:
I - insert
C - current
R - remove
N - next
P - previous
C - current
```

```
S - show list
X - clear list
Q - quit
==> C
GOAT's
Enter one of the following:
I - insert
C - current
R - remove
N - next
P - previous
C - current
S - show list
X - clear list
Q - quit
==> S
 GOAT's BILLY
Enter one of the following:
I - insert
C - current
R - remove
N - next
P - previous
C - current
S - show list
X - clear list
Q - quit
==> I
Enter item: GRUFF
Enter one of the following:
I - insert
C - current
R - remove
N - next
P - previous
C - current
S - show list
X - clear list
Q - quit
==> C
GOAT's
```

```
Enter one of the following:
I - insert
C - current
R - remove
N - next
P - previous
C - current
S - show list
X - clear list
Q - quit
==> S
 GRUFF GOAT's BILLY
Enter one of the following:
I - insert
C - current
R - remove
N - next
P - previous
C - current
S - show list
X - clear list
Q - quit
==> N
Enter one of the following:
I - insert
C - current
R - remove
N - next
P - previous
C - current
S - show list
X - clear list
Q - quit
==> R
Enter one of the following:
I - insert
C - current
R - remove
N - next
P - previous
```

```
C - current
S - show list
X - clear list
Q - quit
==> S
 GRUFF GOAT's
Enter one of the following:
I - insert
C - current
R - remove
N - next
P - previous
C - current
S - show list
X - clear list
Q - quit
==> X
Enter one of the following:
I - insert
C - current
R - remove
N - next
P - previous
C - current
S - show list
X - clear list
Q - quit
==> S

Enter one of the following:
I - insert
C - current
R - remove
N - next
P - previous
C - current
S - show list
X - clear list
Q - quit
==> Q
```

▪ ORDERED LISTS

We can order the items in a linked list. If this is our desire, a somewhat different concept arises; for example, we should no longer be able to insert at any position, because there is only one place an item in an ordered list should be placed (see Figure 13.18).

☐ Class: OrderedList

An `OrderedList` object would have nodes containing `IComparable` items, because the items would need to be compared to each other. Thus, we define an `OrderedListNode` class in Listing 13.10.

Listing 13.10

```
public class OrderedListNode {
      public IComparable datum;
      public OrderedListNode next;
      public OrderedListNode(IComparable item) {
            datum=item;
      }
}
```

An ordered list would not need a current pointer because insertion points are no longer arbitrary; thus, we have only a pointer to the head and tail of an ordered list. The constructor is also listed here:

```
public class OrderedList {

   OrderedListNode head;
   OrderedListNode tail;

   public OrderedList() {//Create an empty list
      head=null;
      tail=null;
   }
}
```

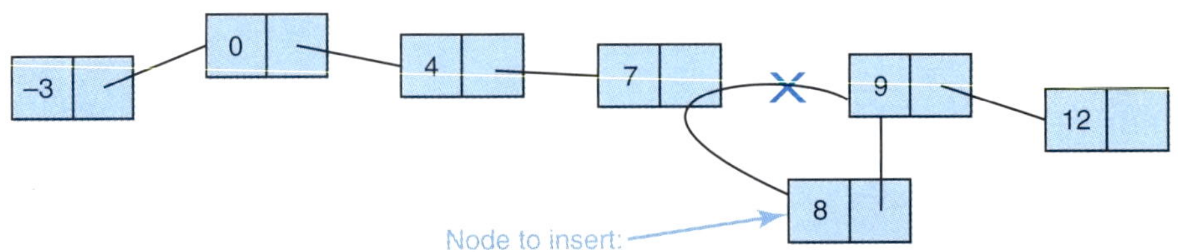

Figure 13.18

The `Insert()` method must first find the proper position in which to insert an item. Of course, there are special cases to consider; for example, is the list empty? The correct position in which to insert an item in an ordered list is just before the first item that is no smaller than the one you are trying to insert. If no such element exists, the insertion is at the tail.

```
public void Insert(IComparable item) {
   OrderedListNode v=new OrderedListNode(item);
   OrderedListNode t=head;
   OrderedListNode p=null;
   while (t!=null&&t.datum.CompareTo(v.datum)<0) {
      p=t;
      t=t.next;
   }
   if (t==null) {
      if (p==null) {
         head=v;
         tail=v;
      } else {
         tail.next=v;
         tail=v;
      }
   } else {
      if (p==null) {
         head=v;
         v.next=t;
      } else {
         p.next=v;
         v.next=t;
      }
   }
}
```

Getting an item from the ordered list, or removing it, means finding it first. Because the list is ordered, a search can stop either when it finds the item or when it comes across an item that is larger than the sought item (in this case, the item sought is not present):

```
public IComparable Get(IComparable target) {
   OrderedListNode travelNode=head;
   OrderedListNode previousNode=null;
   while (travelNode!=null
   && travelNode.datum.CompareTo(target)<0) {
      previousNode=travelNode;
      travelNode=travelNode.next;
   }
   if (travelNode==null) throw
```

```
      new NotFoundException("Item not in list!");
      if (travelNode.datum.CompareTo(target)>0) throw
      new NotFoundException("Item not in list!");
      return travelNode.datum;
   }

   public void Remove(IComparable target) {
      OrderedListNode travelNode=head;
      OrderedListNode previousNode=null;
      while (travelNode!=null
      && travelNode.datum.CompareTo(target)<0) {
         previousNode=travelNode;
         travelNode=travelNode.next;
      }
      if (travelNode==null) throw
      new NotFoundException("Item not in list!");
      if (travelNode.datum.CompareTo(target)>0)
      throw new NotFoundException("Item not in list!");
      if (travelNode==head) head=travelNode.next;
      else previousNode.next=travelNode.next;
      if (travelNode==tail) {
         tail=previousNode;
         tail.next=null;
      }
   }
```

Clearing an ordered list simply means cutting off the tail and the head:

```
public void Clear() {
   head=null;
   tail=null;
}
```

The `Empty` property indicates whether the ordered list is empty:

```
public bool Empty {get{return head==null;}}
```

The `ToString()` method provides a string representation of the list items:

```
public override String ToString() {
      StringBuilder result=new StringBuilder("");
      OrderedListNode traveler=head;
      while (traveler!=null) {
            result.Append(" "+traveler.datum);
            traveler=traveler.next;
      }
      return result.ToString();
}
```

Listing 13.11 provides the `OrderedList` class in its entirety.

Listing 13.11

```
using System;
using System.Text;
public class OrderedList {

   public class OrderedListNode {
         public IComparable datum;
         public OrderedListNode next;
         public OrderedListNode(IComparable item) {
               datum=item;
         }
   }

   OrderedListNode head;
   OrderedListNode tail;

   public OrderedList() {//Create an empty list
      head=null;
      tail=null;
   }

   public bool Empty {get{return head==null;}}

   public void Insert(IComparable item) {
      OrderedListNode v=new OrderedListNode(item);
      OrderedListNode t=head;
      OrderedListNode p=null;
      while (t!=null&&t.datum.CompareTo(v.datum)<0) {
         p=t;
         t=t.next;
      }
      if (t==null) {
         if (p==null) {
            head=v;
            tail=v;
         } else {
            tail.next=v;
            tail=v;
         }
      } else {
         if (p==null) {
            head=v;
            v.next=t;
         } else {
            p.next=v;
            v.next=t;
         }
      }
   }
```

(continued)

```
   public IComparable Get(IComparable target) {
      OrderedListNode travelNode=head;
      OrderedListNode previousNode=null;
      while (travelNode!=null
      && travelNode.datum.CompareTo(target)<0) {
         previousNode=travelNode;
         travelNode=travelNode.next;
      }
      if (travelNode==null) throw
      new NotFoundException("Item not in list!");
      if (travelNode.datum.CompareTo(target)>0) throw
      new NotFoundException("Item not in list!");
      return travelNode.datum;
   }

   public void Remove(IComparable target) {
      OrderedListNode travelNode=head;
      OrderedListNode previousNode=null;
      while (travelNode!=null
      && travelNode.datum.CompareTo(target)<0) {
         previousNode=travelNode;
         travelNode=travelNode.next;
      }
      if (travelNode==null) throw
      new NotFoundException("Item not in list!");
      if (travelNode.datum.CompareTo(target)>0)
      throw new NotFoundException("Item not in list!");
      if (travelNode==head) head=travelNode.next;
      else previousNode.next=travelNode.next;
      if (travelNode==tail) {
         tail=previousNode;
         tail.next=null;
      }
   }

   public void Clear() {
      head=null;
      tail=null;
   }

   public override String ToString() {
         StringBuilder result=new StringBuilder("");
         OrderedListNode traveler=head;
         while (traveler!=null) {
               result.Append(" "+traveler.datum);
               traveler=traveler.next;
         }
         return result.ToString();
   }

}
```

TABLE 13.4

Constructor/Property/Method	*T(n)*
`public OrderedList();`	O(1)
`public bool Empty;`	O(1)
`public void Insert(IComparable item);`	O(n)
`public IComparable Get(IComparable target);`	O(n)
`public void Remove(IComparable target);`	O(n)
`public void Clear();`	O(n)
`public override String ToString();`	O(n)

Note that a list must always be searched sequentially, because you can't get directly to any node without passing through the node before it, or in the case of doubly linked lists, possibly the node behind it. You can write methods that appear to index a list, but the movement through a list is sequential.

So, it can be argued that keeping a list in order is not worthwhile. However, search time can be improved somewhat in an ordered list, because a search can stop at the first item it encounters that is no greater than the item sought. For "small" items, that is, those that would be near the head of the list, this can mean a substantial improvement in search time. (This can help quite a bit if you are looking for an item that isn't in the list.) However, be aware that each time an insertion is made, a search is likewise required to find the proper insertion point. In contrast, an insertion into an unordered list is extremely brief.

See Table 13.4 for an analysis of the `OrderedList` constructors, properties, and methods.

The test program for `OrderedList` is in Listing 13.12.

Listing 13.12

```
using System;
public class TestOrderedList {
    static void Main() {
      OrderedList list=new OrderedList();
      String result="";

      DisplayHeader();
      char option = Console.ReadLine()[0];
      while (option!='Q') {
            switch (option) {
                  case 'I':
                  Console.Write("Enter item: ");
                  list.Insert(Console.ReadLine());
```

(continued)

```
                    break;

                    case 'G':
                    try {
                          Console.Write("Enter item: ");
                          result=(String)list.Get(
                                Console.ReadLine());
                    } catch (NotFoundException ne) {
                          Console.WriteLine(ne);
                    }
                    Console.WriteLine(result);
                    break;

                    case 'R':
                    try {
                          Console.Write("Enter item: ");
                          list.Remove(Console.ReadLine());
                    } catch (NotFoundException ne) {
                          Console.WriteLine(ne);
                    }
                    break;

                    case 'S':
                    Console.WriteLine(list.ToString());
                    break;

                    case 'X':
                    list.Clear();
                    break;

                    default:
                    Console.WriteLine("Invalid option");
                    break;
              }
              DisplayHeader();
              option = Console.ReadLine()[0];
        }
    }

    static void DisplayHeader() {
              Console.WriteLine("Enter one of the following:");
              Console.WriteLine("I - insert");
              Console.WriteLine("G - get");
              Console.WriteLine("R - remove");
              Console.WriteLine("S - show list");
              Console.WriteLine("X - clear list");
              Console.WriteLine("Q - quit");
              Console.Write("==> ");

    }

}
```

Here is the test program running:

```
Enter one of the following:
I - insert
G - get
R - remove
S - show list
X - clear list
Q - quit
==> I
Enter item: THIS
Enter one of the following:
I - insert
G - get
R - remove
S - show list
X - clear list
Q - quit
==> I
Enter item: LIST
Enter one of the following:
I - insert
G - get
R - remove
S - show list
X - clear list
Q - quit
==> I
Enter item: IS
Enter one of the following:
I - insert
G - get
R - remove
S - show list
X - clear list
Q - quit
==> I
Enter item: IN
Enter one of the following:
I - insert
G - get
R - remove
S - show list
X - clear list
```

```
Q - quit
==> I
Enter item: ORDER
Enter one of the following:
I - insert
G - get
R - remove
S - show list
X - clear list
Q - quit
==> S
 IN IS LIST ORDER THIS
Enter one of the following:
I - insert
G - get
R - remove
S - show list
X - clear list
Q - quit
==> G
Enter item: ORDER
ORDER
Enter one of the following:
I - insert
G - get
R - remove
S - show list
X - clear list
Q - quit
==> G
Enter item: CHAOS
NotFoundException: Item not in list!
   at OrderedList.Get(IComparable target)
   at TestOrderedList.Main()
ORDER
Enter one of the following:
I - insert
G - get
R - remove
S - show list
X - clear list
Q - quit
==> R
Enter item: IN
```

```
Enter one of the following:
I - insert
G - get
R - remove
S - show list
X - clear list
Q - quit
==> S
 IS LIST ORDER THIS
Enter one of the following:
I - insert
G - get
R - remove
S - show list
X - clear list
Q - quit
==> R
Enter item: LIST
Enter one of the following:
I - insert
G - get
R - remove
S - show list
X - clear list
Q - quit
==> S
 IS ORDER THIS
Enter one of the following:
I - insert
G - get
R - remove
S - show list
X - clear list
Q - quit
==> R
Enter item: THIS
Enter one of the following:
I - insert
G - get
R - remove
S - show list
X - clear list
Q - quit
==> S
 IS ORDER
```

```
Enter one of the following:
I - insert
G - get
R - remove
S - show list
X - clear list
Q - quit
==> X
Enter one of the following:
I - insert
G - get
R - remove
S - show list
X - clear list
Q - quit
==> S

Enter one of the following:
I - insert
G - get
R - remove
S - show list
X - clear list
Q - quit
==> Q
```

chapter 14

Nonlinear Data Structures

Many of the data structures we developed in the last chapter were dynamic and flexible in the sense that they could grow and shrink as desired. By using self-referencing classes, we developed chains of items. The drawback to such chains is that their search time is linear, whether the items are "sorted" or not. Although linear time can be perfectly acceptable, for many applications it is just too slow. We will discuss data structures now that manage to remain flexible, but exhibit better than linear search times.

■ INDEXERS

We are familiar with using indices with single dimensional and multidimensional arrays. However, you may have noticed that we use indices to access individual characters in a string. Is there anything special about the `String` class? No. You may define an indexer in any class that you write to access individual items in the object. This hasn't really been pertinent until now, as we cover data structures.

An indexer would be defined somewhat like the following:

```
public <TypeA> this [int index] {
      get {
      //...
      return <something of type TypeA at position determined by index>
      }
      set {
            //...
            <Item at position determined by index>=value;
      }
}
```

As an example of a data structure for which an indexer is applicable, consider the data structure I call an "exploding array."

7
6
5
4
3
2
1
0

Figure 14.1

Exploding Arrays

As you know, arrays are fixed in size; they cannot grow or shrink once created. However, because C# lets us allocate memory dynamically, that is, at runtime, we can create a data structure that can grow, and is also easily indexable. Note that a linked list is very flexible and dynamic, but its elements are not directly accessible. In order to get to any item in a linked list, you must first pass through all the elements preceding it. This can be very time consuming, especially if searches are frequent.

Our exploding array will be represented using a jagged two-dimensional array. The first index in the jagged array will be a vector whose elements will point at "subvectors." Figure 14.1 shows that the primary vector will initially be all empty references.

As we add items to this jagged array, we create the subvectors as required. The length of the subvector is determined by the first index, given in Table 14.1.

Figure 14.2 shows what the subvectors look like when created for positions 0, 1, 2, 3, and 4.

TABLE 14.1

First Index in Main Vector	Length of Subvector
0	$2^0 = 1$
1	$2^1 = 2$
2	$2^2 = 4$
3	$2^3 = 8$
4	$2^4 = 16$
...	...
k	2^k

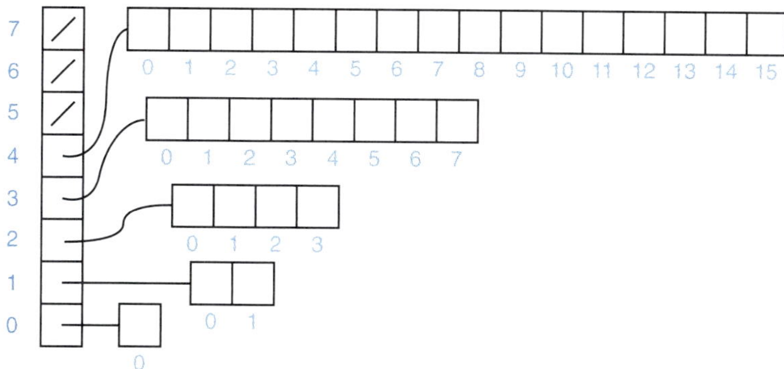

Figure 14.2

The second index of an item will be its position in the subvector. We need not create any subvector until we need to place an item in the exploding array that would map to one of that subvector's positions.

Externally, the exploding array uses a single index, not two. The trick is to map this single index to the dual index in the jagged array using some mathematical trickery. For convenience, suppose the first valid index in an exploding array is 1. Suppose *D* is an exploding array object, and *J* is the underlying jagged array. Then *D*[*i*] would map to *J*[*j*,*k*] if we use this mapping:

j = (position of highest set bit of i) − 1 (low order bit being at position 1)

and

$k = i \bmod 2^j$

As an example, let us consider where an item to be placed at *D*[7] would actually be placed in the underlying jagged array *J*. The binary representation of 7 is 111B, so the position of the highest set bit of 6 in binary is 3. So, 3 − 1 = 2 serves as the first index *j*; that is,

$j = 2$

The second index *k* (we'll call it the offset) is computed by

$k = 7 \bmod 2^j = 7 \bmod 2^2 = 7 \bmod 4 = 3$

So, the item at *D*[7] is actually to be found at *J*[2,3] in the underlying jagged array. See Figure 14.3.

Does this always work? If you check, you will see that it does. Take again, for example, *D*[7], which maps to *J*[2,3]. This happens to be the last position in this subvector; so what happens if we access *D*[8]? By virtue of the length of the subvectors and the mapping chosen, you will see that 8 will map to the next subvector, because the highest set bit of 8 = 1000B is at position 4. The first index then is $j = 4 - 1 = 3$, and the offset is $k = 8 \bmod 2^3 = 8 \bmod 8 = 0$. See Figure 14.4 for the *D*[8] mapping.

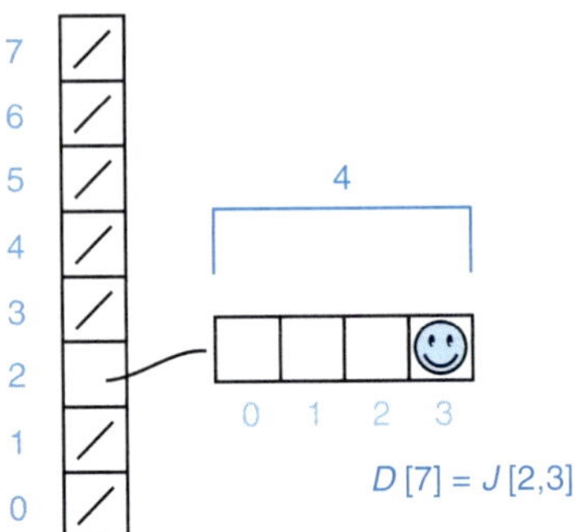

Figure 14.3

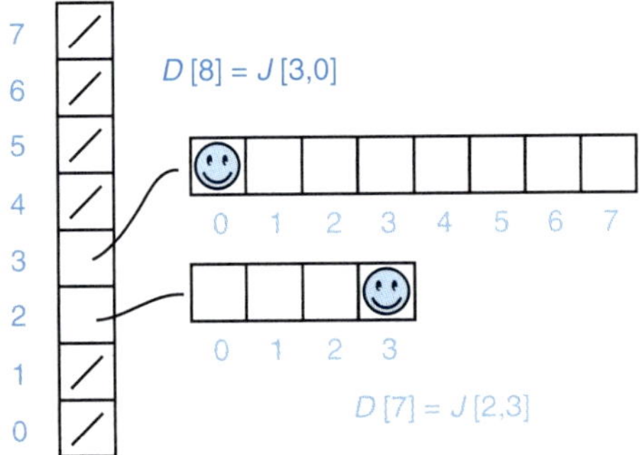

Figure 14.4

Note that this exploding array can grow in size very quickly, doubling in size as each subvector is created. If an exploding array begins with a primary vector of, say, 31 slots, it can hold up to $2^0 + 2^1 + 2^2 + \ldots + 2^{29} + 2^{30} = 2^{31} - 1$, or about 2 billion items. However, it begins as a very memory economical object, and grows only as necessary. And of course, the real benefit is that the items are directly accessible using an index; we need not pass through millions of items to retrieve or modify the object we want.

Listing 14.1 shows the `ExplodingArray` class, which I created to demonstrate this data structure, and to show how an indexer would be created for it. An `ExplodingArray` object would store other objects; its fields consist of the underlying jagged array and some other fields used to store intermediate values when computing the dual index from the single index.

```
using System;
public class ExplodingArray {

    //Exploding array will be represented with a jagged array
    //Each vector at index k in first vector will have 2^k slots
    private Object[][] array;
```

```
    //Fields used to compute the double index from single index
    //maxFirstIndex is largest first index determined by constructor
    private const int maxFirstIndex=30;
    //hiBit represents highest set bit in an index
    private int hiBit;
    //firstIndex is first index in jagged array computed from index
    private int firstIndex;
    //modulus is 2^firstIndex
    private int modulus;
    //offSet computed as index mod modulus-2nd index in jagged array
    private int offSet;
    //Stores the position of highest item in exploding array
    int hiIndex;
//...
}
```

The constructor is parameterless. It creates the primary vector at 31 elements.

```
//Create an ExplodingArray that can hold up to 2^31-1 items
public ExplodingArray() {
      array=new Object[31][];
}
```

Note that 31 is an upper limit, for practical considerations. If your data structure needs to hold more than a couple billion objects, you might want to store them in something other than a gigantic array.

It is convenient to know the item that is at the highest position in the exploding array, so we record this at all times and allow the user to get this value as a property.

```
//HighestIndex property returns index of item at highest
//position in exploding array
public int HighestIndex {
      get {return hiIndex;}
}
```

When computing the dual index, we need to compute the highest set bit from the single index. The private method `hiBitIndex` does this; it takes the single index, continually divides by 2 until a quotient of 1 is achieved (note that you must eventually get a value of 1 if you do this), and counts how many iterations were needed to achieve this. The number of iterations is then the index of the highest set bit.

```
//Returns index (starting with 1) of highest set bit of num
private int hiBitIndex(int num) {
      hiBit=1;
      while (num!=1) {
            num>>=1;
```

```
            hiBit++;
        }
        return hiBit;
}
```

Note that we do not specifically divide by 2; we do the equivalent of that by shifting the integer (stored in binary) to the right one position in each iteration. To see this, take the number

9 = 1001B

and note that

9/2 = 4, or 1001B >> 1 = 0100B = 4

and

4/2 = 2, or 0100B >> 1 = 0010B = 2

and

2/2 = 1, or 0010B >> 1 = 0001B = 1.

The indexer is defined next; it does all the mathematical trickery to compute the dual index, set or get the value at that index, and create the subvectors when necessary (and not before). It also maintains the `hiIndex` field, which remembers the item stored at the highest position in the exploding array. Note that if you attempt to retrieve an item that is not at the specified position in the subvector, or if the subvector itself does not exist, a `get` will return null. The application using the exploding array must know of and handle this condition.

```
//This is the indexer for the exploding array
//Computes a double index into jagged array from single index
public Object this[int index] {
        //get returns null if nothing at valid index
        get {
                if (index<1)
                        throw new IndexOutOfRangeException
                        ("Indices in Exploding array start at 1");

                firstIndex=hiBitIndex(index)-1;
                if (firstIndex>maxFirstIndex)
                        throw new IndexOutOfRangeException
                        ("First index out of range");
                if (array[firstIndex]==null) return null;
                offSet=index%(1<<firstIndex);
                return array[firstIndex][offSet];
        }
```

```
            //set creates subarrays in jagged array as necessary
            set {
                  if (index<1)
                        throw new IndexOutOfRangeException
                        ("Indices in Exploding array start at 1");

                  firstIndex=hiBitIndex(index)-1;
                  if (firstIndex>maxFirstIndex)
                        throw new IndexOutOfRangeException
                        ("First index out of range");
                  modulus=1<<firstIndex;
                  if (array[firstIndex]==null)
                        array[firstIndex]=new Object[modulus];
                  offSet=index%modulus;
                  array[firstIndex][offSet]=value;
                  if (index>hiIndex) hiIndex=index;
            }
      }
```

Listing 14.1

```
using System;
public class ExplodingArray {

      //Exploding array will be represented with a jagged array
      //Each vector at index k in first vector will have 2^k slots
      private Object[][] array;

      //Fields used to compute the double index from single index
      //maxFirstIndex is largest first index determined by constructor
      private const int maxFirstIndex=30;
      //hiBit represents highest set bit in an index
      private int hiBit;
      //firstIndex is first index in jagged array computed from index
      private int firstIndex;
      //modulus is 2^firstIndex
      private int modulus;
      //offSet computed as index mod modulus-2nd index in jagged array
      private int offSet;
      //Stores the position of highest item in exploding array
      int hiIndex;

      //Create an ExplodingArray that can hold up to 2^31-1 items
      public ExplodingArray() {
            array=new Object[31][];
      }
```

(continued)

```
        //This is the indexer for the exploding array
        //Computes a double index into jagged array from single index
        public Object this[int index] {
              //get returns null if nothing at valid index
              get {
                    if (index<1)
                          throw new IndexOutOfRangeException
                          ("Indices in Exploding array start at 1");

                    firstIndex=hiBitIndex(index)-1;
                    if (firstIndex>maxFirstIndex)
                          throw new IndexOutOfRangeException
                          ("First index out of range");
                    if (array[firstIndex]==null) return null;
                    offSet=index%(1<<firstIndex);
                    return array[firstIndex][offSet];
              }
              //set creates subarrays in jagged array as necessary
              set {
                    if (index<1)
                          throw new IndexOutOfRangeException
                          ("Indices in Exploding array start at 1");

                    firstIndex=hiBitIndex(index)-1;
                    if (firstIndex>maxFirstIndex)
                          throw new IndexOutOfRangeException
                          ("First index out of range");
                    modulus=1<<firstIndex;
                    if (array[firstIndex]==null)
                          array[firstIndex]=new Object[modulus];
                    offSet=index%modulus;
                    array[firstIndex][offSet]=value;
                    if (index>hiIndex) hiIndex=index;
              }
        }

        //HighestIndex property returns index of item at highest
        //position in exploding array
        public int HighestIndex {
              get {return hiIndex;}
        }

        //Returns index (starting with 1) of highest set bit of num
        private int hiBitIndex(int num) {
              hiBit=1;
              while (num!=1) {
                    num>>=1;
                    hiBit++;
              }
              return hiBit;
        }

  }
```

TABLE 14.2

Constructor/Indexer/Property	*T*(*n*)
`public ExplodingArray();`	O(1)
`public Object this[int index] {get;}`	O(log*n*)
`public Object this[int index] {set;}`	O(log*n*)
`public int HighestIndex;`	O(1)

Analyzing the efficiency of the `ExplodingArray` class means primarily determining how long it takes to compute an index in the indexer. Say `i` is the supplied index; this involves determining the first index in the jagged array. This is found by finding the highest set bit of `i`, which I have written as a `while` loop. This loop shifts the `int i` to the right until a quantity of 1 is obtained. Because `i` can be as large as $2^{30} - 1$, determining this index will take no more than 30 right shifts, and so runs in time O(log*n*). Computing the offset occurs in constant time, so determining both indices is O(log*n*). Table 14.2 shows the performance of the indexer, the constructor, and the `HighestIndex` property.

To test this class, I provide a `TestExplodingArray` class, seen in Listing 14.2. It continually prompts the user to enter a string and a corresponding index specifying a position to store the string in the exploding array. If the user enters 0 (an invalid index for an `ExplodingArray`), the program iterates through the data structure and displays all the items.

Listing 14.2

```
using System;
public class TestExplodingArray {
    static void Main(String[] args) {
      ExplodingArray ea=new ExplodingArray(); int index; Object item;
      Console.Write("Enter index (0 to stop): ");
      while ((index=Int32.Parse(Console.ReadLine()))>0) {
            Console.Write(
                  "Enter string to store at specified position: ");
            ea[index]=Console.ReadLine();
            Console.Write("Enter index (0 to stop): ");
      }
      for (int i=1;i<=ea.HighestIndex;i++) {
            item=ea[i];
            if (item!=null) Console.WriteLine(i+": "+item);
      }
    }
}
```

Note that the loop goes only as far as needed using the `HighestIndex` property, and does not display any objects that are null. You can see this in our sample run.

```
Enter index (0 to stop): 20000000
Enter string to store at specified position: This is high!
Enter index (0 to stop): 1
Enter string to store at specified position: This is low!
Enter index (0 to stop): 123456
Enter string to store at specified position: This is still
pretty low.
Enter index (0 to stop): 1234567
Enter string to store at specified position: Getting higher...
Enter index (0 to stop): 0
1: This is low!
123456: This is still pretty low.
1234567: Getting higher...
20000000: This is high!
```

The `System.Collections` namespace contains an `ArrayList` class, which provides the functionality of an exploding array, and more. Table 14.3 shows the `ArrayList` members.

An `ArrayList` object is created with an initial capacity. Elements can be added to an `ArrayList` up to this capacity, whereupon it expands to accommodate even more items. An interesting exercise for you may be to modify the `ExplodingArray` class to give it more functionality; that is, to make it more like the `ArrayList` class.

Although a linked list is much more flexible than an array, it must be searched sequentially. What we would like is a data structure that is dynamic i.e., it can grow or shrink as needed), and offers a search time efficiency comparable to a binary search. An exploding array can do this; its elements are directly accessible by an index, so it can be sorted using efficient algorithms and searched using binary search. (One must be careful, however, to ensure that the index can be computed quickly, or the whole point of direct access is lost.)

■ DYNAMIC ARRAYS

Although the exploding array starts out small, a high index can cause an unreasonable request for memory from the operating system, and an `OutOfMemoryException` can be thrown. You may opt to create an array that expands at a constant rate. For lack of a better term, let's call this a "dynamic array."

TABLE 14.3

Public Constructors	Description
`ArrayList` Constructor	Overloaded. Initializes a new instance of the `ArrayList` class.
Public Properties	**Description**
`Capacity`	Gets or sets the number of elements that the `ArrayList` can contain.
`Count`	Gets the number of elements actually contained in the `ArrayList`.
`IsFixedSize`	Gets a value indicating whether the `ArrayList` has a fixed size.
`IsReadOnly`	Gets a value indicating whether the `ArrayList` is read-only.
`IsSynchronized`	Gets a value indicating whether access to the `ArrayList` is synchronized (thread-safe).
`Item`	Gets or sets the element at the specified index. In C#, this property is the indexer for the `ArrayList` class.
`SyncRoot`	Gets an object that can be used to synchronize access to the `ArrayList`.
Public Methods	**Description**
`Adapter`	Creates an `ArrayList` wrapper for a specific `IList`.
`Add`	Adds an object to the end of the `ArrayList`.
`AddRange`	Adds the elements of an ICollection to the end of the `ArrayList`.
`BinarySearch`	Overloaded. Uses a binary search algorithm to locate a specific element in the sorted `ArrayList` or a portion of it.
`Clear`	Removes all elements from the `ArrayList`.
`Clone`	Creates a shallow copy of the `ArrayList`.
`Contains`	Determines whether an element is in the `ArrayList`.
`CopyTo`	Overloaded. Copies the `ArrayList` or a portion of it to a one-dimensional array.
`FixedSize`	Overloaded. Returns a list wrapper with a fixed size, where elements are allowed to be modified, but not added or removed.
`GetEnumerator`	Overloaded. Returns an enumerator that can iterate through the `ArrayList`.
`GetRange`	Returns an `ArrayList` that represents a subset of the elements in the source `ArrayList`.
`IndexOf`	Overload. Returns the zero-based index of the first occurrence of a value in the `ArrayList` or in a portion of it.
`Insert`	Inserts an element into the `ArrayList` at the specified index.
`InsertRange`	Inserts the elements of a collection into the `ArrayList` at the specified index.
`LastIndexOf`	Overloaded. Returns the zero-based index of the last occurrence of a value in the `ArrayList` or in a portion of it.
`ReadOnly`	Overloaded. Returns a list wrapper that is read-only.

(continued)

TABLE 14.3 (continued)

Public Methods	Description
`Remove`	Removes the first occurrence of a specific object from the `ArrayList`.
`RemoveAt`	Removes the element at the specified index of the `ArrayList`.
`RemoveRange`	Removes a range of elements from the `ArrayList`.
`Repeat`	Returns an `ArrayList` whose elements are copies of the specified value.
`Reverse`	Overloaded. Reverses the order of the elements in the `ArrayList` or a portion of it.
`SetRange`	Copies the elements of a collection over a range of elements in the `ArrayList`.
`Sort`	Overloaded. Sorts the elements in the `ArrayList` or a portion of it.
`Synchronized`	Overloaded. Returns a list wrapper that is synchronized (thread-safe).
`ToArray`	Overloaded. Copies the elements of the `ArrayList` to a new array.
`TrimToSize`	Sets the capacity to the actual number of elements in the `ArrayList`.

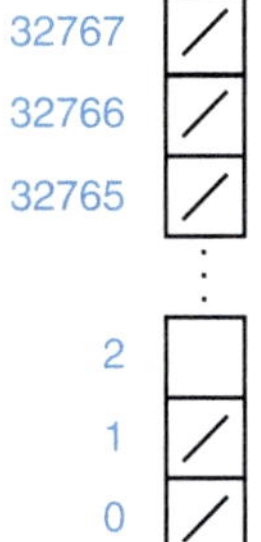

Figure 14.5

Suppose we implement a dynamic array using an underlying two-dimensional array. This time, however, begin with a primary vector of 2^{15} = 32,768 elements, as in Figure 14.5.

Each cell in this primary vector will reference a subvector, each containing 2^{16} or 65,536 elements. No subvector exists until an index determines that an object be placed in it. The application using the dynamic array specifies a single nonnegative index, say `i`. The indexer for the dynamic array class converts this into a dual index, according to the following formula:

Index in primary vector: $j = i / 65{,}536$ (integer division)
Subvector index: $k = i \bmod 65{,}536$

Because 65,536 = 2^{16}, j is the largest 16 bits of i, and k is the smallest 16 bits of i. The highest bit of j is a sign bit, so j ranges in value from 0 to $2^{15} - 1$, and k ranges from 0 to $2^{16} - 1$. But these are exactly the lengths chosen for the primary vector and each of the subvectors.

As an example, suppose D is a dynamic array, and we wish to place something in cell position $D[131076]$. We compute

$j = 131{,}076 / 65{,}536 = 2$

and

$k = 131{,}076 \bmod 65{,}536 = 4$

and the cell we wish to access is at position 2,4 in the underlying two-dimensional array (see Figure 14.6).

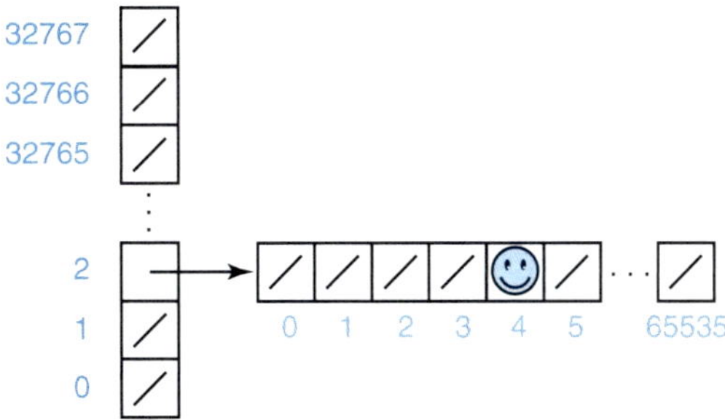

Figure 14.6

Listing 14.3 shows a DynamicArray class. Notice that no subvector exists until it needs to actually hold something.

Listing 14.3

```
using System;
public class DynamicArray {

      //Dynamic array will be represented with a 2D array
      //Each vector at index k in first vector will have 65536 slots
      private Object[][] array;
      //modulus is 65536=2^16
      private const int modulus=65536;
      //maxIndex represents largest accessible index
      private const int maxIndex=Int32.MaxValue-1;

      //Fields used to compute the double index from single index
      //firstIndex is the first index in array computed from index
      private int firstIndex;
      //offSet computed as index mod modulus-2nd index in array
      private int offSet;
      //Stores the position of highest item in dynamic array
      int hiIndex;

      //Create a DynamicArray which holds up to Int32.MaxValue-1 items
      public DynamicArray() {
            array=new Object[Int32.MaxValue/modulus+1][];
      }

      //This is the indexer for the dynamic array
      //Computes a double index into the array from a single index
      public Object this[int index] {
            //get returns null if nothing at valid index
            get {
                  if (index<0||index>maxIndex)
```

(continued)

```
                    throw new IndexOutOfRangeException
                    ("Index must be between 0 and "+maxIndex);

                firstIndex=index/modulus;
                if (array[firstIndex]==null) return null;
                offSet=index%modulus;
                return array[firstIndex][offSet];
            }
            //set creates subarrays in jagged array as necessary
            set {
                if (index<0||index>maxIndex)
                    throw new IndexOutOfRangeException
                    ("Index must be between 0 and "+maxIndex);

                firstIndex=index/modulus;
                if (array[firstIndex]==null)
                    array[firstIndex]=new Object[modulus];
                offSet=index%modulus;
                array[firstIndex][offSet]=value;
                if (index>hiIndex) hiIndex=index;
            }
        }

        //HighestIndex property returns index of item at highest
        //position in dynamic array
        public int HighestIndex {
            get {return hiIndex;}
        }

}
```

Note that the maximum index for a `DynamicArray` is actually $2^{31} - 2$, rather than $2^{31} - 1$. This is simply to allow a `for` loop to traverse the array without exceeding `Int32.MaxValue`, which is, of course, $2^{31} - 1$. This can be seen in the following test program, wherein a `for` loop is used to display the non-null contents of the dynamic array. By placing an item at index $2^{31} - 2 = 2147483646$, the loop control variable can still reach 2147483647, and exit the loop without throwing an exception.

The program in Listing 14.4 demonstrates use of the `DynamicArray` class.

Listing 14.4

```
using System;
public class TestDynamicArray {
    static void Main(String[] args) {
      DynamicArray da=new DynamicArray();
      Console.WriteLine("Minimum index: 0");
      Console.WriteLine("Maximum index: "+(Int32.MaxValue-1));
      int index; Object item;
      Console.Write("Enter index (-1 to stop): ");
      while ((index=Int32.Parse(Console.ReadLine()))>=0) {
            Console.Write(
                  "Enter string to store at specified position: ");
            da[index]=Console.ReadLine();
            Console.Write("Enter index (-1 to stop): ");
      }
      int i;
      for (i=0;i<=da.HighestIndex;i++) {
            item=da[i];
            if (item!=null) Console.WriteLine(i+": "+item);
      }
      Console.WriteLine("Value of loop control variable: "+i);
    }
}
```

Here is a test run:

```
Minimum index: 0
Maximum index: 2147483646
Enter index (-1 to stop): 0
Enter string to store at specified position: I'm so low
Enter index (-1 to stop): 65535
Enter string to store at specified position: I'm in same row as I'm so low
Enter index (-1 to stop): 65536
Enter string to store at specified position: I'm kicking it up a notch
Enter index (-1 to stop): 2147483646
Enter string to store at specified position: I'm at the tail end-single cell
higher than me is always vacant
Enter index (-1 to stop): -1
0: I'm so low
65535: I'm in same row as I'm so low
65536: I'm kicking it up a notch
2147483646: I'm at the tail end-single cell higher than me is always vacant
Value of loop control variable: 2147483647
```

Notice that if $2^{31} - 1 = 2147483647$ were a valid index, the loop control variable would exceed the maximum value of an `int` before it could be tested to exit the `for` loop. You'll note that this also means that the last cell at position 32767,65535 in the 2D array is never used, but this is a small price to pay for this convenience!

I'm sure you've noticed that there is some waste involved in memory allocation with the `ExplodingArray` and `DynamicArray` classes. We can easily wind up allocating memory for huge arrays that are mostly empty. Next we cover a data structure that is consistently economical in terms of memory usage. It also has the search efficiency of a binary search (in the average case), but never needs to be sorted because it maintains its order naturally.

■ BINARY SEARCH TREES

A binary search tree, seen in Figure 14.7, is an arrangement of nodes; each node has a left child reference and a right child reference. Every node in a binary search tree must be larger than its left child (if it has one), and smaller than its right child (likewise, if it has one). The node at the "top" of the tree is called the root. Any node can serve as the root, subject to the previous rules. Note that a binary search tree can only hold data for which an order has been established (for us C# fans, that means `IComparable` items). Also, note that our definition does not allow a binary search tree to contain duplicate items.

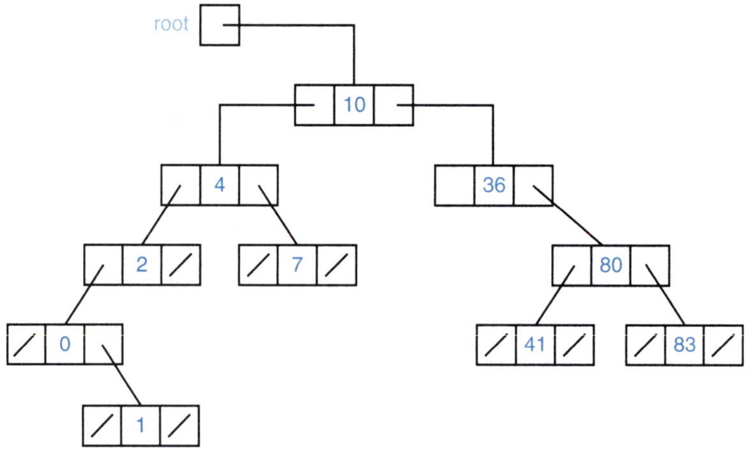

Figure 14.7

Class: BinarySearchTree

The entire `BinarySearchTree` class can be seen in Listing 14.5 (see pages 392–394). Making a `BinarySearchTree` class will first require defining a `BinarySearch-TreeNode` class, with a left child reference and a right child reference:

```
public class BSTNode {
      public IComparable datum;
      public BSTNode leftChild;
      public BSTNode rightChild;
      public BSTNode(IComparable item) {
            datum=item;
      }
}
```

We have access to all items in the binary search tree through the top item, or the root. This is the only field we have defined, and the constructor simply sets it to null:

```
public class BinarySearchTree {

   BSTNode root;

   public BinarySearchTree() {//Create an empty tree
      root=null;
   }
//...
}
```

The `Empty` property tells us whether the tree is empty, and the `Clear()` method chops off the tree at its root.

```
public bool Empty {get{return root==null;}}

public void Clear() {root=null;}
```

Inserting into a binary tree first means finding the place to put the item. Suppose you want to insert the item "6" into the previous binary search tree. We examine first the root; because 6 < 10, so we move to the left child, 4. Because 6 > 4, we move to its right child, 7. Because 6 < 7, and because 7 has no left child, this is where we insert the 6 (see Figure 14.8).

We must attach the parent node reference to the new child node, so we must always be aware as we travel into the tree whether our last movement was to the left or to the right. Of course, inserting an item into an empty tree merely produces the root.

Here is how we insert a node, with special cases taken into account:

```
public void Insert(IComparable item) {
   BSTNode newNode=new BSTNode(item);
   if (root==null) {root=newNode; return;}
```

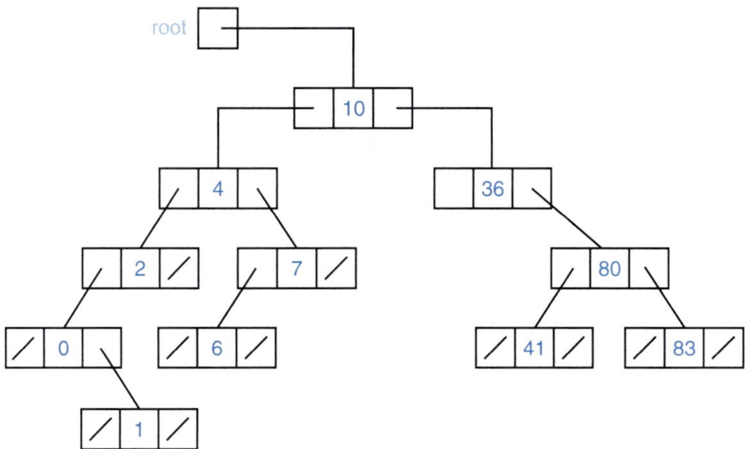

Figure 14.8

```
   BSTNode t=root, p=null;
   bool wentLeft=false;
   while (t!=null) {
      if (t.datum.CompareTo(item)==0) throw new
         ArgumentException("Item already in tree.");
      else if (t.datum.CompareTo(item)<0) {
         p=t;
         t=t.rightChild;
         wentLeft=false;}
      else {
         p=t;
         t=t.leftChild;
         wentLeft=true;}
   }
   if (wentLeft) p.leftChild=newNode;
   else p.rightChild=newNode;
}
```

Retrieving an item from a tree means finding it first. This means comparing the target item to some node, and based on that comparison either stopping (item found), moving left, or moving right. If the item sought is not in the tree, you will eventually encounter a null reference.

Here is the code that finds an item in a tree (if present), and returns it:

```
public IComparable Get(IComparable target) {
   return recursiveGet(root,target);
}

private IComparable recursiveGet(BSTNode treePoint,
```

```
    IComparable target) {
    IComparable answer=null;
    if (treePoint==null) throw new NotFoundException
    ("Item not in tree.");
    else if (treePoint.datum.CompareTo(target)<0)
    answer=recursiveGet(treePoint.rightChild,target);
    else if (target.CompareTo(treePoint.datum)<0)
    answer=recursiveGet(treePoint.leftChild,target);
    else answer=treePoint.datum;
    return answer;
}
```

Note that the method is recursive; recursion actually makes traversing an entire tree much easier, as you will see in the `ToString()` method.

Removing an item from a binary search tree is tricky. Of course, we must first find the item we want to remove:

```
public void Remove(IComparable target) {
    BSTNode t=root, p=null;
    bool wentLeft=false;
    while (t!=null&&t.datum.CompareTo(target)!=0) {
        if (t.datum.CompareTo(target)<0) {
            p=t;
            t=t.rightChild;
            wentLeft=false;
        } else {
            p=t;
            t=t.leftChild;
            wentLeft=true;
        }
    }
    if (t==null) throw new NotFoundException
    ("Item not in tree.");

//More code...

}
```

If the node is found, there are different cases to consider; they are

1. The node to remove has no children.
2. The node to remove has only one child.
3. The node to remove has two children.

Of course, the node we are trying to remove may be the root; we must also consider this.

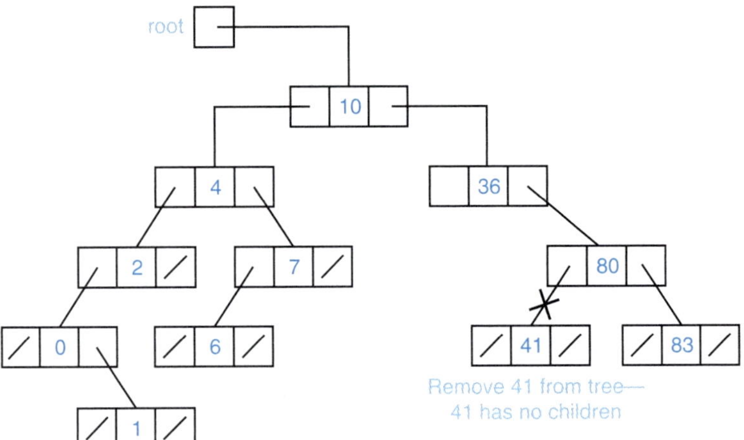

Figure 14.9

Case 1: No Children

If the node we wish to remove has no children, we simply cut the node off from its parent (see Figure 14.9). Of course, we must know whether it is a left child or a right child. If the node to delete is the root, we set the root to null.

```
   public void Remove(IComparable target) {

//...

      if (t.leftChild==null&&t.rightChild==null) {
         if (t==root) {
            root=null;
         } else {
            if (wentLeft) p.leftChild=null;
            else p.rightChild=null;
         }

//More code...

}
```

Case 2: One Child

If the node X we want to remove has exactly one child, we take note of whether this child is a left child or a right child of X (see Figure 14.10). We then connect that child to the parent of X, noting whether X is a left child or a right child of its parent.

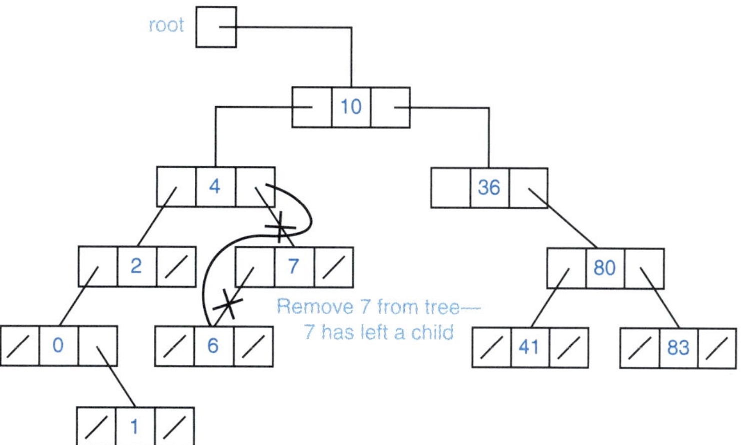

Figure 14.10

```
   public void Remove(IComparable target) {

//...

      } else if (t.leftChild==null) {
         if (t==root) {
            root=t.rightChild;
         } else {
            if (wentLeft) p.leftChild=t.rightChild;
            else p.rightChild=t.rightChild;
         }
       } else if (t.rightChild==null) {
         if (t==root) {
            root=t.leftChild;
         } else {
            if (wentLeft) p.leftChild=t.leftChild;
            else p.rightChild=t.leftChild;
         }

//...

}
```

Case 3: Two Children

If the node X we want to remove has two children, we don't actually delete that node X; we find the largest item in the tree which is still smaller than X (see Figure 14.11). If you

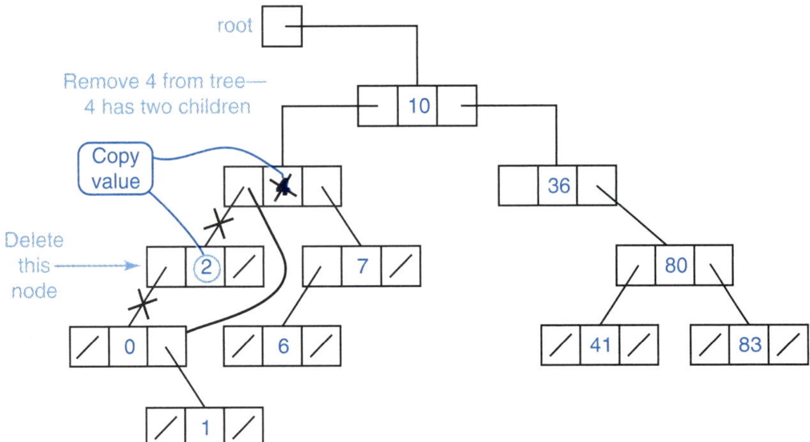

Figure 14.11

think about it, this node Y is the item farthest to the right in the left subtree of X. We copy the data Y to X, then delete the node Y. Because Y cannot have a right child, it simply becomes a matter of connecting Y's left child to Y's parent (of course, Y may not even have a left child).

```
   public void Remove(IComparable target) {

//...

       } else {
       BSTNode tp=t;
       BSTNode travel=t.leftChild;
       while (travel.rightChild!=null) {
              tp=travel;
              travel=travel.rightChild;
       }
       t.datum=travel.datum;
       if (tp==t) tp.leftChild=travel.leftChild;
       else tp.rightChild=travel.leftChild;
       }

//...

}
```

Traversing the entire tree for, say, the `ToString()` method, might seem tricky, but the trick is to use recursion. We can even see the elements in order! Such a traversal is called an in-order traversal.

To do an *in-order* traversal of a binary search tree, begin with the root node:

1. If the node has a left child, do an in-order traversal of the left subtree.
2. Process the node.
3. If the node has a right child, do an in-order traversal of the right subtree.

Processing the entire left subtree before you process a node means all items smaller than that node will be processed first. Likewise, processing the right subtree after any particular node means the larger items will be processed last.

There are other ways to traverse a binary search tree. The most common are as follows

To do a *pre-order* traversal of a binary search tree, begin with the root node:

1. Process the node.
2. If the node has a left child, do a pre-order traversal of the left subtree.
3. If the node has a right child, do a pre-order traversal of the right subtree.

To do a *post-order* traversal of a binary search tree, begin with the root node:

1. If the node has a left child, do a post-order traversal of the left subtree.
2. If the node has a right child, do a post-order traversal of the right subtree.
3. Process the node.

The `ToString()` method does an in-order traversal:

```
public override String ToString() {
   StringBuilder s=new StringBuilder("");
   recursiveToString(root,s);
   return s.ToString();
}

public void recursiveToString(BSTNode p,StringBuilder output) {
   if (p!=null) {
      recursiveToString(p.leftChild,output);
      output.Append("  "+p.datum.ToString());
      recursiveToString(p.rightChild,output);
   }
}
```

Listing 14.5

```
using System;
using System.Text;
public class BinarySearchTree {

   BSTNode root;

   public class BSTNode {
         public IComparable datum;
         public BSTNode leftChild;
         public BSTNode rightChild;
         public BSTNode(IComparable item) {
               datum=item;
         }
   }

   public BinarySearchTree() {//Create an empty tree
      root=null;
   }

   public bool Empty {get{return root==null;}}

   public void Insert(IComparable item) {
      BSTNode newNode=new BSTNode(item);
      if (root==null) {root=newNode; return;}
      BSTNode t=root, p=null;
      bool wentLeft=false;
      while (t!=null) {
         if (t.datum.CompareTo(item)==0) throw new
            ArgumentException("Item already in tree.");
         else if (t.datum.CompareTo(item)<0) {
            p=t;
            t=t.rightChild;
            wentLeft=false;}
         else {
            p=t;
            t=t.leftChild;
            wentLeft=true;}
      }
      if (wentLeft) p.leftChild=newNode;
      else p.rightChild=newNode;
   }

   public void Remove(IComparable target) {
      BSTNode t=root, p=null;
      bool wentLeft=false;
      while (t!=null&&t.datum.CompareTo(target)!=0) {
         if (t.datum.CompareTo(target)<0) {
            p=t;
            t=t.rightChild;
```

(continued)

```
            wentLeft=false;
         } else {
            p=t;
            t=t.leftChild;
            wentLeft=true;
         }
      }
      if (t==null) throw new NotFoundException
      ("Item not in tree.");
      if (t.leftChild==null&&t.rightChild==null) {
         if (t==root) {
            root=null;
         } else {
            if (wentLeft) p.leftChild=null;
            else p.rightChild=null;
         }
      } else if (t.leftChild==null) {
         if (t==root) {
            root=t.rightChild;
         } else {
            if (wentLeft) p.leftChild=t.rightChild;
            else p.rightChild=t.rightChild;
         }
      } else if (t.rightChild==null) {
         if (t==root) {
            root=t.leftChild;
         } else {
            if (wentLeft) p.leftChild=t.leftChild;
            else p.rightChild=t.leftChild;
         }
      } else {
      BSTNode tp=t;
      BSTNode travel=t.leftChild;
      while (travel.rightChild!=null) {
            tp=travel;
            travel=travel.rightChild;
      }
      t.datum=travel.datum;
      if (tp==t) tp.leftChild=travel.leftChild;
      else tp.rightChild=travel.leftChild;
      }
   }

   public IComparable Get(IComparable target) {
      return recursiveGet(root,target);
   }

   private IComparable recursiveGet(BSTNode treePoint,
      IComparable target) {
      IComparable answer=null;
```

(continued)

```
        if (treePoint==null) throw new NotFoundException
        ("Item not in tree.");
        else if (treePoint.datum.CompareTo(target)<0)
        answer=recursiveGet(treePoint.rightChild,target);
        else if (target.CompareTo(treePoint.datum)<0)
        answer=recursiveGet(treePoint.leftChild,target);
        else answer=treePoint.datum;
        return answer;
    }

    public void Clear() {root=null;}

    public override String ToString() {
        StringBuilder s=new StringBuilder("");
        recursiveToString(root,s);
        return s.ToString();
    }

    public void recursiveToString(BSTNode p,StringBuilder output) {
        if (p!=null) {
            recursiveToString(p.leftChild,output);
            output.Append(" "+p.datum.ToString());
            recursiveToString(p.rightChild,output);
        }
    }
}
```

Listing 14.6 is the test program for a binary search tree, based on the model of our other test programs.

Listing 14.6

```
using System;
public class TestBinarySearchTree {
    static void Main() {
      BinarySearchTree bst=new BinarySearchTree();
      String result="";

      DisplayHeader();
      char option = Console.ReadLine()[0];
      while (option!='Q') {
            switch (option) {
                  case 'I':
                  Console.Write("Enter item: ");
                  bst.Insert(Console.ReadLine());
                  break;
```

(continued)

```
                case 'G':
                Console.Write("Enter item: ");
                try {
                      result=(String)bst.Get
                            (Console.ReadLine());
                } catch (NotFoundException ne) {
                      Console.WriteLine(ne);
                }
                Console.WriteLine(result);
                break;

                case 'R':
                Console.Write("Enter item: ");
                try {
                      bst.Remove(Console.ReadLine());
                } catch (NotFoundException ne) {
                      Console.WriteLine(ne);
                }
                break;

                case 'S':
                Console.WriteLine(bst.ToString());
                break;

                case 'X':
                bst.Clear();
                break;

                default:
                Console.WriteLine("Invalid option");
                break;
          }
          DisplayHeader();
          option = Console.ReadLine()[0];
    }
  }

  static void DisplayHeader() {
          Console.WriteLine("Enter one of the following:");
          Console.WriteLine("I - insert");
          Console.WriteLine("G - get");
          Console.WriteLine("R - remove");
          Console.WriteLine("S - show bst");
          Console.WriteLine("X - clear bst");
          Console.WriteLine("Q - quit");
          Console.Write("==> ");

  }

}
```

Here is a sample run of the code:

```
Enter one of the following:
I - insert
G - get
R - remove
S - show bst
X - clear bst
Q - quit
==> I
Enter item: RIGHT
Enter one of the following:
I - insert
G - get
R - remove
S - show bst
X - clear bst
Q - quit
==> I
Enter item: HERE
Enter one of the following:
I - insert
G - get
R - remove
S - show bst
X - clear bst
Q - quit
==> I
Enter item: IS
Enter one of the following:
I - insert
G - get
R - remove
S - show bst
X - clear bst
Q - quit
==> I
Enter item: NIRVANA
Enter one of the following:
I - insert
G - get
R - remove
S - show bst
X - clear bst
```

```
Q - quit
==> S
 HERE IS NIRVANA RIGHT
Enter one of the following:
I - insert
G - get
R - remove
S - show bst
X - clear bst
Q - quit
==> G
Enter item: IS
IS
Enter one of the following:
I - insert
G - get
R - remove
S - show bst
X - clear bst
Q - quit
==> G
Enter item: is
NotFoundException: Item not in tree.
   at BinarySearchTree.recursiveGet(BSTNode treePoint,
IComparable target)
   at BinarySearchTree.recursiveGet(BSTNode treePoint,
IComparable target)
   at BinarySearchTree.recursiveGet(BSTNode treePoint,
IComparable target)
   at BinarySearchTree.recursiveGet(BSTNode treePoint,
IComparable target)
   at BinarySearchTree.Get(IComparable target)
   at TestBinarySearchTree.Main()
IS
Enter one of the following:
I - insert
G - get
R - remove
S - show bst
X - clear bst
Q - quit
==> G
Enter item: NIRVANA
NIRVANA
```

```
Enter one of the following:
I - insert
G - get
R - remove
S - show bst
X - clear bst
Q - quit
==> R
Enter item: NIRVANA
Enter one of the following:
I - insert
G - get
R - remove
S - show bst
X - clear bst
Q - quit
==> S
 HERE IS RIGHT
Enter one of the following:
I - insert
G - get
R - remove
S - show bst
X - clear bst
Q - quit
==> X
Enter one of the following:
I - insert
G - get
R - remove
S - show bst
X - clear bst
Q - quit
==> S

Enter one of the following:
I - insert
G - get
R - remove
S - show bst
X - clear bst
Q - quit
==> Q
```

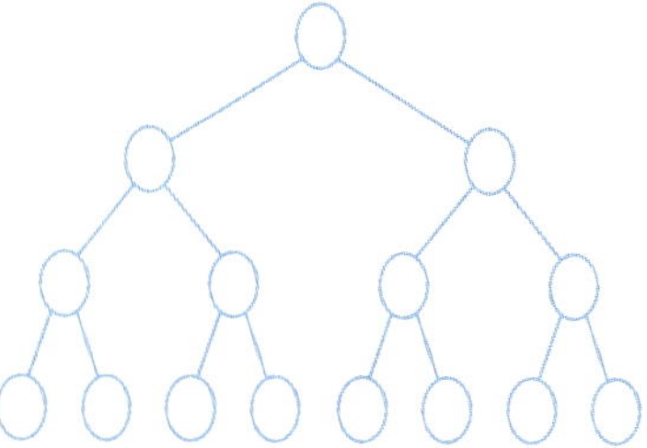

Figure 14.12

Figure 14.13

☐ Efficiency Considerations of Binary Search Trees

Consider the tree in Figure 14.12, which has 15 elements in it.

The tree in Figure 14.13 also has 15 elements (all children are right children, all left children are null).

The search efficiency of the first tree (called a "complete tree") is clearly superior to the second tree (called a "sparse tree"). This complete tree is 4 levels deep. Consider now a similar complete tree that is 30 levels deep; such a tree contains $2^{30} - 1$, or more than a billion elements, but finding any item in such a tree will take no more than 30 lookups! A sparse tree containing that many elements will take an average of 500 million lookups to find an item.

The following observation is obvious:

> A complete binary search tree has the search efficiency of a binary search, whereas a sparse binary search tree approximates a sequential search.

If the data entering a binary search tree comes in random order, a tree approximating a complete tree tends to be formed, but, ironically, if data enters the tree in sorted order, this creates the worst possible sparse tree.

Suppose the data enters a tree in random order. If this is the average case, then Table 14.4 describes our `BinarySearchTree` class performance.

In general, we cannot predict whether the data coming into the tree will be sorted, or nearly sorted, or completely random. A sparse binary search tree will do insertions, retrievals, and removals in linear time versus logarithmic time, *vastly* decreasing performance.

TABLE 14.4

Constructor/Property/Method	*T(n)*
`public BinarySearchTree();`	O(1)
`public bool Empty;`	O(1)
`public void Insert(IComparable item);`	O(logn)
`public void Remove(IComparable target);`	O(logn)
`public IComparable Get(IComparable target);`	O(logn)
`public void Clear();`	O(1)
`public override String ToString();`	O(*n*)

Thus, we must conceive of ways to "rearrange" a binary search tree if necessary for data that produces "long branches." There are various ways of doing this. Among these, the most popular solutions are

- Red-black trees
- AVL trees
- 2–3 trees
- Generalized b-trees

It would be an interesting exercise for you to search the literature and design a class that represents any one of these data structures.

■ HEAPS

A heap is a complete binary tree (i.e., each node has two children) with the condition that the data in each node be larger than both of its children. (An inverted heap has each node smaller than its children.) Only the root can be removed from the heap; the tree must rearrange itself after a removal to maintain heap formation. There are various applications for heaps; for example, priority queues. A priority queue is a queue in which the item with highest priority is always removed first.

For reasons we will go into shortly, it is easy to arrange a heap so that the tree is complete. Actually, a complete tree need not be completely filled out; such a complete tree has the shape shown in Figure 14.14.

Figure 14.14

A complete tree has all levels completely filled out, with the possible exception of the deepest level, which is always filled out left to right.

Inserting an item into a complete tree is easy; we insert the item into the first available spot in the final row (or, if the last row is filled out, by starting another row). In Figure 14.15 we insert the item 17 into this heap:

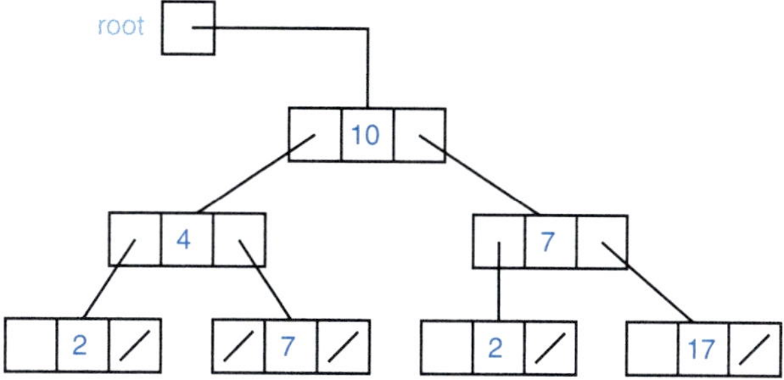

Figure 14.15

Inserting an item can destroy the heap formation, as it does here. When this happens, the new element must "bubble up" to its proper position by repeatedly exchanging places with its parent. When the item eventually becomes larger than both its children, we have a heap again, as seen in Figure 14.16 and Figure 14.17.

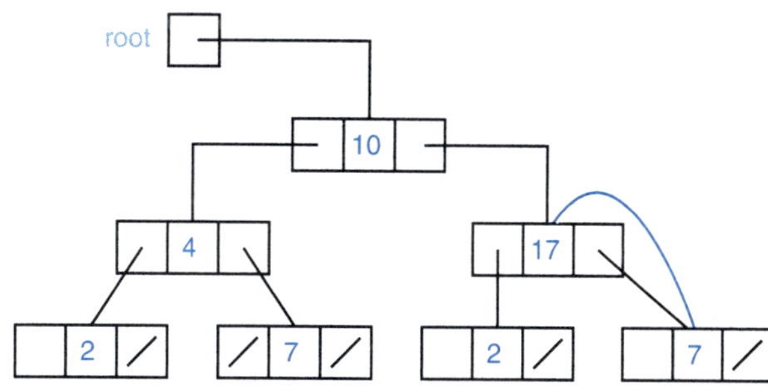

Figure 14.16

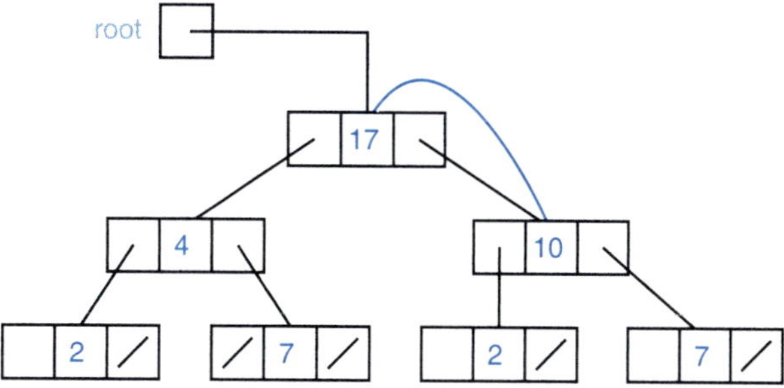

Figure 14.17

It may be necessary for the item to bubble all the way to the root or "top" of the heap. Note that because a heap is a complete tree, it never takes long for an item to bubble up to its proper position.

Only the top of the heap can be removed, so this will certainly require rearranging the tree. Once the data in the root is retrieved, we do the following:

1. If the node has two children, replace it with the data in the larger child. Repeat this step with the larger child until you encounter a node with less than two children.

2. If the node has one child, that child must be the last node in the tree; replace the data in the node with its child's data and delete the child.

3. If the node (call it node X) has no children, copy the data from the last node in the tree to the node, and delete the last node in the tree.

4. The data copied into node X in step 3 may destroy the heap formation. Bubble this up to its proper position in the heap.

You will see that this maintains the order of a heap, and it's not as complicated as it sounds. Let us remove the root from our example heap. We take out the 17, and replace it with the larger of its children, the 10, as in Figure 14.18.

In Figure 14.19 we now replace the 10 with the larger of its two children, the 7.

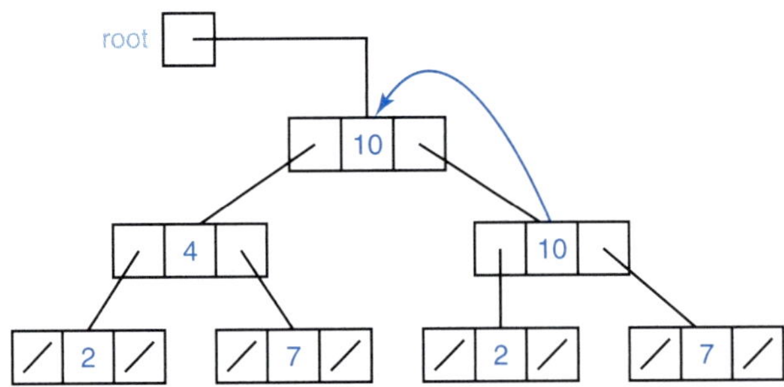

Figure 14.18

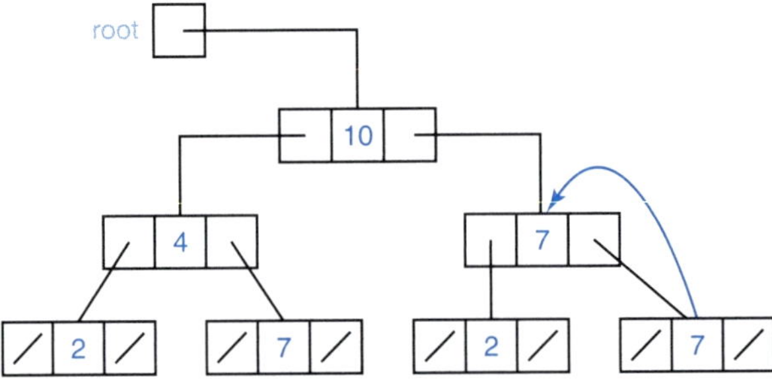

Figure 14.19

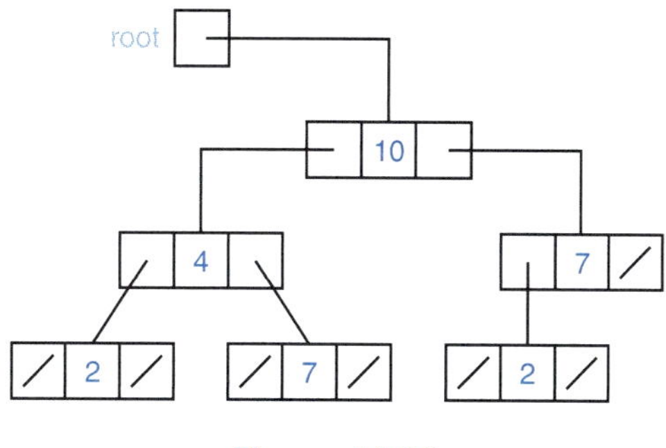

Figure 14.20

The last 7 has no children, so we copy the data in the last node of the tree to this node. In this case the 7 is the last node, so this is redundant. We then delete the last node in the heap, and in this case, there is nothing to bubble up to position (see Figure 14.20).

An interesting thing about heaps is that because they are always complete trees, they can be implemented easily using an array. To see how this is done, put the root in slot 0 of the array, and its children and all other children can be found as shown in Table 14.5.

Also, given any slot in the array, we can easily find the position of its parent (see Table 14.6). As an example, take the heap shown in Figure 14.21. The elements of this heap would be placed in the array as in Figure 14.22.

This manner of representing a heap is actually the conventional one; in fact, you may find it much harder to write the linked version of a heap.

TABLE 14.5

Parent Slot	Left Child Slot	Right Child Slot
0	$2 \times 0 + 1 = 1$	$2 \times 0 + 2 = 2$
1	$2 \times 1 + 1 = 3$	$2 \times 0 + 2 = 4$
2	$2 \times 2 + 1 = 5$	$2 \times 2 + 2 = 6$
3	$2 \times 3 + 1 = 7$	$2 \times 3 + 2 = 8$
…	…	…
k	$2k + 1$	$2k + 2$

TABLE 14.6

Child Slot	Parent Slot
1	(1 − 1)/2 = 0
2	(2 − 1)/2 = 0
3	(3 − 1)/2 = 1
4	(4 − 1)/2 = 1
5	(5 − 1)/2 = 2
6	(6 − 1)/2 = 2
7	(7 − 1)/2 = 3
8	(8 − 1)/2 = 3
...	...
k	(*k* − 1)/2

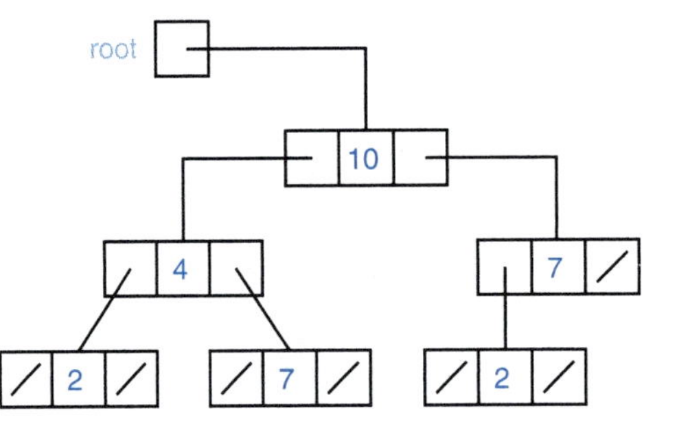

Figure 14.21

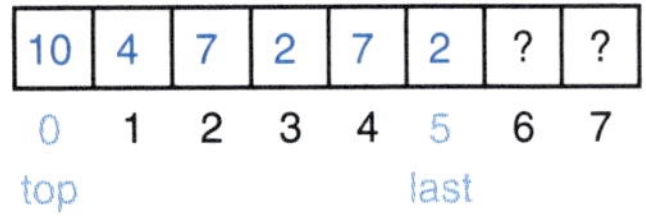

Figure 14.22

☐ Class: Heap

Our `Heap` class (shown in its entirety in Listing 14.7 on pages 407–408) will be represented using an array. There will be a couple of other fields to record the maximum number of elements that can be placed in the heap (i.e., the size of the array), and another to record the number of elements currently in the heap. The constructor creates the array based on an incoming value.

```
public class Heap {

  IComparable[] element;
  int size;
  int maxSize;
```

```
  public Heap(int max) {
    maxSize=max;
    element=new IComparable[max];
    size=0;
  }
//...
}
```

The `Empty` and `Full` properties return whether or not the heap is empty/full. `Size` returns the number of elements on the heap.

```
public bool Full {get{return size==maxSize;}}
public bool Empty {get{return size==0;}}
public int Size {get{return size;}}
```

The `Insert()` method works as described. A new item is inserted just after the last child position in the heap (provided it isn't full), then that item exchanges positions with its parents until it "bubbles up" to its correct position. This bubbling up is handled by a private `bubbleUp()` method.

```
public void Insert(IComparable item) {
  if (Full) throw new FullException("Heap is full.");
  int marker=size++;
  element[marker]=item;
  bubbleUp(marker);
}
```

Here is the `bubbleUp()` method:

```
private void bubbleUp(int marker) {
  int parent=(marker-1)/2;
  while (marker>=1
    &&element[parent].CompareTo(element[marker])<0) {
    IComparable temp=element[marker];
    element[marker]=element[parent];
    element[parent]=temp;
    marker=parent;
    parent=(marker-1)/2;
  }
}
```

The `Remove()` method removes the root of the heap, then rearranges the heap so that it remains in heap formation. It also uses the `bubbleUp()` method after moving the last item in the heap to the last swapped position, and bubbles that item up.

```
public void Remove() {
  if (Empty) throw new EmptyException("Heap is empty.");
  int parent=0;
  int child1=1;
```

```
  int child2=2;
  int smallerChild=0;
  while (child2<=size) {
    if (child2==size) {
      element[parent]=element[child1];
      parent=child1;
      child2++;
    } else {
      if (element[child1].CompareTo(element[child2])<0)
          smallerChild=child2;
      else smallerChild=child1;
      element[parent]=element[smallerChild];
      parent=smallerChild;
      child1=2*parent+1;
      child2=2*parent+2;
    }
  }
  element[parent]=element[--size];
  bubbleUp(parent);
}
```

Of course, the `Peek()` method merely returns the item on top of the heap (without removing it).

```
public IComparable Peek() {
  if (Empty) throw new EmptyException("Heap is empty.");
  return element[0];
}
```

The `Clear()` method passes through the array and cuts off all its items, making them available for garbage collection.

```
public void Clear() {
    for (int i=0;i<size;i++) element[i]=null;
    size=0;
}
```

The `ToString()` method merely passes through the array and adds a string representation of each item to a string, which is returned. The `ToString()` method shows the exact order in which the items are stored in the heap.

```
public override String ToString() {
  String s="";
  for (int i=0;i<size;i++) s=s+" "+element[i].ToString();
  return s;
}
```

Listing 14.7

```
using System;
public class Heap {

  IComparable[] element;
  int size;
  int maxSize;

  public Heap(int max) {
    maxSize=max;
    element=new IComparable[max];
    size=0;
  }

  public bool Full {get{return size==maxSize;}}
  public bool Empty {get{return size==0;}}
  public int Size {get{return size;}}

  public void Insert(IComparable item) {
    if (Full) throw new FullException("Heap is full.");
    int marker=size++;
    element[marker]=item;
    bubbleUp(marker);
  }

  public IComparable Peek() {
    if (Empty) throw new EmptyException("Heap is empty.");
    return element[0];
  }

  public void Remove() {
    if (Empty) throw new EmptyException("Heap is empty.");
    int parent=0;
    int child1=1;
    int child2=2;
    int smallerChild=0;
    while (child2<=size) {
      if (child2==size) {
        element[parent]=element[child1];
        parent=child1;
        child2++;
      } else {
        if (element[child1].CompareTo(element[child2])<0)
            smallerChild=child2;
        else smallerChild=child1;
        element[parent]=element[smallerChild];
        parent=smallerChild;
        child1=2*parent+1;
        child2=2*parent+2;
      }
    }
```

(continued)

```
      element[parent]=element[--size];
      bubbleUp(parent);
    }

    private void bubbleUp(int marker) {
      int parent=(marker-1)/2;
      while (marker>=1
        &&element[parent].CompareTo(element[marker])<0) {
        IComparable temp=element[marker];
        element[marker]=element[parent];
        element[parent]=temp;
        marker=parent;
        parent=(marker-1)/2;
      }
    }

    public void Clear() {
        for (int i=0;i<size;i++) element[i]=null;
        size=0;
    }

    public override String ToString() {
      String s="";
      for (int i=0;i<size;i++) s=s+" "+element[i].ToString();
      return s;
    }

  }
```

Table 14.7 is the analysis of the various methods of the Heap class.

TABLE 14.7

Constructor/Property/Method	***T(n)***
`public Heap(int max);`	O(1)
`public bool Full;`	O(1)
`public bool Empt;`	O(1)
`public int Size;`	O(1)
`public void Insert(IComparable item);`	O(log*n*)
`public IComparable Peek();`	O(1)
`public void Remove();`	O(log*n*)
`public void Clear();`	O(*n*)
`public override String ToString();`	O(*n*)

Note that insertions/removals are O(logn) because of the "bubbling up" process that takes place; the heap is guaranteed to be a complete binary tree, so this activity is assuredly logarithmic.

The `TestHeap` program in Listing 14.8 allows the user to test functions of the `Heap` class.

Listing 14.8

```
using System;
public class TestHeap {
    static void Main() {
      Heap heap=new Heap(1000);
      String result="";

      DisplayHeader();
      char option = Console.ReadLine()[0];
      while (option!='Q') {
            switch (option) {
                  case 'I':
                  Console.Write("Enter item: ");
                  heap.Insert(Console.ReadLine());
                  break;

                  case 'P':
                  try {
                        result=(String)heap.Peek();
                  } catch (EmptyException ne) {
                        Console.WriteLine(ne);
                  }
                  Console.WriteLine(result);
                  break;

                  case 'R':
                  try {
                        heap.Remove();
                  } catch (EmptyException ne) {
                        Console.WriteLine(ne);
                  }
                  break;

                  case 'S':
                  Console.WriteLine(heap.ToString());
                  break;

                  case 'X':
                  heap.Clear();
                  break;

                  default:
                  Console.WriteLine("Invalid option");
```

(continued)

```
                break;
            }
            DisplayHeader();
            option = Console.ReadLine()[0];
        }
    }

    static void DisplayHeader() {
            Console.WriteLine("Enter one of the following:");
            Console.WriteLine("I - insert");
            Console.WriteLine("P - peek");
            Console.WriteLine("R - remove");
            Console.WriteLine("S - show heap");
            Console.WriteLine("X - clear heap");
            Console.WriteLine("Q - quit");
            Console.Write("==> ");

    }

}
```

Here is a sample run of the program:

```
Enter one of the following:
I - insert
P - peek
R - remove
S - show heap
X - clear heap
Q - quit
==> I
Enter item: JOHN
Enter one of the following:
I - insert
P - peek
R - remove
S - show heap
X - clear heap
Q - quit
==> I
Enter item: JACOB
Enter one of the following:
I - insert
P - peek
```

```
R - remove
S - show heap
X - clear heap
Q - quit
==> I
Enter item: JINGLE
Enter one of the following:
I - insert
P - peek
R - remove
S - show heap
X - clear heap
Q - quit
==> I
Enter item: HIEMER
Enter one of the following:
I - insert
P - peek
R - remove
S - show heap
X - clear heap
Q - quit
==> I
Enter item: SCHMIDT
Enter one of the following:
I - insert
P - peek
R - remove
S - show heap
X - clear heap
Q - quit
==> S
 SCHMIDT JOHN JINGLE HIEMER JACOB
Enter one of the following:
I - insert
P - peek
R - remove
S - show heap
X - clear heap
Q - quit
==> R
Enter one of the following:
I - insert
P - peek
```

```
R - remove
S - show heap
X - clear heap
Q - quit
==> S
 JOHN JACOB JINGLE HIEMER
Enter one of the following:
I - insert
P - peek
R - remove
S - show heap
X - clear heap
Q - quit
==> R
Enter one of the following:
I - insert
P - peek
R - remove
S - show heap
X - clear heap
Q - quit
==> S
 JINGLE JACOB HIEMER
Enter one of the following:
I - insert
P - peek
R - remove
S - show heap
X - clear heap
Q - quit
==> R
Enter one of the following:
I - insert
P - peek
R - remove
S - show heap
X - clear heap
Q - quit
==> S
 JACOB HIEMER
Enter one of the following:
I - insert
```

```
P - peek
R - remove
S - show heap
X - clear heap
Q - quit
==> X
Enter one of the following:
I - insert
P - peek
R - remove
S - show heap
X - clear heap
Q - quit
==> S

Enter one of the following:
I - insert
P - peek
R - remove
S - show heap
X - clear heap
Q - quit
==> Q
```

☐ The Heap Sort

Heaps have many marvelous applications. In particular, they can be used to perform an efficient sort. Because of the way a heap is ordered, and because it is always a complete tree, insertions and deletions require fairly little data movement. Also, the largest element in a heap is always on top. Thus, we can perform a sort in this very simple way: Place the unordered elements into a heap, and then remove them. They will come out in descending order.

The `HeapSort()` method is deceptively simple, because the `Heap` class hides the bulk of the body of work:

```
public static void HeapSort(IComparable[] a,int size) {
   Heap heap=new Heap(a.Length);
   foreach(IComparable item in a) heap.Insert(item);
   for(int index=0;index<a.Length;index++) {
         a[index]=heap.Peek();
         heap.Remove();
   }
}
```

If you refer back to the `Sorter` class, you will see the `TestSorter` program, which times the various sorting methods. If you add the `HeapSort` to the list of algorithms being tested, you can test it also, as is done here:

```
Enter # of random integers to sort: 10000
BubbleSort took 15.27196 seconds.
SelectionSort took 5.2876032 seconds.
ShellSort took 0.0801152 seconds.
QuickSort took 0.050072 seconds.
HeapSort took 0.0901296 seconds.
```

Note that the way the heap sort is written, a heap of identical size to the array is created. This is an unnecessary waste of memory, for it is possible to write a heap sort routine that operates on the original array. Consider how this might be done.

▪ HASH TABLES

You may think it impossible to improve on the search efficiency of a complete binary search tree, but theoretically it is possible given an efficient hash table and a very good hash function. A hash table is a table of indexed elements. The index in which some element is placed is determined by a hash function. A hash function maps the data to indices in the table.

Suppose we want to store telephone numbers in a hash table. The hash table has 1000 slots, indexed 0 through 999, and is currently empty. The hash function that maps telephone numbers to indices is

$$f(x) = x \bmod 1000$$

The telephone numbers are regarded as their decimal equivalents after all spaces, parentheses, and dashes are removed. Now, let us store the following telephone numbers in the hash table:

7855551213
6105558765
3455559114
9315552544

By applying the hash function to these numbers, we get the following indices:

$f(7855551213) = 213$
$f(6105558765) = 765$
$f(3455559114) = 114$
$f(9315552544) = 544$

Index	Reference
0	null
...	...
113	null
114	3455559114
115	null
...	...
212	null
213	7855551213
214	null
...	...
543	null
544	9315552544
545	null
...	...
764	null
765	6105558765
766	null
...	...
999	null

Figure 14.23

Obviously, this hash function simply retains the last three decimal digits of the number. These elements would be stored in indices 213, 765, 114, and 544, respectively (see Figure 14.23).

In this example, the data we are mapping (telephone numbers) are numeric, but suppose we want to map strings or other objects into a hash table? This can be overcome simply by regarding the objects as a large binary integer (it's how they're stored anyway).

Now, consider what happens when I try to add the following number:

6115551213

If we produce the hash (the result of the hash function), we get

$f(6115551213) = 213$

This says to place another number in slot 213, which is already occupied. This is known as a collision, and it must be resolved.

☐ Collision Resolution

Collisions are inevitable with hash tables. Even the best hash functions will produce collisions. When a data item hashes to a position in the table that is already occupied, one

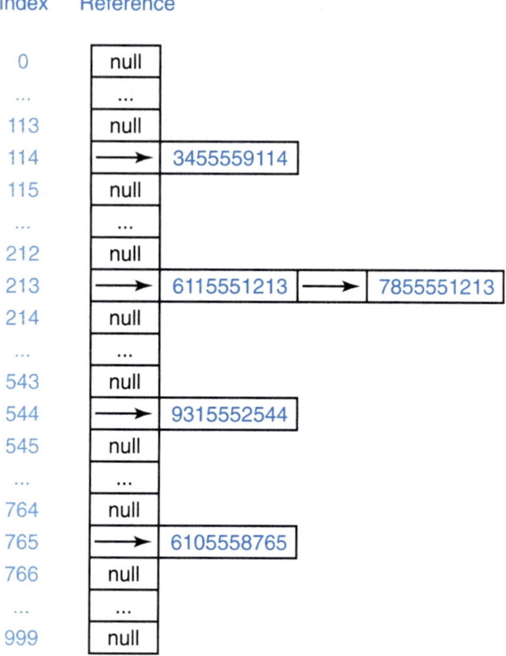

Figure 14.24

must decide what to do about it. There are many methods one can use to resolve collisions, but a very common method (which is also relatively efficient) is called "linear chaining."

With linear chaining, any index in the hash table contains a reference not to an element, but to a linked chain of elements. When an item maps to an index that contains a nonempty chain, we can insert the item anywhere in the chain (and this might as well be the front). If the item maps to an index containing no elements, we simply start a chain with that element.

If you consider the previous example, the number 6115551213 would simply be inserted before the number 7855551213 in a linear chain referenced by index 213 in the hash table (see Figure 14.24).

Searching a hash table using linear chaining for an item may mean searching a chain for the item once you determine the index. If the hash function being used is a good one, then collisions are rare, and any chain should be a short one. Deleting an item from such a hash table simply means removing it from its chain, and if the item is the only one in the chain, making the reference null.

This brings us to the central question: What is a good hash function? In general terms, a hash function should have the following properties:

1. It should compute the hash for a data item quickly.

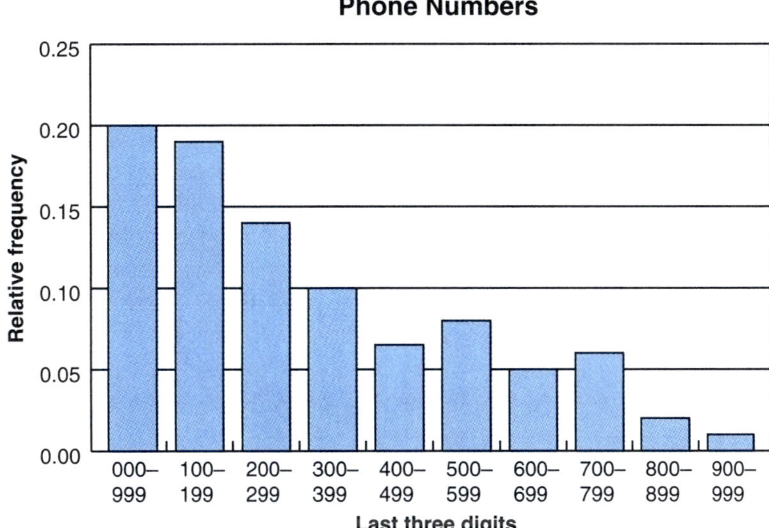

Figure 14.25

2. It should be unbiased in the sense that no index is favored over any other. A biased hash function will produce relatively more collisions (in the favored indices).

Satisfying both of these properties is surprisingly difficult to do in practice. A hash function that is quickly computable often produces too many collisions in certain slots, whereas one that successfully hashes the data to very random-looking indices often takes too long to compute.

It is important to note that the data itself may be biased. For example, telephone numbers in which the last three digits are relatively low may be more frequent than those that are high (see Figure 14.25). This may simply be because low numbers are assigned first (of course, this may not be the real situation; this is hypothetical).

Regardless, a good hash function should be insensitive even to highly skewed data, and the hashes it produces should be uniform across the breadth of the table. Given this, it should be clear that the example hash function

$$f(x) = x \bmod 1000$$

is too sensitive to peculiarities in the inputs (phone numbers) to be considered a good hash function.

☐ Interface: Hashable

Hash tables should store objects for which a hash can be obtained. The truth is, every object in C# already has access to a hash function through its `GetHashCode()` method.

Hash tables are so efficient that the .NET runtime environment uses a hash table to store and retrieve objects.

We can always override the GetHashCode() method in any new data type we define; however, GetHashCode() from Object always produces a different hash, even when the data fields are identical. We can readily see this because the Equals() method from Object (which uses the GetHashCode() method) returns true or false depending on whether the references are the same.

Thus, we create the Hashable interface in Listing 14.9. It requires only two things—that we provide the code for a Hash() method and an Equals() method. The Equals() method is so the programmer can redefine equality in terms of value equality, instead of referential equality.

Listing 14.9

```
public interface Hashable {

  int Hash(int limit);
  //Should produce a "random looking" int x s.t. 0<=x<=n-1
  //Hashable objects supply their own hash function

  bool Equals(Hashable other);
  //Equals should be implemented to override referential equality

}
```

☐ Class: HashTable

The HashTable class in Listing 14.10 (see pages 421–422) is intended to represent a hash table using linear chaining. The obvious manner of representing the table of indices is an array. The array references objects of type HashTableNode; each node contains a Hashable item (the data), and a reference to the next node in the chain. In order to use this HashTable class then, one must implement the Hashable interface.

Here are the fields members of HashTable, plus the nested type HashTableNode and the HashTable constructor:

```
public class HashTable {

  HashTableNode[] data;
  int size;
  int capacity;

  public class HashTableNode {
    public Hashable datum=null;
    public HashTableNode next=null;
    public HashTableNode(Hashable item,HashTableNode link) {
```

```
      datum=item;
      next=link;
    }
  }

  public HashTable(int cap) {
    data=new HashTableNode[cap];
    capacity=cap;
  }
//...
}
```

Inserting a `Hashable` item into the hash table means calculating its hash, and then going to the index and searching the chain there to verify that the item is not already in the hash table. If the item is already in the table, an `ArgumentException` is thrown; otherwise, the item is inserted at the beginning of the chain. The `size` field is incremented to record another item added to the table.

```
public void Insert(Hashable item) {
  //Compute position to insert
  int position=item.Hash(capacity);
  //Check if item is already in the table
  HashTableNode ptr=data[position];
  while (ptr!=null) {
        if (ptr.datum.Equals(item)) throw new ArgumentException
          ("Item is already in list.");
        ptr=ptr.next;
  }
  //Insert at head of list
  HashTableNode newNode=new HashTableNode(item,data[position]);
  data[position]=newNode;
  //Hash table has one more item in it
  size++;
}
```

Getting an item from the table means computing its hash, searching the chain at that index, and returning the `Hashable` item if found. If it is not found, a `NotFoundException` is thrown.

```
public Hashable Get(Hashable target) {
  //No point in looking if table empty
  if (Empty) throw new EmptyException("Hash Table is empty.");
  //Calculate first position of item
  int position=target.Hash(capacity);
  HashTableNode ptr=data[position];
  while (ptr!=null&&!ptr.datum.Equals(target)) ptr=ptr.next;
  if (ptr==null) throw new NotFoundException
```

```
      ("Item is not in table.");
    return ptr.datum;
}
```

Removing an item from the hash table involves determining whether the item is in the table, and if it is, removing it from the chain and decrementing the `size` field. If it is not present, throw a `NotFoundException`.

```
public void Remove(Hashable item) {
  //No point in looking if table empty
  if (Empty) throw new EmptyException("Hash Table is empty.");
  //Calculate hash position of item
  int position=item.Hash(capacity);
  HashTableNode prev=null;
  HashTableNode current=data[position];
  while (current!=null&&!current.datum.Equals(item)) {
    prev=current;
    current=current.next;
  }
  if (current==null) throw new NotFoundException
    ("Item is not in Hash Table.");
  //Point prev past current, the node to delete
  if (prev!=null) prev.next=current.next;
  else data[position]=current.next;
  current.next=null;
  //Hash table has one less item in it
  size--;
}
```

The `Size` and `Empty` properties are read-only properties that return the number of items in the hash table and whether the table is empty, respectively. The `Clear()` method travels down the hash table's array and breaks off each chain, making each suitable for garbage collection.

```
public int Size {get{return size;}}
public bool Empty {get{return size==0;}}
public void Clear() {
    for (int i=0;i<data.Length;i++) data[i]=null;
}
```

The `ToString()` method travels down the array and concatenates each item to a large string, which is returned. For convenience, the index in which an item or group of items are stored is also added to the string.

```
public override String ToString() {
  StringBuilder sb=new StringBuilder("");
  for (int i=0;i<data.Length;i++) {
        if (data[i]!=null) sb.Append("\nIndex "+i+":\n");
```

```
                HashTableNode ptr=data[i];
                while (ptr!=null) {
                      sb.Append(" "+ptr.datum.ToString());
                      ptr=ptr.next;
                }
          }
          return sb.ToString();
        }
```

Listing 14.10

```
using System;
using System.Text;
public class HashTable {

  HashTableNode[] data;
  int size;//Number of items in hash table
  int capacity;//Number of indices in hash table

  public class HashTableNode {
    public Hashable datum=null;
    public HashTableNode next=null;
    public HashTableNode(Hashable item,HashTableNode link) {
      datum=item;
      next=link;
    }
  }

  public HashTable(int cap) {
    data=new HashTableNode[cap];
    capacity=cap;
  }

  public void Insert(Hashable item) {
    //Compute position to insert
    int position=item.Hash(capacity);
    //Check if item is already in the table
    HashTableNode ptr=data[position];
    while (ptr!=null) {
          if (ptr.datum.Equals(item)) throw new ArgumentException
            ("Item is already in list.");
          ptr=ptr.next;
    }
    //Insert at head of list
    HashTableNode newNode=new HashTableNode(item,data[position]);
    data[position]=newNode;
    //Hash table has one more item in it
    size++;
  }
```

(continued)

```
  public void Remove(Hashable item) {
    //No point in looking if table empty
    if (Empty) throw new EmptyException("Hash Table is empty.");
    //Calculate hash position of item
    int position=item.Hash(capacity);
    HashTableNode prev=null;
    HashTableNode current=data[position];
    while (current!=null&&!current.datum.Equals(item)) {
      prev=current;
      current=current.next;
    }
    if (current==null) throw new NotFoundException
      ("Item is not in Hash Table.");
    //Point prev past current, the node to delete
    if (prev!=null) prev.next=current.next;
    else data[position]=current.next;
    current.next=null;
    //Hash table has one less item in it
    size--;
  }

  public Hashable Get(Hashable target) {
    //No point in looking if table empty
    if (Empty) throw new EmptyException("Hash Table is empty.");
    //Calculate first position of item
    int position=target.Hash(capacity);
    HashTableNode ptr=data[position];
    while (ptr!=null&&!ptr.datum.Equals(target)) ptr=ptr.next;
    if (ptr==null) throw new NotFoundException
      ("Item is not in table.");
    return ptr.datum;
  }

  public int Size {get{return size;}}
  public bool Empty {get{return size==0;}}
  public void Clear() {
      for (int i=0;i<data.Length;i++) data[i]=null;
  }

  public override String ToString() {
    StringBuilder sb=new StringBuilder("");
    for (int i=0;i<data.Length;i++) {
          if (data[i]!=null) sb.Append("\nIndex "+i+":\n");
          HashTableNode ptr=data[i];
          while (ptr!=null) {
                sb.Append(" "+ptr.datum.ToString());
                ptr=ptr.next;
          }
    }
    return sb.ToString();
  }

}
```

TABLE 14.8

Constructor/Property/Method	*T(n)*
`public HashTable(int cap);`	O(1)
`public void Insert(Hashable item);`	Depends on hash function from `Hashable`
`public void Remove(Hashable item);`	Depends on hash function from `Hashable`
`public Hashable Get(Hashable target);`	Depends on hash function from `Hashable`
`public int Size;`	O(1)
`public bool Empty;`	O(1)
`public void Clear();`	O(*n*)
`public override String ToString();`	O(*n*)

We can attempt a Big-O analysis of the `HashTable` members in Table 14.8.

Because `Hashable` objects supply their own hash function, we cannot determine how long insertions, removals, and retrievals will take. So, as an example, we will create a class for a `Hashable` type of object called `Customer` in Listing 14.11. Customer contains two fields—`name` and `ssn`.

```
public class Customer:Hashable {

      String name;
      int ssn;

      public Customer(int ssn) {
            this.ssn=ssn;
      }

      public Customer(String name,int ssn) {
            this.name=name;
            this.ssn=ssn;
      }
//...
}
```

The two constructors allow us to create one `Customer` object specifying both the `name` and the `ssn`, and one `Customer` based on only the `ssn`. The second constructor is used when we search the table for a `Customer` using only the `ssn`.

Because `Customer` implements `Hashable`, it provides a `Hash()` method and an `Equals()` method. The `Hash()` method returns an integer between 0 and the size of the hash table minus one. The hash is based on only the `ssn` field.

```
public int Hash(int limit) {
      int temp=ssn;
      int answer=1;
      while (temp>0) {
            if (temp%10!=0)
                  answer=answer*(temp%10)%limit;
            temp/=10;
      }
      return Math.Abs(answer);
}
```

Note that the hash function takes the `ssn` of a `Customer`. The hash value is produced by taking the product of the nonzero decimal digits of the `ssn`. This hash value does not depend on the number of customers in the hash table, so we can say the hash function computes in constant time. However, does this mean the hash function is a good one? No. The hash function may be biased; that is, it may favor some indices over others, hampering the performance of the hash table.

The `Equals()` method regards any two customers as equal if their `ssn`'s are equal. Equality is based on the `ssn` field only, so no two customers may have the same `ssn`.

```
public bool Equals(Hashable other) {
      return this.ssn==((Customer)other).ssn;
}
```

We also override the `ToString()` method from `Object` to turn `Customers` into a string representation:

```
public override String ToString() {return name+" "+ssn;}
```

Having done this, we can insert, retrieve, and remove `Customers` from a `HashTable` object.

Listing 14.11

```
using System;
public class Customer:Hashable {

      String name;
      int ssn;

      public Customer(int ssn) {
            this.ssn=ssn;
      }

      public Customer(String name,int ssn) {
            this.name=name;
            this.ssn=ssn;
      }
```

(continued)

```
    public int Hash(int limit) {
        int temp=ssn;
        int answer=1;
        while (temp>0) {
            if (temp%10!=0)
                answer=answer*(temp%10)%limit;
            temp/=10;
        }
        return Math.Abs(answer);
    }

    public bool Equals(Hashable other) {
        return this.ssn==((Customer)other).ssn;
    }

    public override String ToString() {return name+" "+ssn;}

}
```

The test program of the `HashTable` class is shown in Listing 14.12. It is much like the other test programs of this chapter; using it, we can insert, get, and remove `Hashable` objects (in this case, `Customers`) from the `HashTable`.

Listing 14.12

```
using System;
public class TestHashTable {
    public static void Main() {

        HashTable ht=new HashTable(101);
        Customer result=null;

        String name;
        int ssn;

        DisplayHeader();
        char option=Console.ReadLine()[0];
        while (option!='Q') {
            switch (option) {
            case 'I':
            Console.Write("Enter item name: ");
            name=Console.ReadLine();
            Console.Write("Enter item ssn: ");
            ssn=Int32.Parse(Console.ReadLine());
```

(continued)

```
                try {
                        ht.Insert(new Customer(name,ssn));
                } catch (ArgumentException ae) {
                        Console.WriteLine(ae);
                }
                break;

                case 'G':
                Console.Write("Enter item ssn: ");
                try {
                        result=(Customer)ht.Get(new Customer
                        (Int32.Parse(Console.ReadLine())));
                } catch (EmptyException e) {
                        Console.WriteLine(e);
                } catch (NotFoundException nfe) {
                        Console.WriteLine(nfe);
                }
                Console.WriteLine(result);
                break;

                case 'R':
                Console.Write("Enter item ssn: ");
                try {
                        ht.Remove(new Customer(Int32.Parse
                                (Console.ReadLine())));
                } catch (EmptyException ee) {
                        Console.WriteLine(ee);
                } catch (NotFoundException nfe) {
                        Console.WriteLine(nfe);
                }
                break;

                case 'S':
                Console.WriteLine(ht.ToString());
                break;

                case 'X':
                ht.Clear();
                break;

                default:
                Console.WriteLine("Invalid option");
                break;
                }
                DisplayHeader();
                option=Console.ReadLine()[0];
        }
}
```

(continued)

```
    public static void DisplayHeader() {
        Console.WriteLine("Enter one of the following:");
        Console.WriteLine("I - insert");
        Console.WriteLine("G - get");
        Console.WriteLine("R - remove");
        Console.WriteLine("S - show table");
        Console.WriteLine("X - destroy table");
        Console.WriteLine("Q - quit");
        Console.Write("==> ");
    }

}
```

Note in the test runs that getting or removing an item requires only the `ssn`.

```
Enter one of the following:
I - insert
G - get
R - remove
S - show table
X - destroy table
Q - quit
==> I
Enter item name: LITTLE BOY BLUE
Enter item ssn: 123456789
Enter one of the following:
I - insert
G - get
R - remove
S - show table
X - destroy table
Q - quit
==> I
Enter item name: LITTLE MISS MUFFETT
Enter item ssn: 987654321
Enter one of the following:
I - insert
G - get
R - remove
S - show table
X - destroy table
Q - quit
==> I
```

```
Enter item name: MOTHER GOOSE
Enter item ssn: 111111111
Enter one of the following:
I - insert
G - get
R - remove
S - show table
X - destroy table
Q - quit
==> S

Index 1:
 MOTHER GOOSE 111111111
Index 88:
 LITTLE MISS MUFFETT 987654321 LITTLE BOY BLUE 123456789
Enter one of the following:
I - insert
G - get
R - remove
S - show table
X - destroy table
Q - quit
==> R
Enter item ssn: 101010101
NotFoundException: Item is not in Hash Table.
   at HashTable.Remove(Hashable item)
   at TestHashTable.Main()
Enter one of the following:
I - insert
G - get
R - remove
S - show table
X - destroy table
Q - quit
==> R
Enter item ssn: 987654321
Enter one of the following:
I - insert
G - get
R - remove
S - show table
X - destroy table
Q - quit
==> S
```

```
Index 1:
 MOTHER GOOSE 111111111
Index 88:
 LITTLE BOY BLUE 123456789
Enter one of the following:
I - insert
G - get
R - remove
S - show table
X - destroy table
Q - quit
==> X
Enter one of the following:
I - insert
G - get
R - remove
S - show table
X - destroy table
Q - quit
==> S

Enter one of the following:
I - insert
G - get
R - remove
S - show table
X - destroy table
Q - quit
==> Q
```

■ THE `System.Collections` NAMESPACE

Data structures are so important that it should come as no surprise that C# provides a namespace composed of many different classes representing data structures. The `System.Collections` namespace has declared within it a variety of different interfaces and classes. Table 14.9 lists the classes, interfaces, and structures in the `System.Collections` namespace.

You will notice that this namespace provides many classes we have already discussed, and some that we have not. The data structures we have covered in this text are adequate for an introduction to the topic in C#.

TABLE 14.9

Classes	Class Description
`ArrayList`	Implements the `IList` interface using an array whose size is dynamically increased as required.
`BitArray`	Manages a compact array of bit values, which are represented as Booleans, where true indicates that the bit is on (1) and false indicates the bit is off (0).
`CaseInsensitiveComparer`	Compares two objects for equivalence, ignoring the case of strings.
`CaseInsensitiveHashCodeProvider`	Supplies a hash code for an object, using a hashing algorithm that ignores the case of strings.
`CollectionBase`	Provides the abstract base class for a strongly typed collection.
`Comparer`	Compares two objects for equivalence, where string comparisons are case-sensitive.
`DictionaryBase`	Provides the abstract base class for a strongly typed collection of key-and-value pairs.
`Hashtable`	Represents a collection of key-and-value pairs that are organized based on the hash code of the key.
`Queue`	Represents a first in-first out collection of objects.
`ReadOnlyCollectionBase`	Provides the abstract base class for a strongly typed read-only collection.
`SortedList`	Represents a collection of key-and-value pairs that are sorted by the keys and are accessible by key and by index.
`Stack`	Represents a simple last in-first out collection of objects.
Interfaces	**Interface Description**
`ICollection`	Defines size, enumerators, and synchronization methods for all collections.
`IComparer`	Exposes a method that compares two objects.
`IDictionary`	Represents a collection of key-and-value pairs.
`IDictionaryEnumerator`	Enumerates the elements of a dictionary.
`IEnumerable`	Exposes the enumerator, which supports a simple iteration over a collection.
`IEnumerator`	Supports a simple iteration over a collection.
`IHashCodeProvider`	Supplies a hash code for an object, using a custom hash function.
`IList`	Represents a collection of objects that can be individually accessed by index.
Structures	**Structure Description**
`DictionaryEntry`	Defines a dictionary key-and-value pair that can be set or retrieved.

▪ THE `foreach` STATEMENT AND COLLECTIONS

Traversing through a collection is an important topic. If the only data structure we are concerned with is the array, then this traversal is very simple. We simply pass through all the indices in the array. However, as we have seen, many data structures, such as linked lists, do not use an index to access their elements.

You will recall that C# provides a `foreach` statement. This statement can be used to iterate through the elements of a collection. This collection may be a predefined C# class or a class which you yourself have defined. As an example of the former, see the program in Listing 14.13. It uses an instance of `ArrayList`, which represents a list using an underlying array. However, the `ArrayList` has the convenient ability to expand when necessary as items are added. The `foreach` statement is used to traverse through the collection after some items are added.

Listing 14.13

```
using System;
using System.Collections;
public class ArrayListPassage {
    static void Main() {
      String input;
      ArrayList list=new ArrayList();
      Console.WriteLine("Enter a string (EXIT to quit):");
      while (!(input=Console.ReadLine()).Equals("EXIT")) {
            list.Add(input);
            Console.WriteLine("Enter a string (EXIT to quit):");
      }
      Console.WriteLine("The members in the list are: ");
      foreach (String s in list) Console.WriteLine(s);
    }
}
```

Listing 14.14 is a trial run of this program.

Listing 14.14

```
Enter a string (EXIT to quit):
Hello.
Enter a string (EXIT to quit):
I am fine.
Enter a string (EXIT to quit):
How are you?
Enter a string (EXIT to quit):
EXIT
The members in the list are:
Hello.
I am fine.
How are you?
```

What is it that allows us to use a collection in a `foreach` statement? Any collection that implements the `IEnumerable` interface can use the `foreach` statement to iterate through its elements. It so happens that the `ArrayList` class implements this interface. We can also implement `IEnumerable` when defining a class; if we do, we can then use the `foreach` statement to traverse its members. The `IEnumerable` interface consists of only one public method:

```
public IEnumerator GetEnumerator();
```

This method is to return an object of type `IEnumerator`. Such an object is meant to provide properties and methods to traverse through the items in the data structure. `IEnumerator` is also an interface, consisting of these properties and methods:

```
public Object Current;
```

`Current` should reference some item in the data structure, but it should initially begin before the first item. The methods `Reset` and `MoveNext` move the current pointer through the data structure.

```
public void Reset();
```

`Reset` moves the current pointer back before the first item. The initial call to `MoveNext` moves the pointer to reference the first item, if it exists.

```
public bool MoveNext();
```

`MoveNext` returns a `bool`; false if an attempt is made to move `Current` past the end of the data structure, and true otherwise.

When implementing `IEnumerable`, there is nothing to prevent us from implementing `IEnumerator` as well. I do this in `ListEnumerable`, an implementation of a list that can be traversed with a `foreach` statement (see Listing 14.15).

Note first that `ListEnumerable` implements both `IEnumerable` and `IEnumerator`. The references `head` and `tail` reference the head and tail of the list, and the class provides two constructors—one to create an empty list and one to provide another reference to a list (when we wish to traverse its elements without disturbing the original list's pointers).

```
public class ListEnumerable: IEnumerator,IEnumerable {

   ListNode head;
   ListNode tail;
   ListNode currentPosition;
   //May point at any item, or may be null

   public ListEnumerable() {
      //Create an empty list
      head=null;
      tail=null;
      currentPosition=null;
   }

   public ListEnumerable(ListEnumerable list) {
      //Create another reference to list
      this.head=list.head;
      this.tail=list.tail;
      currentPosition=null;
   }
//...
}
```

`ListEnumerable` provides all the methods and properties described in the interfaces. Note that to produce an enumerator, we simply create additional references to the data structure by using the second constructor.

```
public IEnumerator GetEnumerator() {
   //Returns an enumerator to pass thru list
   //ListEnumerable implements IEnumerator as well as
IEnumerable
   return new ListEnumerable(this);
}

public void Reset() {
   currentPosition=null;
}

public bool MoveNext() {
   if (currentPosition==null&&head!=null) {
         currentPosition=head;
         return true;
   } else if (head==null) {
```

```
            return false;
        } else {
            if (currentPosition.next==null) return false;
            else {
                currentPosition=currentPosition.next;
                return true;
            }
        }
    }

    public Object Current {
        get {
        if (currentPosition==null) return null;
        else return currentPosition.datum;
        }
    }
```

The important thing to remember when implementing these methods is that the current position must start before the first item in the data structure, and `MoveNext` must return true until an attempt is made to move past the last item, and then return false. If you do not do this, it will not work correctly in a `foreach` statement, because these are the conditions the `foreach` statement relies upon.

Of course, `ListEnumerable` also provides methods to insert and remove items from the list, and to destroy the list entirely.

Listing 14.15

```
using System;
using System.Collections;
public class ListEnumerable: IEnumerator,IEnumerable {
    //Implements a doubly linked list which can be traversed
    //using a foreach statement

    ListNode head;
    ListNode tail;
    ListNode currentPosition;
    //May point at any item, or may be null

    public ListEnumerable() {
        //Create an empty list
        head=null;
        tail=null;
        currentPosition=null;
    }

    public ListEnumerable(ListEnumerable list) {
        //Create another reference to list
```

(continued)

```
        this.head=list.head;
        this.tail=list.tail;
        currentPosition=null;
    }

    public void Reset() {
        currentPosition=null;
    }

    public bool MoveNext() {
        if (currentPosition==null&&head!=null) {
                currentPosition=head;
                return true;
        } else if (head==null) {
                return false;
        } else {
                if (currentPosition.next==null) return false;
                else {
                        currentPosition=currentPosition.next;
                        return true;
                }
        }
    }

    public Object Current {
        get {
        if (currentPosition==null) return null;
        else return currentPosition.datum;
        }
    }

    public void Insert(Object item) {
        //Inserts item directly after current position
        ListNode newNode=new ListNode(item);
        if (head==null) { head=newNode; tail=newNode; }
        //If empty list, insert at head
           else if (currentPosition==null) {
        //Current position may be null even if list not empty;
        //new node becomes new head
                  newNode.next=head;
                  head.prev=newNode;
                  head=newNode;
           } else {
        //Insert after current position
                  ListNode nextOne=currentPosition.next;

                  currentPosition.next=newNode;
                  newNode.prev=currentPosition;
```

(continued)

```
            if (currentPosition==tail) tail=tail.next;
         //Inserting after tail; advance tail
            else nextOne.prev=newNode;
         //Inserting before tail nextOne is not null,
         //prev pointer must be set
            newNode.next=nextOne;
      }
}

public void Remove() {
   //if currentPosition null, nothing to remove
         if (currentPosition==null) return;
         //Delete what position is pointing at, advance position
   if (currentPosition!=head&&currentPosition!=tail) {
   //Removing an item from middle
         currentPosition.next.prev=currentPosition.prev;
         currentPosition.prev.next=currentPosition.next;
   } else {
         if (currentPosition==head) {
         //Removing the head
               head=head.next;
               if (head!=null) head.prev=null;
         }
         if (currentPosition==tail) {
               //Removing the tail
               tail=tail.prev;
               if (tail!=null)
               tail.next=null;
         }
      }
   MoveNext();
}

public void Destroy() {
   //Removes all references to list
   head=null;
   tail=null;
   currentPosition=null;
}

public IEnumerator GetEnumerator() {
   //Returns an enumerator to pass thru list
   //ListEnumerable implements IEnumerator as well as IEnumerable
   return new ListEnumerable(this);
}

class ListNode {
   //Class representing the nodes
   public Object datum;
   public ListNode prev;
```

(continued)

```
        public ListNode next;
        public ListNode(Object newdatum) {
              this.datum=newdatum;
        }
    }

}
```

To test ListEnumerable, use TestListEnumerable in Listing 14.16, a command line program to manipulate a ListEnumerable object. The important point to notice in the code is the foreach statement, which traverses the list and then displays its items.

Listing 14.16

```
using System;
public class TestListEnumerable {
    static void Main() {
      ListEnumerable list=new ListEnumerable();
      String result="";

      DisplayHeader();
      char option = Console.ReadLine()[0];
      while (option!='Q') {
            switch (option) {
                  case 'I':
                  Console.Write("Enter item: ");
                  list.Insert(Console.ReadLine());
                  break;

                  case 'C':
                  result=(String)list.Current;
                  Console.WriteLine(result);
                  break;

                  case 'R':
                  list.Remove();
                  break;

                  case 'N':
                  list.MoveNext();
                  break;

                  case 'S':
                  foreach (String z in list) Console.Write(z+" ");
```

(continued)

```
                Console.WriteLine();
                break;

                case 'X':
                list.Destroy();
                break;

                default:
                Console.WriteLine("Invalid option");
                break;
            }
            DisplayHeader();
            option = Console.ReadLine()[0];
        }
    }

    static void DisplayHeader() {
            Console.WriteLine("Enter one of the following:");
            Console.WriteLine("I - insert");
            Console.WriteLine("C - current");
            Console.WriteLine("R - remove");
            Console.WriteLine("N - next");
            Console.WriteLine("S - show list");
            Console.WriteLine("X - clear list");
            Console.WriteLine("Q - quit");
            Console.Write("==> ");

    }

}
```

Here is a sample run of the program:

```
Enter one of the following:
I - insert
C - current
R - remove
N - next
S - show list
X - clear list
Q - quit
==> I
Enter item: HELLO
Enter one of the following:
I - insert
```

```
C - current
R - remove
N - next
S - show list
X - clear list
Q - quit
==> I
Enter item: I LOVE YOU
Enter one of the following:
I - insert
C - current
R - remove
N - next
S - show list
X - clear list
Q - quit
==> I
Enter item: TELL ME YOUR NAME
Enter one of the following:
I - insert
C - current
R - remove
N - next
S - show list
X - clear list
Q - quit
==> S
TELL ME YOUR NAME I LOVE YOU HELLO
Enter one of the following:
I - insert
C - current
R - remove
N - next
S - show list
X - clear list
Q - quit
==> Q
```

chapter 15

Streams and Files

In C#, a stream refers to a stream of data. This stream may be viewed simply as a series of bytes, or these bytes can be given meaning, like say, characters. Streams are represented in C# using, of course, classes. At the top of the hierarchy of the stream classes is the abstract `Stream` class, from the `System.IO` namespace. Figure 15.1 is a diagram displaying part of this tree.

Because streams can represent any kind of data, from raw bytes to any type of object, the `Read` and `Write` methods of the `Stream` class are left abstract. Implementers who wish to create a stream that carries a particular data type provide `Read/Write` methods geared for reading that type.

■ THE `Stream` CLASS

Table 15.1 contains a list of the `Stream` class members.

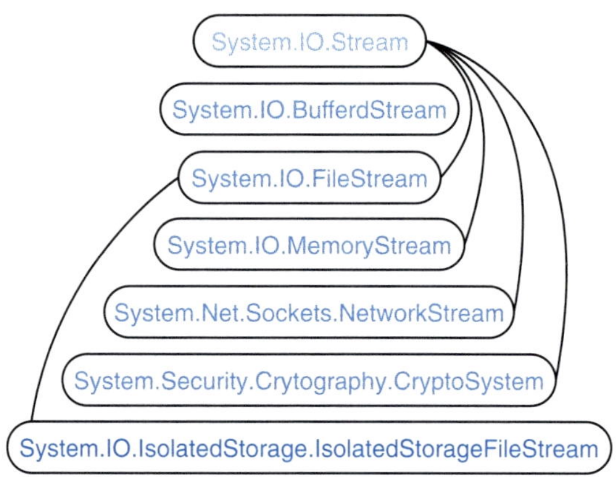

Figure 15.1

TABLE 15.1

Public Fields	
`Null`	A `Stream` with no backing store.
Public Properties	
`CanRead`	When overridden in a derived class, gets a value indicating whether the current stream supports reading.
`CanSeek`	When overridden in a derived class, gets a value indicating whether the current stream supports seeking.
`CanWrite`	When overridden in a derived class, gets a value indicating whether the current stream supports writing.
`Length`	When overridden in a derived class, gets the length in bytes of the stream.
`Position`	When overridden in a derived class, gets or sets the position within the current stream.
Public Methods	
`BeginRead`	Begins an asynchronous read operation.
`BeginWrite`	Begins an asynchronous write operation.
`Close`	Closes the current stream and releases any resources (such as sockets and file handles) associated with the current stream.
`EndRead`	Waits for the pending asynchronous read to complete.
`EndWrite`	Ends an asynchronous write operation.

(continued)

TABLE 15.1 (continued)

Public Methods	
`Flush`	When overridden in a derived class, clears all buffers for this stream and causes any buffered data to be written to the underlying device.
`GetLifetimeService`	(Inherited from `MarshalByRefObject`.) Retrieves the current lifetime service object that controls the lifetime policy for this instance.
`InitializeLifetimeService`	(Inherited from `MarshalByRefObject`.) Obtains a lifetime service object to control the lifetime policy for this instance.
`Read`	When overridden in a derived class, reads a sequence of bytes from the current stream and advances the position within the stream by the number of bytes read.
`ReadByte`	Reads a byte from the stream and advances the position within the stream by one byte, or returns −1 if at the end of the stream.
`Seek`	When overridden in a derived class, sets the position within the current stream.
`SetLength`	When overridden in a derived class, sets the length of the current stream.
`Write`	When overridden in a derived class, writes a sequence of bytes to the current stream and advances the current position within this stream by the number of bytes written.
`WriteByte`	Writes a byte to the current position in the stream and advances the position within the stream by one byte.
Protected Constructors	
`Stream` Constructor	Initializes a new instance of the `Stream` class.
Protected Methods	
`CreateWaitHandle`	Allocates a `WaitHandle` object.

Notice that the `Stream` constructor is protected, and exists only so that a derived class can call this base constructor.

▪ THE `StreamReader` AND `StreamWriter` CLASSES

The `StreamReader` and `StreamWriter` classes are useful for reading/writing character data to and from streams. Thus, the bytes received by a `StreamReader` are interpreted as characters, and the bytes sent by a `StreamWriter` into a stream are likewise intended as characters. This is the purpose of the `Read` and `Write` methods.

Table 15.2 lists the StreamReader members, and Table 15.3 gives the SteamWriter members.

TABLE 15.2

Public Constructors	
StreamReader Constructor	Overloaded. Initializes a new instance of the StreamReader class for the specified stream.
Public Fields	
Null	A StreamReader around an empty stream.
Public Properties	
BaseStream	Returns the underlying stream.
CurrentEncoding	Gets the current character encoding that the current StreamReader is using.
Public Methods	
Close	Overridden. Closes the StreamReader and releases any system resources associated with the reader.
CreateObjRef	(Inherited from MarshalByRefObject.) Creates an object that contains all the relevant information required to generate a proxy used to communicate with a remote object.
DiscardBufferedData	Allows a StreamReader to discard its current data.
GetLifetimeService	(Inherited from MarshalByRefObject.) Retrieves the current lifetime service object that controls the lifetime policy for this instance.
InitializeLifetimeService	(Inherited from MarshalByRefObject.) Obtains a lifetime service object to control the lifetime policy for this instance.
Peek	Overridden. Returns the next available character but does not consume it.
Read	Overloaded. Overridden. Reads the next character or next set of characters from the input stream.
ReadBlock	(Inherited from TextReader.) Reads a maximum of count characters from the current stream and writes the data to buffer, beginning at index.
ReadLine	Overridden. Reads a line of characters from the current stream and returns the data as a string.
ReadToEnd	Overridden. Reads the stream from the current position to the end of the stream.
Protected Methods	
Dispose	Overridden. Releases the unmanaged resources used by the StreamReader and optionally releases the managed resources.

TABLE 15.3

Public Constructors	
`StreamWriter` Constructor	Overloaded. Initializes a new instance of the `StreamWriter` class.
Public Fields	
`Null`	Provides a `StreamWriter` with no backing store that can be written to, but not read from.
Public Properties	
`AutoFlush`	Gets or sets a value indicating whether the `StreamWriter` will flush its buffer to the underlying stream after every call to `Console.Write` or `Console.WriteLine`.
`BaseStream`	Gets the underlying stream that interfaces with a backing store.
`Encoding`	Overridden. Gets the encoding in which the output is written.
`FormatProvider`	(Inherited from `TextWriter`.) Gets an object that controls formatting.
`NewLine`	(Inherited from `TextWriter`.) Gets or sets the line terminator string used by the current `TextWriter`.
Public Methods	
`Close`	Overridden. Closes the current `StreamWriter` and the underlying stream.
`CreateObjRef`	(Inherited from `MarshalByRefObject`.) Creates an object that contains all the relevant information required to generate a proxy used to communicate with a remote object.
`Flush`	Overridden. Clears all buffers for the current writer and causes any buffered data to be written to the underlying stream.
`GetLifetimeService`	(Inherited from `MarshalByRefObject`.) Retrieves the current lifetime service object that controls the lifetime policy for this instance.
`InitializeLifetimeService`	(Inherited from `MarshalByRefObject`.) Obtains a lifetime service object to control the lifetime policy for this instance.
`Write`	Overloaded. Overridden. Writes to the stream.
`WriteLine`	(Inherited from `TextWriter`.) Overloaded. Writes some data as specified by the overloaded parameters, followed by a line terminator.
Protected Fields	
`CoreNewLine`	(Inherited from `TextWriter`.) Stores the new line characters used for this `TextWriter`.
Protected Methods	
`Dispose`	Overridden. Releases the unmanaged resources used by the `StreamWriter` and optionally releases the managed resources.
`Finalize`	Overridden. Frees the resources of the current `StreamWriter` before it is reclaimed by the garbage collector. In C# and C++, finalizers are expressed using destructor syntax.

There are a variety of useful constructors from `StreamReader` and `StreamWriter`. They can be used to attach them to an existing stream or to a file. Here are some of the various `StreamReader` constructors:

```
public StreamReader(Stream);//Connects to an existing stream
public StreamReader(string);//String represents a file path/name
public StreamReader(Stream, Encoding);//Specifies encoding method
public StreamReader(string, Encoding);//File name, encoding method
```

Some of these constructors allow you to specify how the characters are encoded in the stream. Many character representation schemes exist, like ASCII, UTF-8, UTF-16, and so on. If you do not specify how the characters are coded, UTF-8 is assumed.

The `StreamWriter` constructors have similar functionality:

```
public StreamWriter(Stream);
public StreamWriter(string);
public StreamWriter(Stream, Encoding);
public StreamWriter(string, bool);
public StreamWriter(Stream, Encoding, int);
public StreamWriter(string, bool, Encoding);
public StreamWriter(string, bool, Encoding, int);
```

Here, a `Stream` parameter always refers to an existing stream, and a `string` always refers to a file path and name. `Encoding` is a class that refers to different encoding methods. An `int` refers to a buffer size, and a `bool` determines whether data will be appended to an existing file (true) or replace an existing file (false). If the file does not exist, it will be created.

☐ Text Files

We can use `StreamReader` to read from a text file. The constructor opens the file (if it exists) and prepares it for reading. The `StreamReader` class conveniently has a `ReadLine` method, for capturing an entire line at a time from the text file. We can use a loop to read a series of lines; when the `ReadLine` method returns null, we know we have reached the end of the text file.

We show this in the following program, which counts the number of lines, characters, and words in a text file.

☐ Program: CountCharsWordsLinesFile

This program (Listing 15.1) is a modification of `CountCharsWordsLines`; words are defined as any group of nonspace characters separated by whitespace. The program counts these, plus the number of lines and nonspace characters from a file using a `StreamReader` object.

Listing 15.1

```
using System;
using System.IO;
class CountCharsWordsLinesFile {
    static void Main() {
      //Variables to record #lines, words, chars (nonblanks)
      int numWords=0, numChars=0, numLines=0;

      //Represents a line read from file
      String line;

      //line will be split into this array
      String[] words;

      //Split string on the space character
      char[] delimiter={' '};

      //Contents of file will be placed in a stream
      StreamReader sr=null;

      //Prompt the user for the file name
      Console.Write("Enter file name: ");
      String fileName=Console.ReadLine();

      try {
            //Create the StreamReader and point to the text file
            sr = new StreamReader(fileName);

            //Loop will terminate when ReadLine returns null
            while((line=sr.ReadLine())!=null) {

                  //A line was read in
                  numLines++;

                  //Split the string into an array
                  //separated by blanks
                  words=line.Split(delimiter);

                  //Pass thru the array
                  foreach (String word in words) {
                        //Add length of each word to numChars
                        numChars+=word.Length;
                        //If nonblank word found,
                        //increment numWords
                        if (word.Length>0) numWords++;
                  }
            }
```

(continued)

```
            //Close the StreamReader (and underlying object being
            //read from; in this case, a file)
            sr.Close();
            //Report results
            Console.WriteLine("There are \n"
                  +numChars+" non-space characters, \n"
                  +numWords+" words, and \n"
                  +numLines+" lines in \n"
                  +fileName);
      //A series of exceptions if a problem with file or stream occurs
      } catch (ArgumentException ae) {
            Console.WriteLine(ae.ToString());
      } catch (FileNotFoundException fnfe) {
            Console.WriteLine(fnfe.ToString());
      } catch (NullReferenceException nre) {
            Console.WriteLine(nre.ToString());
      }
    }
}
```

Note the `try ... catch` block, which reports errors, like say, when the specified file does not exist. Also, note that the `StreamReader` object is closed using the `Close` method. It is particularly important to call this method when you are finished reading, because this closes the `StreamReader` and the underlying stream and, in this case, file. If the file is left open even for reading purposes only, it can prevent other programs from using the file.

Here is a run of this program. The text file that it reads in this case is CountCharsWordsLinesFile, the same source file from which the program was compiled.

```
Enter file name: CountCharsWordsLinesFile.cs
There are
1445 non-space characters,
208 words, and
66 lines in
CountCharsWordsLinesFile.cs
```

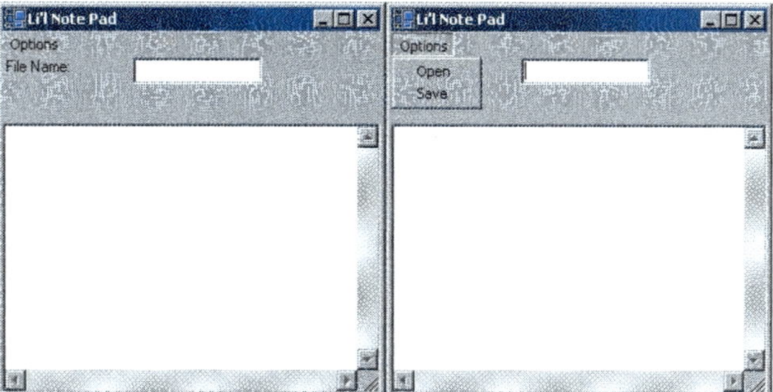

Figure 15.2

Program: LilNotepad

The program in Listing 15.2 is a GUI that functions like a little notepad. It has a menu that contains options to open and close text files. We can edit them as well using a multiline text box on the GUI. Figure 15.2 shows some shots of the Li'l Note Pad window and its options.

The `File` Class

In order to write the little notepad program, we will make use of the `File` class, which has methods to conveniently manipulate files. In particular, we use the `File.Exists()` method to determine whether the file we wish to open exists. If it doesn't, we use the method `File.Create(String)` to create the file from the specified path and name. `File.Create` returns a `FileStream` object, which is a `Stream` by inheritance. This program deals with text files, so we pass this `Stream` into a `StreamReader` constructor.

This would be done something like this:

```
//Assume fileName is String specifying path and file name of
//text file
                  if (!File.Exists(fileName))
                        streamr=new StreamReader(
                              File.Create(fileName));
```

Table 15.4 shows the methods from the `File` class. They are all static.

TABLE 15.4

Public Methods	
`AppendText`	Creates a `StreamWriter` that appends UTF-8 encoded text to an existing file.
`Copy`	Overloaded. Copies an existing file to a new file.
`Create`	Overloaded. Creates a file in the specified fully qualified path.
`CreateText`	Creates or opens a new file for writing UTF-8 encoded text.
`Delete`	Deletes the file specified by the fully qualified path. An exception is not thrown if the specified file does not exist.
`Exists`	Determines whether the specified file exists.
`GetAttributes`	Gets the `FileAttributes` of the file on the fully qualified path.
`GetCreationTime`	Returns the creation date and time of the specified file or directory.
`GetLastAccessTime`	Returns the date and time the specified file or directory was last accessed.
`GetLastWriteTime`	Returns the date and time the specified file or directory was last written to.
`Move`	Moves a specified file to a new location, providing the option to specify a new file name.
`Open`	Overloaded. Opens a `FileStream` on the specified path.
`OpenRead`	Opens an existing file for reading.
`OpenText`	Opens an existing UTF-8 encoded text file for reading.
`OpenWrite`	Opens an existing file for writing.
`SetAttributes`	Sets the specified `FileAttributes` of the file on the specified path.
`SetCreationTime`	Sets the date and time the file was created.
`SetLastAccessTime`	Sets the date and time the specified file was last accessed.
`SetLastWriteTime`	Sets the date and time that the specified file was last written to.

The `Form.Closing` Event

How many times have you almost exited a program without saving the file you were working on? Even though you attempted to close the window, a prompt popped up to inquire if you were sure you wanted to do this. If our little notepad is to be useful, it should also do this, and it can do so by making use of the `Closing` event from the `Form` class.

The `Closing` event is fired whenever the form is being closed. The `Closing` event's delegate is a `CancelEventHandler`. This delegate must reference a method that takes an `Object` and a `CancelEventArgs` object as parameters. `CancelEventArgs` is in the `System.ComponentModel` namespace, so make sure to include it. The `CancelEventArgs` class has one very important property called `Cancel`. If it is set to true, the operation is cancelled and the form does not close. Otherwise, it does.

To use a `CancelEventHandler` for the closing event, set it up in the same way as any other event handler.

```
//This is a Form-Leaving is a void method
      this.Closing+=new CancelEventHandler(Leaving);
```

The delegate, of course, refers to a method that must have a particular signature:

```
private void Leaving(Object sender, CancelEventArgs cea) {
  //...
  //if you want to really close
  //...
  cea.Cancel=false;
  //...
  //don't close the form
  //...
  cea.Cancel=true;
}
```

Knowing these things, we can create the `LilNotepad` class. It prompts the user if he or she attempts to exit or to open a new file if the contents of the text box have been modified, and allows them the opportunity to save the contents. We use the `Modified` property from `TextBox` to give us this information. Here is the `LilNotepad` class.

Listing 15.2

```
using System;
using System.Windows.Forms;
using System.IO;
using System.ComponentModel;
public class LilNotepad:Form {

    //Create some menu items
    MenuItem fileOptions = new MenuItem();
    MenuItem open = new MenuItem();
    MenuItem save = new MenuItem();

    //Create a main menu
    MainMenu mm=new MainMenu();

    //File name will be entered in text box
    Label fileNameLabel = new Label();
    TextBox fileName = new TextBox();

    //LilNotepad will be a multi-line editable text box on a panel
    Panel notepadPanel = new Panel();
    TextBox typingArea=new TextBox();

    public LilNotepad() {
      this.Text="Li'l Note Pad";
```

(continued)

```
    //Add Options to main menu
    fileOptions.Text="Options";
    mm.MenuItems.Add(fileOptions);

    //Put save and open as menu items of fileOptions
    open.Text="Open";
    fileOptions.MenuItems.Add(open);
    save.Text="Save";
    fileOptions.MenuItems.Add(save);

    //Bind the main menu to the form
    this.Menu=mm;

    //Make the file name prompt label and box
    fileNameLabel.Text="File Name:";
    this.Controls.Add(fileNameLabel);
    fileName.Left=100;
    this.Controls.Add(fileName);

    //Put the panel on the form
    notepadPanel.Top=50;
    notepadPanel.Width=ClientSize.Width;
    notepadPanel.Height=ClientSize.Height-50;
    notepadPanel.Anchor=AnchorStyles.Top
          |AnchorStyles.Left
          |AnchorStyles.Right
          |AnchorStyles.Bottom;
    this.Controls.Add(notepadPanel);

    //Put the typing area on the panel
    //Stretch it across the panel using DockStyle.Fill
    typingArea.Multiline=true;
    typingArea.Dock=DockStyle.Fill;
    typingArea.ScrollBars=ScrollBars.Both;
    typingArea.WordWrap=false;
    notepadPanel.Controls.Add(typingArea);

    //Add Click event handlers for save and open
    open.Click+=new EventHandler(DoOpen);
    save.Click+=new EventHandler(DoSave);

    //Put a CancelEventHandler on Form
    //in case user tries to quit without saving
    this.Closing+=new CancelEventHandler(Leaving);
  }

  private void DoOpen(Object Sender,EventArgs ea) {
    //Check if typing area was changed since last save
    if (typingArea.Modified) {
          //If it was, prompt user if they want to open or not
          DialogResult choice = DialogResult.None;
```

(continued)

```
            choice=MessageBox.Show(
                  "Work not saved; Open anyway?",
                  "Whoops!",
                  MessageBoxButtons.OKCancel);
            if (choice==DialogResult.OK) {
                  //User wants to open
                  //Open a StreamReader, place contents of file
                  //into typing area
                  //If specified file does not exist, create it
                  StreamReader streamr;
                  if (!File.Exists(fileName.Text))
                        streamr=new StreamReader(
                              File.Create(fileName.Text));
                  else streamr=new StreamReader(fileName.Text);
                  typingArea.Text=streamr.ReadToEnd();
                  streamr.Close();
            }//User does not want to open-do nothing
      }
   }

   private void DoSave(Object sender, EventArgs ea) {
      //Open a StreamWriter, place contents of text box into file
      //Set Modified property of text box to false
      //this is so an exit will not prompt for a save
      //Modified will revert to true if you type in box again
      StreamWriter streamw=new StreamWriter(fileName.Text);
      streamw.Write(typingArea.Text);
      streamw.Close();
      typingArea.Modified=false;
   }

   private void Leaving(Object sender, CancelEventArgs cea) {
      //Check if typing area was changed since last save
      if (typingArea.Modified) {
            //If it was, prompt user if they want to quit or not
            DialogResult choice = DialogResult.None;
            choice=MessageBox.Show(
                  "Work not saved; Quit anyway?",
                  "Whoops!",
                  MessageBoxButtons.OKCancel);
            if (choice==DialogResult.OK) {
                  //User wants to quit-do not cancel operation
                  cea.Cancel=false;
            } else {
                  //Else Cancel property set to true
                  //Form is not closed
                  cea.Cancel=true;
            }
      }
   }
```

(continued)

```
    static void Main(String[] args) {
      Application.Run(new LilNotepad());
    }

}
```

Figure 15.3 is a shot of the program. We type in the name of the file we wish to open. In Figure 15.4 we select Options, then Open, and the text from the file is placed in the text box. We save the file by choosing Options, then Save (see Figure 15.5). Because we have not specified a path, it is saved in the same path the program is running in.

In Figure 15.6 we make some changes, and attempt to exit. The program prompts with a message box, as in Figure 15.7. Here we can choose whether or not to cancel the closing of the window.

■ BINARY FILES AND STREAMS

The term *binary file* has characteristically been used to refer to any kind of file other than text. At the lowest level, any file or stream is merely a series of bytes. It is how those bytes are interpreted that determines, for example, the type of file it is.

C# imposes no structure on files or streams. If we want structure, we must use a preexisting class, or define our own.

Suppose we want a file that contains information for various individuals; say their name, age, and weight. The file stores this information not as text, but in a binary format similar to (or the same as) the way they are stored in memory. For example, the `int`

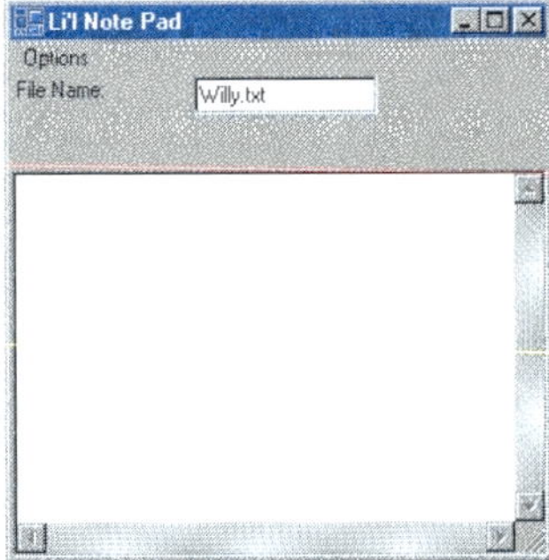

Figure 15.3

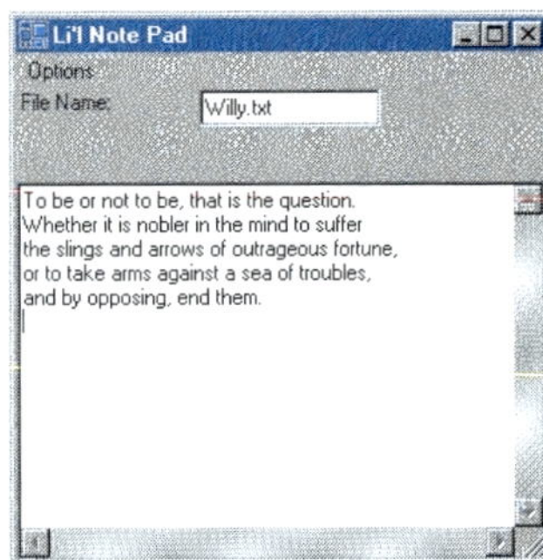

Figure 15.4

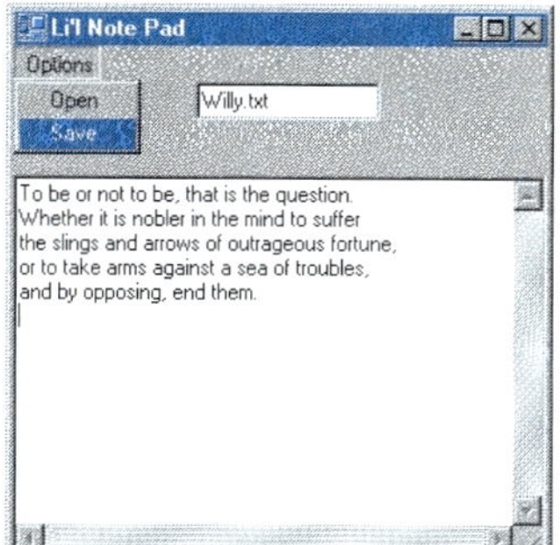

Figure 15.5

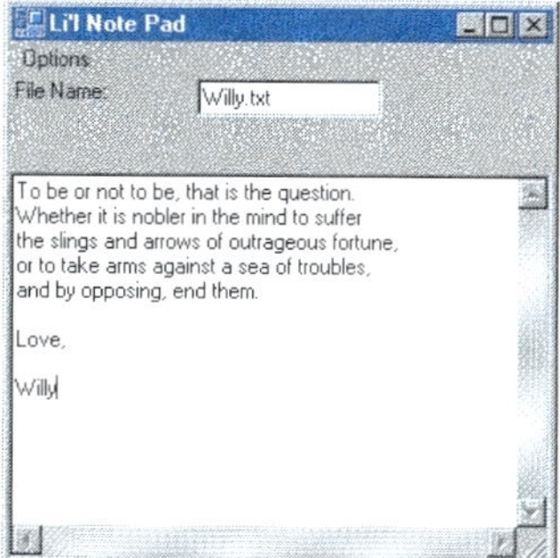

Figure 15.6

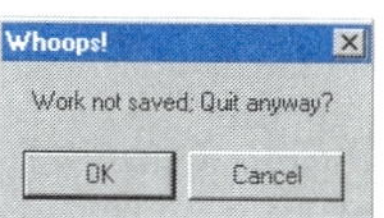

Figure 15.7

`345` would not be stored as the characters '`3`', '`4`', and '`5`', but as the binary representation of 345.

To accomplish this, we can use the `BinaryWriter` class for writing to the file, and the `BinaryReader` class to read from it. `BinaryWriter` contains methods for writing simple types to a file in a binary format. It can also write strings to these files, and because strings can be of variable length, it writes the *length* of the string into the file as well.

Table 15.5 shows the members of the `BinaryWriter` class.

Of particular importance is the `Write` method, which is overloaded. The many versions of `Write` can write different data types to the file depending on the type of the parameter passed in. Here are the `Write` methods:

- `public virtual void Write(bool);`
- `public virtual void Write(byte);`
- `public virtual void Write(byte[]);`
- `public virtual void Write(char);`
- `public virtual void Write(char[]);`
- `public virtual void Write(decimal);`
- `public virtual void Write(double);`
- `public virtual void Write(short);`
- `public virtual void Write(int);`
- `public virtual void Write(long);`
- `public virtual void Write(sbyte);`
- `public virtual void Write(float);`
- `public virtual void Write(string);`
- `public virtual void Write(ushort);`
- `public virtual void Write(uint);`
- `public virtual void Write(ulong);`
- `public virtual void Write(byte[], int, int);`
- `public virtual void Write(char[], int, int);`

TABLE 15.5

Public Constructors	
`BinaryWriter` Constructor	Overloaded. Initializes a new instance of the `BinaryWriter` class that writes to a stream.
Public Fields	
`Null`	A `BinaryWriter` with no backing store.
Public Properties	
`BaseStream`	Gets the `BinaryWriter`'s underlying stream.
Public Methods	
`Close`	Closes the current `BinaryWriter` and the underlying stream.
`Flush`	Clears all buffers for the current writer and causes any buffered data to be written to the underlying device.
`Seek`	Sets the position within the current stream.
`Write`	Overloaded. Writes a value to the current stream.
Protected Constructors	
`BinaryWriter` Constructor	Overloaded. Initializes a new instance of the `BinaryWriter` class that writes to a stream.
Protected Fields	
`OutStream`	Holds the underlying stream.
Protected Methods	
`Dispose`	Releases the unmanaged resources used by the `BinaryWriter` and optionally releases the managed resources.
`Write7BitEncodedInt`	Writes a 32-bit integer in a compressed format.

☐ Program: WriteBinaryFile

For our file, we will store a person's name as a `string`, their age as an `int`, and their weight as a `double`. The WriteBinaryFile program (Listing 15.3) prompts for a file name, then asks you to enter the name, age, and weight of some people. It writes this info to the file.

Listing 15.3

```
using System;
using System.IO;
public class WriteBinaryFile {
  public static void Main(String[] args) {
    try {

      //Prompt the user for the file name
      Console.Write("Enter the path and/or file name: ");
      String fileName = Console.ReadLine();

      //Create a BinaryWriter to write to a file
      BinaryWriter bw;
      //Create the file if it doesn't exist
      if (!File.Exists(fileName))
            bw=new BinaryWriter(File.Create(fileName));
      //Connect the writer to the file if it does exist
      //Truncate anything in the file
      else bw=new BinaryWriter(File.Open(fileName,FileMode.Truncate));

      //Loop for individuals' names, ages, and weights
      //Write each to the file
      Console.Write("Enter someone's name (ENTER to quit): ");
      String name = Console.ReadLine();
      while (name.Length>0) {
            bw.Write(name);
            Console.Write("Enter this person's age: ");
            int age = Int32.Parse(Console.ReadLine());
            bw.Write(age);
            Console.Write("Enter this person's weight: ");
            double weight = Double.Parse(Console.ReadLine());
            bw.Write(weight);
            Console.Write("Enter someone's name (ENTER to quit): ");
            name = Console.ReadLine();
      }

      //Close the file
      bw.Close();

    } catch (Exception e) {
      Console.Write(e.StackTrace);
    }
  }
}
```

Note that the program checks if the file already exists, and if not, calls File.Create, which creates the file and returns a FileStream object. The BinaryWriter constructor we use takes this Stream (by inheritance) as an argument and associates the BinaryWriter to the file.

```
if (!File.Exists(fileName))
     bw=new BinaryWriter(File.Create(fileName));
```

If, on the other hand, the file does exist, we use File.Open, which likewise returns a FileStream.

```
else bw=
      new BinaryWriter(File.Open(fileName,FileMode.Truncate));
```

File.Open takes an additional parameter of type FileMode, which is an enumeration. The valid values and their meaning follow:

- FileMode.Append—Opens the file if it exists and seeks to the end of the file, or creates a new file.
- FileMode.Create—Specifies that the operating system should create a new file. If the file already exists, it will be overwritten.
- FileMode.CreateNew—Specifies that the operating system should create a new file.
- FileMode.Open—Specifies that the operating system should open an existing file. A System.IO.FileNotFoundException is thrown if the file does not exist.
- FileMode.OpenOrCreate—Specifies that the operating system should open a file if it exists; otherwise, a new file should be created.
- FileMode.Truncate—Specifies that the operating system should open an existing file. Once opened, the file should be truncated so that its size is zero bytes.

Some FileMode values are intended only for writing purposes, like FileMode.Truncate. Because we want to write over any data that may be in the file, we open our file in this mode. If we were to append data to the end of the file, we would use FileMode.Append.

Here we run the WriteBinaryFile program. Note that it stops processing when we enter an empty string when prompted for a name.

```
Enter the path and/or file name: BinaryFile.fil
Enter someone's name (ENTER to quit): David Bishop
Enter this person's age: 103
Enter this person's weight: 1033.3
Enter someone's name (ENTER to quit): Humpty Frumpty
Enter this person's age: 56
Enter this person's weight: 123.4
Enter someone's name (ENTER to quit): Little Boy Blue
Enter this person's age: 8
```

```
Enter this person's weight: 40
Enter someone's name (ENTER to quit):
```

Let's display the contents of this file using the `type` command from the prompt. The `type` command expects text, so we get something that just looks like garbage. Of course, this is because much of the data is not stored as characters.

```
C:\C#>type BinaryFile.fil

♀David Bishopg   33333%É@♬Humpty Frumpty8   ÜÖÖÖ┘^@☼Little Boy Blu

D@
```

Program: ReadBinaryFile

To properly read this file, we create another program for this purpose. It makes use of the `BinaryReader` class. Table 15.6 gives the members.

TABLE 15.6

Public Constructors	
`BinaryReader` Constructor	Overloaded. Initializes a new instance of the `BinaryReader` class.
Public Properties	
`BaseStream`	Exposes access to the underlying stream of the `BinaryReader`.
Public Methods	
`Close`	Closes the current reader and the underlying stream.
`PeekChar`	Returns the next available character and does not advance the byte or character position.
`Read`	Overloaded. Reads characters from the underlying stream and advances the current position of the stream.
`ReadBoolean`	Reads a Boolean from the current stream and advances the current position of the stream by 1 byte.
`ReadByte`	Reads the next byte from the current stream and advances the current position of the stream by 1 byte.
`ReadBytes`	Reads `count` bytes from the current stream into a byte array and advances the current position by `count` bytes.
`ReadChar`	Reads the next character from the current stream and advances the current position of the stream in accordance with the encoding used and the specific character being read from the stream.

(continued)

TABLE 15.6 (continued)

Public Methods	
`ReadChars`	Reads `count` characters from the current stream, returns the data in a character array, and advances the current position in accordance with the encoding used and the specific character being read from the stream.
`ReadDecimal`	Reads a decimal value from the current stream and advances the current position of the stream by 16 bytes.
`ReadDouble`	Reads an 8-byte floating point value from the current stream and advances the current position of the stream by 8 bytes.
`ReadInt16`	Reads a 2-byte signed integer from the current stream and advances the current position of the stream by 2 bytes.
`ReadInt32`	Reads a 4-byte signed integer from the current stream and advances the current position of the stream by 4 bytes.
`ReadInt64`	Reads an 8-byte signed integer from the current stream and advances the current position of the stream by 4 bytes.
`ReadSByte`	Reads a signed byte from this stream and advances the current position of the stream by 1 byte.
`ReadSingle`	Reads a 4-byte floating point value from the current stream and advances the current position of the stream by 4 bytes.
`ReadString`	Reads a `String` from the current stream. The `String` is prefixed with the length, encoded as an integer 7 bits at a time.
`ReadUInt16`	Reads a 2-byte unsigned integer from the current stream using little-endian encoding and advances the position of the stream by 2 bytes.
`ReadUInt32`	Reads a 4-byte unsigned integer from the current stream and advances the position of the stream by 4 bytes.
`ReadUInt64`	Reads an 8-byte unsigned integer from the current stream and advances the position of the stream by 8 bytes.
Protected Methods	
`Dispose`	Releases the unmanaged resources used by the `BinaryReader` and optionally releases the managed resources.
`FillBuffer`	Fills the internal buffer with the specified number of bytes read from the stream.
`Read7BitEncodedInt`	Reads in a 32-bit integer in a compressed format.

Note that there are many different methods for reading. Each is for the purpose of reading in a simple data type, like a signed 16-bit integer versus an unsigned 64-bit integer. A `ReadString` method reads in strings; this method expects the string to be prefixed by its length.

The ReadBinaryFile program (Listing 15.4) prompts the user for the file name, then opens the file if it exists or displays an error if it doesn't. We read each record in a loop, display each value, and jump out of the loop when an attempt to read past the end of the file is made. The `ReadString` method will throw an `EndOfStreamException` when the program tries to read past the last record, and we jump to the `catch` block. This displays a message that the job is complete. We then close the `BinaryReader` (and the underlying file) and exit.

Listing 15.4

```
using System;
using System.IO;
public class ReadBinaryFile {
  public static void Main(String[] args) {
    try {

      //Prompt the user for the file name
      Console.Write("Enter the path and/or file name: ");
      String fileName = Console.ReadLine();

      //Create a BinaryReader to read from a file
      BinaryReader br;
      //Display error if it doesn't exist
      if (!File.Exists(fileName))
            Console.WriteLine("This doesn't exist!");
      //Connect the reader to the file if it does exist
      else {

            br=new BinaryReader(File.Open(fileName,FileMode.Open));

            //Loop for individual's names, ages, and weights
            //Read each from the file-EndOfStreamException thrown
            //when we try to read past the end of the file
            try {
                //Jump out of loop when exception is thrown
                for(;;) {
                  String name=br.ReadString();
                  Console.Write(name+" ");
                  int age = br.ReadInt32();
                  Console.Write(age+" ");
                  double weight = br.ReadDouble();
                  Console.WriteLine(weight);
                }
            } catch (EndOfStreamException) {
```

(continued)

```
                Console.WriteLine("\nAll done.");
            }

            //Close the reader/file
            br.Close();

        }

      } catch (Exception e) {
        Console.Write(e.StackTrace);
      }
    }
  }
```

Here is a run of the program, which appears to read the file correctly.

```
Enter the path and/or file name: BinaryFile.fil
David Bishop 103 1033.3
Humpty Frumpty 56 123.4
Little Boy Blue 8 40

All done.
```

■ OBJECTS IN FILES AND STREAMS

The previous program allowed us to send simple types and strings through a stream, but what about sending objects through a stream? This would be very convenient, because you wouldn't have to pick the object apart to send it, and you wouldn't have to put it back together once received. C# allows us to send objects through a stream, provided the objects are serializable. Serialization simply refers to the process required to turn data into a linear array of bytes for passage through a stream, and deserialization refers to reconstituting the data from those bytes.

In C#, we denote that a class or field is serializable by using the `[Serializable]` attribute, which precedes the declaration. The members of a type marked `[Serializable]` should be serializable as well. In C#, all the simple types and strings are serializable.

☐ Class: SerializablePerson

Listing 15.5 creates a `SerializablePerson` class. We mark it `[Serializable]`, and note that its members, name, age, and weight are also serializable. The constructor sets the fields, and we also have `Name`, `Age`, and `Weight` properties to provide read access to the fields.

Listing 15.5

```
using System;
//A Person object is marked Serializable
[Serializable] public class SerializablePerson {
      //All the fields are Serializable
      String name;
      int age;
      double weight;

      public SerializablePerson(String name,int age,double weight) {
            this.name=name;
            this.age=age;
            this.weight=weight;
      }

      public String Name {get {return name;}}
      public int Age {get {return age;}}
      public double Weight {get {return weight;}}

}
```

We can place a serializable object into a stream by serializing it. In C#, we can do this by calling the `Serialize` method from a `BinaryFormatter` object. The `BinaryFormatter` class is in the namespace `System.Runtime.Serialization.Formatters.Binary`. Here is an example of how this is done; suppose `name`, `age`, and `weight` have value, and that `s` refers to some type of stream.

```
//Create a BinaryFormatter object
BinaryFormatter bformatter=new BinaryFormatter();

//Create the person object and serialize it
SerializablePerson p=new SerializablePerson(name,age,weight);
bformatter.Serialize(s,p);
```

We will see next an application that writes a series of `SerializablePerson` objects to a file.

☐ Program: WriteBinarySerializedFile

The program in Listing 15.6 uses a `BinaryFormatter` to serialize some `SerializablePerson` objects, and write them to a file. The way they are stored is determined by the `BinaryFormatter`. The program first prompts for a file name, then the info on a series of individuals. It writes these as `SerializablePerson` objects to the file.

Listing 15.6

```
using System;
using System.IO;
using System.Runtime.Serialization.Formatters.Binary;
public class WriteBinarySerializedFile {
  public static void Main(String[] args) {
    try {

      //Create a BinaryFormatter object
      BinaryFormatter bformatter=new BinaryFormatter();

      //Prompt the user for the file name
      Console.Write("Enter the path and/or file name: ");
      String fileName = Console.ReadLine();

      //Create the stream to write to
      //bformatter will serialize objects into this stream
      FileStream fs;

      //Create the file if it doesn't exist
      if (!File.Exists(fileName)) fs=File.Create(fileName);
      //Truncate anything in the file
      else fs=File.Open(fileName,FileMode.Truncate);

      //Loop for individuals' names, ages, and weights
      //Write each to the file AS AN OBJECT
      Console.Write("Enter someone's name (ENTER to quit): ");
      String name = Console.ReadLine();
      while (name.Length>0) {
            Console.Write("Enter this person's age: ");
            int age = Int32.Parse(Console.ReadLine());
            Console.Write("Enter this person's weight: ");
            double weight = Double.Parse(Console.ReadLine());

            //Create the person object and serialize it
            SerializablePerson p=
                  new SerializablePerson(name,age,weight);
            bformatter.Serialize(fs,p);

            Console.Write("Enter someone's name (ENTER to quit): ");
            name = Console.ReadLine();
      }

      //Close the file
      fs.Close();

    } catch (Exception e) {
      Console.Write(e.StackTrace);
    }
  }
}
```

Here is the output of a run of this program:

```
Enter the path and/or file name: BinarySerializedFile.fil
Enter someone's name (ENTER to quit): David Bishop
Enter this person's age: 55
Enter this person's weight: 475.1
Enter someone's name (ENTER to quit): Jim Slim
Enter this person's age: 103
Enter this person's weight: 123.4
Enter someone's name (ENTER to quit): Frita Frink
Enter this person's age: 32
Enter this person's weight: 89.9
Enter someone's name (ENTER to quit):
```

If we use the `type` command to examine the contents of the file created by this, we get some clue as to how C# serializes objects.

```
C:\C#>type BinarySerializedFile.fil

 ☺        ☺         ♀☻   ISerializablePerson, Version=0.0.0.0, Culture=neutral,

Pub

licKeyToken=null♣☺   ↕SerializablePerson♥   ♦name♥age♠weight☺♠☻   ♠♥   ♀David

Bi

shop7   ÜÖÖÖ▒}@♂ ☺        ☺         ♀☻   ISerializablePerson, Version=0.0.0.0,

Cul

ture=neutral, PublicKeyToken=null♣☺   ↕SerializablePerson♥

♦name♥age♠weight☺

♠☻   ♠♥ Jim Slimg   ÜÖÖÖ┘^@♂ ☺        ☺         ♀☻   ISerializablePerson,

Version=

0.0.0.0, Culture=neutral, PublicKeyToken=null♣☺   ↕SerializablePerson♥

♦name♥a

ge♠weight☺♠☻   ♠♥   ♂Frita Frink   ÜÖÖÖyV@♂
```

☐ Program: ReadBinarySerializedFile

Listing 15.7 is another program to read this file. We deserialize the objects one by one from the stream using the `Deserialize` method from `BinaryFormatter`. This method returns an `Object`, so we must cast the result back to an object of type `SerializablePerson`.

Listing 15.7

```
using System;
using System.IO;
using System.Runtime.Serialization;
using System.Runtime.Serialization.Formatters.Binary;
public class ReadBinarySerializedFile {
  public static void Main(String[] args) {
    try {

      //Create a BinaryFormatter object
      BinaryFormatter bformatter=new BinaryFormatter();

      //Prompt the user for the file name
      Console.Write("Enter the path and/or file name: ");
      String fileName = Console.ReadLine();

      //Create a FileStream-bformatter will read from this
      FileStream fs;

      //Display error if file doesn't exist
      if (!File.Exists(fileName))
            Console.WriteLine("This doesn't exist!");
      //otherwise, deserialize each object from the file
      else {

          fs=File.Open(fileName,FileMode.Open);
          try {
            //Loop to read individuals from stream as objects
            //A SerializationException is thrown when attempt is
            //made to read past last object in stream
            for(;;) {
                  //Deserialize one object at a time
                  //Cast each to a SerializablePerson
                  SerializablePerson p=(SerializablePerson)
                        bformatter.Deserialize(fs);
                  //Display the properties of the person
                  Console.WriteLine(p.Name+" "+p.Age+" "+p.Weight);
            }
          } catch (SerializationException) {
            Console.WriteLine("\nAll objects retrieved.");
          }
```

(continued)

```
            //Close the stream
            fs.Close();

        }

    } catch (Exception e) {
      Console.Write(e+"\n"+e.StackTrace);
    }
  }
}
```

Note that the deserialization of each object occurs in an infinite `for` loop. We exit the loop when we attempt to deserialize past the last object in the stream. When this happens, a `SerializationException` is thrown and we jump to the `catch` block, which merely reports the end of processing.

Note also that the receiving application really doesn't need to know anything about the internal structure of a `SerializablePerson` in order to read it from the stream. Any reconstruction is done by the `BinaryFormatter`. This goes a long way toward protecting the private internal structure of an object, and is more in keeping with the object-oriented philosophy of C#. Besides, it's convenient as well!

Here we run the program, and it appears to read everything just fine.

```
Enter the path and/or file name: BinarySerializedFile.fil
David Bishop 55 475.1
Jim Slim 103 123.4
Frita Frink 32 89.9

All objects retrieved.
```

There are alternatives to using binary formatting; after all, other systems may use a different form of binary coding, and would not be able to communicate through such a stream.

■ RELATIONAL DATABASES

Convenient and efficient information management is the objective of any database, which is a collection of files managed by a database management system (DBMS). Early databases were not easily modifiable; the structure of such databases was static, and changing it often required significant reprogramming.

Products : Table

	ID	Name	Price	Cost
+	1	Rubber Dog Poop	$1.49	$0.03
+	2	Fake Vomit	$3.99	$1.75
+	3	Itching Powder	$1.79	$0.99
+	4	Sneezing Powder	$3.89	$2.17
+	5	Hand Buzzer	$5.99	$3.25
▶	(AutoNumber)		$0.00	$0.00

Record: 6 of 6

Figure 15.8

Retailers : Table

	ID	Name	Street	City	State	Zip
+	1	Bill's Gag Shop	321 Hoboken	Crabtree	KS	00111
+	2	Joe's Gas	1230 True Love Street	Des Moines	IA	32119
+	3	Millie's	555 Dark Lane	St. Paul	MN	55555
▶	(AutoNumber)					

Record: 4 of 4

Figure 15.9

Sales : Table

	TransactionNumber	TransactionDate	ProductID	RetailerID	Quantity
	1	11/11/2000	3	1	12
	2	11/23/2001	1	2	12
	3	1/31/2002	5	3	7
	4	12/31/2002	1	3	60
	5	1/12/2003	2	2	36
	6	1/27/2003	4	1	15
	7	4/1/2003	4	1	24
▶	(AutoNumber)		0	0	0

Record: 8 of 8

Figure 15.10

Modern relational databases provide convenient access to the data, and are easily modified by users with the proper permissions. A relational database can be viewed as a collection of tables joined by relationships. The columns in each table are referred to as fields, whereas the rows are called "records." The rows represent a real-world entity, and a column-row intersection represents a value for an entity.

Figure 15.8 shows an example of a table called `Products`, which is part of the Gags.mdb database in our C# folder. This database was created by Microsoft Access.

The table has four fields and five records. A table should have a field called the "primary key" that identifies each record. In the `Products` table, `ID` is the primary key. No two records may have the same primary key value.

The `Retailers` table is seen in Figure 15.9. It also has a primary key labeled `ID`.

Finally, the `Sales` table in Figure 15.10 records transactions involving products and retailers. Each transaction has a unique `TransactionNumber`, and this field is used as the primary key of this table.

Note that the `Sales` table also makes references to products and retailers via the `ProductID` and `RetailerID` fields. These fields serve as foreign keys in this database; that is, these foreign keys refer to primary keys in another database. The relationship between the three tables is also set up in Microsoft Access, and is seen in Figure 15.11.

Figure 15.11

The purpose of foreign keys, primary keys, and the relationships between them is twofold:

- A foreign key always identifies a record in another table uniquely because it references the unique primary key in that table. (Using another nonunique field, like name or address, for example, may produce ambiguity.)
- The relationship between primary and foreign keys reduces data redundancy; for example, if the `Sales` table had retailer name, street, city, state, and ZIP fields, this data would need to be rekeyed for every transaction involving that client in the `Sales` table. Such redundancy is not efficient and is error-prone because changing the values in one row does not change any of the other values. This causes entries to likely contain outdated and incorrect information.

C# provides classes to retrieve data from, manipulate data in, and remove records from relational databases. We will do this by submitting Structured Query Language (SQL) statements to the database. SQL is a powerful language that interacts with databases that support it, and practically every relational database does. SQL statements look like simple questions/directions to the database. We cannot hope to cover the huge scope of SQL here, but we will see some SQL examples in the programs to follow.

Because Gags.mdb is an OLE (Object Linking and Embedding) database, we will use the classes from `System.Data.OleDb` to interface with it. We will not use the advanced abilities an OLE database provides, however; we simply use SQL to query and modify the database. There is also a `System.Data.Sql` namespace, and the examples could be rewritten using it.

☐ Program: DBQuery

DBQuery (Listing 15.8) is a program designed to submit SQL queries to a database. Queries do not modify the contents of tables; they only retrieve data from them. SQL queries begin with the keyword `SELECT`.

We must first make a connection to the database. To do this, we must have access to a data provider; we use the JET provider from Microsoft. A provider is easily obtained by going to

```
http://msdn.microsoft.com/downloads
```

We make a connection to the provider by passing in a specially formatted string to an `OleDbConnection` constructor. In our case, it is the following:

```
"Provider=Microsoft.Jet.OLEDB.4.0;Data Source=Gags.mdb"
```

The Gags.mdb database is in the same folder as the DBQuery program, so we need not specify a path. If it exists elsewhere on your local machine, you can supply a path in the string as well.

The `OleDbConnection` constructor accepts the string, and creates a connection with the database:

```
OleDbConnection connection = new OleDbConnection(
"Provider=Microsoft.Jet.OLEDB.4.0;Data Surce=Gags.mdb");
```

Connections should be closed once access is no longer required. We do this by using the `OleDBConnection Close` method:

```
connection.Close();
```

Once a connection exists, we issue a command to the database by creating a `OleDbCommand` object. This constructor takes in a SQL command as a string, plus the `OleDbConnection`. Next, we prepare the command for execution by calling the `Open` method from the `Connection` property of `OleDBCommand` (which returns the `OleDbConnection` that exists between client and database).

```
OleDbCommand command =
      new OleDbCommand(query,connection);
command.Connection.Open();
```

If you are issuing a query, that is, a `SELECT` statement, there are many ways to capture the data, but I think the most direct way is to use an `OleDbDataReader` object. We create such a reader by calling the `ExecuteReader` method from the `OleDbCommand` object. This returns an `OleDbReader` object.

```
OleDbDataReader reader = command.ExecuteReader(
      CommandBehavior.CloseConnection);
```

Note that we pass a `CommandBehavior` value to this constructor. `CommandBehavior` is an enumeration from `System.Data`. The `Close` value simply says that the connection will be closed when the reader is closed. Incidentally, the `OleDbDataReader` is closed using its `Close` method:

```
reader.Close();
```

An `OleDbDataReader` reads a row of data at a time. This row may come from an actual table or be a row of data generated by the query itself. We read a single row by calling the `Read` method from `OleDbDataReader`. The `Read` method returns a Boolean; true if a row was successfully read, and false otherwise. A false value means there is no more data to read.

```
while (reader.Read()) {
//Play with the row here

}
```

Once we have obtained a row, we can access the `index`-th field (where indexing starts with 0) by using one of the many `get` methods from `reader`. Here are some:

- `string GetString(int index);`
- `int GetInt32(int index);`
- `DateTime GetDateTime(int index);`
- `double GetDouble(int index);`

How do we know what type the `index`-th field is? By calling the instance `OleDbDataReader` method

```
Type GetFieldType(int index);
```

Once we know the type, we know how to capture that value from the row. There are many `get` methods from `OleDbDataReader` that can capture values of types other than those I've shown here; an interesting exercise may be for you to modify DBQuery to capture correctly as many types as possible.

This is all we need to know to write DBQuery. This program allows only `SELECT` queries. The path and file name to the database are passed in through the command line.

Listing 15.8

```
using System;
using System.Data;
using System.Data.OleDb;
public class DBQuery {
   public static void Main(String[] args) {
     try {
      //Form the string used to connect to the database
      //We will use the JET data provider from Microsoft
      //Path name of database will be passed in thru command line
      String connectionString = "Provider=Microsoft.Jet.OLEDB.4.0;"
            +"Data Source="+args[0];
      //Create the connection
      OleDbConnection connection =
            new OleDbConnection(connectionString);

      //User enters query at prompt
      Console.Write("Enter select query: ");
      String query = Console.ReadLine();

      //Only select queries are allowed
      if (query.ToUpper().Trim().StartsWith("SELECT")) {
```

(continued)

```
            //Create a command and open
            OleDbCommand command =
                  new OleDbCommand(query,connection);
            command.Connection.Open();

            //Create a data reader to read results
            OleDbDataReader reader = command.ExecuteReader(
                  CommandBehavior.CloseConnection);

            //Call Read first-returns false if no more data
            while (reader.Read()) {
              //Pass thru the fields in each row
              //Determine type of each
              //Call appropriate Get method from the reader
              for (int i=0;i<reader.FieldCount;i++) {
                Type theFieldType=reader.GetFieldType(i);
                if (theFieldType==typeof(System.Int32)) {
                  Console.Write(reader.GetInt32(i)+" ");
                } else if (theFieldType==typeof(System.String)) {
                  Console.Write(reader.GetString(i)+" ");
                } else if (theFieldType==typeof(System.Double)) {
                  Console.Write(reader.GetDouble(i)+" ");
                } else if (theFieldType==typeof(System.DateTime)) {
                  Console.Write(reader.GetDateTime(i)+" ");
                }
              }
              Console.WriteLine();
            }

            //Close the reader and connection
            reader.Close();
            connection.Close();

      } else {
            Console.WriteLine("Only SELECT queries are allowed.");
      }
     } catch (Exception e) {
      Console.WriteLine(e + "\n" + e.StackTrace);
     }
   }
}
```

Here are some example queries to the Gags.mdb database:

```
C:\C#>DBQuery Gags.mdb
Enter select query: select * from Products
1 Rubber Dog Poop 1.49 0.03
2 Fake Vomit 3.99 1.75
```

```
3 Itching Powder 1.79 0.99
4 Sneezing Powder 3.89 2.17
5 Hand Buzzer 5.99 3.25

C:\C#>DBQuery Gags.mdb
Enter select query: select * from Sales,Retailers where
Sales.RetailerID = Retailers.ID
1 11/11/2000 12:00:00 AM 3 1 12 1 Bill's Gag Shop 321 Hoboken
Crabtree KS 00111
2 11/23/2001 12:00:00 AM 1 2 12 2 Joe's Gas 1230 True Love
Street Des Moines IA 32119
3 1/31/2002 12:00:00 AM 5 3 7 3 Millie's 555 Dark Lane St. Paul
MN 55555
4 12/31/2002 12:00:00 AM 1 3 60 3 Millie's 555 Dark Lane St.
Paul MN 55555
5 1/12/2003 12:00:00 AM 2 2 36 2 Joe's Gas 1230 True Love
Street Des Moines IA 32119
6 1/27/2003 12:00:00 AM 4 1 15 1 Bill's Gag Shop 321 Hoboken
Crabtree KS 00111
7 4/1/2003 12:00:00 AM 4 1 24 1 Bill's Gag Shop 321 Hoboken
Crabtree KS 00111

C:\C#>DBQuery Gags.mdb
Enter select query: select Sales.Quantity, Retailers.Name from
Sales,Retailers where Sales.RetailerID=Retailers.ID and
Sales.Quantity > 10
12 Bill's Gag Shop
12 Joe's Gas
60 Millie's
36 Joe's Gas
15 Bill's Gag Shop
24 Bill's Gag Shop

C:\C#>DBQuery Gags.mdb
Enter select query: select Sales.ProductID, Sales.Quantity *
Products.Price from Sales, Products where
Sales.ProductID=Products.ID
3 21.48
1 17.88
5 41.93
1 89.4
2 143.64
4 58.35
4 93.36
```

```
C:\C#>DBQuery Gags.mdb
Enter select query: select Sales.ProductID, sum(Sales.Quantity
* Products.Price) from Sales,Products where
Sales.ProductID=Products.ID group by Sales.ProductID
1 107.28
2 143.64
3 21.48
4 151.71
5 41.93

C:\C#>DBQuery Gags.mdb
Enter select query: select sum(Sales.Quantity*Products.Price)
from Sales, Products where Sales.ProductID=Products.ID
466.04

G:\C#>DBQuery Gags.mdb
Enter select query: select sum(Sales.Quantity*Products.Price)
from Sales, Products
2846.9
```

Notice that no path is specified for Gags.mdb when we run DBQuery. This means, of course, that Gags.mdb and DBQuery.exe are in the same directory. Note also that the SQL is clearly not case sensitive.

☐ Program: DBModify

We can also use SQL to modify a database, and I have written a DBModify program to do this (see Listing 15.9). DBModify accepts only `UPDATE`, `INSERT`, and `DELETE` statements. An interesting exercise for you would be to allow it to accept more types of SQL statements.

Setting up the connection, creating the command, and opening it is done in exactly the same way as in the previous example DBQuery. The only difference is that when the command is executed, we call the `ExecuteNonQuery` method from the `OleDbCommand` object.

```
//sql is a string containing the SQL statement
//connection is the OleDbConnection between client and database
OleDbCommand cmd = new OleDbCommand(sql,connection);
cmd.Connection.Open();
cmd.ExecuteNonQuery();
connection.Close();
```

Of course, we still close the connection after the SQL statement has executed.

Listing 15.9

```
using System;
using System.Data.OleDb;
public class DBModify {
   public static void Main(String[] args) {
     try {
      //Form the string used to connect to the database
      //We will use the JET data provider from Microsoft
      //Path name of database will be passed in thru command line
      String connectionString = "Provider=Microsoft.Jet.OLEDB.4.0;"
            +"Data Source="+args[0];
      //Create the connection
      OleDbConnection connection =
            new OleDbConnection(connectionString);

      //User enters SQL at prompt
      Console.Write("Enter non-query SQL: ");
      String sql = Console.ReadLine();
      String testsql = sql.ToUpper().Trim().Split()[0];

      //Only certain statements are allowed
      if (testsql=="DELETE"
            ||testsql=="INSERT"
            ||testsql=="UPDATE") {

            //Create, open, execute, command
            OleDbCommand cmd =
                  new OleDbCommand(sql,connection);
            cmd.Connection.Open();
            cmd.ExecuteNonQuery();

            //Don't forget to close connection
            connection.Close();

      } else {
            Console.WriteLine("This statement is not allowed.");
      }
     } catch (Exception e) {
      Console.WriteLine(e + "\n" + e.StackTrace);
     }
   }
}
```

Here are some examples of the use of INSERT, UPDATE, and DELETE statements in SQL. Periodic queries are also made with DBQuery to show the effect of these statements.

```
C:\C#>DBQuery Gags.mdb
Enter select query: select * from Products
```

```
1 Rubber Dog Poop 1.49 0.03
2 Fake Vomit 3.99 1.75
3 Itching Powder 1.79 0.99
4 Sneezing Powder 3.89 2.17
5 Hand Buzzer 5.99 3.25

C:\C#>DBModify Gags.mdb
Enter non-query SQL: insert into Products (ID, name, price,
cost) values (6, 'Whoopie Cushion', 7.99, 3.49)

C:\C#>DBQuery Gags.mdb
Enter select query: select * from Products
1 Rubber Dog Poop 1.49 0.03
2 Fake Vomit 3.99 1.75
3 Itching Powder 1.79 0.99
4 Sneezing Powder 3.89 2.17
5 Hand Buzzer 5.99 3.25
6 Whoopie Cushion 7.99 3.49

C:\C#>DBModify Gags.mdb
Enter non-query SQL: update products set price=8.99 where ID=6

C:\C#>DBQuery Gags.mdb
Enter select query: select * from Products
1 Rubber Dog Poop 1.49 0.03
2 Fake Vomit 3.99 1.75
3 Itching Powder 1.79 0.99
4 Sneezing Powder 3.89 2.17
5 Hand Buzzer 5.99 3.25
6 Whoopie Cushion 8.99 3.49

G:\C#>DBModify Gags.mdb
Enter non-query SQL: delete from products where id=6

G:\C#>DBQuery Gags.mdb
Enter select query: select * from products
1 Rubber Dog Poop 1.49 0.03
2 Fake Vomit 3.99 1.75
3 Itching Powder 1.79 0.99
4 Sneezing Powder 3.89 2.17
5 Hand Buzzer 5.99 3.25
```

chapter 16

Concurrency

Modern operating systems can run many programs at the same time. Because these programs are sharing common resources, one must ensure that jobs do not interfere with each other, either intentionally or accidentally. *Concurrency* is a term used to describe the safe management of multiple programs.

The first computer systems could run only one program at a time. Each had to be manually set up and executed, and then the results had to be accumulated. After a time, simple operating systems were developed that would do the sequential setup and execution of these jobs; this was often done overnight. The set of jobs to run was called a "batch," and the system that ran them was called a "batch system."

Later, more sophisticated operating systems were constructed. A multiprogramming system not only set up and executed the programs, but also decided when to run the jobs, and in what order. It could interrupt running jobs, save their state, run other jobs, and reactivate the interrupted job in the same place it left. Eventually, operating systems were developed that could perform this switching so quickly that a user would not be aware of it; that is, it seemed as though each program the user ran had its own processor. These systems are called "time-sharing" or "multitasking systems."

In order for an operating system to schedule and control the programs, it must store additional information about each of them. A program plus all this system information is called a "process." Here are some items the operating system must store for every process:

- A number to identify the process
- A value indicating the priority of the process
- The state the process was in when last interrupted
- The address of the next instruction to execute in the process
- The values the registers contained when the process was interrupted
- Values denoting the memory limitations imposed on the process
- A list of files the process has opened

This information allows the operating system (OS) to interrupt and resume processes seamlessly.

CREATING PROCESSES

C# allows us to create and start processes from within a C# application, and to obtain information on any running process as well. We do this by using the `Process` class from the `System.Diagnostics` namespace.

Table 16.1 contains a breakdown of the members of the `Process` class.

TABLE 16.1

Public Constructors	
`Process` Constructor	Initializes a new instance of the `Process` class.
Public Properties	
`BasePriority`	Gets the base priority of the associated process.
`Container`	(Inherited from `Component`.) Gets the `IContainer` that contains the `Component`.
`EnableRaisingEvents`	Gets or sets whether the `Exited` event should be raised when the process terminates.
`ExitCode`	Gets the value that the associated process specified when it terminated.
`ExitTime`	Gets the time that the associated process exited.
`Handle`	Returns the associated process's native handle.
`HandleCount`	Gets the number of handles opened by the process.
`HasExited`	Gets a value indicating whether the associated process has been terminated.

(continued)

TABLE 16.1 (continued)

Public Properties	
`Id`	Gets the unique identifier for the associated process.
`MachineName`	Gets the name of the computer the associated process is running on.
`MainModule`	Gets the main module for the associated process.
`MainWindowHandle`	Gets the window handle of the main window of the associated process.
`MainWindowTitle`	Gets the caption of the main window of the process.
`MaxWorkingSet`	Gets or sets the maximum allowable working set size for the associated process.
`MinWorkingSet`	Gets or sets the minimum allowable working set size for the associated process.
`Modules`	Gets the modules that have been loaded by the associated process.
`NonpagedSystemMemorySize`	Gets the nonpaged system memory size allocated to this process.
`PagedMemorySize`	Gets the paged memory size.
`PagedSystemMemorySize`	Gets the paged system memory size.
`PeakPagedMemorySize`	Gets the peak paged memory size.
`PeakVirtualMemorySize`	Gets the peak virtual memory size.
`PeakWorkingSet`	Gets the peak working set size.
`PriorityBoostEnabled`	Gets or sets a value indicating whether the associated process priority should temporarily be boosted by the operating system when the main window has the focus.
`PriorityClass`	Gets or sets the overall priority category for the associated process.
`PrivateMemorySize`	Gets the private memory size.
`PrivilegedProcessorTime`	Gets the privileged processor time for this process.
`ProcessName`	Gets the name of the process.
`ProcessorAffinity`	Gets or sets the processors on which the threads in this process can be scheduled to run.
`Responding`	Gets a value indicating whether the user interface of the process is responding.
`Site`	(Inherited from `Component`.) Gets or sets the `ISite` of the `Component`.
`StandardError`	Gets a `StreamReader` through which to read error output from the application.
`StandardInput`	Gets a `StreamWriter` through which the application can write input to the process.

(continued)

TABLE 16.1 (continued)

Public Properties	
`StandardOutput`	Gets a `StreamReader` through which the application can read output from the process.
`StartInfo`	Gets or sets the properties to pass to the `Start` method of the process.
`StartTime`	Gets the time that the associated process was started.
`SynchronizingObject`	Gets or sets the object used to marshal the event handler calls that are issued as a result of a process exit event.
`Threads`	Gets the set of threads that are running in the associated process.
`TotalProcessorTime`	Gets the total processor time for this process.
`UserProcessorTime`	Gets the user processor time for this process.
`VirtualMemorySize`	Gets the size of the process's virtual memory.
`WorkingSet`	Gets the associated process's physical memory usage.
Public Methods	
`Close`	Frees all the resources that are associated with this component.
`CloseMainWindow`	Closes a process that has a user interface by sending a close message to its main window.
`CreateObjRef`	(Inherited from `MarshalByRefObject`.) Creates an object that contains all the relevant information required to generate a proxy used to communicate with a remote object.
`Dispose`	(Inherited from `Component`.) Overloaded. Releases the resources used by the `Component`.
`EnterDebugMode`	Puts a `Process` component in state to interact with operating system processes that run in a special mode.
`GetCurrentProcess`	Gets a new `Process` component and associates it with the currently active process.
`GetLifetimeService`	(Inherited from `MarshalByRefObject`.) Retrieves the current lifetime service object that controls the lifetime policy for this instance.
`GetProcessById`	Overloaded. Creates a new `Process` component, and associates it with the existing process resource that you specify.
`GetProcesses`	Overloaded. Creates an array of new `Process` components and associates them with existing process resources.
`GetProcessesByName`	Overloaded. Creates an array of new Process components and associates them with the existing process resources that all share the specified process name.
`InitializeLifetimeService`	(Inherited from `MarshalByRefObject`.) Obtains a lifetime service object to control the lifetime policy for this instance.

(continued)

TABLE 16.1 (continued)

Public Methods	
`Kill`	Immediately stops the associated process.
`LeaveDebugMode`	Takes a `Process` component out of the state that lets it interact with operating system processes that run in a special mode.
`Refresh`	Discards any information about the associated process that has been cached inside the process component.
`Start`	Overloaded. Starts a process resource and associates it with a `Process` component.
`ToString`	Overridden. Formats the process's name as a string, combined with the parent component type, if applicable.
`WaitForExit`	Overloaded. Sets the period of time to wait for the associated process to exit, and blocks the current thread of execution until the time has elapsed or the process has exited.
`WaitForInputIdle`	Overloaded. Causes the `Process` component to wait for the associated process to enter an idle state.
Public Events	
`Disposed`	(Inherited from `Component`.) Adds an event handler to listen to the `Disposed` event on the component.
`Exited`	Occurs when a process exits.
Protected Properties	
`DesignMode`	(Inherited from `Component`.) Gets a value that indicates whether the `Component` is currently in design mode.
`Events`	(Inherited from `Component`.) Gets the list of event handlers that are attached to this `Component`.
Protected Methods	
`Dispose`	Overloaded. Overridden. Disposes of this process.
`GetService`	(Inherited from `Component`.) Returns an object that represents a service provided by the `Component` or by its `Container`.
`OnExited`	Raises the `Exited` event.

These properties and methods allow us to obtain information on processes, to start processes, and to manipulate them.

☐ Program: ProcessInfo

The static `GetCurrentProcess()` method allows us to capture the currently running process; that is, the program you are running. Listing 16.1 is an example that does this, then displays information on the process.

Listing 16.1

```
using System;
using System.Diagnostics;
public class ProcessInfo {
  public static void Main(String[] args) {
//if we are here, this is the current process
    Process me=Process.GetCurrentProcess();
//Display the process ID, machine name, process name,
//total time actually running, &
//total time from start to finish
    Console.WriteLine("Id: "+me.Id);
    Console.WriteLine("Machine name: "+me.MachineName);
    Console.WriteLine("Process name: "+me.ProcessName);
    Console.WriteLine("User processor time: "+me.UserProcessorTime);
    Console.WriteLine("Total processor time: "+me.TotalProcessorTime);
  }
}
```

The application starts running and becomes a process in the system. It first executes the `GetCurrentProcess()` method, which captures the process and represents it as a C# `Process` object. We then display the ID number of the process, the machine it is running on, the name of the process, the time the application spent running, and the total time the process used from the time it started until it finished. This information, and much more, can all be obtained through the various properties and methods in the `Process` class.

Here is an example run of this application:

```
Id: 3856
Machine name: .
Process name: ProcessInfo
User processor time: 00:00:00.0937500
Total processor time: 00:00:00.2343750
```

The process ID is assigned by the system, which uses it to identify and manipulate the process. Here, the machine name is simply ".", which means the process is running on the local computer. We can also use the `Process` class to obtain information on a process running on a remote computer on a network. In this case, the process name is the same as the class name.

The difference between user processor time and total processor time is explained by the multitasking nature of the OS. When a process is started, it enters a queue awaiting

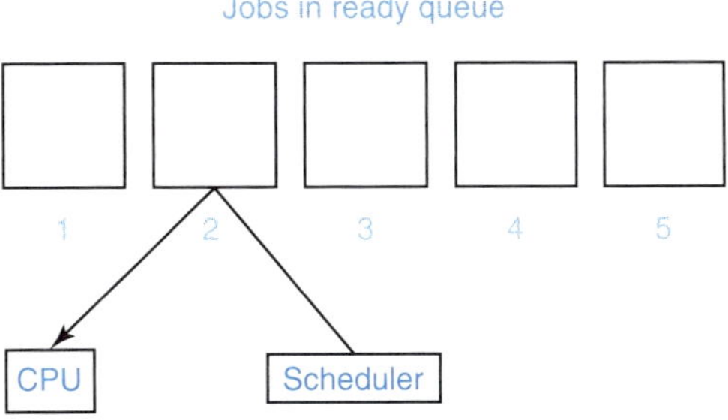

Figure 16.1

the processor. A system program called the "scheduler" eventually selects it to run, and gives it to the processor. (See Figure 16.1.)

The process may be interrupted periodically by the scheduler as other processes compete for the processor. User processor time refers to the time the process spent actually running, whereas total processor time refers to this plus the time the process spent in the ready queue.

The `Process` class can also obtain information on all processes on a system using the static `GetProcesses()` method, which returns an array of `Process` objects. Once we have these processes, we can obtain information on them and manipulate them using the methods of the `Process` class.

☐ Program: ProcessesDisplay

Listing 16.2 is an application that captures the processes on the local machine, and displays the ID and name of each process.

Listing 16.2

```
using System;
using System.Diagnostics;
//Gets and displays all running processes
public class ProcessesDisplay {
    public static void Main(String[] args) {
      //GetProcesses returns processes on system as array
      Process[] pa = Process.GetProcesses();

      //Display name and id of each process
      Console.WriteLine("ID\tNAME");
      foreach (Process p in pa)
          Console.WriteLine(p.Id+"\t"+p.ProcessName);
    }
}
```

Once we have obtained these processes in an array, we can access them by index or, because we now have the names and IDs of the processes, we can also use the `GetProcessById()` method or the `GetProcessesByName()` method.

Here is this application running. It shows all processes on my local machine at the time I ran the program.

```
ID      NAME
424     pccntupd
316     Grxp4exe
524     winlogon
1272    mdm
1688    cmd
188     hpztsb04
180     hkcmd
396     PNTIOMON
1036    Lexpps
500     csrss
1032    spoolsv
1352    ZipToA
1672    Explorer
812     svchost
1988    WebTrapNT
164     Imgicon
912     svchost
1980    Pop3trap
568     services
1228    ActivityDisk
1972    qttask
580     lsass
3040    NOTEPAD
788     svchost
1960    igfxtray
996     LexBceS
888     svchost
244     INSTAN~1
1312    Tmntsrv
348     VAServ
1624    tgcmd
444     SMSS
2900    iexplore
328     AD2KClient
3964    ProcessesDisplay
4       System
0       Idle
```

▪ SPAWNING PROCESSES

The `Process` class can also be used to start a new process. When a process creates another process, it is sometimes referred to as "spawning." Depending on the environment, a spawned process can be either a copy of its parent or a new process with some program loaded into it. Windows actually supports both methods.

We spawn processes in C# by using both the `Process` class and the `ProcessStartInfo` class. (`ProcessStartInfo` is also in `System.Diagnostics.`) We create a `ProcessStartInfo` object by using one these constructors:

- `public ProcessStartInfo();`
- `public ProcessStartInfo(String file);`
- `public ProcessStartInfo(String file,String args);`

The first constructor does not specify a file name, but you can set the `FileName` property after you create the `ProcessStartInfo` object. The second constructor allows you to specify the file name of the application you wish to run (or the document you wish to open). The third constructor allows you to pass in command line arguments to the application as well.

Once we have determined the file name in a `ProcessStartInfo` object, named say, `psi`, we can create a `Process` object `p` and set its `StartInfo` property to `psi`. We then start the process using `p.Start()`. Table 16.2 contains a partial listing of the members of the `ProcessStartInfo` class.

TABLE 16.2

Public Constructors	
`ProcessStartInfo` Constructor	Overloaded. Initializes a new instance of the ProcessStartInfo class.
Public Properties	
`Arguments`	Gets or sets the set of command line arguments to use when starting the application.
`CreateNoWindow`	Gets or sets a value indicating whether to start the process in a new window.
`EnvironmentVariables`	Gets search paths for files, directories for temporary files, application-specific options, and other similar information.
`ErrorDialog`	Gets or sets a value indicating whether an error dialog is displayed to the user if the process cannot be started.
`ErrorDialogParentHandle`	Gets or sets the window handle to use when an error dialog is shown for a process that cannot be started.

(continued)

TABLE 16.2 (continued)

Public Properties	
`FileName`	Gets or sets the application or document to start.
`RedirectStandardError`	Gets or sets a value indicating whether the process's error output is written to the `Process` instance's StandardError member, enabling you to write to a destination other than the standard error stream (usually the monitor screen). Used to write error data to a file or a log, for example.
`RedirectStandardInput`	Gets or sets a value indicating whether the process command input is read from the `Process` instance's `StandardInput` member, enabling you to read from a source other than the standard input stream (usually the keyboard). Used to read data from a file, for example.
`RedirectStandardOutput`	Gets or sets a value indicating whether the process output is written to the `Process` instance's `StandardOutput` member, enabling you to write to a destination other than the standard output stream (usually the monitor screen). Used to write data to a file, for example.
`UseShellExecute`	Gets or sets a value indicating whether to use the operating system shell to start the process.
`Verb`	Gets or sets the verb to use when opening the application or document specified by the `FileName` property.
`Verbs`	Gets the set of verbs associated with the type of file specified by the `FileName` property.
`WindowStyle`	Gets or sets the window state to use when the process is started.
`WorkingDirectory`	Gets or sets the initial directory for the process to be started.

□ Program: ProcessSpawning

Listing 16.3 is an application that runs $n - 1$ copies of itself, where n is a positive integer passed in through the command line. The application launches itself $n - 1$ more times, where n is reduced by one in each call. We pass this value in through the command line, so we use the form of the `ProcessStartInfo` constructor, which allows us to do this. Eventually $n = 1$, and the application stops making and running copies of itself.

Listing 16.3

```
using System;
using System.Windows.Forms;
using System.Diagnostics;
//This class starts and runs n-1 copies of itself
//n is passed in thru command line
public class ProcessSpawning {
    public static void Main(String[] args) {
      //Capture command line parameter-3 is default
      int processNumber=args.Length==1?Int32.Parse(args[0]):3;

      //Throw up a message box-user clicks OK
      MessageBox.Show("Process "+processNumber+" running");

      //Spawn a new copy of this process
      //until command line parameter reaches 1
      if (processNumber!=1) {
            //Create new process-not running yet
            Process p=new Process();

            //Create a ProcessStartInfo object
            //This constructor takes file name and
            //command line arguments
            ProcessStartInfo psi=new ProcessStartInfo(
                  "ProcessSpawning.exe",
                  (processNumber-1).ToString());

            //Set StartInfo property of this process
            p.StartInfo=psi;

            //Start the process
            p.Start();
      }

      //Exit THIS process
    }
}
```

Figure 16.2 shows screenshots of the application. The default value for the command line argument is 3.

Figure 16.2

Although it is very convenient to be able to launch and manipulate processes through the `Process` class, it is more convenient, efficient, and flexible to use threads. Thus, further development will be done with them.

■ THREADS

The runtime environment of .NET allows us to use threads, which are often referred to as "lightweight processes." This is because a single process can have many "threads" of execution, and much of the information the OS stores on a process can be shared by these many threads.

When a process launches, it can spawn many threads, and these threads compete for processor time just as processes do. These threads can all be executing code within the process that spawned them, and they can do so concurrently (see Figure 16.3).

□ The `Thread` Class

C# provides a `Thread` class to enable us to do multithreaded programming. Table 16.3 provides a breakdown of the `Thread` class, which is in the `System.Threading` namespace.

You create a thread in a C# application by using the `Thread` constructor, which takes this form:

```
public Thread(ThreadStart);
```

You must pass in a `ThreadStart` object to the constructor. A `ThreadStart` is a delegate; that is, it references a method rather than object data. Specifically, `ThreadStart` is a `void` delegate of this form:

```
public delegate void ThreadStart();
```

The `ThreadStart` delegate passed into a `Thread` constructor works this way:

1. The `ThreadStart` delegate is created first. Because it references some method, say `m()`, that method must have the same number and type of parameters as specified in the delegate; in the case of `ThreadStart`, that means no parameters.

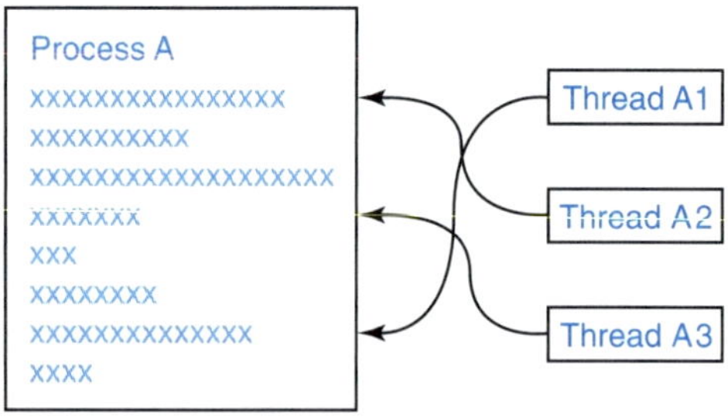

Figure 16.3

TABLE 16.3

Public Constructors	
`Thread` Constructor	Initializes a new instance of the `Thread` class.
Public Properties	
`ApartmentState`	Gets or sets the apartment state of this thread.
`CurrentContext`	Gets the current context in which the thread is executing.
`CurrentCulture`	Gets or sets the culture for the current thread.
`CurrentPrincipal`	Gets or sets the thread's current principal (for role-based security).
`CurrentThread`	Gets the currently running thread.
`CurrentUICulture`	Gets or sets the current culture used by the Resource Manager to look up culture-specific resources at run time.
`IsAlive`	Gets a value indicating the execution status of the current thread.
`IsBackground`	Gets or sets a value indicating whether or not a thread is a background thread.
`Name`	Gets or sets the name of the thread.
`Priority`	Gets or sets a value indicating the scheduling priority of a thread.
`ThreadState`	Gets a value containing the states of the current thread.
Public Methods	
`Abort`	Overloaded. Raises a `ThreadAbortException` in the thread on which it is invoked, to begin the process of terminating the thread. Calling this method usually terminates the thread.
`AllocateDataSlot`	Allocates an unnamed data slot on all the threads.
`AllocateNamedDataSlot`	Allocates a named data slot on all the threads.
`FreeNamedDataSlot`	Frees a previously allocated named data slot.
`GetData`	Retrieves the value from the specified slot on the current thread, within the current thread's current domain.
`GetDomain`	Returns the current domain in which the current thread is running.
`GetDomainID`	Returns a unique application domain identifier.
`GetNamedDataSlot`	Looks up a named data slot.
`Interrupt`	Interrupts a thread that is in the `WaitSleepJoin` thread state.
`Join`	Overloaded. Blocks the calling thread until a thread terminates.
`ResetAbort`	Cancels an `Abort` requested for the current thread.
`Resume`	Resumes a thread that has been suspended.
`SetData`	Sets the data in the specified slot on the currently running thread, for that thread's current domain.

(continued)

TABLE 16.3 (continued)

Public Methods	
`Sleep`	Overloaded. Blocks the current thread for the specified number of milliseconds.
`SpinWait`	Causes a thread to wait the number of times defined by the `iterations` parameter.
`Start`	Causes the operating system to change the state of the current instance to `ThreadState.Running`.
`Suspend`	Either suspends the thread or, if the thread is already suspended, has no effect.

The `ThreadStart` delegate is void, so `m()` must likewise return no value. The name of the method is passed into the `ThreadStart` declaration, as in the following example:

```
ThreadStart ts = new ThreadStart(m);
```

2. The `ThreadStart` object is passed into the Thread constructor, which creates a `Thread` object with a reference to the method `m()`. This method will be called after the `Thread` is started. Here is an example of creating the thread:

```
Thread t = new Thread(ts);
```

3. The thread is started using the `Start()` method from the `Thread` class.

```
t.Start();
```

When this happens, the thread is set up to run, and waits in the ready queue for the processor. When selected, it calls the method `m()`, and begins executing the code within `m()`. When it is finished, the thread "dies" and is removed from the ready queue.

☐ Program: TestThreads

Listing 16.6 is an example of a program that creates a couple of threads that run concurrently. One is set up to find prime numbers in a specified range, whereas the other finds perfect squares in a specified range.

First we create two classes—`PrimeFinder`, which contains a method to search for the primes, and `PerfectSquareFinder`, which likewise contains a method to find the perfect squares.

First, we will look at the `PrimeFinder` class (Listing 16.4). It has two fields, `minNumber` and `maxNumber`, which will define the search range for primes, and are set in the constructor. The `FindPrimes()` method searches for and displays all primes between minNumber and maxNumber. Note that FindPrimes() is void, and accepts no parameters. This is the only way it can be referenced by a ThreadStart delegate.

Listing 16.4

```
public class PrimeFinder {
  int minNumber;
  int maxNumber;

  //Constructor sets min and max in range
  public PrimeFinder(int min,int max) {
     if (min<=0||max<=0) throw new ArgumentException(
      "Only positive values allowed!");
     minNumber=min;
     maxNumber=max;
  }

  public void FindPrimes() {
         //Finds all primes between minNumber and maxNumber
         if (minNumber==1) minNumber++;//Don't test 1-skip to 2
         for (int testnum=minNumber;testnum<=maxNumber;testnum++) {
             bool isprime=true;//Assume the test number is prime.
             for (int divisor=2;
            divisor<=(int)Math.Sqrt(testnum);
            divisor++) {
                 if (testnum%divisor==0) {isprime=false; break;}
             }
             if (isprime) Console.Write(testnum+"-prime ");
         }
  }
}
```

The PerfectSquareFinder (Listing 16.5) is practically the same as PrimeFinder; it has a FindSquares method that will be passed into a ThreadStart delegate.

Listing 16.5

```
public class PerfectSquareFinder {
  int minNumber;
  int maxNumber;

  //Constructor sets min and max in range
  public PerfectSquareFinder(int min,int max) {
     if (min<=0||max<=0) throw new ArgumentException(
      "Only positive values allowed!");
     minNumber=min;
```

(continued)

```
 maxNumber=max;
  }

  //Called after squareThread starts
public void FindSquares() {
     //Finds all perfect squares between minNumber and maxNumber
     for (int testnum=minNumber;testnum<=maxNumber;testnum++)
        if (Math.Sqrt(testnum)==Math.Round(Math.Sqrt(testnum)))
           Console.Write(testnum+"-square ");
  }
}
```

Both of the two previous classes are in TestThreads.cs (Listing 16.6), which contains the `Main` method for this program as well. (Recall that C# does not care whether we place our classes in separate files or not.) The `Main` method first prompts the user for the search range. We create a `PrimeFinder` object and a `PerfectSquareFinder` object, passing this range into their constructors. Finally, we create a couple of `Thread` objects—one references the `FindPrimes` method and the other references the `FindSquares` method. When the threads are started, each begins doing its respective job—one to find and display primes, the other to find and display perfect squares.

Listing 16.6

```
using System;
using System.Threading;
public class TestThreads {
  public static void Main(String[] args) {
      int n=0,n2=0;

      Console.WriteLine("Find primes and squares in a range.");

      //Prompt user to enter min,max values
      try {
            Console.Write("Enter minimum positive int to test: ");
            n=Int32.Parse(Console.ReadLine());
            Console.Write("Enter maximum positive int to test: ");
            n2=Int32.Parse(Console.ReadLine());
      } catch (ArgumentException ae) {
            Console.WriteLine(ae.ToString());
      }

      //Create a PrimeFinder object
      PrimeFinder p=new PrimeFinder(n,n2);
      //Create a ThreadStart object; references Findprimes method of p
      ThreadStart pts=new ThreadStart(p.FindPrimes);
```

(continued)

```
        //Create the thread-doesn't run until Start() called
        Thread primeThread=new Thread(pts);

        //Do same setup for squareThread
        PerfectSquareFinder s=new PerfectSquareFinder(n,n2);
        ThreadStart sts=new ThreadStart(s.FindSquares);
        Thread squareThread=new Thread(sts);

        //Start both threads-method specified by delegate called now
        primeThread.Start();
        squareThread.Start();
    }
}
```

Here is a demonstration run of the program. Note how the processor switches between the threads. Also, I interrupted the application using Ctrl+C here to avoid an enormous amount of output:

```
Find primes and squares in a range.
Enter minimum positive int to test: 2000000000
Enter maximum positive int to test: 2100000000
2000000011-prime 2000000033-prime 2000000063-prime 2000000087-prime
2000000089-prime 2000000099-prime 2000000137-prime 2000000141-prime
2000000143-prime 2000000153-prime 2000000203-prime 2000000227-prime
2000000239-prime 2000000243-prime 2000000269-prime 2000000273-prime
2000000279-prime 2000000293-prime 2000000323-prime 2000000333-prime
2000000357-prime 2000000381-prime 2000000393-prime 2000000407-prime
2000057284-square 2000146729-square 2000236176-square 2000325625-square
2000415076-square 2000504529-square 2000593984-square 2000683441-square
2000000413-prime 2000000441-prime 2000000503-prime 2000000507-prime
2000000531-prime 2000000533-prime 2000000579-prime 2000000603-prime
2000000609-prime 2000772900-square 2000862361-square 2000951824-square
2001041289-square 2001130756-square 2001220225-square 2001309696-square
001399169-square 2001488644-square 2001578121-square 2001667600-square
001757081-square 2001846564-square 2000000621-prime 2000000641-prime
2000000659-prime 2000000671-prime 2000000693-prime 2000000707-prime
2000000731-prime 2000000741-prime 2000000767-prime 2001936049-square
2002025536-square 2002115025-square 2002204516-square 2002294009-square
2002383504-square 2002473001-square 2000000771-prime 2000000773-prime
2000000789-prime 2000000797-prime 2000000809-prime 2000000833-prime
2000000837-prime 2000000843-prime 2000000957-prime 2000000983-prime
2000001001-prime 2000001013-prime 2002562500-square 2002652001-square
2002741504-square 2002831009-square 2002920516-square 2003010025-square
```

```
2003099536-square 2000001043-prime 2000001049-prime 2000001089-prime
2000001097-prime 2000001103-prime 2000001109-prime 2000001119-prime
2000001127-prime 2000001137-prime 2003189049-square 2003278564-square
2003368081-square 2003457600-square 2003547121-square 2003636644-square
2003726169-square 2000001149-prime 2000001151-prime 2000001167-prime
2000001173-prime 2000001187-prime 2000001229-prime 2000001233-prime
2000001247-prime 2000001257-prime 2003815696-square 2003905225-square ^C
```

Thread States

A thread can be in one or more of many states at any given time. The state(s) a thread is in determines how it is handled by the system; that is, if it is waiting in the ready queue to run, waiting in some other queue, or is dead (stopped) and awaiting disposal.

C# threads have the following states, determined by the `ThreadState` enumeration:

- `ThreadState.Unstarted`
- `ThreadState.Running`
- `ThreadState.WaitSleepJoin`
- `ThreadState.SuspendRequested`
- `ThreadState.Suspended`
- `ThreadState.AbortRequested`
- `ThreadState.Stopped`

We change the state of a `Thread` object by calling various methods; for example, we place a thread in the `Running` state when we call the `Start()` method. A thread may also have its state changed by the system as it manages them; for example, when a thread is finished executing its code, the system automatically changes its state to `Stopped`.

Table 16.4 contains a listing of how the `ThreadState` property of a `Thread` can change. Further explanation will be provided as we proceed.

It is important to note that a C# thread can be in more than one state at a time. Also, the state does not necessarily indicate what the thread is doing; for example, being in the `Running` state does not necessarily mean the thread currently has the processor—it may simply be in the ready queue. To avoid confusion, you should become familiar with the `ThreadState` values, and exactly how a thread moves among them.

Scheduling Threads and Thread Priority

Recall that a special system program called the scheduler must select from the ready queue the next process/thread to run. There are many ways of scheduling; some are quite simple, whereas others are not. Here are some examples of scheduling methods; for this discussion I use the word *job* to mean either thread or process, because it pertains to both.

- **First come, first served (FCFS)**—A scheduler that uses FCFS simply runs jobs in their entirety in the order they arrive in the ready queue. The FCFS scheduler will not normally interrupt a running job unless it determines that the current job is hung, causing damage to the system, or otherwise misbehaving. When a

TABLE 16.4

ThreadState	Action
`Unstarted`	A thread is created.
`Running`	A thread calls `Start`.
`Running`	The thread starts running.
`WaitSleepJoin`	The thread calls `Sleep`.
`WaitSleepJoin`	The thread calls `Wait` on another object.
`WaitSleepJoin`	The thread calls `Join` on another thread.
`Running`	Another thread calls `Interrupt`.
`SuspendRequested`	Another thread calls `Suspend`.
`Suspended`	The thread responds to a `Suspend` request.
`Running`	Another thread calls `Resume`.
`AbortRequested`	Another thread calls `Abort`.
`Stopped`	The thread responds to a `Abort` request.
`Stopped`	A thread is terminated.

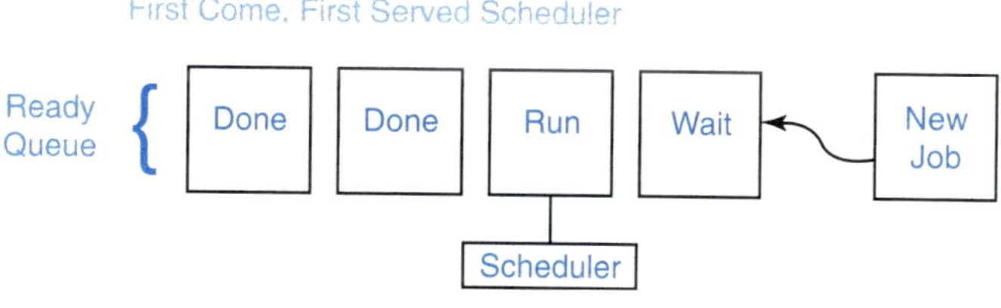

Figure 16.4

scheduler does not interrupt a job in favor of another, it is called "non-preemptive scheduling." Figure 16.4 is a diagram of a FCFS scheduler.

- **Shortest job first (SJF)**—It should be reasonable to anyone that running the shortest jobs first in a queue reduces the average amount of time jobs wait in the queue (think about it). Of course, determining *in advance* which job is the shortest can be quite a trick. An SJF scheduler must make pretty good guesses about runtime in order to work effectively. There are non-preemptive and preemptive SJF schedulers. A preemptive version will interrupt running job A if job B enters the ready queue and has less remaining execution time than A. The non-preemptive version will allow A to finish, then will select and run B (assuming an even shorter job does not arrive in the mean time).
- **Priority**—This type of scheduler selects as next to run the job with the highest priority. The priority of a thread can be based on anything. You could view FCFS as a non-preemptive priority scheduler in which the job with highest priority is

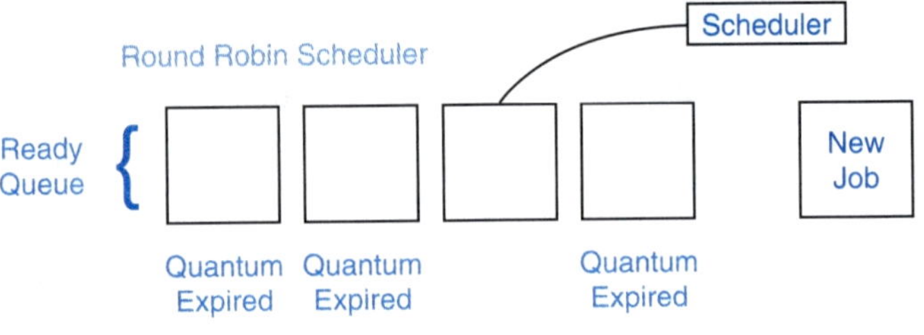

Figure 16.5

the job in the front of the queue. Or SJF could be viewed as a priority scheduler in which the job with the shortest remaining execution time has highest priority. There are preemptive and non-preemptive priority schedulers. Some priority schedulers allow the priority of a job to *change* while it is in the queue.

- **Round robin**—A round robin scheduler is preemptive. It runs the jobs in the order they arrive in the queue, but switches among them quickly and frequently based on a time period called a "quantum." If a job is running and exceeds the quantum, the scheduler interrupts it and loads the next job from the queue, wrapping around to the beginning of the queue when necessary. When a job is finished or aborted, it is removed from the queue, and the scheduler continues to hop from one job to the next in round robin fashion. Figure 16.5 shows how a round robin scheduler works.

The Runtime Environment Scheduler

The C# runtime environment uses a preemptive priority scheduler; that is, if a job with higher priority than the running job arrives, it will become the running job. Among jobs with the same priority, the scheduler uses a round robin algorithm; for example, if a set of jobs are all of priority X or lower in the ready queue, the scheduler will switch among all jobs of priority X in round robin fashion, as long as no job with a priority higher than X arrives. It does this until all jobs with priority X are finished. It will then proceed with jobs having priority lower than X.

We can also change the priority of a running thread; in fact, this is how we can preempt other jobs from within our application.

The priority values a C# thread can assume are defined by the `ThreadPriority` enumeration; the values are

- `ThreadPriority.Highest`
- `ThreadPriority.AboveNormal`
- `ThreadPriority.Normal`
- `ThreadPriority.BelowNormal`
- `ThreadPriority.Lowest`

Class: RoundRobinScheduler

The scheduler used by the runtime environment is very general in nature. By manipulating priorities in such a scheduler, we can achieve any behavior desired. For example, Listing 16.7 is a class that is an example of a round robin scheduler, named, appropriately, RoundRobinScheduler.

The private fields are a queue in which the threads will line up and an int that represents the time quantum allowed each process. These are both set in the RoundRobinScheduler constructor.

```
//A round robin scheduler
using System;
using System.Threading;
public class RoundRobinScheduler {
   private Queue queue;
   private int timeSlice;

   //Constructor establishes time quantum for threads to run in
   //and creates a queue to hold the threads
   public RoundRobinScheduler(int quantum) {
      timeSlice = quantum;
      queue = new Queue(5);
   }
//...other methods
}
```

This class also contains the AddThread(Thread) method, which sets the priority of the incoming thread to Normal, then inserts it in the queue.

```
//Adds a thread to the queue, setting priority to Normal
public void AddThread(Thread t) {
   t.Priority=ThreadPriority.Normal;
   queue.Insert(t);
}
```

Finally, the void RunRoundRobin() method does the work of the scheduler. First, so that it cannot be interrupted by some other thread, it set its own priority to the highest level. Then it pulls the thread from the head of the queue, and raises its priority above normal. The scheduler then goes to sleep for a quantum. When this happens, the single thread with above normal priority starts running. When the quantum expires, the scheduler interrupts the running thread (because the scheduler was given highest priority). It then puts the interrupted thread back in the queue, and lowers its priority to normal again. All this can be seen in the following code:

```
public void RunRoundRobin() {
   Thread current;

   // set the priority of the scheduler to the highest priority
   Thread.CurrentThread.Priority=ThreadPriority.Highest;
```

```
    //Scheduler runs forever
    for (;;) {
    if (!queue.Empty) {
          //Pull a thread from head of queue
          current = (Thread)queue.Peek();
          queue.Remove();

          //Raise priority of this thread
          current.Priority=ThreadPriority.AboveNormal;

          //other threads in queue still have Normal priority
          //current will begin running when the scheduler sleeps
          Console.WriteLine(current.Name+" running");

          //Put scheduler to sleep for a quantum
          Thread.Sleep(timeSlice);

          //When scheduler wakes, it preempts current
          //Scheduler has Highest priority
          //Put current back in queue
          //lowering its priority back to Normal
          AddThread(current);
    }
    }
}
```

Note that this scheduler periodically announces which thread it is running. Also note that the round robin scheduler puts itself to sleep for a time period as soon as it selects the next job to run.

```
Thread.Sleep(timeSlice);
```

It does this so that the selected job can run, because when it calls `Sleep(timeSlice)` it moves to the `WaitSleepJoin` state. When the thread moves to this state, it gives up the processor and is removed from the ready queue. When the number of milliseconds determined by `timeSlice` elapses, it is returned to the ready queue. Because the scheduler has higher priority than the running job, it will interrupt the running job and take over.

Listing 16.7

```
//A round-robin scheduler
using System;
using System.Threading;
public class RoundRobinScheduler {
   private Queue queue;
   private int timeSlice;

 //Constructor establishes time quantum for threads to run in
   //and creates a queue to hold the threads
   public RoundRobinScheduler(int quantum) {
      timeSlice = quantum;
      queue = new Queue(5);
   }

 //Adds a thread to the queue, setting priority to Normal
   public void AddThread(Thread t) {
      t.Priority=ThreadPriority.Normal;
      queue.Insert(t);
 }

 public void RunRoundRobin() {
      Thread current;

// set the priority of the scheduler to the highest priority
      Thread.CurrentThread.Priority=ThreadPriority.Highest;

//Scheduler runs forever
      for (;;) {
      if (!queue.Empty) {
            //Pull a thread from head of queue
            current = (Thread)queue.Peek();
            queue.Remove();

            //Raise priority of this thread
            current.Priority=ThreadPriority.AboveNormal;

            //other threads in queue still have Normal priority
            //current will begin running when the scheduler sleeps
  Console.WriteLine(current.Name+" running");

            //Put scheduler to sleep for a quantum
            Thread.Sleep(timeSlice);

            //When scheduler wakes, it preempts current
            //Scheduler has Highest priority
            //Put current back in queue
            //lowering its priority back to Normal
            AddThread(current);
      }
      }
   }
}
```

To test RoundRobinScheduler, we will create a Job class (Listing 16.8). A Job object just spins its wheels forever, doing nothing. We would, of course, use objects more useful than Job objects in a real application using the RoundRobin scheduler, but this works fine as a demonstration here.

Listing 16.8

```
//Job objects just run forever
public class Job {
      //This method is referenced by the ThreadStart delegate
      public void SpinWheels() {
            for (;;);
      }
}
```

Finally, Listing 16.9 is a test program for the RoundRobinScheduler class. The program first gives itself highest priority so that it won't be interrupted by the round robin scheduler it will create. The Main method has to be active long enough to create the scheduler and the threads it will run.

The next step is to create the RoundRobinScheduler object, and a Thread for it to run in. The ThreadStart delegate will of course be the void RunRoundRobin() method. The scheduler is then started.

Finally, the Main method creates three Job objects and three threads for them to run in. Each thread references the SpinWheels() method of one of the Job objects.

Listing 16.9

```
public class TestScheduler {
   public static void Main(String[] args) {
      //Must run at highest priority so scheduler cannot interrupt it
      Thread.CurrentThread.Priority=ThreadPriority.Highest;

      //Create the scheduler and its thread
      RoundRobinScheduler scheduler = new RoundRobinScheduler(10);
      Thread schedThread =
    new Thread(new ThreadStart(scheduler.RunRoundRobin));

      schedThread.Start();

      //Create three job threads, start them, and put them in queue
      //Scheduler runs them round robin in the order they entered queue
      Job job1 = new Job();
      Thread t1 = new Thread(new ThreadStart(job1.SpinWheels));
      t1.Name="Thread 1";
      t1.Start();
      scheduler.AddThread(t1);
```

(continued)

```
        Job job2 = new Job();
        Thread t2 = new Thread(new ThreadStart(job2.SpinWheels));
        t2.Name="Thread 2";
        t2.Start();
        scheduler.AddThread(t2);

        Job job3 = new Job();
        Thread t3 = new Thread(new ThreadStart(job3.SpinWheels));
        t3.Name="Thread 3";
        t3.Start();
        scheduler.AddThread(t3);
    }
}
```

All of the classes in this example are found in RoundRobinScheduler.cs. If you compile it to an executable file and run it, you will get the following:

```
Thread 1 running
Thread 2 running
Thread 3 running
Thread 1 running
Thread 2 running
Thread 3 running
Thread 1 running
Thread 2 running
Thread 3 running
Thread 1 running
Thread 2 running
Thread 3 running
Thread 1 running
^C
```

Note how the scheduler runs the threads in the order in which they entered the queue; that is, 1, 2, 3, 1, 2, 3, ... At no time does any thread "break rank."

You will note that this scheduler does not check to see if a thread is already finished, and if it is, to remove it from the queue for good. This works fine for our `Job` objects, however, because they intentionally run forever. An interesting exercise for you would be to modify the scheduler so that it removes threads that have finished from the queue.

■ RACE CONDITIONS

I know what you're thinking: "Multithreaded programming can't possibly be this easy!" You're right; it isn't. Anytime two or more threads have to share a resource—that is, a file, a printer, or even a variable—problems arise.

Consider an integer type variable, say `i`, which is incremented from time to time by two threads, say `A` and `B`. This increment can be expressed simply as the C# statement:

```
i++;
```

Although this is a single statement in C#, it actually consists of multiple machine language statements; say, something like

1. Load the value of `i` from memory into the accumulator.
2. Increment the value in the accumulator.
3. Write the value in the accumulator back to the address of `i`.

Generally speaking, a machine language instruction cannot be interrupted in the middle of its execution. Such instructions are considered *atomic actions*. If C# statements were atomic actions, we would have no difficulty with this scenario, but they are not, and the difficulty soon becomes apparent:

1. Suppose `i` currently has the value 10, and thread `A` has the processor.
2. Suppose `A` executes machine language statements 1 and 2, then is interrupted. The system stores the values in the registers (including the accumulator) for `A`, then switches to thread `B`.
3. `B` takes over and also executes statements 1 and 2, then is interrupted. The values in the registers are stored for thread `B`, then the values for `A` are reloaded.
4. **Notice that at this point, the value of `i` is still 10.**
5. `A` executes statement 3, and the value in the accumulator (11) is copied to `i`'s location. Say `A` is interrupted again here, and a switch to `B` occurs.
6. The last value `B` had in the accumulator was 11, and this value is again copied to `i`'s location as `B` executes statement 3.

At this point, we notice that `i` has the value 11, but it should be 12, because `i` was meant to be incremented once by both `A` and `B`.

When threads share a common resource, we can obtain erroneous results; this is called a "race condition." The next program should convince you that this problem is real.

☐ Program: RaceCondition

The `RaceCondition` class (Listing 16.10) should be enough to convince any cynic of the seriousness of race conditions. First, the class declares some variables to use as counters.

```
using System;
using System.Threading;
public class RaceCondition {

    //Incrementing thread increments upCounter
```

```
    public static long upCounter=0;

    //Decrementing thread decrements downCounter
    public static long downCounter=0;

    //Incrementing thread increments globalCounter
    //Decrementing thread decrements globalCounter
    public static long globalCounter=0;

    public static long max=1000000000;

// Methods here-including Main

}
```

The `Main` method merely creates and starts two threads. One increments a global variable (called `globalCounter`) `max` times (where `max` is a positive integer), and the other decrements it `max` times. When both threads are finished, the `Main` method displays the value of `globalCounter`. Each thread also maintains a separate counter to verify that it counted up/down to the correct value.

```
public static void Main(String[] args) {

  //Maximum value to inc/dec passed in thru command line
  if (args.Length==1) max=Int32.Parse(args[0]);

  //Set up and start incrementing and decrementing Threads
  Thread t=new Thread(new ThreadStart(Inc));
  Thread t2=new Thread(new ThreadStart(Dec));
    t.Start();
    t2.Start();

  //Main loops until both threads are finished (and dead)
  //This is called a BUSY WAIT; very inefficient, but works
  while (t.IsAlive||t2.IsAlive);

  //Report the global counter total-should be ZERO
  Console.WriteLine("GLOBAL COUNTER TOTAL: "+globalCounter);
}
```

Note that the value of `max` is passed through the command line, but if no value is passed in, a default value of 1 billion is used.

The incrementing thread calls the static `void` method `Inc()` via its `ThreadStart` delegate, and this method increments `upCounter` and `globalCounter`. It reports the value of `upCounter` before terminating.

```
static void Inc() {
  //increment upCounter and globalCounter
  while (upCounter<max) {upCounter++;globalCounter++;}

  //Report upCounter value
  Console.WriteLine("Up counter total: "+upCounter);
}
```

The decrementing thread similarly calls `Dec()`, which decrements `downCounter` and `globalCounter`. It reports the value of `downCounter` before terminating.

```
static void Dec() {
  //decrement downCounter and globalCounter
  while (downCounter>-max) {downCounter--;globalCounter--;}

  //Report downCounter value
  Console.WriteLine("Down counter total: "+downCounter);
}
```

`Inc()` and `Dec()` are called exactly the same number of times, so the final value of `globalCounter` should be ZERO. Here is a trial run using the default value of 1 billion:

```
Up counter total: 1000000000
Down counter total: -1000000000
GLOBAL COUNTER TOTAL: 121026678
```

Note that both threads counted correctly up/down 1 billion times, but the global counter is *way* off!

Listing 16.10

```
using System;
using System.Threading;
public class RaceCondition {

    //Incrementing thread increments upCounter
    public static long upCounter=0;
    //Decrementing thread decrements downCounter
    public static long downCounter=0;
    //Incrementing thread increments globalCounter
    //Decrementing thread decrements globalCounter
    public static long globalCounter=0;
    public static long max=1000000000;

    public static void Main(String[] args) {

      //Maximum value to inc/dec passed in thru command line
      if (args.Length==1) max=Int32.Parse(args[0]);
```

(continued)

```
      //Set up and start incrementing and decrementing Threads
      Thread t=new Thread(new ThreadStart(Inc));
      Thread t2=new Thread(new ThreadStart(Dec));
        t.Start();
        t2.Start();

      //Main loops until both threads are finished (and dead)
      //This is called a BUSY WAIT; very inefficient, but works
      while (t.IsAlive||t2.IsAlive);

      //Report the global counter total-should be ZERO
      Console.WriteLine("GLOBAL COUNTER TOTAL: "+globalCounter);
    }

    static void Inc() {
      //increment upCounter and globalCounter
      while (upCounter<max) {upCounter++;globalCounter++;}

      //Report upCounter value
      Console.WriteLine("Up counter total: "+upCounter);
    }

    static void Dec() {
      //decrement downCounter and globalCounter
      while (downCounter>-max) {downCounter--;globalCounter--;}

      //Report downCounter value
      Console.WriteLine("Down counter total: "+downCounter);
    }

}
```

☐ The `Thread.IsAlive` Property

We should take another look at the `Main` method of the `RaceCondition` class; in particular, this line:

```
while (t.IsAlive||t2.IsAlive);
```

This looks like it could be an infinite loop, because nothing happens in the loop to change anything. However, the `Main` method is merely one of three threads competing for processor time in this application. While the `Main` method is running at this point, it merely checks (over and over again) if either of the other two threads is still alive. Eventually, the `Main` method uses up its quantum, and the scheduler selects another thread.

The `IsAlive` property returns true if this thread has been started and has not terminated normally or aborted; otherwise, it returns false. When the counting threads eventually finish counting, they will be placed in the `Stopped` state by the system.

This `while` loop as written works, but it is very inefficient because it spends its entire quantum repeatedly checking a condition that will not change. Such a waste of processor time is called a *busy wait*. There should be a mechanism whereby this thread could voluntarily give up the processor before it is forced to do so. We can do this by using `Thread.Sleep`, but this seems inappropriate because the thread may wake up much later than it needs to, and we can't reliably calculate this. There is a mechanism by which threads can notify each other, and we will examine how to do this later when we discuss the Wait and Pulse methods for the Monitor class.

The Critical Section Problem

Race conditions come about when threads are interrupted in the middle of changing the state of some resource, and another thread is allowed to do an update with invalid (old) data. As we have seen, this can be as simple as an interrupt occurring within a single statement, like

```
i++;
```

A region of code that is susceptible to creating a race condition is called a *critical section*, and the race conditions that result from multiple threads entering the critical section at the same time are known as the *critical section problem*.

How do we resolve this? We cannot tell the scheduler when to interrupt and when not to, so we would like some mechanism that allows only one thread in a particular critical section at a time. The runtime environment does provide such a mechanism, called a *monitor*.

Every object has a private field called a monitor. A monitor is not used for applications that are not multithreaded; for multithreaded applications, it regulates entry of threads into a critical section. C# represents monitors with the `Monitor` class.

The `Monitor` Class

Once we have identified a critical section of code in an instance method, we can regulate entry into this section by using the following:

```
Monitor.Enter(obj);//this is the object representing the
                   //resource

//Critical section code

Monitor.Exit(obj);
```

When a thread executes the `void Enter(Object r)` method, the thread attempts to *obtain the lock* on the object. Obtaining the lock means that the object `r` records in its monitor field the thread that currently has exclusive access to the object. `Monitor.Enter` marks the beginning of a critical section. As long as some thread has possession of the lock for object `r`, no other thread will be able to enter a critical section of `r`.

Even if, say, thread A is interrupted in the critical section, a thread B that takes over the processor cannot enter that same critical section. If B attempts to execute Monitor.Enter, it will discover that A has the lock, and B will *immediately give up the processor* and go back to a wait queue. Eventually A will be scheduled to run again. It will eventually complete the critical section and execute Monitor.Exit, and B will be allowed to obtain the lock and enter the critical section.

There is another way to enter/exit a critical section; namely, by using the lock statement in C#.

```
lock(obj) {

//Critical Section code

}
```

It is equivalent to using Monitor.Enter(obj) and Monitor.Exit.(obj).

The following class is a demonstration of the use of a monitor to define a critical section and restrict access to it.

Program: OrnamentalGarden

The ornamental garden is a classic example used in lectures dealing with concurrency. The garden has two turnstiles through which people enter—one to the east and one to the west. The turnstiles should update a counter so that the we know exactly how many people have entered the park.

To simulate this, the OrnamentalGarden.cs file (Listing 16.11 on pages 512–515) contains all of the following classes:

- OrnamentalGarden—Contains Main
- Counter—A global counter that is not thread safe
- SafeCounter—A thread-safe version, derived from Counter
- Turnstile—Represents the east and west turnstiles
- Timer—Runs the test for a specified time period

It may be best to first look at the Timer class. At some point we must end the simulation, and the Timer class allows us to do this. A method in a Timer object is first started via a thread. It maintains a Boolean sentinel value initialized to true, and which eventually becomes set to false when the test duration time expires. The turnstiles (which are also running as threads) continually check this value through the KeepGoing property. Here is the Timer class:

```
public class Timer {

      int duration;

      //sentinel set to false when time to stop test
      bool sentinel=true;
```

```
        //KeepGoing property allows read access to sentinel
        public bool KeepGoing {
              get {return sentinel;}
        }

        //Set the time for this thread to sleep
        public Timer(int duration) {this.duration=duration;}

        public void Run() {
              Thread.Sleep(duration);
              //When timer awakens, set sentinel to false
              sentinel=false;
        }

  }
```

Note that this `Timer` class could be effectively used in any simulation.

The `Counter` class provides access to the global counter, which will be shared by the two turnstiles. The `Increment()` method does this, and it is called periodically by both the east and west turnstiles.

```
public class Counter {

    int value;
    public Random randomint=new Random();

    //Counter starts at 0
    public Counter() {value=0;}

    //This method increments the counter; not threadsafe
    public virtual void Increment() {
      //Save the old value
        int temp = value;

      //Simulate an interrupt-occurs with about 50% probability
      //If occurs, sleep for 200 milliseconds
        if (randomint.Next()<Int32.MaxValue/2) Thread.Sleep(200);

      //Increment the value AFTER a possible interrupt
        value=temp+1;

      //Report the value of the counter
        Console.WriteLine(Thread.CurrentThread.Name+
             " increments global count to: "+value);
    }
}
```

Note there is nothing to prevent both threads from entering `Increment()` and updating the counter at around the same time. This is breeding ground for a race condition. This method also purposefully interrupts the thread in the middle of the update (about half the time). This is so we can see the race condition develop using relatively small numbers.

A thread-safe version of the `Counter` class is a simple modification. Identify the critical section in the `Increment` method, and protect it using a monitor. The `SafeCounter` class does exactly that.

```
//Thread-safe version of Counter
public class SafeCounter:Counter {

   //Turnstiles calling this method increment counter safely
   public override void Increment() {

      //Turnstile calling method obtains lock on SafeCounter
      Monitor.Enter(this);

      //Even if interrupted, no OTHER thread can enter here
        base.Increment();

      //Tunrstile releases lock before exiting
      Monitor.Exit(this);
   }
}
```

Of course, the `Turnstile` class represents the turnstiles. These merely simulate people walking through them at random intervals, and update the counter as this happens. Each turnstile also maintains its own local counter, which keeps count of only those who have passed through a single turnstile. The total of these local counts should equal the global counter.

```
public class Turnstile {

  //Global counter shared by all turnstiles
  Counter people;

  //Local counter used by individual turnstile
  int turnstileCount=0;

  Timer t;
  public Random randomint=new Random();

  //Pass global counter and timer to turnstile
  public Turnstile(Counter c,Timer t) {
        people = c;
```

```
        this.t=t;
    }

    public void Run() {
        //Continue until KeepGoing property becomes false
        while (t.KeepGoing) {

        //Sleep for a random interval-simulates customers entering
          Thread.Sleep(randomint.Next()%400+100);

        //Increment local counter and report
          Console.WriteLine("Turnstile "+Thread.CurrentThread.Name+
              " activated-increase local count to "+(++turnstileCount));

        //Increment global counter
        //possibly unsafe unless SafeCounter used
          people.Increment();
        }
    }
}
```

The `OrnamentalGarden` class contains the `Main` method. It merely sets up the `Timer` and both `Turnstile` objects as threads, and starts them. It also prompts the user for the duration of the test, and asks them if they want to use a `Counter` or a `SafeCounter`.

```
using System;
using System.Threading;
public class OrnamentalGarden {

    public static Turnstile west;
    public static Turnstile east;
    public static Counter counter;
    public static Timer timer;
    public static int duration;

    public static void Main(String[] args) {

      Console.Write("Run the threadsafe version? ");
      //Make a thread-safe counter, or not
      if (Console.ReadLine().ToUpper().Trim()=="Y")
      counter=new SafeCounter();
      else counter=new Counter();

      //Timer sleeps for a specified interval
```

```
        //When it wakes, sets a variable telling the threads to stop
        Console.Write("Enter the duration of the test in seconds: ");
        duration=Int32.Parse(Console.ReadLine());
        timer=new Timer(duration*1000);
        Thread timeThread=new Thread(new ThreadStart(timer.Run));
        timeThread.Start();

        //Set up east & west turnstile threads
        west= new Turnstile(counter,timer);
        east= new Turnstile(counter,timer);
        Thread wt=new Thread(new ThreadStart(west.Run));
        //Give the west thread a name
        wt.Name="West";
        Thread et=new Thread(new ThreadStart(east.Run));
        //Give the east thread a name
        et.Name="East";

        wt.Start();
        et.Start();
    }

}
```

First, let's simulate the ornamental garden scenario using a regular counter:

```
Run the threadsafe version? n
Enter the duration of the test in seconds: 2
Turnstile West activated-increase local count to 1
West increments global count to: 1
Turnstile East activated-increase local count to 1
East increments global count to: 2
Turnstile West activated-increase local count to 2
West increments global count to: 3
Turnstile East activated-increase local count to 2
Turnstile West activated-increase local count to 3
East increments global count to: 4
West increments global count to: 4
Turnstile West activated-increase local count to 4
West increments global count to: 5
Turnstile East activated-increase local count to 3
East increments global count to: 6
Turnstile East activated-increase local count to 4
Turnstile West activated-increase local count to 5
East increments global count to: 7
West increments global count to: 7
```

```
Turnstile West activated-increase local count to 6
Turnstile East activated-increase local count to 5
West increments global count to: 8
East increments global count to: 8
```

The global count is clearly wrong, as you can verify by totaling the final values of both turnstiles. If we use a `SafeCounter`, however, we get correct results.

```
Run the threadsafe version? y
Enter the duration of the test in seconds: 2
Turnstile West activated-increase local count to 1
West increments global count to: 1
Turnstile East activated-increase local count to 1
East increments global count to: 2
Turnstile West activated-increase local count to 2
Turnstile East activated-increase local count to 2
West increments global count to: 3
East increments global count to: 4
Turnstile West activated-increase local count to 3
West increments global count to: 5
Turnstile East activated-increase local count to 3
Turnstile West activated-increase local count to 4
East increments global count to: 6
Turnstile East activated-increase local count to 4
West increments global count to: 7
Turnstile West activated-increase local count to 5
East increments global count to: 8
West increments global count to: 9
```

Listing 16.11

```
using System;
using System.Threading;
public class OrnamentalGarden {

    public static Turnstile west;
    public static Turnstile east;
    public static Counter counter;
    public static Timer timer;
    public static int duration;

    public static void Main(String[] args) {

      Console.Write("Run the threadsafe version? ");
      //Make a thread-safe counter, or not
      if (Console.ReadLine().ToUpper().Trim()=="Y")
      counter=new SafeCounter();
```

(continued)

```
            else counter=new Counter();

 //Timer sleeps for a specified interval
       //When it wakes, sets a variable telling the threads to stop
       Console.Write("Enter the duration of the test in seconds: ");
       duration=Int32.Parse(Console.ReadLine());
       timer=new Timer(duration*1000);
       Thread timeThread=new Thread(new ThreadStart(timer.Run));
       timeThread.Start();

       //Set up east & west turnstile threads
         west= new Turnstile(counter,timer);
         east= new Turnstile(counter,timer);
       Thread wt=new Thread(new ThreadStart(west.Run));
       //Give the west thread a name
       wt.Name="West";
       Thread et=new Thread(new ThreadStart(east.Run));
       //Give the east thread a name
       et.Name="East";

       wt.Start();
       et.Start();
     }

 }

 public class Timer {

       int duration;

       //sentinel set to false when time to stop test
       bool sentinel=true;

       //KeepGoing property allows read access to sentinel
       public bool KeepGoing {
             get {return sentinel;}
       }

       //Set the time for this thread to sleep
       public Timer(int duration) {this.duration=duration;}

       public void Run() {
             Thread.Sleep(duration);
             //When timer awakens, set sentinel to false
             sentinel=false;
       }

 }
```

(continued)

```
//A global counter incremented by all turnstiles-not thread-safe
public class Counter {

    int value;
    public Random randomint=new Random();

    //Counter starts at 0
    public Counter() {value=0;}

    //This method increments the counter; not thread-safe
    public virtual void Increment() {
      //Save the old value
        int temp = value;

      //Simulate an interrupt-occurs with about 50% probability
      //If occurs, sleep for 200 milliseconds
        if (randomint.Next()<Int32.MaxValue/2) Thread.Sleep(200);

      //Increment the value AFTER a possible interrupt
        value=temp+1;

      //Report the value of the counter
        Console.WriteLine(Thread.CurrentThread.Name+
            " increments global count to: "+value);
    }
}

//Thread-safe version of Counter
public class SafeCounter:Counter {

   //Turnstiles calling this method increment counter safely
   public override void Increment() {

      //Turnstile calling method obtains lock on SafeCounter
      Monitor.Enter(this);

      //Even if interrupted, no OTHER thread can enter here
        base.Increment();

      //Tunrstile releases lock before exiting
      Monitor.Exit(this);
   }
}

public class Turnstile {

  //Global counter shared by all turnstiles
  Counter people;

  //Local counter used by individual turnstile
  int turnstileCount=0;
```

(continued)

```
  Timer t;
  public Random randomint=new Random();

  //Pass global counter and timer to turnstile
  public Turnstile(Counter c,Timer t) {
        people = c;
      this.t=t;
  }

  public void Run() {
      //Continue until KeepGoing property becomes false
      while (t.KeepGoing) {

      //Sleep for a random interval-simulates customers entering
        Thread.Sleep(randomint.Next()%400+100);

      //Increment local counter and report
        Console.WriteLine("Turnstile "+Thread.CurrentThread.Name+
            " activated-increase local count to "+(++turnstileCount));

      //Increment global counter
      //possibly unsafe unless SafeCounter used
        people.Increment();
      }
  }
}
```

☐ `Monitor.Wait` and `Monitor.Pulse`

Recall the busy wait from the RaceCondition program:

```
while (t.IsAlive||t2.IsAlive);
```

This loop is very inefficient because the thread running it spends its entire quantum checking conditions that will not change during that quantum. There should be a mechanism whereby the thread testing this condition can give up the processor immediately, and it can via the `Wait()` method from the `Monitor` class.

By executing `Monitor.Wait(object r)`, the executing thread gives up the processor and puts itself into a wait queue immediately. To be placed back in the ready queue, some *other* thread must make the call `Monitor.Pulse(object r)` or `Monitor.PulseAll(object r)`. `Monitor.Pulse` removes only a *single* thread from the wait queue. `Monitor.PulseAll`, however, removes *all* threads from the wait queue, where they all compete for the processor.

An example of how `Wait` and `Pulse` are used follows.

Program: ProducerConsumer

The producer-consumer scenario is another classic example in concurrency. A common memory cell is shared by the producer and the consumer. The producer writes values to

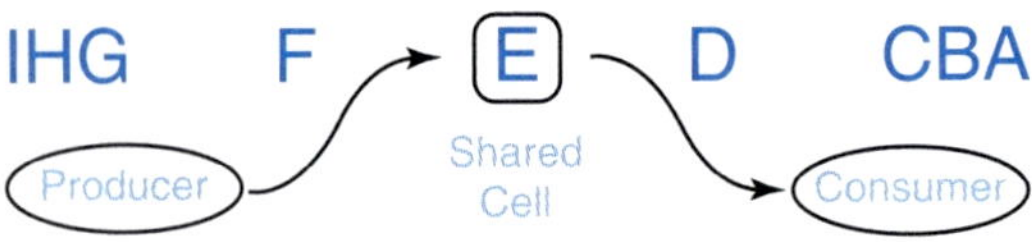

Figure 16.6

this cell, while the consumer reads them (see Figure 16.6); however, this must be done in such a way so that

- The producer does not write a new value into the cell before the consumer has read the previous value.
- The consumer does not read before the producer has placed anything in the cell, and also does not read the same value more than once.

We will simulate producer/consumer behavior using `Monitor.Wait` and `Monitor.Pulse`. The file ProducerConsumer.cs contains the source for this example (Listing 16.12 on pages 526–530); it contains the following classes:

- `ProducerConsumer`—Contains `Main` and starts `Producer` and `Consumer` threads
- `Cell`—Represents the cell shared by `Producer` and `Consumer`; not thread-safe
- `BusyCell`—Version of a `Cell` using a busy wait
- `SafeCell`—Thread-safe version of a `Cell`
- `Producer`—Writes values into the shared cell
- `Consumer`—Reads from the shared cell

First, let us examine the `Cell` class. The value it contains is a single character, initialized to `'*'`. This value is set by the `Producer` via the `Set(char)` method, and is read by the `Consumer` via the `Get()` method. Notice that neither `Set` nor `Get` restricts access to the cell contents.

```
//Cell is not thread-safe
public class Cell {

   //The cell contains a single character
   protected char commonCell = '*';

   //Producer calls Set method to set the value of shared cell
   public virtual void Set( char value ) {
      Console.WriteLine( Thread.CurrentThread.Name +
    " Setting cell to " + value );
      commonCell = value;
   }
```

`Producer` obtains a reference to the cell it shares with the `Consumer` via its constructor. The `RunProducer()` method will be called by a `ThreadStart` delegate. It produces 26 values, `'A'` through `'Z'`, and writes each into the shared cell. Before completion, it announces the values it wrote into the cell. If the `Producer` and `Consumer` are working in tandem, the `Consumer` will retrieve each value exactly once.

```
public class Producer {

   //Reference to the shared cell
   private Cell sharedCell;

   //Reference to shared cell passed thru constructor
   public Producer(Cell shared) {
      sharedCell = shared;
   }

   public void RunProducer() {
      StringBuilder messages=new StringBuilder();
      for ( char c = 'A'; c <= 'Z'; c++ ) {

         //Sleep for a random interval
         Thread.Sleep(ProducerConsumer.rand.Next()%300);

         //Get the value in the shared cell
         sharedCell.Set(c);

         //Add value produced to the others
         messages.Append(c);
      }

      //Report all values produced
      Console.WriteLine(Thread.CurrentThread.Name +
    " produced these messages: "+messages);
   }

}
```

`Consumer` is similar to the `Producer` class. It will also run as a thread with its `RunConsumer()` method. It reads at random intervals from the shared cell, and stops when it retrieves the value `'Z'`. It displays at the end all values retrieved. If all goes well, these should be "ABCDEFGHIJKLMNOPQRSTUVWXYZ".

```
public class Consumer {

   //Reference to the shared cell
   private Cell sharedCell;

   //Reference to shared cell passed thru constructor
```

```
    public Consumer(Cell shared) {
       sharedCell = shared;
    }

    public void RunConsumer() {

       char value;
       StringBuilder messages=new StringBuilder();

       do {
          //Sleep for a random interval
          Thread.Sleep(ProducerConsumer.rand.Next()%300);

          //Get the value in the shared cell
          value = sharedCell.Get();

          //Add retrieved value to the others
          messages.Append(value);

       } while ( value != 'Z' );

       //Report all values consumed
       Console.WriteLine(Thread.CurrentThread.Name +
     " retrieved these messages: " + messages);
    }

}
```

The `Main` method is in the `ProducerConsumer` class; it first prompts the user to run a version of the program:

- Version 1 creates a `Cell` as the shared cell.
- Version 2 creates a `BusyCell` as the shared cell.
- Version 3 creates a `SafeCell` as the shared cell.

We will cover the `BusyCell` and `SafeCell` versions later. `Main` then creates the `Producer` and `Consumer` and runs them as threads.

```
using System;
using System.Threading;
using System.Text;
public class ProducerConsumer {

   //Producer and Consumer use this to sleep for random intervals
   public static Random rand = new Random();
```

```
    //Represents the cell the Producer writes to
    //and the Consumer reads from
    static Cell sharedCell;

    public static void Main(String[] args) {

        Console.WriteLine("1-No waiting, no critical sections");
        Console.WriteLine("2-Busy waiting, no critical sections");
        Console.WriteLine("3-Wait/Pulse, critical sections (default)");
        Console.Write("Run which version? ");

        //Create a cell
        int reply= Int32.Parse(Console.ReadLine().ToUpper().Trim());

        if (reply==1) sharedCell=new Cell();
        else if (reply==2) sharedCell=new BusyCell();
        else sharedCell=new SafeCell();

        //Create the producer and consumer
        //each references the shared cell
        Producer producer = new Producer(sharedCell);
        Consumer consumer = new Consumer(sharedCell);

        //Make the threads, specify the delegates, and set their names
        Thread tproducer =
        new Thread(new ThreadStart(producer.RunProducer));
        tproducer.Name="Producer";
        Thread tconsumer =
        new Thread(new ThreadStart(consumer.RunConsumer));
        tconsumer.Name="Consumer";

        tproducer.Start();
        tconsumer.Start();
    }
}
```

Suppose we run Version 1 using a `Cell` object as the shared cell.

```
1-No waiting, no critical sections
2-Busy waiting, no critical sections
3-Wait/Pulse, critical sections (default)
Run which version? 1
Consumer retrieving cell value *
Producer Setting cell to A
Producer Setting cell to B
```

```
Producer Setting cell to C
Consumer retrieving cell value C
Producer Setting cell to D
Consumer retrieving cell value D
Consumer retrieving cell value D
Consumer retrieving cell value D
Producer Setting cell to E
Consumer retrieving cell value E
Producer Setting cell to F
Consumer retrieving cell value F
Producer Setting cell to G
Producer Setting cell to H
Consumer retrieving cell value H
Consumer retrieving cell value H
Producer Setting cell to I
Consumer retrieving cell value I
Producer Setting cell to J
Producer Setting cell to K
Consumer retrieving cell value K
Producer Setting cell to L
Consumer retrieving cell value L
Producer Setting cell to M
Consumer retrieving cell value M
Producer Setting cell to N
Producer Setting cell to O
Consumer retrieving cell value O
Producer Setting cell to P
Producer Setting cell to Q
Consumer retrieving cell value Q
Producer Setting cell to R
Consumer retrieving cell value R
Consumer retrieving cell value R
Consumer retrieving cell value R
Producer Setting cell to S
Consumer retrieving cell value S
Producer Setting cell to T
Producer Setting cell to U
Consumer retrieving cell value U
Consumer retrieving cell value U
Producer Setting cell to V
Consumer retrieving cell value V
Consumer retrieving cell value V
Producer Setting cell to W
Consumer retrieving cell value W
```

```
Producer Setting cell to X
Producer Setting cell to Y
Consumer retrieving cell value Y
Consumer retrieving cell value Y
Producer Setting cell to Z
Producer produced these messages: ABCDEFGHIJKLMNOPQRSTUVWXYZ
Consumer retrieving cell value Z
Consumer retrieved these messages: *CDDDEFHHIKLMOQRRRSUUVVWYYZ
```

We shouldn't be surprised with the erroneous results we've obtained here. The `Get()` and `Set()` methods of the `Cell` class did nothing to restrict the `Producer` or `Consumer` from entering at any time. Both the `Producer` and `Consumer` threads accessed the `Cell` object freely at random intervals.

In order to "synchronize" the `Producer` and `Consumer`, we create a different cell class, `SafeCell`, which is derived from `Cell`. First, it defines a Boolean variable called `readAccess`, which works like this:

- If `readAccess` is false, the `Consumer` will enter a wait queue using `Wait()` until the `Producer` changes `readAccess` to true, and signals using `Pulse()`.
- If `readAccess` is true, the `Producer` will enter a wait queue using `Wait()` until the `Consumer` changes `readAccess` to true, and signals using `Pulse()`.

Note that `readAccess` is initialized to false, and so the `Producer` will go first, as it should.

We also define critical sections in both `Set()` and `Get()` using the `lock(object)` statement. As we shall see later, this is necessary.

```
//SafeCell is thread-safe and synchronizes Producer and Consumer
public class SafeCell:Cell {

   //Variable to toggle between producer/consumer
   bool readAccess=false;

   //Producer calls Set method to set the value of shared cell
   public override void Set( char value ) {
      lock(this) {
            //Uses the monitor to put itself in wait queue
            while (readAccess) Monitor.Wait(this);
            base.Set(value);

            //Allow consumer to read
            readAccess=true;

            //Notify other thread(s) of completion
            Monitor.Pulse(this);
      }//End of critical section
   }
```

```
   //Consumer calls Get to retrieve cell contents
   public override char Get() {
      lock (this) {
            //Uses the monitor to put itself in wait queue
            while (!readAccess) Monitor.Wait(this);
            char c=base.Get();

            //Allow producer to write
            readAccess=false;

            //Notify other thread(s) of completion
            Monitor.Pulse(this);
            return c;
      }//End of critical section
   }
}
```

Version 3 of this application produces the correct results. The Producer and Consumer still attempt to write and read at random intervals, but they are forced to move in a stepwise fashion by the readAccess variable, and the fact that only the Producer or the Consumer can have exclusive access to the shared cell at a time.

```
1-No waiting, no critical sections
2-Busy waiting, no critical sections
3-Wait/Pulse, critical sections (default)
Run which version? 3
Producer Setting cell to A
Consumer retrieving cell value A
Producer Setting cell to B
Consumer retrieving cell value B
Producer Setting cell to C
Consumer retrieving cell value C
Producer Setting cell to D
Consumer retrieving cell value D
Producer Setting cell to E
Consumer retrieving cell value E
Producer Setting cell to F
Consumer retrieving cell value F
Producer Setting cell to G
Consumer retrieving cell value G
Producer Setting cell to H
Consumer retrieving cell value H
Producer Setting cell to I
Consumer retrieving cell value I
Producer Setting cell to J
```

```
Consumer retrieving cell value J
Producer Setting cell to K
Consumer retrieving cell value K
Producer Setting cell to L
Consumer retrieving cell value L
Producer Setting cell to M
Consumer retrieving cell value M
Producer Setting cell to N
Consumer retrieving cell value N
Producer Setting cell to O
Consumer retrieving cell value O
Producer Setting cell to P
Consumer retrieving cell value P
Producer Setting cell to Q
Consumer retrieving cell value Q
Producer Setting cell to R
Consumer retrieving cell value R
Producer Setting cell to S
Consumer retrieving cell value S
Producer Setting cell to T
Consumer retrieving cell value T
Producer Setting cell to U
Consumer retrieving cell value U
Producer Setting cell to V
Consumer retrieving cell value V
Producer Setting cell to W
Consumer retrieving cell value W
Producer Setting cell to X
Consumer retrieving cell value X
Producer Setting cell to Y
Consumer retrieving cell value Y
Producer Setting cell to Z
Producer produced these messages: ABCDEFGHIJKLMNOPQRSTUVWXYZ
Consumer retrieving cell value Z
Consumer retrieved these messages: ABCDEFGHIJKLMNOPQRSTUVWXYZ
```

It appears that the `readAccess` variable is solely what keeps the `Producer` and `Consumer` in tandem. We might think it possible to forego the use of `Wait/Pulse`, and discard the critical sections. This would be a mistake; to see this, consider the `BusyCell` class, which is also derived from `Cell`.

The `BusyCell` object uses a busy wait in both the `Set` and `Get` methods; that is, if `readAccess` is true, for example, the `Producer` thread will waste its entire quantum checking this fact repeatedly. Although this doesn't necessarily produce errors, it cannot be denied that this is very inefficient. Once the `Producer` gets past this busy wait, it sets readAccess to true, simulates an interrupt, and sets the value in the shared cell. As long as the Consumer does not enter the Get method during the simulated interrupt, it will obtain the new value from the cell, and not the previous value for the second time. However, because there are no critical regions defined, there is nothing to prevent this.

Likewise, if you look at the Get method, there is nothing to prevent the Producer from entering the Set method during the simulated interrupt in Get. By defining critical sections in SafeCell, neither of these situation can occur.

```
//BusyCell is not thread-safe
public class BusyCell:Cell {

   //readAccess allows producer to write when false
   //and allows consumer to read when true
   protected bool readAccess=false;

   //Producer calls Set method to set the value of shared cell
   public override void Set( char value ) {
      while (readAccess);//Busy wait

      readAccess=true;

      //Interrupt here
      if (ProducerConsumer.rand.Next()<Int32.MaxValue/2)
          Thread.Sleep(300);

      base.Set(value);

   }

   //Consumer calls Get to retrieve cell contents
   public override char Get() {
      while (!readAccess);//Busy wait

      readAccess=false;

      //Interrupt here
      if (ProducerConsumer.rand.Next()<Int32.MaxValue/2)
          Thread.Sleep(300);
      char c=base.Get();

      return c;
   }
}
```

As you can see from this run of Version 2, we cannot rely merely on the value of `readAccess` and the busy wait.

```
1-No waiting, no critical sections
2-Busy waiting, no critical sections
3-Wait/Pulse, critical sections (default)
Run which version? 2
Producer Setting cell to A
Consumer retrieving cell value A
Producer Setting cell to B
Consumer retrieving cell value B
Producer Setting cell to C
Consumer retrieving cell value C
Consumer retrieving cell value C
Producer Setting cell to D
Producer Setting cell to E
Producer Setting cell to F
Consumer retrieving cell value F
Consumer retrieving cell value F
Producer Setting cell to G
Consumer retrieving cell value G
Producer Setting cell to H
Consumer retrieving cell value H
Producer Setting cell to I
Consumer retrieving cell value I
Consumer retrieving cell value I
Producer Setting cell to J
Consumer retrieving cell value J
Producer Setting cell to K
Producer Setting cell to L
Consumer retrieving cell value L
Producer Setting cell to M
Consumer retrieving cell value M
Producer Setting cell to N
Consumer retrieving cell value N
Producer Setting cell to O
Consumer retrieving cell value O
Producer Setting cell to P
Producer Setting cell to Q
Consumer retrieving cell value Q
Consumer retrieving cell value Q
Producer Setting cell to R
Consumer retrieving cell value R
Producer Setting cell to S
```

```
Producer Setting cell to T
Consumer retrieving cell value T
Consumer retrieving cell value T
Producer Setting cell to U
Consumer retrieving cell value U
Producer Setting cell to V
Consumer retrieving cell value V
Producer Setting cell to W
Consumer retrieving cell value W
Producer Setting cell to X
Consumer retrieving cell value X
Producer Setting cell to Y
Consumer retrieving cell value Y
Producer Setting cell to Z
Producer produced these messages: ABCDEFGHIJKLMNOPQRSTUVWXYZ
Consumer retrieving cell value Z
Consumer retrieved these messages: ABCCFFGHIIJLMNOQQRTTUVWXYZ
```

Listing 16.12

```
using System;
using System.Threading;
using System.Text;
public class ProducerConsumer {

   //Producer and Consumer use this to sleep for random intervals
   public static Random rand = new Random();

   //Represents the cell the Producer writes to
   //and the Consumer reads from
   static Cell sharedCell;

   public static void Main(String[] args) {

      Console.WriteLine("1-No waiting, no critical sections");
      Console.WriteLine("2-Busy waiting, no critical sections");
      Console.WriteLine("3-Wait/Pulse, critical sections (default)");
      Console.Write("Run which version? ");

      //Create a cell
      int reply= Int32.Parse(Console.ReadLine().ToUpper().Trim());

      if (reply==1) sharedCell=new Cell();
      else if (reply==2) sharedCell=new BusyCell();
      else sharedCell=new SafeCell();
```

(continued)

```
        //Create the producer and consumer
        //each references the shared cell
        Producer producer = new Producer(sharedCell);
        Consumer consumer = new Consumer(sharedCell);

        //Make the threads, specify the delegates, and set their names
        Thread tproducer =
        new Thread(new ThreadStart(producer.RunProducer));
        tproducer.Name="Producer";
        Thread tconsumer =
        new Thread(new ThreadStart(consumer.RunConsumer));
        tconsumer.Name="Consumer";

        tproducer.Start();
        tconsumer.Start();
    }
}

//Cell is not thread-safe
public class Cell {

    //The cell contains a single character
    protected char commonCell = '*';

    //Producer calls Set method to set the value of shared cell
    public virtual void Set( char value ) {
        Console.WriteLine( Thread.CurrentThread.Name +
        " Setting cell to " + value );
        commonCell = value;
    }

    //Consumer calls Get to retrieve cell contents
    public virtual char Get() {
        Console.WriteLine( Thread.CurrentThread.Name +
        " retrieving cell value " + commonCell );
        return commonCell;
    }
}

//BusyCell is not thread-safe
public class BusyCell:Cell {

    //readAccess allows producer to write when false
    //and allows consumer to read when true
    protected bool readAccess=false;

    //Producer calls Set method to set the value of shared cell
    public override void Set( char value ) {
        while (readAccess);//Busy wait
```

(continued)

```
      readAccess=true;

      //Interrupt here
      if (ProducerConsumer.rand.Next()<Int32.MaxValue/2)
         Thread.Sleep(300);

      base.Set(value);

   }

   //Consumer calls Get to retrieve cell contents
   public override char Get() {
      while (!readAccess);//Busy wait

      readAccess=false;

      //Interrupt here
      if (ProducerConsumer.rand.Next()<Int32.MaxValue/2)
         Thread.Sleep(300);
      char c=base.Get();

      return c;
   }
}

//SafeCell is thread-safe and synchronizes Producer and Consumer
public class SafeCell:Cell {

   //Variable to toggle between producer/consumer
   bool readAccess=false;

   //Producer calls Set method to set the value of shared cell
   public override void Set( char value ) {
      lock(this) {
            //Uses the monitor to put itself in wait queue
            while (readAccess) Monitor.Wait(this);
            base.Set(value);

            //Allow consumer to read
            readAccess=true;

            //Notify other thread(s) of completion
            Monitor.Pulse(this);
      }//End of critical section
   }

   //Consumer calls Get to retrieve cell contents
   public override char Get() {
      lock (this) {
            //Uses the monitor to put itself in wait queue
            while (!readAccess) Monitor.Wait(this);
```

(continued)

```
            char c=base.Get();

            //Allow producer to write
            readAccess=false;

            //Notify other thread(s) of completion
            Monitor.Pulse(this);
            return c;
      }//End of critical section
   }
}

public class Consumer {

   //Reference to the shared cell
   private Cell sharedCell;

   //Reference to shared cell passed thru constructor
   public Consumer(Cell shared) {
      sharedCell = shared;
   }

   public void RunConsumer() {

      char value;
      StringBuilder messages=new StringBuilder();

      do {
         //Sleep for a random interval
         Thread.Sleep(ProducerConsumer.rand.Next()%300);

         //Get the value in the shared cell
         value = sharedCell.Get();

         //Add retrieved value to the others
         messages.Append(value);

      } while ( value != 'Z' );

      //Report all values consumed
      Console.WriteLine(Thread.CurrentThread.Name +
    " retrieved these messages: " + messages);
   }

}

public class Producer {

   //Reference to the shared cell
   private Cell sharedCell;
```

(continued)

```
    //Reference to shared cell passed thru constructor
    public Producer(Cell shared) {
        sharedCell = shared;
    }

    public void RunProducer() {
        StringBuilder messages=new StringBuilder();
        for ( char c = 'A'; c <= 'Z'; c++ ) {

            //Sleep for a random interval
            Thread.Sleep(ProducerConsumer.rand.Next()%300);

            //Get the value in the shared cell
            sharedCell.Set(c);

            //Add value produced to the others
            messages.Append(c);
        }

        //Report all values produced
        Console.WriteLine(Thread.CurrentThread.Name +
        " produced these messages: "+messages);
    }

}
```

■ INTERPROCESS COMMUNICATION

Processes and threads can also communicate by way of built-in data structures. In the case of C#, we call this a pipe. We can send messages from one process to another simply by redirecting the standard output of one process away from the console, and toward the other process. We do this by setting the `RedirectStandardOutput` property of `Process` to true. When this process writes to the console, it actually sends its output to the other process. These messages come out perfectly on the other end, so the pipe is synchronized.

As an example of this, let's model the producer-consumer relationship using a pipe. First, look at the consumer in Listing 16.13.

Listing 16.13

```
using System;
using System.Diagnostics;
public class ConsumerPiped {
    public static void Main(String[] args) {

      //This is the consumer
      //Start the producer as another process
      Process producer = new Process();
      producer.StartInfo.FileName = "ProducerPiped.exe";

      //May not use the shell if redirecting standard output
      producer.StartInfo.UseShellExecute = false;
      producer.StartInfo.RedirectStandardOutput = true;

      //Start the producer
      producer.Start();

  //Read all output coming from producer
      Console.WriteLine(producer.StandardOutput.ReadToEnd());

//Producer waits for consumer to finish reading and exit
      producer.WaitForExit();
    }
}
```

The consumer starts the producer as another process, redirecting the producer's standard output. It starts the producer, then reads all output from the producer using the `ReadToEnd()` method of the `StandardOutput` property (which returns a `StreamWriter`). The producer is directed to wait for the consumer to exit before it terminates.

Notice also that in order to redirect standard output, one must set the `UseShellExecute` property to false. The shell allows us to open processes that are not executable programs (like documents). The shell has the information required to open a file properly based on its type, and to launch the proper application for it. You may not use the shell if you plan to create a pipe in this manner.

There is nothing special about the producer (Listing 16.14); as far as it knows, it is sending its output to the console. In fact, if you ran it from the command line (instead of spawning it via the consumer), that is exactly what it would do.

Listing 16.14

```
using System;
public class ProducerPiped {
      public static void Main(String[] args) {
            //Producer sends a series of chars to standard output
            for (char c='A';c<='Z';c++) Console.Write(c);
      }
}
```

Here is the output when the consumer is run. The output comes from the consumer, which it received from the producer.

```
C:\C#>ConsumerPiped
ABCDEFGHIJKLMNOPQRSTUVWXYZ
```

■ DEADLOCK

In the early days of concurrency, a condition arose wherein a machine or application would lock up for reasons not encountered before. The system would pass through the ready queue to select jobs, but they would not run. This is quite different from the typical "freeze" an application creates via an infinite loop. This condition was called "deadlock," and its explanation was simple, although it didn't seem so during those early days.

Deadlock occurs when at least two threads are waiting for a resource held by the other. Deadlock can involve any number of threads, but all such threads are waiting for resources that will never be released.

As a classic example of deadlock, consider the dining philosophers problem. There is a round table around which are seated *N* philosophers. There are *N* forks on the table, one fork between each philosopher; that is, one fork serves as the right-hand fork for one philosopher, and as the left-hand fork for another (see Figure 16.7, in which $N = 5$).

The philosophers sit and think, and periodically become hungry. When hungry, a philosopher attempts to pick up her right fork. If this fork is being used, she waits; otherwise, she picks it up, then attempts to pick up her left fork. If this fork is being used, she waits; otherwise, she picks it up, and begins eating. When she finishes eating, she places both forks down, and resumes thinking.

When does deadlock occur in this scenario? Suppose all five philosophers get hungry at the same time. Each picks up their right fork, then attempts to pick up their left fork. However, no philosopher can get their left fork because it is held by the philosopher to their left. Progress has now halted (see Figure 16.8).

Figure 16.7

To model the dining philosophers problem, consider the following DiningPhilosophers program. DiningPhilosophers.cs (Listing 16.15 on page 543) contains the classes necessary for this; namely,

- `DiningPhilosophers`—Main method here; sets up philosophers and forks
- `Fork`—Represents the shared resource
- `Philosopher`—Simulates a philosopher; runs in a thread
- `SmartPhilosopher`—A type of philosopher that prevents deadlock

We should begin with the `Fork` class. The `Fork` represents the shared resource in this application, so we expect the critical sections to be here.

First, because there are N `Forks` on the table, we assign each `Fork` a number. Likewise, we will assign each philosopher a number. Figure 16.9 shows this numbering scheme where $N = 5$.

Note that we have chosen the right `Fork` for philosopher k as `Fork` k, and the left `Fork` to be Fork $k - 1$. Of course, philosopher 0 is a special case; her left `Fork` is `Fork` $N - 1$.

Next, a `Fork` object has a Boolean field called `taken`, which records whether the `Fork` is in use. Two operations can be performed on a `Fork` object—it can be picked up and put down. There is a `Get()` and `Put()` method to model these operations:

Figure 16.8

Figure 16.9

- Get tests if the Fork is taken, and waits if it is (using Monitor.Wait), or takes possession of it if not, and sets taken to true.
- Put signifies putting a Fork down by setting the variable taken to false, then using Monitor.Pulse to notify any threads waiting for this Fork.

Examine the following code to verify this description.

```
public class Fork {

  //This records whether or not fork is in use
  private bool taken=false;

  //Each fork has a number
  private int identity;

  //Constructor gives the fork its number
  public Fork(int id) { identity = id;}

  //Philosopher calls this when hungry; may be a right OR a left fork
  public void Get() {
      lock (this) {

           //Wait if desired fork is taken
           while (taken) Monitor.Wait(this);

           //Fork is free; grab it
           taken=true;

           Console.WriteLine("Fork "+identity+ " picked up.");
      }
  }

  //Philosopher calls this to put a fork down when finished eating
  public void Put() {
      lock (this) {

  //Put the fork down; mark it as free
           taken=false;
           Console.WriteLine("Fork "+identity+ " put down.");

           //Announce to other thread fork is available
           Monitor.Pulse(this);
      }
  }
}
```

A `Philosopher` object represents the behavior of a philosopher. As was done with the `Forks`, each `Philosopher` is assigned a number. Each `Philosopher` will also have two `Fork` fields—one references the right `Fork` and the other references the left `Fork`. The `Philosopher` calls the `Fork.Get` method for either `Fork` to test whether it is in use, and to acquire said `Fork`.

The `RunPhilosopher()` method will be called via a `ThreadStart` delegate for a thread. It starts by

- Thinking for a random interval.
- Getting hungry, and attempting to pick up the right `Fork`.
- If the previous step was successful, it continues by attempting to pick up the left `Fork`.
- If the previous step was successful, philosopher simulates eating for a random interval.
- Putting down both `Forks`.

Barring deadlock (or a system crash), each philosopher repeats this cycle *ad infinitum*.

```
public class Philosopher {

  //Each philosopher has a number
  protected int identity;

  //Each philosopher has a fork on left, and one on right
  protected Fork left;
  protected Fork right;

  public Philosopher(int id, Fork left, Fork right) {
    identity = id;
  this.left = left;
  this.right = right;
  }

  public void RunPhilosopher() {
      while (true) {

      //thinking
      Console.WriteLine("Philosopher "+identity+" is THINKING.");

      //hungry
      Console.WriteLine("Philosopher "+identity+" is HUNGRY.");

      right.Get();
      //got right fork
      Console.WriteLine("Philosopher "+identity+
            " got the RIGHT FORK.");
```

```
      left.Get();
      //got left fork

      //eating
      Console.WriteLine("Philosopher "+identity+
            " got the LEFT FORK and is EATING.");

      //put both forks down
      right.Put();
      left.Put();
      }
   }
}
```

The `Main` method is in the `DiningPhilosophers` class. It must set up an array of *N* `Philosopher` objects and *N* `Fork` objects. It must also associate each `Philosopher` with the proper left and right `Fork`, and start each `Philosopher` as a thread. It does this by calling the `MakePhilosopher` method, also in the `DiningPhilosophers` class.

First, examine the `makePhilosopher` method:

```
using System;
using System.Threading;
public class DiningPhilosophers {

    //Declare the philosopher & fork array
    static Thread[] phil;
    static Fork[] fork;

    //User chooses deadlock-prone version or safe version
    static bool noDeadlock = false;

    //The number of philosophers
    static int numPhil;

    //Method either creates a philosopher thread
  //or a smart philosopher thread; these prevent deadlock
    public static Thread MakePhilosopher(
            int id, Fork left, Fork right) {
        if (noDeadlock) {
            SmartPhilosopher p=new SmartPhilosopher(id,left,right);
            return new Thread(
                  new ThreadStart(p.RunSmartPhilosopher));
        } else {
            Philosopher p=new Philosopher(id,left,right);
```

```
            return new Thread(
                  new ThreadStart(p.RunPhilosopher));
        }
    }

//Main method here

}
```

Note the use of a Boolean variable called noDeadLock, the value of which is determined in the Main method. If false, it creates Philosopher objects; otherwise, it creates SmartPhilosopher objects. SmartPhilosopher objects behave in such a way as to prevent deadlock in this scenario; we will discuss how they do this later.

The Main method follows:

```
public static void Main(String[] args) {

 Console.Write("Enter the number of philosophers: ");
   numPhil=Int32.Parse(Console.ReadLine());

   Console.Write("Run the deadlock prone version? ");
   char ans=Console.ReadLine().Trim().ToUpper()[0];
   noDeadlock=ans=='Y'?false:true;

   //Create the array of philosophers and forks
   phil= new Thread[numPhil];
   fork = new Fork[numPhil];

   //Create each fork and put in array
   for (int i =0; i<numPhil; i++)
        fork[i] = new Fork(i);

   //Create each philosopher and put in array, start each thread
   //Philosopher i's right fork is fork #i
   //Philosopher i's left fork is i-1 (with wrap-around for 0)
   for (int i =0; i<numPhil; i++){
        phil[i] = MakePhilosopher(
                    i,
                    fork[(i-1+numPhil)% numPhil],
                    fork[i]);
        phil[i].Start();
   }
}
```

Here is an example test run of `DiningPhilosophers` in which the number of philosophers and forks is 5. Not all the output is shown here, because it happens to take a while before becoming deadlocked.

```
Enter the number of philosophers: 5
Run the deadlock prone version? y

...

Philosopher 4 is THINKING.
Philosopher 4 is HUNGRY.
Fork 4 picked up.
Philosopher 4 got the RIGHT FORK.
Fork 0 picked up.
Philosopher 0 got the RIGHT FORK.
Fork 1 picked up.
Philosopher 1 got the RIGHT FORK.
Fork 2 picked up.
Philosopher 2 got the RIGHT FORK.
Fork 3 picked up.
Philosopher 3 got the RIGHT FORK.
```

The program appeared to freeze after the last line was output. If you check, you can see why; each of the philosophers 0, 1, 2, 3, and 4 have picked up their right fork, and are waiting to pick up their left fork. None can do so; hence, they continue to wait indefinitely.

With the dining philosophers, the cause of deadlock is clear: Each philosopher reaches for her right fork first, so it is possible that each has her right fork, waiting for the left fork being held by the philosopher to the left. How do we fix this? The easiest answer is: At least one philosopher goes for her left fork first. If this is our approach, there is no way the dining philosophers can deadlock; hence, we create the `SmartPhilosopher` class, which is derived from `Philosopher`.

A `SmartPhilosopher` inherits the members from `Philosopher`, so the `Identity`, left `Fork`, and right `Fork` are from the base class, and are determined via a base constructor. The `RunSmartPhilosopher()` method is called via a `ThreadStart` delegate. In this method, even-numbered philosophers go for the *left* fork first, and odd-numbered philosophers go for the *right* fork. This will prevent deadlock, and is easily handled by a couple of `if` statements.

This class also declares a `successCount` variable, which is incremented every time this philosopher eats. This is just so I can run this program for a long period and show the trailing output, verifying the stability of the program.

```
public class SmartPhilosopher:Philosopher {

  //inherits all fields from Philosopher

  int successCount = 0;

  //Specify base constructor to call
  public SmartPhilosopher(int identity, Fork left, Fork right)
      :base(identity,left,right) {}

  public void RunSmartPhilosopher() {
      while (true) {

        //thinking
        Console.WriteLine("Philosopher "+identity+" is THINKING.");

        //hungry
        Console.WriteLine("Philosopher "+identity+" is HUNGRY.");

      //get a fork
      if (identity%2 == 0) {
            //even-numbered philosophers go left first
            left.Get();
            Console.WriteLine("Philosopher "+identity+
                  " got the LEFT FORK.");
      } else {
            //odd-numbered philosophers go right first
            right.Get();
            Console.WriteLine("Philosopher "+identity+
                  " got the RIGHT FORK.");
      }
      //get the other fork
      if (identity%2 == 0) {
            right.Get();
            Console.WriteLine("Philosopher "+identity+
                  " got the RIGHT FORK:EATING for the "
                  +(++successCount)+"th time.");
      } else {
            left.Get();
            Console.WriteLine("Philosopher "+identity+
                  " got the LEFT FORK:EATING for the "
                  +(++successCount)+"th time.");
      }
```

```
//put both forks down
      right.Put();
      left.Put();
      }
  }
}
```

Now we will run the deadlock-proof version of this application, and again the number of philosophers/forks is five. Note how the even-numbered philosophers do indeed go for the right fork first. Here I show only the trailing output after having run the application for a long period. It appears to be stable.

```
...
Philosopher 2 got the LEFT FORK.
Fork 2 picked up.
Philosopher 0 is THINKING.
Philosopher 0 is HUNGRY.
Philosopher 2 got the RIGHT FORK:EATING for the 28501th time.
Fork 2 put down.
Fork 1 put down.
Fork 1 picked up.
Philosopher 1 got the RIGHT FORK.
Fork 0 picked up.
Philosopher 1 got the LEFT FORK:EATING for the 23367th time.
Fork 1 put down.
Fork 0 put down.
Philosopher 1 is THINKING.
Philosopher 1 is HUNGRY.
Fork 1 picked up.
Philosopher 1 got the RIGHT FORK.
Fork 0 picked up.
Philosopher 1 got the LEFT FORK:EATING for the 23368th time.
Fork 1 put down.
Fork 0 put down.
Philosopher 1 is THINKING.
Philosopher 1 is HUNGRY.
Fork 1 picked up.
Philosopher 1 got the RIGHT FORK.
Fork 0 picked up.
Philosopher 1 got the LEFT FORK:EATING for the 23369th time.
Fork 1 put down.
Fork 0 put down.
Philosopher 1 is THINKING.
Philosopher 1 is HUNGRY.
Fork 1 picked up.
```

```
Philosopher 1 got the RIGHT FORK.
Fork 0 picked up.
Philosopher 1 got the LEFT FORK:EATING for the 23370th time.
Fork 1 put down.
Fork 0 put down.
Philosopher 1 is THINKING.
Philosopher 1 is HUNGRY.
Fork 1 picked up.
Philosopher 1 got the RIGHT FORK.
Philosopher 4 got the RIGHT FORK:EATING for the 17894th time.
Fork 4 put down.
Fork 3 put down.
Philosopher 4 is THINKING.
Philosopher 4 is HUNGRY.
Fork 3 picked up.
Philosopher 4 got the LEFT FORK.
Fork 4 picked up.
Philosopher 4 got the RIGHT FORK:EATING for the 17895th time.
Fork 4 put down.
Fork 3 put down.
Philosopher 4 is THINKING.
Philosopher 4 is HUNGRY.
Fork 3 picked up.
Philosopher 4 got the LEFT FORK.
Fork 4 picked up.
Philosopher 4 got the RIGHT FORK:EATING for the 17896th time.
Fork 4 put down.
Fork 4 picked up.
Philosopher 0 got the LEFT FORK.
Fork 3 put down.
Fork 3 picked up.
Philosopher 3 got the RIGHT FORK.
Fork 2 picked up.
Philosopher 3 got the LEFT FORK:EATING for the 26900th time.
Fork 3 put down.
Fork 2 put down.
Philosopher 3 is THINKING.
Philosopher 3 is HUNGRY.
Fork 3 picked up.
Philosopher 3 got the RIGHT FORK.
Fork 2 picked up.
Philosopher 3 got the LEFT FORK:EATING for the 26901th time.
Fork 3 put down.
Fork 2 put down.
Philosopher 3 is THINKING.
```

Listing 16.15

```
using System;
using System.Threading;
public class DiningPhilosophers {

    //Declare the philosopher & fork array
    static Thread[] phil;
    static Fork[] fork;

    //User chooses deadlock-prone version or safe version
    static bool noDeadlock = false;

    //The number of philosophers
    static int numPhil;

    //Method either creates a philosopher thread
    //or a smart philosopher thread; these prevent deadlock
    public static Thread MakePhilosopher(
            int id, Fork left, Fork right) {
        if (noDeadlock) {
            SmartPhilosopher p=new SmartPhilosopher(id,left,right);
            return new Thread(
                  new ThreadStart(p.RunSmartPhilosopher));
        } else {
            Philosopher p=new Philosopher(id,left,right);
            return new Thread(
                  new ThreadStart(p.RunPhilosopher));
        }
    }

    public static void Main(String[] args) {

       Console.Write("Enter the number of philosophers: ");
       numPhil=Int32.Parse(Console.ReadLine());

       Console.Write("Run the deadlock prone version? ");
       char ans=Console.ReadLine().Trim().ToUpper()[0];
       noDeadlock=ans=='Y'?false:true;

       //Create the array of philosophers and forks
       phil= new Thread[numPhil];
       fork = new Fork[numPhil];

       //Create each fork and put in array
       for (int i =0; i<numPhil; i++)
            fork[i] = new Fork(i);

       //Create each philosopher and put in array, start each thread
       //Philosopher i's right fork is fork #i
       //Philosopher i's left fork is i-1 (with wrap-around for 0)
```

(continued)

```
        for (int i =0; i<numPhil; i++){
             phil[i] = MakePhilosopher(
                         i,
                         fork[(i-1+numPhil)% numPhil],
                         fork[i]);
             phil[i].Start();
        }
    }

}

public class Fork {

  //This records whether or not fork is in use
  private bool taken=false;

  //Each fork has a number
  private int identity;

  //Constructor gives the fork its number
  public Fork(int id) { identity = id;}

  //Philosopher calls this when hungry; may be a right OR a left fork
  public void Get() {
      lock (this) {

           //Wait if desired fork is taken
           while (taken) Monitor.Wait(this);

           //Fork is free; grab it
           taken=true;

           Console.WriteLine("Fork "+identity+ " picked up.");
      }
  }

  //Philosopher calls this to put a fork down when finished eating
  public void Put() {
      lock (this) {

  //Put the fork down; mark it as free
           taken=false;
           Console.WriteLine("Fork "+identity+ " put down.");

           //Announce to other thread fork is available
           Monitor.Pulse(this);
      }
  }
}
```

(continued)

```
public class Philosopher {

  //Each philosopher has a number
  protected int identity;

  //Each philosopher has a fork on left, and one on right
  protected Fork left;
  protected Fork right;

  public Philosopher(int id, Fork left, Fork right) {
    identity = id;
  this.left = left;
  this.right = right;
  }

  public void RunPhilosopher() {
      while (true) {

      //thinking
      Console.WriteLine("Philosopher "+identity+" is THINKING.");

      //hungry
      Console.WriteLine("Philosopher "+identity+" is HUNGRY.");

      right.Get();
      //got right fork
      Console.WriteLine("Philosopher "+identity+
            " got the RIGHT FORK.");
      left.Get();
      //got left fork

      //eating
      Console.WriteLine("Philosopher "+identity+
            " got the LEFT FORK and is EATING.");

      //put both forks down
      right.Put();
      left.Put();
      }
  }
}

public class SmartPhilosopher:Philosopher {

  //inherits all fields from Philosopher

  int successCount = 0;

  //Specify base constructor to call
  public SmartPhilosopher(int identity, Fork left, Fork right)
      :base(identity,left,right) {}
```

(continued)

```
  public void RunSmartPhilosopher() {
      while (true) {

        //thinking
        Console.WriteLine("Philosopher "+identity+" is THINKING.");

        //hungry
        Console.WriteLine("Philosopher "+identity+" is HUNGRY.");

      //get a fork
      if (identity%2 == 0) {
            //even-numbered philosophers go left first
            left.Get();
            Console.WriteLine("Philosopher "+identity+
                  " got the LEFT FORK.");
      } else {
            //odd-numbered philosophers go right first
            right.Get();
            Console.WriteLine("Philosopher "+identity+
                  " got the RIGHT FORK.");
      }
      //get the other fork
      if (identity%2 == 0) {
            right.Get();
            Console.WriteLine("Philosopher "+identity+
                  " got the RIGHT FORK:EATING for the "
                  +(++successCount)+"th time.");
      } else {
            left.Get();
            Console.WriteLine("Philosopher "+identity+
                  " got the LEFT FORK:EATING for the "
                  +(++successCount)+"th time.");
      }

//put both forks down
      right.Put();
      left.Put();
      }
  }

}
```

■ STARVATION

Solving the deadlock problem isn't the end of the story. Starvation of processes/threads can also occur. Starvation occurs when threads keep another thread continually unable to obtain the resources it needs to run. For example, if philosopher 2 and philosopher 4 always eat at the same time, philosopher 3 will never be able to eat. Of course, our model arranges it so that the philosophers become hungry randomly; in a real situation, however, threads may not be governed by random forces.

The most apparent solution to starvation is to allow a starving thread to interrupt another. In C#, this is easily done by modifying thread priorities. But how to determine that a thread is starving? One way is to maintain a counter that records the number of times the thread tried to run, but was unable to. After a certain number of tries, the thread is allowed to interrupt other threads. An interesting exercise would be for you to rewrite the dining philosophers problem so that the possibility of starvation is prevented.

chapter 17

Distributed Processing

Modern applications must be able to function through networks and internets. Such programs commonly share data, send and receive information, and execute programs remotely on other machines. The more transparent this functionality is, the better. This is known as distributed processing. All the problems we face in local programming, such as concurrency, we also come across in distributed applications.

C# provides a wide range of classes to use for writing distributed apps, and many of them are found in the `System.Net` and `System.Net.Sockets` namespaces. The first topic we will cover is identifying machines on the Internet.

■ IP ADDRESSES AND DOMAIN NAMES

In the beginning, machines were identified on the Internet by a 4-byte number, called an IP address. It was usually written in dotted-quad format—four decimal integers separated by periods, like 127.0.0.1. The range of each integer was 0 through 255, the range of an unsigned byte. Numbers were notoriously hard for humans to remember, however, and the concept of a domain name came about. When someone wished to obtain a domain name, they would request one from a central authority, and it would be issued (for a nominal fee). Because machines still used IP addresses to identify each other, Internet requests would be routed through domain name servers (DNS). These servers maintain a database of domain name/IP address mappings. Identifying the machine in this manner is known as domain name resolution or "resolving the host."

The System.Net namespace contains a Dns class that is used to resolve hosts. It has some handy methods to retrieve IP addresses from domain names, and vice versa. It can also obtain information about the local machine. Table 17.1 contains a listing of Dns members.

☐ Program: FindHosts

Listing 17.1 is an example of how the Dns methods are used. We first call Dns.GetHostName to retrieve the name of the local machine as a string. We then pass this name to Dns.Resolve, which returns an IPHostEntry object. IPHostEntry objects contain the domain names and IP addresses of the resolved host, and we obtain these by getting values from the AddressList and Aliases properties. You should note that a domain name may have multiple IP addresses, and an IP address could likewise be associated with multiple names, so these properties return arrays. AddressList returns an array of IPAddress objects, and Aliases returns an array of Strings. IPHostEntry and IPAddress are also in System.Net.

TABLE 17.1

Public Methods	
BeginGetHostByName	Begins an asynchronous request for IPHostEntry information about the specified DNS host name.
BeginResolve	Begins an asynchronous request to resolve a DNS host name or IP address in dotted-quad notation to an IPAddress instance.
EndGetHostByName	Ends an asynchronous request for DNS information.
EndResolve	Ends an asynchronous request for DNS information.
GetHostByAddress	Overloaded. Gets DNS host information for an IP address.
GetHostByName	Gets the DNS information for the specified DNS host name.
GetHostName	Gets the host name of the local computer.
Resolve	Resolves a DNS host name or IP address in dotted-quad notation to an IPHostEntry instance.

Here is the code to resolve the local host and display its IP addresses and aliases:

```
String thisMachine = Dns.GetHostName();
Console.WriteLine("Local machine's name: "+thisMachine);

IPHostEntry localHost = Dns.Resolve(thisMachine);

IPAddress[] localAddresses = localHost.AddressList;

Console.Write("Local machine's IP address(es): ");
foreach (IPAddress ipa in localAddresses)
      Console.Write(ipa);
Console.WriteLine();

String[] localNames = localHost.Aliases;

Console.Write("Local machine's aliases: ");
foreach (String name in localNames)
      Console.Write(name);
Console.WriteLine();
```

The FindHosts program resolves the local host, and also resolves a host input from the command line. You can also pass an IP address as a string in dotted-quad format into the `Dns.Resolve` method.

Listing 17.1

```
using System;
using System.Net;
public class FindHosts {
      public static void Main(String[] args) {

          try {

            //Get name of local machine
            //Dns.GetHostName returns a string
            String thisMachine = Dns.GetHostName();
            Console.WriteLine("Local machine's name: "+thisMachine);

            //Use Dns.Resolve to return IPHostEntry object
            //We get the IP addresses using its AddressList property
            IPHostEntry localHost = Dns.Resolve(thisMachine);

            //AddressList is an array since a name may have
            //multiple addresses
            IPAddress[] localAddresses = localHost.AddressList;
```

(continued)

```
            //Display these addresses
            Console.Write("Local machine's IP address(es): ");
            foreach (IPAddress ipa in localAddresses)
                  Console.Write(ipa);
            Console.WriteLine();

            //A host may have multiple names as well
            String[] localNames = localHost.Aliases;

            //Display these aliases
            Console.Write("Local machine's aliases: ");
            foreach (String name in localNames)
                  Console.Write(name);
            Console.WriteLine();

            //Do this for a host specified by user
            //Pass host name in thru command line
            //www.grinnell.edu is default
            String host;
            if (args.Length>0) host=args[0];
            else host="www.grinnell.edu";

            IPHostEntry inputHost = Dns.Resolve(host);
            IPAddress[] inputAddresses = inputHost.AddressList;
            Console.Write(host+"'s IP address(es): ");
            foreach (IPAddress ipa in inputAddresses)
                  Console.Write(ipa);
            Console.WriteLine();

            String[] inputNames = inputHost.Aliases;

            Console.Write(host+"'s aliases: ");
            foreach (String name in inputNames)
                  Console.Write(name);
            Console.WriteLine();

          } catch (Exception e) {
            Console.WriteLine(e+" "+e.StackTrace);
          }
      }
}
```

Here is a sample run of the program:

```
C:\C#>FindHosts www.grinnell.edu
Local machine's name: PC1290
Local machine's IP address(es): 132.161.1.99
Local machine's aliases:
www.grinnell.edu's IP address(es): 132.161.10.35
www.grinnell.edu's aliases:
```

A special IP address, 127.0.0.1, can be used to refer to the local host. It is often used by programmers to test their network programs, and it will be used in many of the following programs as well.

■ THE `HttpWebRequest` AND `HttpWebResponse` CLASSES

The `HttpWebRequest` and `HttpWebResponse` classes (from `System.Net`) are very handy for handling Hypertext Transfer Protocol (HTTP) activity over the Internet. These classes embody all the complicated messages that browsers and HTTP servers exchange to retrieve Hypertext Markup Language (HTML) documents, post information, and so forth.

The most common type of message an HTTP client (usually a browser, but not necessarily) sends to a server is a `GET` request. Say a user types

```
http://www.whatever.com/dave.html
```

into the browser. The corresponding `GET` request looks something like this:

```
GET /dave.html HTTP/1.1
Accept: image/gif, image/x-xbitmap, image/jpeg, image/pjpeg,
application/vnd.ms-
powerpoint, application/vnd.ms-excel, application/msword, */*
Accept-Language: en-us
Accept-Encoding: gzip, deflate
User-Agent: Mozilla/4.0 (compatible; MSIE 6.0; Windows NT 5.1; .NET CLR
1.0.3705
)
Host: 127.0.0.1
Connection: Keep-Alive
```

The first line tells the server what resource is required; only the path and file name are sent, not the entire domain name. In this case, dave.html is supposed to be in the root of the servers Web directory. (Every Web server has such a directory, and all HTTP requests are mapped to it.) The last entry, "HTTP/1.1", tells the server which version of HTTP the client is using.

The HTTP server then sends a response. The first line contains a code that tells the client what is coming back. A 200 code says the file was found, and is being sent. Two other common codes are 404-File not found and 501-Service not implemented. There are many others.

```
HTTP/1.1 200 OK\r\n
Date: 12:31PM August 28, 2003\r\n
Server: HTTPServer 1.0\r\n
Content-type: image/jpeg\r\n
Content-length: 2133\r\n
\r\n
<THE FILE IS SENT NOW, AFTER THE HEADER>
```

Another important line is the content-type, which tells the client what type of file is being sent. This is important information for the client, so it will know how to handle the file properly. Modern browsers often check the file to determine its type as well (rather than trusting the server). Content-length tells the length of the file in bytes, so the client will receive it properly.

Here I have terminated each line specifically with a carriage return/line feed (\r\n). The HTTP protocol makes it clear that HTTP servers should terminate header lines with this pair of characters.

The C# `HttpWebRequest` and `HttpWebResponse` classes handle the nuisance of creating and parsing HTTP headers. These classes handle many different types of HTTP activity.

☐ Program: ViewSource

Listing 17.2 demonstrates the use of `HttpWebRequest` and `HttpWebResponse`. We send a request for an HTML document, then display the returned HTML source on the console.

First, we create an `HttpWebRequest` object. We do not use a constructor, but the static method

```
public static WebRequest Create (String resource);
```

from the `WebRequest` class. (`HttpWebRequest` is derived from `WebRequest`.)

`WebRequest.Create` returns a `WebRequest` object, which we must cast into an `HttpWebRequest` object.

```
HttpWebRequest request = (HttpWebRequest)
       WebRequest.Create("http://www.whatever.com);
```

This makes the connection and sends the request. To obtain the response, we must use the `GetResponse()` method from `HttpWebRequest`:

```
public HttpWebResponse GetResponse();
```

which returns an `HTTPWebResponse` object. We can turn this response into a stream by using `GetResponseStream()` from `HttpWebResponse`, as follows:

```
StreamReader sr = new StreamReader(
     request.GetResponse().GetResponseStream());
```

This is all we need to know to view the source of any HTML document.

Listing 17.2

```
using System;
using System.Net;
using System.IO;
public class ViewSource {
   public static void Main(String[] args) {
     try {
      String resource;

      //Page to retrieve comes from command line
      if (args.Length==1) resource=args[0];
      else resource="http://www.cs.grinnell.edu";

      //Make an HTTP request-note a cast is required
      HttpWebRequest request =
            (HttpWebRequest)WebRequest.Create(resource);

      //Set up StreamReader to get response
      StreamReader sr = new StreamReader(
            request.GetResponse().GetResponseStream());

      //Read the response and close the stream
      String response=sr.ReadToEnd();
      sr.Close();

      Console.Write(response);
     } catch (Exception exc) {
      Console.WriteLine(exc+" "+exc.StackTrace);
     }
   }
}
```

The resource can come in through the command line; if no string is entered, a default URL is used. Note also that the default

```
http://www.cs.grinnell.edu
```

specifies no file. When this happens, HTTP servers may still send back a document, usually index.html or index.htm.

```
C:\C#>ViewSource http://www.cs.grinnell.edu/~bishopd
<!DOCTYPE HTML PUBLIC "-//W3C//DTD HTML 3.2 Final//EN">
<HTML>
 <HEAD>
  <TITLE>Index of /~bishopd</TITLE>
 </HEAD>
 <BODY>
```

```
<H1>Index of /~bishopd</H1>
<PRE><IMG SRC="/icons/blank.gif" ALT="     "> <A HREF="?N=D">Name</A>
         <A HREF="?M=A">Last modified</A>       <A HREF="?S=A">Size</A>  <A HREF
="?D=A">Description</A>
<HR>
<IMG SRC="/icons/back.gif" ALT="[DIR]"> <A HREF="/">Parent Directory</A>
18-Aug-2003 10:26      -
<IMG SRC="/icons/folder.gif" ALT="[DIR]"> <A HREF="bio/">bio/</A>
     08-Mar-2002 08:21      -
<IMG SRC="/icons/folder.gif" ALT="[DIR]"> <A HREF="crypbook/">crypbook/</A>
          18-Oct-2002 11:52      -
<IMG SRC="/icons/folder.gif" ALT="[DIR]"> <A HREF="csc105/">csc105/</A>
        12-Dec-2001 13:15      -
<IMG SRC="/icons/folder.gif" ALT="[DIR]"> <A HREF="csc152/">csc152/</A>
        09-May-2003 10:59      -
<IMG SRC="/icons/folder.gif" ALT="[DIR]"> <A HREF="csc213/">csc213/</A>
        10-Dec-2002 11:15      -
<IMG SRC="/icons/folder.gif" ALT="[DIR]"> <A HREF="csc223/">csc223/</A>
        02-Apr-2003 13:11      -
<IMG SRC="/icons/folder.gif" ALT="[DIR]"> <A HREF="csc395/">csc395/</A>
        21-Feb-2002 14:01      -
<IMG SRC="/icons/folder.gif" ALT="[DIR]"> <A HREF="gabepics/">gabepics/</A>
          06-May-2002 18:20      -
<IMG SRC="/icons/folder.gif" ALT="[DIR]"> <A HREF="projectdelta/">projectdelta/<
/A>          15-Oct-2002 13:06      -
<IMG SRC="/icons/folder.gif" ALT="[DIR]"> <A HREF="publisherdocs/">publisherdocs
/</A>          15-May-2002 11:24      -
</PRE><HR>
<ADDRESS>Apache/1.3.19 Server at <A HREF="mailto:webmaster@math.grinnell.edu">ww
w.cs.grinnell.edu</A> Port 80</ADDRESS>
</BODY></HTML>
```

Note that we didn't have to manually send or parse any HTTP headers; they are nicely handled by the `HttpWebRequest` and `HttpWebResponse` classes.

☐ Program: ViewPage

The ViewPage program does the same job as ViewSource, but displays the source in a GUI. The code for this program is shown in Listing 17.3.

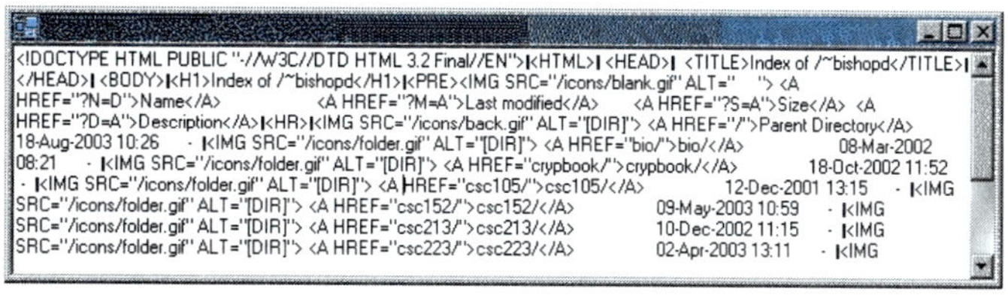

```
<!DOCTYPE HTML PUBLIC "-//W3C//DTD HTML 3.2 Final//EN">|<HTML>| <HEAD>| <TITLE>Index of /~bishopd</TITLE>|
</HEAD>| <BODY>|<H1>Index of /~bishopd</H1>|<PRE><IMG SRC="/icons/blank.gif" ALT="     "> <A
HREF="?N=D">Name</A>                    <A HREF="?M=A">Last modified</A>       <A HREF="?S=A">Size</A>  <A
HREF="?D=A">Description</A>|<HR>|<IMG SRC="/icons/back.gif" ALT="[DIR]"> <A HREF="/">Parent Directory</A>
18-Aug-2003 10:26    - |<IMG SRC="/icons/folder.gif" ALT="[DIR]"> <A HREF="bio/">bio/</A>              08-Mar-2002
08:21    - |<IMG SRC="/icons/folder.gif" ALT="[DIR]"> <A HREF="crypbook/">crypbook/</A>          18-Oct-2002 11:52
 - |<IMG SRC="/icons/folder.gif" ALT="[DIR]"> <A HREF="csc105/">csc105/</A>            12-Dec-2001 13:15    - |<IMG
SRC="/icons/folder.gif" ALT="[DIR]"> <A HREF="csc152/">csc152/</A>            09-May-2003 10:59    - |<IMG
SRC="/icons/folder.gif" ALT="[DIR]"> <A HREF="csc213/">csc213/</A>            10-Dec-2002 11:15    - |<IMG
SRC="/icons/folder.gif" ALT="[DIR]"> <A HREF="csc223/">csc223/</A>            02-Apr-2003 13:11    - |<IMG
```

Figure 17.1

Listing 17.3

```
using System;
using System.Net;
using System.IO;
using System.Windows.Forms;
public class ViewPage:Form {
   TextBox viewer=new TextBox();
   public ViewPage(String resource) {
     try {
      viewer.ScrollBars=ScrollBars.Vertical;
      viewer.Multiline=true;
      viewer.Dock=DockStyle.Fill;
      this.Controls.Add(viewer);
      HttpWebRequest request =
            (HttpWebRequest)WebRequest.Create(resource);
      StreamReader sr = new StreamReader(
            request.GetResponse().GetResponseStream());
      String response=sr.ReadToEnd();
      sr.Close();
      viewer.Text=response;
     } catch (Exception exc) {
      viewer.Text=exc+" "+exc.StackTrace;
     }
   }
   public static void Main(String[] args) {
      String resource;
      if (args.Length==1) resource=args[0];
      else resource="http://www.cs.grinnell.edu";
      Application.Run(new ViewPage(resource));
   }
}
```

Figure 17.1 shows a sample run.

An interesting exercise for you would be to render the HTML in a browser-like window.

■ THE TcpClient AND TcpListener CLASSES

HTTP is considered a "high end" protocol, meaning that it depends on lower-level protocols for the actual transfer of data, which is actually quite complicated. Some protocols, like User Datagram Protocol (UDP), do not guarantee (or even check) that messages have been received, whereas others, like Transmission Control Protocol (TCP), do.

Networks send data in packets, or datagrams. Because of varying conditions on the network or Internet, these datagrams may arrive at the destination corrupted or out of order, or they may not arrive at all. TCP is actually a complicated protocol that represents an exchange between client and server that ensures the message received is the same as was sent.

Communication between TCP clients and servers in C# resembles normal stream communication. This is because the NetworkStream class is derived from stream; thus, all the ugly details of actual packet exchange and checking is hidden from the programmer. The TcpClient and TcpListener classes allow us to create a TCP connection.

□ Program: DaytimeClient

The TCP version of the Daytime protocol allows a client to connect to a Daytime server listening on port 13. (There are 65,536 logical ports available. Server ports for well-established protocols are standard; the OS picks a port for the client, and it can be anything.) Once the server establishes the connection, it immediately sends the time (in no standard format) as text. The server then closes the connection.

We create a connection with a Daytime server using a TcpClient constructor and the Connect method, like so:

```
TcpClient client = new DaytimeClient("time.nist.gov");
client.Connect();
```

Once the connection exists, we need to capture the data stream between client and server. This is easily done using the GetStream() method from TcpClient, which returns a NetworkStream:

```
NetworkStream ns = client.GetStream();
```

However, if we know the message is text (and in the case of the Daytime protocol, we do), we can produce a StreamReader to easily read text from the stream.

```
StreamReader sr = new StreamReader(ns);
```

This constructor takes a Stream as a parameter (and a NetworkStream is a Stream by inheritance). From this point on, we can read the message(s) sent by the server using the convenient reading methods from StreamReader.

Listing 17.4 is the `DaytimeClient` class, which is derived from `TcpClient`. DaytimeClient has a `Main` method, which is the entry point for execution.

Listing 17.4

```
using System;
using System.Net.Sockets;
using System.Windows.Forms;
using System.IO;
public class DaytimeClient:TcpClient {

   //Daytime client connects when constructor called
   public DaytimeClient(String host) {
      //Uses the Connect method from TcpClient
      //Daytime protocol is thru port 13 on server
      base.Connect(host,13);
   }
   public static void Main(String[] args) {

     DaytimeClient dtreceiver=null;
     StreamReader sr=null;

     try {
      //Host name comes from command line
      //If no host specified, local machine is host
      String host=args.Length==1?args[0]:"127.0.0.1";

      //Connect to Daytime server
      dtreceiver=new DaytimeClient(host);

      //Get the stream between server and client
      //Create a user-friendly StreamReader
      //Daytime servers send ASCII
      sr=new StreamReader(dtreceiver.GetStream());

      //Get the daytime from the server
      String returndata=sr.ReadToEnd();
      MessageBox.Show("Time at "+host+": "+returndata);
     } catch (Exception e) {
      MessageBox.Show(e+" "+e.StackTrace);
     } finally {
      if (sr!=null) sr.Close();
      if (dtreceiver!=null) dtreceiver.Close();
     }
   }
}
```

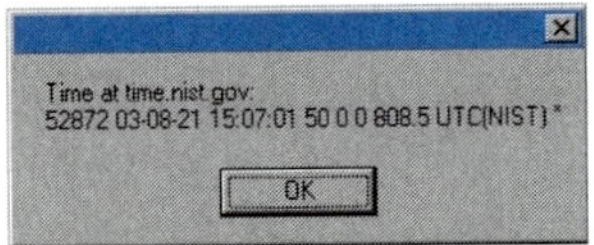

Figure 17.2

The host name of the Daytime server comes in through the command line. If no host is specified, the local machine is expected to be a Daytime server. Here, we connect to time.nist.gov, a well-known Daytime server:

```
G:\C#>DaytimeClient time.nist.gov
```

Figure 17.2 shows the time when the program was run.

This program assumes the local host is a Daytime server if no host is specified on the command line. To test this, we will write a Daytime server using the `TcpListener` class.

☐ Program: DaytimeServer

Writing a Daytime server first means listening for incoming connections (that's what servers do) on port 13. This is called binding to a port; `TcpListener` objects can do this via the constructor and their `Start` method:

```
TcpListener server = new TcpListener(13);//Bind to port
server.Start();//Start listening
```

A `TcpListener` captures a connection with a client via its `AcceptTcpClient()` method, which returns a `TcpClient` object. This particular method blocks until a connection is actually established.

```
TcpClient connection = server.AcceptTcpClient();
```

The `TcpClient` returned represents the connection. You can use it to get I/O streams on the server side in the same ways the client can use this class. In the case of a `DaytimeServer`, we produce a `StreamWriter` through which we send the date and time.

Listing 17.5 is the `DaytimeServer` class.

Listing 17.5

```
using System;
using System.Net.Sockets;
using System.IO;
public class DaytimeServer {
  public static void Main(String[] args) {
    TcpListener server=null;
    try {
      //Daytime servers listen on port 13
      int portNumber = 13;

      //Daytime server first binds to port 13
      server = new TcpListener(portNumber);
      //Server starts listening
      server.Start();

      //Daytime server loops forever, listening for clients
      for(;;) {
      Console.WriteLine("Waiting for a connection....");
      //Accept the pending client connection and return a
      //client initialized for communication.
      //This method will block until a connection is made
      TcpClient client = server.AcceptTcpClient();
      Console.WriteLine("Connection accepted.");

      //Prepare response
      String responseString = DateTime.Now.ToString();
      //Make a user-friendly StreamWriter from the stream
      StreamWriter sw=new StreamWriter(client.GetStream());
      sw.WriteLine(responseString);
      Console.WriteLine("Message Sent: " + responseString);

      //Close the StreamWriter, stream, connection
      sw.Close();
      client.Close();
      }
    } catch (Exception e) {
      Console.WriteLine(e+" "+e.StackTrace);
    } finally {
      //Release the port and stop the server
      server.Stop();
    }
  }
}
```

We start the server here, which halts as it waits for a connection.

```
C:\C#>DaytimeServer
Waiting for a connection....
```

Figure 17.3

Now, we will run DaytimeClient from the same machine. Since we passed in no host name, the local machine is assumed to be running as a Daytime server.

```
C:\C#>DaytimeClient
```

Figure 17.3 shows the time from the local machine.

Note that the time does not need to be in any particular format. This is a mixed blessing for the Daytime protocol. It makes it very easy for a server to send the time in the format it prefers, but harder for clients that must parse these various strings and make sense of them.

Our DaytimeServer continues to run after each client is disconnected, because a server must continually listen for other clients. Thus, we must interrupt the DaytimeServer program to stop it.

```
G:\C#>DaytimeServer
Waiting for a connection....
Connection accepted.
Message Sent: 8/20/2003 9:49:52 PM
Waiting for a connection....
^C
G:\C#>
```

Note also how the server closes the connection, using the Close() method from TcpClient. It also closes the StreamWriter (and the underlying stream). It is particularly important for the server to close the connection when it is finished with a client. It does not matter if either party closes the connection when it has already been closed, so the client should have provisions to close as well.

```
sw.Close();
client.Close();
```

If the server should ever be stopped, it should release the port it was bound to. We do this in C# by using the Stop method.

```
try {//do your thing
} catch (...){
} finally {
  //Release the port and stop the server
  server.Stop();
}
```

We stop the server using a finally block. This guarantees that the port will be released whether exceptional condition arise or not.

■ MULTITHREADED SERVERS

If a server has to carry on a long session with any particular client, it should be threaded; that is, each time a client connects with the server, we should spawn a new thread to handle the exchange. This allows the server to loop back and wait for another connection while other threads talk to their client. In the case of the Daytime server, you can argue against threading it, because the connection is open for such a short time. However, other protocols can keep a connection open for a very long time. Case in point: the `Echo` protocol.

A server supporting the `Echo` protocol listens for incoming connections on port 7. When a client connects, the server waits for a message. When it receives a message from the client, it sends the message back, provided the message is not "." (a period). If the message is ".", the server disconnects from this client.

It could be quite a while (possibly never) before the client sends a period to the server, and this connection could be open indefinitely, preventing the server from communicating with other clients. An unthreaded version of an Echo server follows.

☐ Class: `EchoServerNoThread`

The Echo server in Listing 17.6 waits in an infinite loop servicing clients, in the same way the Daytime server does. However, because two-way communication exists in the `Echo` protocol, we create both a `StreamReader` and a `StreamWriter`. Note that the `StreamWriter` calls `Flush()` after every response. This is to ensure that the message is sent even though the internal buffer is not yet full.

Listing 17.6

```
using System;
using System.Net.Sockets;
using System.IO;
public class EchoServerNoThread {
  public static void Main(String[] args) {
    StreamReader sr=null;
    StreamWriter sw=null;
    TcpClient client=null;
    TcpListener server=null;
    try {
      //Echo servers listen on port 7
      int portNumber = 7;

      //Echo server first binds to port 7
      server = new TcpListener(portNumber);
      //Server starts listening
      server.Start();
```

(continued)

```
      //Echo server loops forever, listening for clients
      for(;;) {
      Console.WriteLine("Waiting for a connection....");
      //Accept the pending client connection and return a client
      //initialized for communication
      //This method will block until a connection is made
      client = server.AcceptTcpClient();
      Console.WriteLine("Connection accepted.");

      //Make a user-friendly StreamReader from the stream
      sr=new StreamReader(client.GetStream());

      //Make a user-friendly StreamWriter from the stream
      sw=new StreamWriter(client.GetStream());

      String incoming=sr.ReadLine();
      while (incoming!=".") {
            Console.WriteLine("Message received: "+incoming);
            sw.WriteLine(incoming);
            sw.Flush();
            Console.WriteLine("Message Sent back: " + incoming);
            incoming=sr.ReadLine();
      }
      Console.WriteLine("Client sent '.': closing connection.");
      sr.Close();
      sw.Close();
      client.Close();
      }
    } catch (Exception e) {
      Console.WriteLine(e+" "+e.StackTrace);
    } finally {
      if (sr!=null) sr.Close();
      if (sw!=null) sw.Close();
      if (client!=null) client.Close();
      //Release the port and stop the server
      server.Stop();
    }
  }
}
```

Class: `EchoClient`

The `EchoClient` class (Listing 17.7) is derived from `TcpClient`, and it connects to a host specified on the command line, or uses the local machine if no host is specified. Once the client sends the disconnect message ("."), it jumps out of its loop and terminates.

Listing 17.7

```
using System;
using System.Net.Sockets;
using System.IO;
public class EchoClient:TcpClient {

   //Echo client connects when constructor called
   public EchoClient(String host) {
      //Uses the Connect method from TcpClient
      //Echo protocol is thru port 7 on server
      base.Connect(host,7);
   }

   public static void Main(String[] args) {
     EchoClient conversant=null;
     StreamWriter sw=null;
     StreamReader sr=null;
     try {
      //Host name comes from command line
      //If no host specified, local machine is host
      String host=args.Length==1?args[0]:"127.0.0.1";

      //Connect to Echo server
      conversant=new EchoClient(host);

      //Get the stream between server and client
      NetworkStream ns=conversant.GetStream();

      //Create a user-friendly StreamWriter
      sw=new StreamWriter(ns);

      //Create a user-friendly StreamReader
      sr=new StreamReader(ns);

      //Prompt user for message to send to server
      //Period "." tells server to end session
      String input;
      Console.Write("Enter text: '.' to stop: ");

      while ((input=Console.ReadLine())!=".") {
            //Send message to server
            sw.WriteLine(input);
            sw.Flush();

            //Get the Echo from the server
            String returndata=sr.ReadLine();
            Console.WriteLine("Reply from "+host+": "+returndata);
            Console.Write("Enter text: '.' to stop: ");
      }
```

(continued)

```
            //Send final message and scram
            sw.WriteLine(".");
            sw.Flush();

          } catch (Exception e) {
            Console.WriteLine(e+" "+e.StackTrace);
          } finally {
            //Close the connection whether exception thrown or not
            if (sw!=null) sw.Close();
            if (sr!=null) sr.Close();
            if (conversant!=null) conversant.Close();
          }
       }

}
```

Here is the `EchoClient` conversing with the `EchoServer` already running on the local host:

```
C:\C#>EchoClient
Enter text: '.' to stop: Dear John:
Reply from 127.0.0.1: Dear John:
Enter text: '.' to stop: I don't love you anymore.
Reply from 127.0.0.1: I don't love you anymore.
Enter text: '.' to stop: Goodbye.
Reply from 127.0.0.1: Goodbye.
Enter text: '.' to stop: .
```

Here is the exchange from the server side:

```
C:\C#>EchoServerNoThread
Waiting for a connection....
Connection accepted.
Message received: Dear John:
Message Sent back: Dear John:
Message received: I don't love you anymore.
Message Sent back: I don't love you anymore.
Message received: Goodbye.
Message Sent back: Goodbye.
Client sent '.': closing connection.
Waiting for a connection....
```

This server attempts to make no new connections while it is conversing with its client. This is unacceptable; we must rewrite the server so that it can converse with many clients concurrently.

Class: EchoServer

The trick to threading a server is to move all the code to handle the exchange between client and server into a method referenced by a ThreadStart delegate. The connection that exists between client and server can be set in an instance variable within a constructor. The EchoServer in Listing 17.8 does this.

```
TcpClient client=null;

public EchoServer(TcpClient tcpc) {client=tcpc;}

//Main method
for(;;) {
   //...
   EchoServer es = new EchoServer(server.AcceptTcpClient());
   Thread serverThread = new Thread(
      new ThreadStart(es.Conversation));
   serverThread.Start();
   //...
}
//end of Main

public void Conversation() {
      //all the talkie-talkie goes here
}
```

Note that the for loop is blocked only for a short time as it spawns the new thread. It then immediately loops back and waits for another client. By continually spawning threads, it can hold conversations with any number of clients at the same time, each in its own thread.

Listing 17.8

```
using System;
using System.Net.Sockets;
using System.IO;
using System.Threading;
public class EchoServer {

  StreamReader sr=null;
  StreamWriter sw=null;
  TcpClient client=null;

  public EchoServer(TcpClient tcpc) {client=tcpc;}

  public void Conversation() {
    try {
```

(continued)

```
      Console.WriteLine("Connection accepted.");

      //Make a user-friendly StreamReader from the stream
      sr=new StreamReader(client.GetStream());

      //Make a user-friendly StreamWriter from the stream
      sw=new StreamWriter(client.GetStream());

      String incoming=sr.ReadLine();
      while (incoming!=".") {
            Console.WriteLine("Message received: "+incoming);
            sw.WriteLine(incoming);
            sw.Flush();
            Console.WriteLine("Message Sent back: " + incoming);
            incoming=sr.ReadLine();
      }

      Console.WriteLine("Client sent '.': closing connection.");
      sr.Close();
      sw.Close();
      client.Close();
    } catch (Exception e) {
      Console.WriteLine(e+" "+e.StackTrace);
    } finally {
      if (sr!=null) sr.Close();
      if (sw!=null) sw.Close();
      if (client!=null) client.Close();
    }
  }

  public static void Main(String[] args) {

    TcpListener server=null;

    try {
      //Echo servers listen on port 7
      int portNumber = 7;

      //Echo server first binds to port 7
      server = new TcpListener(portNumber);
      //Server starts listening
      server.Start();

      //Echo server loops forever, listening for clients
      for(;;) {
      //Accept the pending client connection and return a client
      //initialized for communication
      //This method will block until a connection is made
      EchoServer es = new EchoServer(server.AcceptTcpClient());
```

(continued)

```
      //Allow this conversation to run in a new thread
      Thread serverThread = new Thread(
            new ThreadStart(es.Conversation));
      serverThread.Start();

      //Loop back up and wait for another client
      //Another thread is servicing this client
      }
    } catch (Exception e) {
      Console.WriteLine(e+" "+e.StackTrace);
    } finally {
      //Release the port and stop the server
      server.Stop();
    }

  }

}
```

If you test this server, you will note that you can connect clients from multiple machines and carry on conversations with this server concurrently.

☐ Class: `HTTPOneFileServer`

There is no reason why we can't write an HTTP server using `TcpListener` and `TcpClient`. All we need to know is how to parse an HTTP request, and how to send a proper response. We already covered HTTP responses to `GET` requests earlier; the format is like the following:

```
HTTP/1.1 200 OK\r\n
Date: 12:31PM August 28, 2003\r\n
Server: HTTPServer 1.0\r\n
Content-type: text/html\r\n
Content-length: 2133\r\n
\r\n
<THE FILE IS SENT NOW, AFTER THE HEADER>
```

This is what the server sends back if the file exists. The first line always comes first; the following header lines may come in a different order or may not always be present, or different header entries may appear. Content-length is a particularly important entry, however.

We will write an HTTP server that does a very simple job—it fires back the same HTML page for *every* request. Thus, we don't need to parse the `GET` request from the client; everybody gets the same file no matter what they ask for. It is arguable as to whether a server throwing a tiny file back to everyone should be threaded; we will thread it because we can write a better service based on the same code.

HTTP servers normally listen on port 80, so our `HTTPOneFileServer` does this by default. The code for this one-file server is in Listing 17.9.

Listing 17.9

```
using System;
using System.Net.Sockets;
using System.IO;
using System.Threading;
public class HTTPOneFileServer {

  //browser represents the client
  TcpClient browser;

  //Constructor sets the connection to incoming client
  public HTTPOneFileServer(TcpClient tcpc) {
    browser = tcpc;
  }

  public static void Main(String[] args) {

    int thePort;
    TcpListener server;

    //Set the port to listen on
    try {
      Console.Write("Enter the port to bind to: ");
      thePort = Int32.Parse(Console.ReadLine());
      //If an invalid port is entered, set the port to 80
      if (thePort < 0 || thePort > 65535) thePort = 80;
    } catch (Exception) {
      //If anything goes wrong, use default port 80
      thePort = 80;
    }

    try {
      //Bind to the port and start server
      server = new TcpListener(thePort);
      Console.WriteLine("Accepting connections on port " + thePort);
      server.Start();

      //Start accepting connections
      //each serviced in a separate thread
      for(;;) {

        HTTPOneFileServer https = new HTTPOneFileServer(
            server.AcceptTcpClient());
      Thread serverThread = new Thread(new ThreadStart(
            https.ProcessRequest));
        serverThread.Start();
```

(continued)

```
      //Loop back for more requests

      }

    } catch (Exception e) {
      Console.WriteLine(e+" "+e.StackTrace);
    }
  }

  //The method referred to by thread delegate
  public void ProcessRequest() {
    try {

      //Announce connection
      Console.WriteLine("HTTP request incoming.");

      //Set up the I/O streams
      //HTTP response headers are text
      StreamWriter ostream = new StreamWriter(browser.GetStream());

      //StreamReader reads the client's request,
      //even though we totally ignore its contents
      StreamReader istream = new StreamReader(browser.GetStream());
      String request=null;
      while ((request = istream.ReadLine()) != null) {
            //Display these lines on console
            Console.WriteLine(request);
            if (request.Trim().Equals("")) break;
      }

      //Send the SAME HTML document, no matter what they ask for
      SendHeader(ostream,
      "HTTP/1.0 200 OK\r\n",
      "text/html");
      //Send the HTML page to the client
      ostream.Write("\r\n<HTML><BODY><H1>THIS IS ALL YOU GET!");
      ostream.Write("</H1></BODY></HTML>\r\n");
      ostream.Close();

      //Close the connection
      browser.Close();

    } catch (Exception e) {
      //Report any other problem
      Console.WriteLine(e+" "+e.StackTrace);
    }

  }
```

(continued)

```
   public void SendHeader(StreamWriter ostream,
       String code,
       String contentType) {
             DateTime now = DateTime.Now;
             ostream.Write(code);
             ostream.Write("Date: " + now + "\r\n");
             ostream.Write("Server: HTTPServer 1.0\r\n");
             ostream.Write("Content-type: " + contentType + "\r\n");
   }

 }
```

Note that even though we create a connection with the client and read in its entire request, we do absolutely nothing with it:

```
StreamReader istream = new StreamReader(browser.GetStream());
String request=null;
while ((request = istream.ReadLine()) != null) {
      //Display these lines on console
      Console.WriteLine(request);
      if (request.Trim().Equals("")) break;
}
```

We then send the same header and HTML file to every request. (Actually, we don't send a file, but have hard-coded the HTML into the program. The client doesn't know the difference.)

```
SendHeader(ostream,
"HTTP/1.0 200 OK\r\n",
"text/html");
ostream.Write("\r\n<HTML><BODY><H1>THIS IS ALL YOU GET!");
ostream.Write("</H1></BODY></HTML>\r\n");
ostream.Close();
```

Note that the connection is closed by the server immediately after it serves the file (this is specified in the HTTP protocol). The `SendHeader` method simply forms and sends the header from the strings input to it:

```
public void SendHeader(StreamWriter ostream,
    String code,
    String contentType) {
          DateTime now = DateTime.Now;
          ostream.Write(code);
          ostream.Write("Date: " + now + "\r\n");
          ostream.Write("Server: HTTPServer 1.0\r\n");
          ostream.Write("Content-type: " + contentType + "\r\n");
}
```

Figure 17.4

In the case of `HTTPOneFileServer`, this header is always the same, but we can use `SendHeader` later on as we construct a better HTTP server. We now run `HTTPOne-FileServer`, which prompts for the port to listen on, and then proceeds to wait for incoming requests.

```
C:\C#>HTTPOneFileServer
Enter the port to bind to: 80
Accepting connections on port 80
```

Regardless of the request, this server sends back the same HTML document; namely, the one shown in Figure 17.4.

Here is the server displaying the `GET` request it received during this run. The HTTP server continues to wait for requests while servicing others in separate threads.

```
C:\C#>HTTPOneFileServer
Enter the port to bind to: 80
Accepting connections on port 80
HTTP request incoming.
GET / HTTP/1.1
Accept: image/gif, image/x-xbitmap, image/jpeg, image/pjpeg,
application/vnd.ms-
powerpoint, application/vnd.ms-excel, application/msword, */*
Accept-Language: en-us
Accept-Encoding: gzip, deflate
User-Agent: Mozilla/4.0 (compatible; MSIE 6.0; Windows NT 5.1; .NET CLR
1.0.3705
)
Host: 127.0.0.1
Connection: Keep-Alive
```

Now we can attempt to write a simple HTTP server that actually retrieves requested files or else reports errors.

☐ Class: `HTTPServer`

The simple HTTP server in Listing 17.10 can respond only to `GET` requests. The following are the only server responses it will make:

- 200 OK
- 404 File Not Found
- 501 Not Implemented

TABLE 17.2

MIME Type	Extension
text/plain	.txt
text/html	.htm and .html
image/gif	.gif
image/jpeg	.jpeg and .jpg

The server can send back files of any type, but all files will be characterized by one of the MIME types shown in Table 17.2, based on the extension of the requested file.

If the file extension is not any of those shown in Table 17.2, the server labels it in the header as text/plain. You can modify this server to produce more advanced behavior.

Now that we are writing a server that actually tries to find the file that is requested, we must set up a mapping between the path specified in a URL and the actual path on the server where the file should be. For example, if our domain name is http://www.whatever.com, we would like requests such as

```
http://www.whatever.com/stuff/deeperstuff/howdy.html
```

mapped to a local directory like

```
c:\webroot\stuff\deeperstuff\howdy.html
```

The HTTP server must capture the path and file name from the `GET` request, minus the domain name:

```
/stuff/deeperstuff/howdy.html
```

Fortunately, the client already does this in the `GET` request. The server must then append this to c:\webroot to obtain a full reference to the file. Of course, this root directory is determined when the server is started. In this `HTTPServer`, the variable `docroot` records this directory:

```
  //docroot is local directory that resource requests are mapped to
  static String docroot;

  //if file not specified in URI, index.html is assumed
  static String indexfile = "index.html";

//...

    //Prompt for the Document root
    Console.Write("Enter the root directory of the Web server: ");

    //The String represents the path to the file
    docroot = Console.ReadLine();
```

When we parse the GET request from the client, we split it up into tokens separated by white space; for example:

```
GET /dir1/zippity.html HTTP/1.1
```

would be split into

GET /dir1/zippity.html HTTP/1.1

We can easily do this by using the Split method from the String class. Suppose request is a String containing the first line of the GET request:

```
//Split it into tokens, separated by white space
String[] st = request.Split();

//First token should be keyword GET
method = st[0];

if (method.Equals("GET")) {

      //Next token should be the path and file name
  String file = st[1];

  //If no file specified, must be requesting "index.html"
  if (file.EndsWith("/")) file += indexfile;

//...

//If there is another token, it must be the version: HTTP/X.X
  if (st.Length>2) {
    httpVersion = st[2];
  }
```

Once we get the path and file name from the GET request, we can append it to the document root string to search for the file. The server also needs to know the MIME type of the file, which it determines by examining the file extension of the requested file and passing it to a "guess" function:

```
      //Next token should be the path and file name
      String file = st[1];

//...

      //Returns a MIME type string based on file extension
      contentType = GuessContentTypeFromName(file);

//...
```

```
public String GuessContentTypeFromName(String name) {

  //Determine the MIME type from the specified file extension
  if (name.EndsWith(".html")
    || name.EndsWith(".htm")) return "text/html";
  else if (name.EndsWith(".txt")) return "text/plain";
  else if (name.EndsWith(".gif") ) return "image/gif";
  else if (name.EndsWith(".jpg")
    || name.EndsWith(".jpeg")) return "image/jpeg";
  else return "text/plain";

}
```

Knowing the version is rather important as well. Pre-HTTP 1.0 requests look like this:

```
GET /dir1/dir2/whatever.html
```

without a version specified. The server must respond to such requests *without* sending a header; that is, only the requested file or some HTML message is sent. HTTP server response headers simply didn't exist prior to HTTP 1.0. This `HTTPServer` does look for a version, and sends no header if no version is specified.

Suppose `httpVersion` is a string formed by parsing the `GET` request. `SendHeader` is a static method that sends the header; it is the same as `SendHeader` in `HTTPOne-FileServer`. The variable `ostream` represents a `StreamWriter` to the client. The variable `theData` is an array of bytes containing the contents of the requested file (read in via a `FileStream`).

```
      //If there is another token, it must be the version: HTTP/X.X
        if (st.Length>2) {
          httpVersion = st[2];
        }

//...

          // send a MIME header if version was specified
          if (httpVersion.StartsWith("HTTP/")) {
            SendHeader(ostream,"HTTP/1.0 200 OK\r\n",contentType);
            ostream.Write("Content-Length: "
                  + theData.Length + "\r\n\r\n");
          }

          // send the file-possibly without a header
          //Use a BufferedStream-requested file may not be text
          BufferedStream byteStream=new BufferedStream(
            browser.GetStream());
          byteStream.Write(theData,0,theData.Length);
```

```
//Closing the stream flushes the buffer
//HTTP connections are closed after EVERY request
byteStream.Close();
```

Notice that we don't use the `StreamWriter` to send the file to the client, because `StreamWriters` are made to send text, and the requested file may not be text (such as a GIF image, for example). To send it, we set up a `BufferedStream` and use its `Write` method. Even if the requested file is text, we can still send it this way.

From this discussion, we now have all we need to write the `HTTPServer` class.

Listing 17.10

```
using System;
using System.Net.Sockets;
using System.IO;
using System.Threading;
using System.Text;
public class HTTPServer {

  //browser represents the client
  TcpClient browser;

  //docroot is local directory that resource requests are mapped to
  static String docroot;

  //if file not specified in URI, index.html is assumed
  static String indexfile = "index.html";

  //Constructor sets the connection to incoming client
  public HTTPServer(TcpClient tcpc) {
    browser = tcpc;
  }

  public static void Main(String[] args) {

    int thePort;
    TcpListener server;

    //Prompt for the Document root
    Console.Write("Enter the root directory of the Web server: ");

    //The String represents the path to the file
    docroot = Console.ReadLine();

    //Set the port to listen on
    try {
      Console.Write("Enter the port to bind to: ");
      thePort = Int32.Parse(Console.ReadLine());
      //If an invalid port is entered, set the port to 80
```

(continued)

```
      if (thePort < 0 || thePort > 65535) thePort = 80;
    } catch (Exception) {
      //If anything goes wrong, use default port 80
      thePort = 80;
    }

    try {
      //Bind to the port and start server
      server = new TcpListener(thePort);
      Console.WriteLine("Accepting connections on port " + thePort);
      Console.WriteLine("Document Root: " + docroot);
      server.Start();

      //Start accepting connections-each serviced in a separate thread
      for(;;) {

        HTTPServer https = new HTTPServer(server.AcceptTcpClient());
      Thread serverThread = new Thread(new ThreadStart(
            https.ProcessRequest));
        serverThread.Start();
      //Loop back for more requests

      }

    } catch (Exception e) {
      Console.WriteLine(e+" "+e.StackTrace);
    }
  }

  //The method referred to by thread delegate
  public void ProcessRequest() {

    String method;
    String contentType;
    String httpVersion = "";
    String fileName;

    try {

      //Announce connection-for debugging
      Console.WriteLine("HTTP request incoming");

      //Set up the I/O streams
      //HTTP response headers are text
      StreamWriter ostream = new StreamWriter(browser.GetStream());

      //HTTP requests are always text
      StreamReader istream = new StreamReader(browser.GetStream());
```

(continued)

```
//Read the first line from the client-the GET line
String request = istream.ReadLine();

//Display the request-for debugging
Console.WriteLine(request);

//Split it into tokens, separated by white space
String[] st = request.Split();

//First token should be keyword GET
method = st[0];

if (method.Equals("GET")) {

      //Next token should be the path and file name
  String file = st[1];

  //If no file specified, must be requesting "index.html"
  if (file.EndsWith("/")) file += indexfile;

  //Call the GuessContentTypeFromName() method-see below
//Returns a MIME type string based on file extension
  contentType = GuessContentTypeFromName(file);

//If there is another token, it must be the version: HTTP/X.X
  if (st.Length>2) {
    httpVersion = st[2];
  }

  // loop through the rest of the input lines
//this server will not use this client info
  while ((request = istream.ReadLine()) != null) {
      //Display these lines (for the heck of it)
      Console.WriteLine(request);
      if (request.Trim().Equals("")) break;
  }

//Now determine if requested resource exists on server
  try {

    //Form a full local path and file name
    fileName = docroot + file;

    //Open the file for reading
    //This throws FileNotFoundException if file doesn't exist
    FileStream fileStream = new FileStream(
      fileName,FileMode.Open);

    //Create an array of bytes-same Length as the file to read in
    byte[] theData = new byte[(int)fileStream.Length];
```

(continued)

```
        //Read the file into the array and close
        fileStream.Read(theData,0,theData.Length);
        fileStream.Close();

        // send a MIME header if version was specified
        if (httpVersion.StartsWith("HTTP/")) {
          SendHeader(ostream,"HTTP/1.0 200 OK\r\n",contentType);
          ostream.Write("Content-Length: "
                + theData.Length + "\r\n\r\n");
        }

        // send the file-possibly without a header
        //Use a BufferedStream-requested file may not be text
        BufferedStream byteStream=new BufferedStream(
          browser.GetStream());
        byteStream.Write(theData,0,theData.Length);
        //Closing the stream flushes the buffer
        //HTTP connections are closed after EVERY request
        byteStream.Close();

      } catch (FileNotFoundException) {

        //can't find the file-send a 404 code
        if (httpVersion.StartsWith("HTTP/")) {
          SendHeader(ostream,
          "HTTP/1.0 404 File Not Found\r\n",
          "text/html");
        }
        //Send some HTML to the client describing error
        ostream.Write("\r\n<HTML><BODY><H1>HTTP Error 404: ");
        ostream.Write("File Not Found</H1></BODY></HTML>\r\n");
        ostream.Close();

      }

    } else {

          // method token does not equal "GET"-send a 501 code
      if (httpVersion.StartsWith("HTTP/")) {
          SendHeader(ostream,
          "HTTP/1.0 501 Not Implemented\r\n",
          "text/html");
      }
      //Send some HTML to the client describing error
      ostream.Write("\r\n<HTML><BODY><H1>HTTP Error 501: ");
      ostream.Write("Not Implemented</H1></BODY></HTML>\r\n");
      ostream.Close();
    }
```

(continued)

```
      //Close the connection
      browser.Close();

    } catch (Exception e) {
      //Report any other problem
      Console.WriteLine(e+" "+e.StackTrace);
    }

  }

  public String GuessContentTypeFromName(String name) {

    //Determine the MIME type from the specified file extension
    if (name.EndsWith(".html")
      || name.EndsWith(".htm")) return "text/html";
    else if (name.EndsWith(".txt")) return "text/plain";
    else if (name.EndsWith(".gif") ) return "image/gif";
    else if (name.EndsWith(".jpg")
      || name.EndsWith(".jpeg")) return "image/jpeg";
    else return "text/plain";

  }

  public void SendHeader(StreamWriter ostream,
      String code,
      String contentType) {
            DateTime now = DateTime.Now;
            ostream.Write(code);
            ostream.Write("Date: " + now + "\r\n");
            ostream.Write("Server: HTTPServer 1.0\r\n");
            ostream.Write("Content-type: " + contentType + "\r\n");
  }

}
```

When we run this program, we are first prompted for the directory all requests will be mapped to and the port to bind the HTTP server to. Here, we map requests to the same directory the server is running from ".", and we use the default HTTP port 80:

```
C:\C#>HTTPServer
Enter the root directory of the Web server: .
Enter the port to bind to: 80
Accepting connections on port 80
Document Root: .
```

The same directory that holds HTTPServer.cs contains a couple of HTML files we can reference to test the server. Listing 17.11 is dave.html.

Listing 17.11

```
<html>
<title>
Brainiac Alert!
</title>
<body>
<h1>Crazed Professor on the Loose!</h1>
<img src=dave.jpg>
<h2>
If you have seen this egomaniac
<a href="dave2.html">
Click here Now!!!
</a>
</h2>
</body>
</html>
```

Figure 17.5

Note that this HTML file has an image reference:

```
<img src=dave.jpg>
```

(View Figure 17.5 to see the image.) How is this handled? The browser issues a *separate* `GET` request for dave.jpg when it parses this tag. Hence, you should note that some HTTP requests are initiated not by the user, but by the document.

There is also an anchor tag in dave.html that references another document:

```
<a href="dave2.html">
Click here Now!!!
</a>
```

This tag appears as a hyperlink, and clicking on it will issue a `GET` request to which the server responds. Listing 17.12 is dave2.html:

Listing 17.12

```
<html>
<title>
This site hosted by: Crazed Professor!!!!!
</title>
<body>
<h1>You're too late! HA HA HA HA HA!!!!!</h1>
<img src=dave.jpg>
</body>
</html>
```

Now that `HTTPServer` is running on the local host, open the browser and type

```
http://127.0.0.1/dave.html
```

in the address line. The document in Figure 17.6 appears, complete with image and hyperlink.

Click on the hyperlink, and the page in Figure 17.7 appears.

If we request a document that doesn't exist, like

```
http://127.0.0.1/
```

Figure 17.6

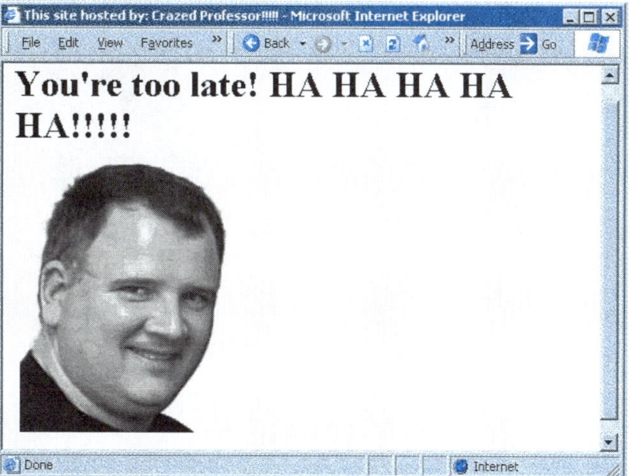

Figure 17.7

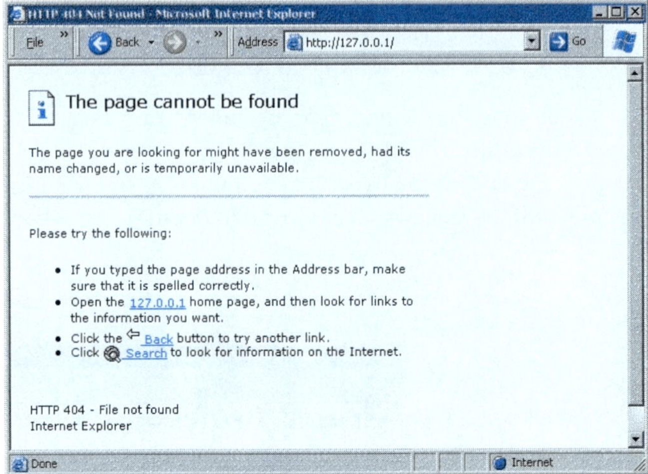

Figure 17.8

`HTTPServer` searches the root directory for a file named index.html; when such a file is not found, it returns the 404 error code (see Figure 17.8).

Note that the browser did not display the HTML that `HTTPServer` sends, but instead displays its own document. This particular browser only retrieves the server code in this case, and sends its own HTML to the window.

Here is a record of the `GET` requests as they arrived at the server during this session:

```
C:\C#>HTTPServer
Enter the root directory of the Web server: .
Enter the port to bind to: 80
Accepting connections on port 80
Document Root: .
HTTP request incoming
GET /dave.html HTTP/1.1
Accept: image/gif, image/x-xbitmap, image/jpeg, image/pjpeg,
application/vnd.ms-
powerpoint, application/vnd.ms-excel, application/msword, */*
Accept-Language: en-us
Accept-Encoding: gzip, deflate
User-Agent: Mozilla/4.0 (compatible; MSIE 6.0; Windows NT 5.1; .NET CLR
1.0.3705; .NET CLR 1.1.4322)
Host: 127.0.0.1
Connection: Keep-Alive
```

```
HTTP request incoming
GET /dave.jpg HTTP/1.1
Accept: */*
Referer: http://127.0.0.1/dave.html
Accept-Language: en-us
Accept-Encoding: gzip, deflate
User-Agent: Mozilla/4.0 (compatible; MSIE 6.0; Windows NT 5.1; .NET CLR
1.0.3705; .NET CLR 1.1.4322)
Host: 127.0.0.1
Connection: Keep-Alive

HTTP request incoming
GET /dave2.html HTTP/1.1
Accept: image/gif, image/x-xbitmap, image/jpeg, image/pjpeg,
application/vnd.ms-
powerpoint, application/vnd.ms-excel, application/msword, */*
Referer: http://127.0.0.1/dave.html
Accept-Language: en-us
Accept-Encoding: gzip, deflate
User-Agent: Mozilla/4.0 (compatible; MSIE 6.0; Windows NT 5.1; .NET CLR
1.0.3705; .NET CLR 1.1.4322)
Host: 127.0.0.1
Connection: Keep-Alive

HTTP request incoming
GET /dave.jpg HTTP/1.1
Accept: */*
Referer: http://127.0.0.1/dave2.html
Accept-Language: en-us
Accept-Encoding: gzip, deflate
User-Agent: Mozilla/4.0 (compatible; MSIE 6.0; Windows NT 5.1; .NET CLR
1.0.3705; .NET CLR 1.1.4322)
Host: 127.0.0.1
Connection: Keep-Alive

HTTP request incoming
GET / HTTP/1.1
Accept: image/gif, image/x-xbitmap, image/jpeg, image/pjpeg,
application/vnd.ms-
powerpoint, application/vnd.ms-excel, application/msword, */*
Accept-Language: en-us
Accept-Encoding: gzip, deflate
```

```
User-Agent: Mozilla/4.0 (compatible; MSIE 6.0; Windows NT 5.1; .NET CLR
1.0.3705; .NET CLR 1.1.4322)
Host: 127.0.0.1
Connection: Keep-Alive
```

This HTTP server is clearly limited in what it can do. Even though you could get much more functionality just by using the `HttpWebRequest` and `HttpWebResponse` classes, I think this is a case where doing the dirty work really teaches you something. An interesting exercise for you would be to study the HTTP protocol, and give `HTTPServer` more functionality.

▪ REMOTE OBJECTS

Ask any programmer familiar with distributed processing what they think of remote objects, and this is what you're likely to hear:

```
"SWEET!!!!!"
```

A remote object is an object that you can manipulate just like any other object on your local machine; that is, by referencing properties and fields, calling methods, and using delegates, except the object *does not exist on your machine*, but on another. You can change the state of the object and retrieve data from it within a program that treats it just like any local object.

If the remote object is thread-safe and properly synchronized, it can be safely accessed from multiple clients connected via a network or Internet. This represents the ultimate framework in which programmers writing distributed applications can work. Sweet indeed!

☐ Program: MessageQueue

We will create a `MessageQueue` class and use it as an example of remoting. See Listing 17.13 for the `MessageQueue` source code. A `MessageQueue` object can be set up on a remote machine. A producer on another machine writes values to the `MessageQueue`, and a consumer retrieves values from it. The methods of `MessageQueue` are so that the producer and consumer behave in a synchronized fashion. Both producer and consumer treat the `MessageQueue` as a local object, merely using method calls to the object. The only difference is how the object is set up.

We will not go into the `Send` and `Receive` methods of `MessageQueue`; they are merely thread-safe methods that block the producer while the consumer is reading, and likewise block the consumer while the producer is writing. A discussion of the producer–consumer problem can be seen in Chapter 16.

What is different is that `MessageQueue` registers itself as a well-known service type using the HTTP protocol on port 12345 of the local machine. Newer versions of HTTP allow us to remotely manipulate objects, so we can use HTTP for this purpose. Other protocols, such as Sun's RMI (Remote Method Invocation) can do remoting as well. The MessageQueue server would execute this program.

Classes register as a well-known service type by calling this method:

```
static void RegisterWellKnownServiceType(
      Type theObjectType,
      String Url;
      WellKnownObjectMode
);
```

from the `RemotingConfiguration` class in `System.Runtime.Remoting`. The `Type` parameter refers to the type of remote object you will create, the `String` is a URL to that service, and `WellKnownObjectMode` is an enumeration that can attain one of these two values:

- `SingleCall`
- `Singleton`

`SingleCall` creates a new object of the specified type for each method call, whereas `Singleton` uses only one instance of the object to service all requests. For our producer–consumer example, we want the same queue to serve the many requests from both producer and consumer, so we use the `Singleton` value.

Listing 17.13

```
using System;
using System.Collections;
using System.Runtime.Remoting;
public class MessageQueue {

   //The message queue is implemented as an ArrayList
   //It can be a remote object after registered
   private ArrayList queue;

   //Constructor
   public MessageQueue() {
      queue = new ArrayList();
   }

   //Send implements a nonblocking send
   //Producer calls this method remotely
   public void Send(Object item) {
      lock(this) {
            queue.Add(item);
            //Announce the item placed in message queue
            Console.WriteLine("REMOTE QUEUE: Producer entered "
                  + item + ". size = " + queue.Count);
      }
   }
```

(continued)

```
    //Receive implements a nonblocking receive
    //Consumer calls this method remotely
    public Object Receive() {
       lock(this) {
       Object item;
       //Method may return null if queue empty
       if (queue.Count == 0) return null;
       else {
             item = queue[0];
             queue.RemoveAt(0);
             //Announce the item removed
             Console.WriteLine("REMOTE QUEUE: Consumer removed "
                   + item + ". size = " + queue.Count);
             return item;
         }
       }
    }

    public static void Main(String[] args) {
       try {
             //Register the MessageQueue as a well-known service
             //using HTTP for object remoting on server port 12345
             //Singleton mode means only one message queue
             //is created to service all requests
                RemotingConfiguration.RegisterWellKnownServiceType(
                  typeof(MessageQueue),
                  "http://127.0.0.1:12345/",
                  WellKnownObjectMode.Singleton);
             Console.WriteLine("Message queue service on port 12345");
       } catch(Exception e) {
             Console.WriteLine(e);
       }

    }
}
```

Note that the Main method does not create a MessageQueue object; no constructor is called anywhere in the code. We will actually create the remote object when we create the producer and consumer. To start the service, we run MessageQueue:

```
C:\C#>MessageQueue
Message queue service on port 12345
```

☐ Program: PCFactory

The PCFactory class in Listing 17.14 sets up the remote MessageQueue object. It does this not by calling a constructor, but by calling the CreateInstance method from the Activator class. This is considered such a fundamental action that the C# developers put Activator in the System namespace.

```
static Object CreateInstance(
      Type typeOfObject,
      Object[] constructorArgs,
      Object[] activationArgs
);
```

The Type parameter is the type of object we wish to create. The second parameter is an array of objects. These objects are matched against the set of parameters in the constructor list of the object we are trying to create. The best match is chosen, if a match can be made. If this array is empty, a parameterless constructor is assumed.

The last parameter is an array of objects used to activate the object. In this example, we pass in only a UrlAttribute, which reveals the location of the service. This is most often all you need.

Note that CreateInstance returns an Object (actually a reference to an object, which may be at a remote location). Hence, a cast is usually necessary to produce the desired type.

The rest of PCFactory is completely normal; the producer and consumer are created, and they call the remote object in the same way they call a local one, and that's the beauty of it.

Listing 17.14

```
using System;
using System.Runtime.Remoting;
using System.Runtime.Remoting.Activation;
using System.Threading;
public class PCFactory {

   //An array of arguments to pass to MessageQueue constructor
   //Only MessageQueue constructor takes no arguments,
   //so this array is empty
   Object[] constructorArgs={};

   //An array of arguments that can be passed for activation purposes
   Object[] activationArgs= new Object[1];

   //Producer and Consumer use this to sleep for random intervals
   Random rnd = new Random();

   public PCFactory(String server) {
      //This is the remote object
      MessageQueue mailBox;

      //Only activation argument is a UrlAttribute
      //giving location of the MessageQueue service
```

(continued)

```
      activationArgs[0]=new UrlAttribute("http://"+server+":12345/");

      try {

            //Use Activator.CreateInstance method to create the
            //remote MessageQueue object
            //Registering does NOT CREATE THE OBJECT
            mailBox = (MessageQueue)Activator.CreateInstance(
                  typeof(MessageQueue),
                  constructorArgs,
                  activationArgs);

                //Now create and run the producer and consumer threads
            //Pass in the MessageQueue object
            //Each treats it as though it were a local object
            Prod producer = new Prod(mailBox,rnd);
            Thread pThread = new Thread(new ThreadStart(producer.Run));
            pThread.Start();
            Cons consumer = new Cons(mailBox,rnd);
            Thread cThread = new Thread(new ThreadStart(consumer.Run));
            cThread.Start();

      } catch (Exception e) {
            Console.WriteLine(e+"\n"+e.StackTrace);
      }
   }

   public static void Main(String[] args) {
      //We can pass in the MessageQueue server name thru cmd line
      //Local machine assumed if no server specified
      String serverName="127.0.0.1";
      if (args.Length>0) serverName=args[0];
      //Create the remote queue, producer and consumer
      PCFactory client = new PCFactory(serverName);
   }

}

public class Cons {

   private  MessageQueue mbox;
   Random rnd;

   public Cons(MessageQueue m,Random rnd) {
      mbox = m;
      this.rnd = rnd;
   }

   public void Run() {
```

(continued)

```
      //Loop eternally, sleeping then removing messages fm queue
      for(;;) {
       Thread.Sleep(rnd.Next()%10000);
       try {
       Object obj = mbox.Receive();

       //Queue may be empty-consumer reports this if so
       if (obj!=null) {
             DateTime message=(DateTime)obj;
             Console.WriteLine("CONSUMER: RETRIEVING "+message);
       } else Console.WriteLine("CONSUMER: BUFFER EMPTY");
       } catch (Exception e) {
             Console.WriteLine(e+"\n"+e.StackTrace);
       }
      }
   }
}

public class Prod {

   private  MessageQueue mbox;
   Random rnd;

   public Prod(MessageQueue m,Random rnd) {
      mbox = m;
      this.rnd=rnd;
   }

   public void Run() {
      DateTime message;

      //Loop eternally, sleeping then placing messages in queue
      for(;;) {
        Thread.Sleep(rnd.Next()%10000);
        //Produce a date & time, & enter it into the buffer
        message = DateTime.Now;
      try {
            mbox.Send(message);
            Console.WriteLine("PRODUCER: ENTERING "+message);
      } catch (Exception e) {
            Console.WriteLine(e+"\n"+e.StackTrace);
      }
      }
   }
}
```

We assume the MessageQueue program has already run, and the service exists on our local machine. When I ran PCFactory here I ran it also on the local machine. You can run it from any other machine, however, as long as you supply the address to the service in the `CreateInstance` method.

Note from the following output the synchronized behavior of producer and consumer:

```
CONSUMER: BUFFER EMPTY
REMOTE QUEUE: Producer entered 8/24/2003 8:14:37 PM. size = 1
PRODUCER: ENTERING 8/24/2003 8:14:37 PM
REMOTE QUEUE: Consumer removed 8/24/2003 8:14:37 PM. size = 0
CONSUMER: RETRIEVING 8/24/2003 8:14:37 PM
CONSUMER: BUFFER EMPTY
REMOTE QUEUE: Producer entered 8/24/2003 8:14:39 PM. size = 1
PRODUCER: ENTERING 8/24/2003 8:14:39 PM
REMOTE QUEUE: Producer entered 8/24/2003 8:14:39 PM. size = 2
PRODUCER: ENTERING 8/24/2003 8:14:39 PM
REMOTE QUEUE: Consumer removed 8/24/2003 8:14:39 PM. size = 1
CONSUMER: RETRIEVING 8/24/2003 8:14:39 PM
REMOTE QUEUE: Consumer removed 8/24/2003 8:14:39 PM. size = 0
CONSUMER: RETRIEVING 8/24/2003 8:14:39 PM
CONSUMER: BUFFER EMPTY
REMOTE QUEUE: Producer entered 8/24/2003 8:14:46 PM. size = 1
PRODUCER: ENTERING 8/24/2003 8:14:46 PM
REMOTE QUEUE: Consumer removed 8/24/2003 8:14:46 PM. size = 0
CONSUMER: RETRIEVING 8/24/2003 8:14:46 PM
REMOTE QUEUE: Producer entered 8/24/2003 8:14:53 PM. size = 1
PRODUCER: ENTERING 8/24/2003 8:14:53 PM
REMOTE QUEUE: Producer entered 8/24/2003 8:14:55 PM. size = 2
PRODUCER: ENTERING 8/24/2003 8:14:55 PM
REMOTE QUEUE: Producer entered 8/24/2003 8:14:57 PM. size = 3
PRODUCER: ENTERING 8/24/2003 8:14:57 PM
REMOTE QUEUE: Consumer removed 8/24/2003 8:14:53 PM. size = 2
CONSUMER: RETRIEVING 8/24/2003 8:14:53 PM
^C
```

Hopefully, you can see the power and flexibility that remote objects have to offer the programmer.

appendix

C# Rules

OPERATORS

The following table lists categories of operators, the name and example usage of each, and also denotes which operators may be overloaded. The operator categories are listed in precedence order, so that operators in each category have higher precedence than operators in subsequent categories. Within a category, execution of operators is done left to right.

Name	Usage	May Be Overloaded
Primary		
Parentheses	(expression)	
Member Access, aka the dot operator	object.member	
Struct pointer member access	structObject → member	
Method call	method(parameters)	
Indexing	object[index]	
Postincrement	variable**++**	Yes
Postdecrement	variable**––**	Yes
Memory allocation	**new**	
Array stack allocation	**stackalloc**	
Obtaining type	**typeof** object	
Obtaining struct size	**sizeof** structObject	
Switch arithmetic checker on	**checked**	
Switch arithmetic checker off	**unchecked**	
Unary		
Positive value	**+**value	Yes
Negate value	–value	Yes
Logical NOT	**!**	Yes
Bitwise complement	**~**	Yes
Preincrement	**++**variable	Yes
Predecrement	**––**variable	Yes
Type casting	(Type) object	
Value at address	*location	
Address of value	&variable	
Multiplicative		
Multiply	a*b	Yes
Divide	a/b	Yes
Remainder of integer division	a%b	Yes
Additive		
Add	a+b	Yes
Subtract	a–b	Yes

Name	Usage	May Be Overloaded
Shift		
Left bit shift	value<<positions	Yes
Right bit shift	value>>positions	Yes
Relational		
Less than	a<b	Yes
Greater than	a>b	Yes
Less than or equal to	a<=b	Yes
Greater than or equal to	a>=b	Yes
Type testing	object **is** Type	
Equality		
Equal to	a==b	Yes
Not equal to	a!=b	Yes
Logical Bitwise		
AND	a&b	Yes
OR	a|b	Yes
Exclusive OR	a^b	Yes
Logical Boolean		
AND	a&&b	
OR	a||b	
Conditional	condition?value1:value2	
Assignment		
Assign	a=b	
Multiply/assign	a*=b	
Divide/assign	a/=b	
Remainder/assign	a%=b	
Add/assign	a+=b	
Subtract/assign	a–=b	
Left bit shift/assign	a<<=positions	
Right bit shift/assign	a>>=positions	
Bitwise AND/assign	a&=b	
Bitwise exclusive OR/assign	a^=b	
Bitwise OR/assign	a|=b	

■ THE FOUR ACCESS MODIFIERS

Modifier	Accessibility	Default for
public	Fully accessible.	enum members, interface members
private	Members within a type are accessible only within that type.	class members, struct members
internal	Accessible only within its own assembly.	nonnested types, classes, structs, enums
protected	Members within a type are accessible only from that type, or from other types that inherit from it.	

■ COMPILER OPTIONS

OUTPUT FILES

/out:<file>	Output file name (default: base name of file with main class or first file).
/target:exe	Build a console executable (default). (Short form: /t:exe)
/target:winexe	Build a Windows executable. (Short form: /t:winexe)
/target:library	Build a library. (Short form: /t:library)
/target:module	Build a module that can be added to another assembly. (Short form: /t:module)
/define:<symbol list>	Define conditional compilation symbol(s). (Short form:/d)
/doc:<file>	XML documentation file to generate.

INPUT FILES

/recurse:<wildcard>	Include all files in the current directory and subdirectories according to the wildcard specifications.
/reference:<file list>	Reference metadata from the specified assembly files. (Short form: /r)
/addmodule:<file list>	Link the specified modules into this assembly.

RESOURCES

/win32res:<file> Specifies Win32 resource file. (.res)

/win32icon:<file> Use this icon for the output.

/resource:<resinfo> Embeds the specified resource. (Short form: /res)

/linkresource:<resinfo> Links the specified resource to this assembly. (Short form: /linkres)

CODE GENERATION

/debug[+ | –] Emit debugging information.

/debug:{full | pdbonly} Specify debugging type. ("full" is default, and enables attaching a debugger to a running program.)

/optimize[+ | –] Enable optimizations. (Short form: /o)

/incremental[+ | –] Enable incremental compilation. (Short form: /incr)

ERRORS AND WARNINGS

/warnaserror[+ | –] Treat warnings as errors.

/warn:<n> Set warning level (0–4). (Short form: /w)

/nowarn:<warning list> Disable specific warning messages.

LANGUAGE

/checked[+ | –] Generate overflow checks.

/unsafe[+ | –] Allow "unsafe" code.

MISCELLANEOUS

@<file> Read response file for more options.

/help Display this usage message. (Short form: /?)

/nologo Suppress compiler copyright message.

/noconfig Do not auto-include CSC.RSP file.

ADVANCED

/baseaddress:<address> Base address for the library to be built.

/bugreport:<file> Create a "Bug Report" file.

/codepage:<n> Specifies the code page to use when opening source files.

/utf8output Output compiler messages in UTF-8 encoding.

/main:<type> Specifies the type that contains the entry point (ignore all other possible entry points). (Short form: /m)

/fullpaths Compiler generates fully qualified paths.

/filealign:<n> Specify the alignment used for output file sections.

/nostdlib[+ | –] Do not reference standard library (mscorlib.dll).

/lib:<file list> Specify additional directories to search in for references.

■ RULES FOR DECLARING CLASSES

Classes are declared using the `keyword` class. The declaration takes the form:

```
[attributes] [modifiers] class identifier [:base-list] { class-body }[;]
```

where:

`attributes` (Optional)	Additional declarative information.
`modifiers` (Optional)	The allowed modifiers are `new`, `abstract`, `sealed`, and the four access modifiers.
`identifier`	The class name.
`base-list` (Optional)	A list that contains the one base class and any implemented interfaces, all separated by commas.
`class-body`	Declarations of the class members.

A class can contain declarations of the following members:

- Constructors
- Destructors
- Constants
- Fields
- Methods
- Properties
- Indexers
- Operators
- Nested types

Unlike C++, only single inheritance is allowed in C#. In other words, a class can inherit implementation from one base class only. However, a class can implement more than one interface. The access levels `protected` and `private` are allowed only on nested classes.

■ RULES FOR DECLARING STRUCTURES

A `struct` type is a value type that can contain the following:

- Constructors
- Constants
- Fields
- Methods
- Properties

- Indexers
- Operators
- Nested types

The declaration of a struct takes the following form:

```
[attributes] [modifiers] struct identifier [:interfaces] body [;]
```

where:

attributes (Optional)	Additional declarative information.
modifiers (Optional)	The allowed modifiers are new and the four access modifiers.
identifier	The struct name.
interfaces (Optional)	A list that contains the interfaces implemented by the struct, all separated by commas.
body	The struct body that contains member declarations.

It is an error to declare a parameterless constructor for a struct. A default constructor is provided to initialize the struct members to their default values. It is an error to initialize an instance field in a struct.

When you create a struct object using the new operator, it is created and the appropriate constructor is called. Unlike classes, structs can be instantiated without using the new operator. If you do not use new, the fields will remain unassigned and the object cannot be used until all of the fields are initialized.

A struct cannot inherit from another struct or class, and it cannot be the base of a class. A struct, however, inherits from the base class Object. A struct can implement interfaces in the same way classes do.

RULES FOR DECLARING ENUMERATIONS

The enum keyword is used to declare an enumeration, a type consisting of a set of named constants called the "enumerator list." Every enumeration type has an underlying type, which can be any integral type except char. The declaration of an enum variable takes the form:

```
[attributes] [modifiers] enum identifier [:base-type] {enumerator-list};
```

where:

attributes (Optional)	Additional declarative information.
modifiers (Optional)	The allowed modifiers are new and the four access modifiers.
identifier	The enum name.

`base-type` (Optional)	The underlying type that specifies the storage allocated for each enumerator. It can be any of the integral types except `char`. The default is `int`.
`enumerator-list`	The enumerators' identifiers separated by commas, optionally including a value assignment.

The default underlying type of the enumeration elements is the `int` type. By default, the first enumerator has the value zero, and the value of each successive enumerator is increased by one.

The underlying type specifies how much storage is allocated for each enumerator. A cast is needed to convert from an `enum` type to an integral type.

appendix B

More C# Books

C# and the .NET Platform
by Andrew Troelsen
Paperback: 970 pages
Publisher: APress
ISBN: 1893115593
1st edition (June 2001)

OOP with Microsoft Visual Basic .NET and Microsoft Visual C# .NET Step by Step
by Robin A. Reynolds-Haertle
Paperback: 416 pages
Publisher: Microsoft Press
ISBN: 0735615683
1st edition (January 23, 2002)

Programming C#
by Jesse Liberty
Paperback: 656 pages
Publisher: O'Reilly & Associates
ISBN: 0596003099
2nd edition (February 2002)

Programming Windows with C# (Core Reference)
by Charles Petzold
Hardcover: 1200 pages
Publisher: Microsoft Press
ISBN: 0735613702
1st edition (December 19, 2001)

Index

Symbols

A

D

U

V